SILVERSTONE
An Historical Mosaic

Researched and compiled by Elaine Lovell

Assisted by

Anne Austins
Joe da Casa
Gerald Lovell
Martin Marix Evans
Nigel Read

Edited by Martin Marix Evans

SILVERSTONE
An Historical Mosaic

Foreword by Sir Stirling Moss

Published in 2001 by: Silverstone Appraisal Group, 7 Church Street, Silverstone, Towcester, Northamptonshire NN12 8XA

Production Editor: Joe da Casa
Designer: Pam Higgins
Layout: Chris Sanders
Proofreading: Chris Lovell, Gillian Marix Evans and Pat Read
Production Manager: Martin Marix Evans, Book Packaging and Marketing.

Printed in England by: Gemini Press, Towcester

Half-title photograph: A Top-dog and an Under-dog working in a saw-pit, cutting planks. (Courtesy Geoff Blackwell)

Title page photograph: Harry Lovell's carting team, behind the Compasses, looking towards Church Street. (Courtesy Sam Linnell)

In addition to the gratitude owed to innumerable contributors of information and illustrations, including Northamptonshire Heritage Sites and Monuments, the publishers acknowledge the permission to publish material of which the copyright is the property of the bodies listed below. The abbreviations in brackets are used to indicate the text or illustration used. The Royal Commission on the Historical Monuments of England (RCHM), reference B9398/98/99, for © Crown Copyright material; the Ordnance Survey for the 1999 map, based upon Ordnance Survey (OS) mapping, on behalf of The Controller of Her Majesty's Stationery Office © Crown Copyright, MC100013836, and for other, older, OS mapping; the Cambridge University Collection of Air Photographs (CU) and the Northamptonshire Record Office (NRO). We are grateful to Northamptonshire Newspapers for permission to reproduce the articles from the Independent and to Central Counties Newspapers for permitting the use of the article from the Brackley and Towcester Advertiser.

As so much of the material has been donated by private individuals from their own collections it may be that material has been reproduced without the knowledge that it is in copyright. The publishers would be grateful of notification of any such inadvertent trespass and trust that, as any surplus of revenues is to be donated to causes of benefit to the village, the copyright owners will be willing to grant permission both retrospectively and gratis.

The publishers also wish to express their gratitude to the Lottery Millennium Festival "Awards for All" Programme and to Silverstone Circuits Ltd for outright grants and to South Northamptonshire Council for a grant/loan under their Millennium Grant-Aid Scheme. Advance subscribers' act of faith in ordering and paying before publication has produced the revenue for 315 copies, adding to the financial support. Further help has been given in the form of services rendered over and above any contractual obligation by John Rudland and the Gemini Press.

Contents

PART 5: **The Twentieth Century**

PART 6: **The Village in 2000**

Foreword

Silverstone has been synonymous with motor racing to me for almost as long as I can remember. I first drove a small racing car there when the wartime airfield had just been converted into a racing circuit. In those days I had family friends living near Buckingham, and lodged with them, so I had little time or opportunity to get to know much about this ancient village or its much older and more varied background.

I had no idea that its origins dated back to the Bronze Age, nor that the names of features on the circuit which I came to know so well, such as Abbey Curve, Chapel, Luffield, or Woodcote were so closely intertwined with the ancient traditions of a forest based community such as is described in this book.

You don't have to be a motor racing enthusiast to enjoy discovering the older Silverstone, and that its place in history was well established in the days of Richard the Lionheart or the Princes in the Tower. We of the motor racing fraternity have perhaps helped to put the name of Silverstone firmly on the modern international map, but that name was on the map of English history long before the invention of the internal combustion engine.

Enjoy reading about the "whole" Silverstone.

Sir Stirling Moss, August 2000.

Preface

Silverstone is known the world over - for the Grand Prix. By and large this is all that most people know of it, almost as if the village is a by-product of the circuit and not vice-versa. Silverstone circuit is a big part of our contemporary history, but "Silson" as it was known by its natives of a bygone age, has been much more than that. For more than two millennia, in fact as far back as the Bronze age, there has been a settlement here.

Through the pages of this book we attempt to reveal something of the history of this intriguing village and the people in it.

The account we give is anything but complete, but perhaps this historical mosaic of archive and anecdote will challenge readers to find the missing details.

Elaine Lovell (Researcher).

Introduction

There is a feeling about the village; it has a character all of its own and a history that has formed the very fabric and heart of it. In the early 1970s there was a group of ladies who had not long moved into the village and helped to swell the numbers of the already well established Womens' Institute. These ladies were struck by this character and wondered what went into the spirit and make-up of the people that lived here. At some time they came across a copy of Old Oak, written during the 19th century by the Rev J.E.Linnell (discussed elsewhere in these pages). This inspired them to set out on a project to preserve memories of the recent past of the village and its people as much as possible, starting where Old Oak had left off.

Joy Townsend ran the Post Office in the High Street along with her husband Tony. The WI group decided to make an audio diary involving as many of the older residents as possible, and it was Joy who headed the project. The WI interviews have proved to be priceless. The group consisted of Joy Townsend, Jenny Tero, Connie Cowley, Jenny Plummer, Dorothy Brown, Joan Lidgard, Heather Coles, and Sara Hughes. Joy had also started collecting information and facts from the Records Office in Northampton. Armed with tapes, records, and photographs, some of which were donated by those interviewed, Joy's ultimate intention was to compile a book about Silverstone by Silsoners within living memory of past times. Sadly Joy has since died, as did, recently, her husband Tony. The project was abandoned and all the tapes and information were put in a box and given to Ruth Denney for safekeeping by Joy and Tony's children.

In 1997 another band of residents gathered to form a village appraisal group. They consisted of Nigel Read, Martin Marix Evans, Gerald Lovell, Anne Austins and Elaine Lovell. It was during their regular meetings and appraisal discussions that the same idea of a book about Silverstone came into being. They, with the help of others, including Joe da Casa and John Oates, have carried on where Joy left off. Further research and new interviews, added to the information already gathered, has brought about finally the long awaited book.

In recognition of Joy's work and contribution to the community, her introduction to the book that she never completed is reproduced below. It is given here in a slightly edited form. The changes made correct a number of matters of fact which, we are confident, she would have been keen to see altered.

"Silverstone is a fairly ancient settlement situated in the once very extensive Royal Forest of Whittlewood. It is mentioned in the Anglo-Saxon Chronicle of 942 AD and listed in the Domesday Book. As a forest village we can be sure that earlier inhabitants had to work hard hunting, cutting timber and getting a living where and how they could. Living in wooden hovels in small groups and families, we can imagine that the place names within the village identified such groups: Cattle End, West End, Olney, Stocks Hill, Little London.

"An early historical claim to fame is the association of the Queen's Oak of Whittlewood Forest with Elizabeth Wydville (usually written Woodville). She was a beautiful but impoverished aristocratic widow who lived at Grafton Regis in the time of the Wars of the Roses. Her relatives, the Greys, who were

Lancastrians, had been beaten by Richard Neville, Earl of Warwick, at Bamburgh Castle in 1464. The Yorkist king, Edward IV, was tall, handsome and a keen huntsman both of deer and women. Having failed to get their way on the field of battle, the Greys sought to regain power through Elizabeth.

"Elizabeth was, so the legend goes, stationed by the great oak tree, clad in her most eye-catching outfit where the King couldn't help but see her. Moved by her great beauty and distinguished appearance, the King was attracted to her and, on learning that she was widowed, in poor circumstances, and with two or three small children, he naturally wished to help her. The long and short of it was that, at Grafton Regis on 1 May 1464, Elizabeth and Edward were married. The King then fell out with Warwick, so the Wydvilles and their kin became the influential force. In July 1469 Edward's supporters were beaten by Warwick's allies at the Battle of Edgecote, near Banbury, but Edward managed to rally support and won the Battle of Losecote Field, near Empingham, in March 1470.

"Elizabeth was the mother of the two little princes alleged to have been murdered in the Tower of London by order of Richard II, but she had another daughter, also named Elizabeth, who married Henry Tudor, later King Henry VII. Elizabeth Wydville was, therefore, an important person in the history of England, never mind that of Silverstone and Whittlewood.

Joy goes on to mention the Royal Hunting Lodge, the Fishponds and the monks of Luffield Abbey.

"While there are signs of Holy living all around Silverstone at this time, the natives weren't exactly God fearing people, or at any rate didn't believe in building any permanent structure to be a church at that date. We must remember of course, that their houses were all still built of wood, since that was the most plentiful material obtainable, and there may possibly have been a wooden church placed near to the site of the present church. The map of 1656, whilst showing the Church of Saint Mary at Whittlebury, shows nothing of that kind in Silverstone. However a few buildings are marked and the main paths that would have just been tracks at that time, are quite clearly shown. You will notice "Crarves" the footpath from the "Craftsmen's" Fields.

"By 1756, there are many more buildings and the Church is already shown. If you have read or heard tales of "Old Oak" you will know what a rowdy lot we were in the 18th century. Very independent, fierce fighters and hard workers; this goes on into the 19th century, despite the enclosure of much of the traditional working grounds of the inhabitants.

"The Parish Award of 1827 shows how the village was split up to try and be fair to the locals, although of course it was mostly of benefit to the gentry and aristocracy of the neighbourhood. If you look at the maps you can see that the village had grown both in house numbers, and therefore in population, at a fairly steady rate until there were about 900 at the start of the 20th century.

"For many of the changes since that time, we have spoken to some of the oldest inhabitants, many of whom had their own highly individual views on life in their Silson back then."

As Joy points out, the contents of this collection are the opinions of a large number of individuals. Their ideas are not always the same but are reported here as told to the compilers and should not be taken as fact except where they are supported by solid evidence. Within the bounds of practicality some evidence, such as photographs of maps, copies of official records and reproductions of published reports, have been assembled to provide readers with a foundation for their own research.

What is most important of all is that those who do not know it already will become aware of the depth and richness of the history of this little village. The evidence of the past is all around us, in the shaping of the land, in the texture and substance of the walls, in the jinks, turns and names of the paths and roads, and in the words of those who lived here before us. Such wealth is worth preserving as part of the new village that every generation in turn creates.

We therefore dedicate this book to those who came before and those who will follow, thus:

To the Once and Future Oaks of Silverstone
and to the late Joy Townsend
Silverstone Postmistress 1966-1994
who planted the acorn which grew into this book

PART 1 🏺 **Ancient Times**

GEOLOGY

Silverstone, geologically speaking is an odd shape that nestles in a moderately small dell.

Its shape was formed at the end of the last Ice Age. During the thaw, great glaciers were on the move taking with them parts of whatever landscape lay beneath them. The dell that formed Silverstone is where some of the glacial deposits came to rest. Creating a new landscape, it had left among its deposits large bedrocks of boulder clay, patches of glacial sands and gravel, and bands of Oolite limestone found in the newly created valley walls to the north (now the area along the route of the main A43 road). In the centuries since, the limestone was dug out for building houses and barns. The clay left by the glacier was extracted to make bricks for further building, and limestone was burnt to produce the lime needed for mortar in brick and stone buildings. Various sites of stone quarries, lime kilns and clay pits are shown on recent maps. The remains of a clay pit can still be seen at the junction of West End and Puddledock, where the pond, locally known as Brickle (Brick hole), fills the old workings. Even the gravel and pebbles left by the glacier have been put to use; gravel was used to maintain local roads until the use of tarmac became widespread.

THE BRONZE AGE

Silverstone has evidence of many early settlements but the one that has been most fully excavated and detailed is a Bronze age barrow or grave mound.

It is said that the site lay mostly in Lillingstone Dayrell. This mound is on the site of what later became the aerodrome which led to an investigation by the Ministry of Defence (then the War Ministry) in November 1941, putting the find firmly in Silverstone. We and the rest of the world know this area through its latest incarnation as Silverstone motor racing circuit.

This mound occupied an isolated position in open fields on one of the many knolls or ridges which make up the east Midlands, on a plateau of medium height intersected by the Nene and Ouse river systems. The trigonometrical station beside the mound had a spot height of 513 ft. On the O.S. six-inch sheet 8NW (NGR 42/670419), the mound lay just to the south of the Northamptonshire and Buckinghamshire boundary, and belongs therefore to the parish of Lillingstone Dayrell in Buckinghamshire, although the aerodrome which led to this investigation was named as being in Silverstone, Northamptonshire. The mound had the appearance of a disturbed bell-barrow. As such it was the only recorded example of its type in this locality. But there was the possibility that it might have been of later date, serving some different purpose, possibly, for instance, as a windmill mound. Although the hope of recovering datable material in such disturbed conditions seemed unlikely, it was nevertheless desirable that, if possible, its true character should be determined.

The centre of the mound had been dug out in one large irregular lobed pit which penetrated to a depth of nearly 18 ins. below the natural surface. Scraps of pottery suggested that filling may have taken place in the Middle Ages. In spite of the absence of earlier finds there can be no doubt that the mound was originally a barrow. The manner of disturbance is in itself a strong

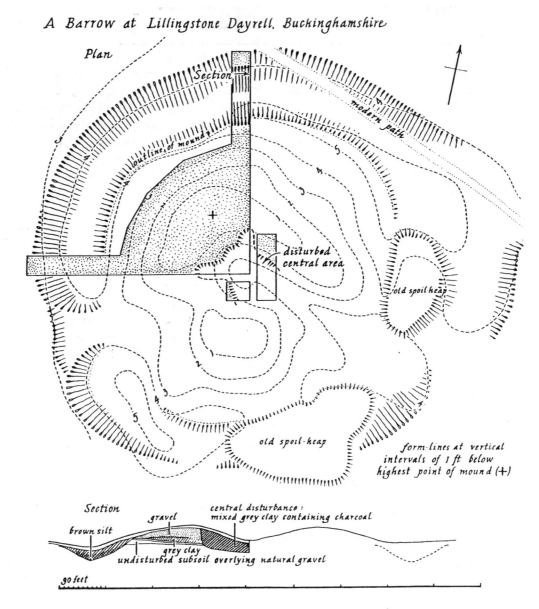

A Barrow at Lillingstone Dayrell, Buckinghamshire

Plan

Section

outline of mound

modern path

disturbed central area

old spoil-heap

old spoil-heap

form-lines at vertical intervals of 1 ft below highest point of mound (+)

Section

gravel

central disturbance: mixed grey clay containing charcoal

brown silt

grey clay

undisturbed subsoil overlying natural gravel

90 feet

indication of this, for a mediaeval windmill mound would not have been so dug out. The natural surface was a clayey layer overlying gravel; the mound displayed these materials in reverse, its base being a low heap of grey clay overlain by gravel, all clearly derived from the digging of the ditch. The latter, in its one fully exposed section, was a wide V, with a depth of up to 3ft. Its filling was a normal silt with a varying gravel content in the usual sagging layers. The filling of the disturbed central area was a mixed clay which contained finely broken charcoal. To the extent that this charcoal might be derived from a cremation or burial, the barrow could belong to the Middle to Late Bronze Age.

Based on: W. F. Grimes, Excavations on Defence Sites 1939-45, London, 1968.

ROMAN TIMES

There is evidence of a Roman settlement in Silverstone. To the North of the parish, in the bank of a small stream near Silverstone Fields farm, were found ashes, animal bones and the neck and handles of a large Roman amphora, (Ref. RCHM, Northamptonshire vol 4). At one time a Roman road passed to the East of the village to a Roman settlement in Wood Burcote. Additional evidence of such a settlement in Silverstone is the recent find by a village resident, Mrs Patricia Baker-Cassidy. This came about when one of the utility companies, water or gas, excavated the road alongside The Compasses in the High Street. When Mrs Cassidy looked into the trench, where men were digging about 5ft down, she saw what appeared to be the edges of a Roman road. This find suggests that there was a Roman road that went through the centre of the village joining with the main route near Wood Burcote. There has also been a find by some archaeologists (who were logging finds in Wood Burcote) that there was a Roman kiln near the small fish ponds in Little London.

It is said that, when the Roman armies were leaving Britain, their commanders gave their men the opportunity to remain, a particularly welcome proposal to those who had fathered children on British women. The men were not permitted to marry while still in service and the offer of a parcel of land as severance pay permitted them to regularise their unions. Such concessions would also have been extended to retiring soldiers who could then become traders supplying the military's needs. As Towcester, then Lactodorum, was an important settlement and fort on Watling Street, the discovery of kilns and bake houses in the surrounding area comes as no surprise, and their enterprise might well have extended to the exploitation of the forest at Silverstone.

THE MISTS OF TIME
Just how old is our village?

It certainly dates back at least to the early 12th Century, for the royal hunting lodge is mentioned in documents from 1130 A.D. But how far back beyond this did people live here? To the north of the village, in a bank of a small stream near Silverstone Fields Farm, ashes, animal bones, and the neck and parts of the handles of a large Roman amphora (large vase) were once found. At one time, a Roman road passed to the east side of the village, to the site at Wood Burcote, where a Roman villa, temple and pottery kiln have been excavated. There is also the site of a Roman villa close to the road from Abthorpe to Towcester. Could the village itself be as old?

When I was clearing the ruins of an old bakehouse in our garden, I found even deeper foundations and cobbling, and, scattered at this level, some small turquoise coloured rings. I recently showed these to an archaeologist who said they were almost certainly Roman. One of our neighbours has also found some deep foundations of a large building.

It has been said that the name of the village has Roman origins, Silva-tun [wood town], but I looked up the name in a book on the origins of place names, which gave the origin as Siegwuld's town, which suggests an even earlier date.

Written for News and Views by John Oates

PART 2 ⤙ **The Middle Ages**

MEDIAEVAL SILVERSTONE

Humble Beginnings

At the time of the Norman Conquest a large area of the forest had already been cleared. Domesday Book states that there were three estates and seven families in Silverstone in 1086. One estate lay to the immediate West of the village in two fields on either side of the Silverstone brook and was shared with the Charlock farmers on the Abthorpe side of the brook. Apart from Charlock there were other family settlements on West End (attracting trade from the main drovers road), Cattle End (with fields for rent to the drovers to overnight their cattle or for weekends before continuing to market), Stocks Hill (built around the original chapel of ease in the village centre). These places became more populated after the demise of the hamlet of Charlock. It is not documented, but speculation suggests that Charlock hamlet was affected by plague in the 13th or 14th century and was thus abandoned.

A Lake, Ponds and a Vanished Hamlet

To find out some details of the history of the Silverstone fishponds, a copy of the archaeological survey of South Northants was obtained from the Towcester Library. Not only did this reveal detail about the fishponds, but also several other pieces of information about that part of the village. It seems that there was indeed a very large lake in the valley where the playing fields are now located. Apparently this lake was the largest artificial pond in the county in mediaeval times.

The present courses of the streams around the edge of the lake area, are actually man made "*leats*". The two main streams have reverted to their original course about two-thirds of the way down the lake area where they join and flow through a breach in what was once a complete dam. It is possible that there was once a small breeding pond at the eastern end of this dam. The ponds and the lake are recorded in several 13th century records, but nothing seems to be known of them after the early 14th century when the use of the royal hunting lodge declined.

John Oates.

Rotating the Carp

Seeing a house being built on the site of the village fishponds, in Little London, set me to thinking about what the ponds were like when they were in use. They were very important to those who relied on them to supply a regular source of fresh meat, particularly in the Winter months when the only other meat was either game or cured and smoked joints. Fishponds usually had more than one compartment and this was so that a simple but effective two year crop rotation could be followed. In one year a pond had fish growing in it and in the next year it was drained. When a good, lush growth of grass had been made, fertilised by the nutrient-rich sediment, cattle would be grazed there. Their cowpats then supplied food for the fish when the pond was flooded again for the next year. The fish grown were usually carp (large goldfish to most people) because they are a tough and hardy species, not too particular about their food. Not exactly exciting eating, but probably very

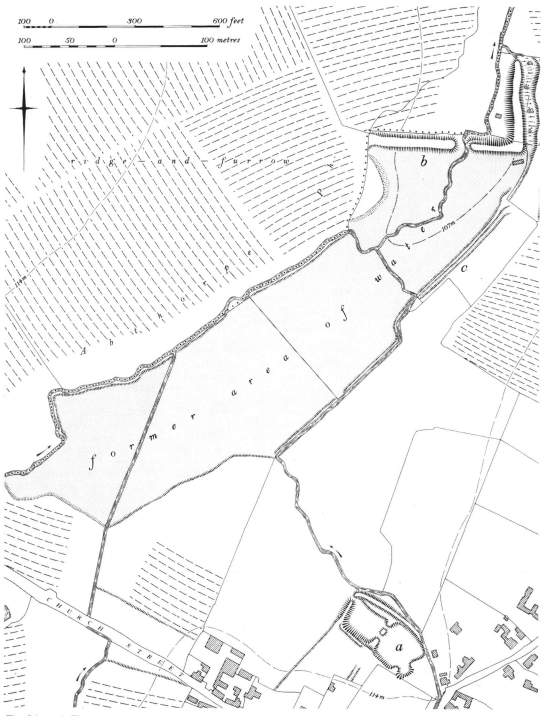

The fishponds. The small ponds (a) are next to the footpath off Little London and the south-eastern bank of the large pond can be seen today where the footbridges on the same path crosses the stream on the way to the playing fields. The dam of the large pond (b) can be viewed from where the track north of New Rookery Farm ends and joins the footpath going south-west to Rookery Farm. The 107m. contour indicates the possible area of a mill head pond.

welcome on a cold winter's evening, grilled by a wood fire and flavoured with dried fennel, dill-weed and tossed on the flames. The Silverstone ponds may also have raised fish to stock the great fishpond. With the forest coming to its edge it would have been a favoured watering place for the deer, many of which no doubt fell to the hunter's arrow. All in all, fishponds were once a much more prominent part of the village than their remains would now suggest.

John Oates.

53 SILVERSTONE
(OS 1:10000 [a] SP 64 SE, [b] SP 64 NE, [c] SP 64 SW)

The parish covers about 760 hectares and is of irregular shape, sloping gently N. from the higher ground on the S. boundary with Buckinghamshire, at 155 m. above OD, to a N.E.-flowing stream on the N.W. boundary at about 105 m. above OD. It is entirely covered by Boulder Clay except for some small patches of glacial sands and gravels, and bands of Oolite limestone along the valley sides in the N. The most important monuments are the medieval fishponds (2) which are well documented because of their royal association.

PREHISTORIC AND ROMAN

Worked flints are said to have been found in the parish (OS Record Cards). The probable Bronze Age barrow said to be in Silverstone parish and which was excavated in 1940 actually lay just S. of the county boundary, in Buckinghamshire (*Ant. J.*, 28 (1948), 27; W. F. Grimes, *Excavations on Defence Sites*, I (1960), 245–7).

[b](1) ROMAN SETTLEMENT (?) (SP 677456), in the N. of the parish, on river gravels at 105 m. above OD. The neck and parts of the handles of a large Roman amphora were discovered in the bank of a small stream, together with ashes and animal bones (OS Record Cards).

MEDIEVAL AND LATER

The Benedictine Priory of Luffield lay partly in the extreme S. of the parish, and partly in Buckinghamshire. Nothing remains on the site, which is now occupied by Abbey Farm (SP 674421; VCH *Northants.*, II (1906), 95–7).

The site of the well-documented royal hunting lodge at Silverstone has not been located. It is mentioned as early as 1121–30 and was rebuilt and altered several times before 1317 when it was abandoned (R. A. Brown, H. M. Colvin and A. J. Taylor, *History of The King's Works*, II (1963), 1002–3). It may have been located near the present parish church, close to the smaller of the two fishponds (2) (SP 668443), for the area was known as Hall Garth in 1600 (NRO, map of Whittlewood Forest).

There are records of a deer park in the parish in the 13th century but this also has not been located (*Northants. P. and P.*, 5 (1975), 231).

[a](2) FISHPONDS (SP 667446; Fig. 104), lie to the N.W. of the village, in the bottom of a broad open valley draining N.E. and in one of its tributary valleys, on alluvium be-

tween 105 m. and 112 m. above OD. The ponds are associated with a royal hunting lodge at Silverstone (see above) and are referred to in a number of 13th-century documents. For example in 1227 the sheriff of Northampton was ordered 'to cause the broken ponds of the Kings stews of Silverston . . . and the bays of the same to be repaired' (*Cal. Lib.* I, 23). In 1241 the bailiffs of Silverstone were asked to 'aid William the Kings fisherman, whom he is to send to fish in his stews at Silverston and to send the fish that he shall catch to the King without delay' (*Cal. Lib.* II, 31) and in 1244 the keepers of the 'stew of Silverstone' were told to 'aid Geoffrey Corburn and William the Kings fisherman, whom he is sending to fish there, to carry their fish to the King at Woodstock' (*Cal. Lib.* II, 217). Soon after, the King ordered that his servants were to 'search out nets in the town of Oxford with which William the Kings fisherman, whom he is sending to Silverstone, can fish in the Kings stews there and to carry them to Woodstock' (*Cal. Lib.* III, 83–3). In 1257 the King allocated the men of Silverstone '4 shillings spent in taking 20 pike in the Kings stews at Silverstone and in salting them and carrying them to London' (*Cal. Lib.* IV, 415). The later history of the ponds is unknown for royal interest in the hunting lodge ceased in the early 14th century. The ponds are not marked on a map of Whittlewood Forest of about 1600 (NRO).

At the S.E. end of the area ('a' on plan) are two small conjoined rectangular ponds cut back into the side of small steep-sided valley to a depth of 2.5 m. A large dam up to 3 m. high along the N.W. and N.E. sides has a later cut through it in the N. corner. The remains of a second dam 2 m. high, cut through in two places, form a division between the two ponds. These ponds were probably breeding tanks for the main pond which lies to the N. and N.W. The latter, when filled, was probably the largest artificial pond in the county in medieval times. The water was retained by a large dam spanning the open valley ('b' on plan). This is flat-topped and up to 3 m. high and has a later gap cut through the centre. At its E. end the dam turns N. and there is a large marshy depression along its E. side, perhaps where the surplus water from the pond was returned around the edge of the dam and into the stream. The depression received water from an artificial leat which ran above the former pond along its E. side ('c' on plan). However the depression is larger than it would need to be for these purposes and it may be another fishpond or a mill-pond. The area of the former pond is defined by a number of features. On the S.E. side it is marked by a high-level leat ('c' on plan) which once carried water from the tributary valley and from the small fishponds to the S.E. along the side of the pond and around the E. end of the dam. The S. side of the pond is marked by a low scarp or bank less than 0.25 m. high, now largely ploughed down or completely destroyed by the construction of a playing field at the extreme S.W. end but clearly visible on air photographs taken in 1947 (RAF VAP CPE/UK/ 1926, 3230–2). Most of the N.W. side of the pond is marked by another embanked leat which carries the water of the stream which occupied the valley bottom before the construction of the ponds. This leat returns the water into the valley bottom a little to the S.W. of the dam.

Another point of considerable interest is the fact that though the parish boundary between Silverstone and Abthorpe follows the stream in the valley for most of its length, in the vicinity of the pond it follows the N.W. edge of the pond as far as the dam and then returns to the original stream. This suggests that the parish boundary was moved in order to ensure that the whole pond lay in Silverstone parish. If this is so it was probably carried out by Royal Command in order to avoid the legal and administrative problems involved in having the pond in two parishes. (*Northants. P. and P.*, 4 (1970), 308; CUAP, AWN68)

[2](3) SETTLEMENT REMAINS (centred SP 662437), formerly part of Silverstone village, lie on the E. side of the road, in the S. part of West End, on Boulder Clay at 128 m. above OD. The area is under cultivation and only a scatter of stone-rubble and pottery of 13th to 18th-century date is visible. This marks the sites of at least four houses which are shown here on the map of Whittlewood Forest of about 1600 (NRO) but which had gone by 1827 (NRO, Enclosure Map). These remains contribute to an understanding of the development of Silverstone village which, before 19th-century and later changes consisted of three distinct parts. To the E., around the church, lay a compact settlement at a cross-roads. To the W. was a single long street, now known as West End, and to the S. lay another street, known as Cattle End. No explanation for this unusual settlement pattern can be suggested, except that it might be the result of piecemeal forest-edge development. (RAF VAP CPE/UK/1926, 3230–2, 5230–1)

(4) CULTIVATION REMAINS. The common fields of the parish were enclosed by an Act of Parliament of 1827 (NRO, Enclosure Map). At that time there were five open fields of very different sizes. Between the main part of the village and West End lay the small Backside Field, and to the E. lay the equally small Ridge Knoll Field. Hall Hills and Blackspit Fields were to the N.E. of the village, with Swinney Field beyond. Old enclosures surrounded the various parts of the village to the S., W. and E.

The S. part of the present parish was not in Silverstone parish in 1827 but in Whittlewood Forest and is not depicted on the Enclosure Map. An earlier map of Whittlewood Forest of about 1600 (NRO) shows a similar situation, though with some additional information. Backside Field was then known as Wood Crafts Field and all the others were grouped into two large areas known as Silson Field and Whittlebury Field. All the old enclosures S. and W. of the village are shown as on the later map but their names, for example Grindons Sart, Dancome Sart, Elms Sart and Fryers Assart, all indicate their origins as woodland clearances. These are probably some of the assarts mentioned as being in Silverstone in 1273 (*Cal. IPM* II, 49). The 1600 map also shows that all the S. part of the parish as far as the county boundary was then under woodland.

Ridge-and-furrow of these fields exists on the ground or can be traced on air photographs in some parts of the parish. A few fragments can be seen in the former Backside or Wood Crafts Field and other small areas, now built over, are visible on air photographs in the former Ridge Knoll Field. To the N.W. of the village very little ridge-and-furrow is traceable in the area of the other three former open fields and the pattern is not recoverable anywhere.

Ridge-and-furrow occurs in the old enclosure W. of the village (SP 659440 and 663433), much of it in exceptionally narrow ridges only 4 m.–5 m. across. For the most part the furlongs lie within existing fields or are bounded by shallow ditches or slight banks indicating former hedges. Further S., both in the area of old enclosures S. of the village and within the former wooded areas, wide ridge-and-furrow, exactly straight and fitted within fields of regular shape, appears to be the result of late 19th-century ploughing (e.g. SP 661429 and 673433). (RAF VAP CPE/UK/1926, 1231–3, 2231–4, 3228–34, 5229–32)

R.C.H.M. Vol. 4, South Northamptonshire

A Millpond?

In 1970 an archaeological survey was carried out on the upper part of the mediaeval Fishponds beyond the dam. Depressions in its outline and other factors led the researchers to pursue the possibility of a post mediaeval industrial site here. On further investigation evidence was found to suggest that this area had a water mill and mill pond. Whether this was an original feature before the pond was enlarged has yet to be established. Referring to the map of the former large fishpond, the area around the dam which may have been a millpond follows the 107m. contour.

Aerial photograph, taken in the afternoon of 20 January 1969, of the dam of the large pond. The small ponds, with light reflecting from standing water, are top right and Little London top centre. (Cambridge University Collection of Air Photographs: copyright reserved)

OLD CHARLOCK

But I also found out something quite unexpected. I have often looked at the earthworks in the large fields behind Watergate, wondering what they might have been for, and trying to see some sort of pattern in them. It turns out that they are in fact all that is left of what once was a complete hamlet: the settlement of Old Charlock. So, we have our own mediaeval village! (it's actually in the adjacent parish of Abthorpe). The hamlet is first recorded in the mid thirteenth century, although it is probably much older than that. Shown on the map below, are the main outlines of it, and one can see how a large area is

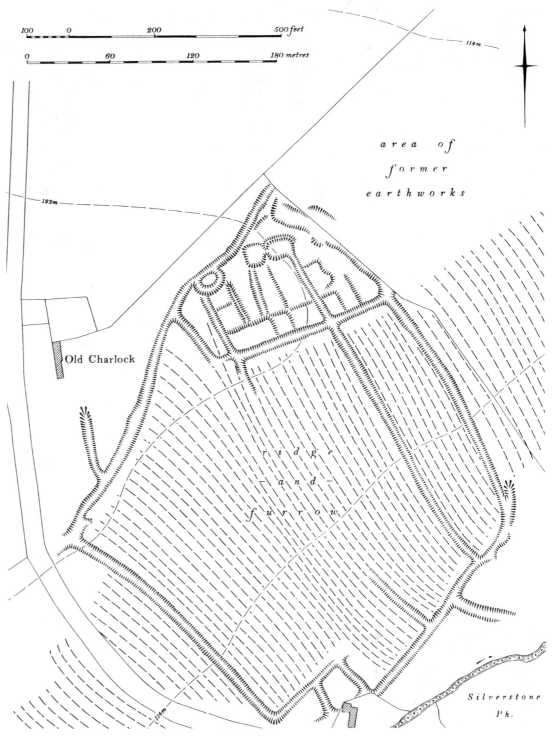

Plan of the hamlet of Charlock from RCHM, Northampton, Volume 4, which says that the date of the enclosure of the common fields of the deserted hamlet of Charlock is also unknown but was certainly before 1726, and was probably much earlier than that. The stream beside the playing fields can be seen bottom right.

enclosed by banks and ditches, (this was probably the main cultivated area). The buildings were in the north corner and here too are traces of possibly two more ponds. The main street probably led down to the lake: this old *"hollow-way"* is the most visible remain nowadays. If you look over the other side of the stream, towards Bucknell Wood, the next time you are on the playing field, and when the sun is casting long shadows, you'll be able to see it quite clearly.

So that corner of our village was once very different from what it is now. In fact, there are traces of Ridge and Furrow cultivation all along the Western side of the lake valley, so imagine yourself as an inhabitant of Silverstone 700 years ago, looking down from Little London, across the fish ponds to the lake, and seeing on the far side of Charlock, people working their fields. Will we one day see a new development and old Charlock rise again as New Charlock?

John Oates

LUFFIELD ABBEY

The Bronze Age barrow became the site of Luffield Priory in the 9th century, a house of Benedictine monks. There must be something very special about this site because something of great importance has always been built to occupy that space. Now it is the turn of Luffield Priory. According to Bakers History Vol.3 the name Luffield means lovely field. This is a quotation from that book:

Luffield, according to the etymology of Buowne Willis, 'Ager amabilis or Lovely field' from its situation, is a secluded spot within the forest of Whittlewood, or Whittlebury. Here, at the junction of the two counties of Buckingham and Northampton, the conventual buildings

and offices being principally in the parish of Lillingston Dayrell in the former county, and the church wholly in the precincts of Silveston, stood a small priory of the Benedictine order, dedicated to the Virgin Mary. It was founded in the reign of Henry I by Robert Bossu, Earl of Leicester, who, for the souls of William, King of England, and Queen Matilda, and Roger de Bellamont and Adeliza his wife and Robert his father, and for the health of the souls of himself and Waleran his brother, gave in alms to Malger the monk, the servant of God, a small land. King Henry I commanded R. Basset, A. de Vere, and Hugh de Chalian, and all his foresters of "Whitlewode", to permit the prior and monks of Luffield to have, as they were accustomed, all convenient accommodation in his forest without waste, and to protect them from all injury and contumely so long as they were under his patronage.

This was given in a charter headed *"The Foundation of the Monastery of the Blessed Mary of Luffield in the County of Northamptonshire within the Forest of Whittlewode"*. Henry's daughter, the Empress Matilda, issued a similar command to maintain Malgar the Monk and his servants in the peaceable enjoyment of what the king had granted them.

The Village

Later Henry III made another charter in the 42nd year of his reign, dated 1258 at *"Selverston"*, and took into his special care, protection and defence all the men, lands and other possessions of the Priory and Convent of Luffield, whose church was of his patronage. The priory was very wealthy, it had donations made to it by charters from Dodford, Hayford, Maidford, Greens Norton, Silveston and Whittelburry, also Challock, Cosgrave, Eltington, Milton Malsor, Northampton, Paulersprury, Slapton and Towcester. In Buckinghamshire the

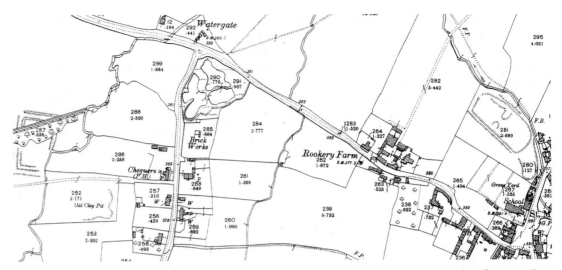

A detail from the 1900 Ordnance Survey map. On the extreme left, behind the Chequers, three sides of a rectangle of moat are shown by hatching. This is the suggested site of the Royal residence. The area marked by dotted lines behind St Michael's Church School is the possible site of Hall Garth and the hunting lodge.

monks of Luffield had considerable possessions and wealth. Lord Hamon de Wolverton gave them the tithes of, *"The Bread of His House"*, wheresoever it might be on his land, and 10 shillings yearly forever out of his mill in Wolverton, in lieu of the tithes of bread of his house. The priory being partly in Lillingston Dayrell came about because Sir Robert de Areial gave them *"the place in his wood Lillingstone"*, in which was built the chapel of St. Thomas a Becket the Archbishop and Martyr. The name Lillingston Dayrell is a corruption of Sir Robert's name of *"de Areial"*. Robert's son Ralph added his gift of *"all his wood in length from St. Thomas's chapel to great Holebeck'*; and Hugh de St. Martin gave them the chapel of St. John the Baptist in his court of Lillingston. Rents paid to the priory came from some of the villages in many forms. The village of Brackhole paid one pound of pepper, a place called Acle paid one pound of wax, Dodford and Hayford paid thirty capons and seventy-seven hens. These were amoung the 25 or so villages that had to pay rents to the priory as was recorded in *"The annual rental of this priory"*, in the time of Edward I (1289) as entered in the cartulary.

Through the prosperity of Luffield it was little surprise that a Royal residence should be built in Silverstone together with a Royal hunting lodge as the surrounding woods were richly stocked. In looking at what scanty documentary evidence survives, it seems probable that the Royal residence and the Royal hunting lodge were definitely two separate buildings. The hunting lodge (according to RCHM Vol IV) may have been located near the present parish church close to the smaller of the two fishponds. This area, known as Hall Garth, is shown on the 1640 map of Whittlewood forest (see Plate 1). The existence of the Royal residence has been well documented but not clearly located.

The Royal residence is mentioned as early as 1121-30 and was rebuilt and altered several times before 1317 when it was abandoned. It may be that this considerable building was located behind what is now West End and before Bucknells Wood, between the road to Blackmires Farm and the road to Abthorpe. It would have commanded a prominent view of the larger fishing lake. There are also records of a deer park in the parish in the 13th century. Rebuilding was often done to the Royal

Residence, specifically mentioned are the hall and cellar. Both house and ponds were regularly repaired during the reigns of Richard I and John I in 1210-11. John had built a *"new chamber and stables"*. In 1236 Henry III had long and beautiful windows put in the walls of the king's and queen's chambers, and in 1247-50 he built a new chapel and wardrobe for the queen. There was a king's chapel and king's new chamber to which a porch was added. There were repairs and alterations to the kitchen, the wall round the court yard, and the bridge before the gate to the entrance. All this suggests a much larger area than the land where the parish church now stands. The hunting lodge fits that area. According to Bridges the house was in the neighbouring parish of Syresham (as shown in maps). The kings who stayed in the royal residence were:

Henry I (1121),

Henry II (1164),
(rebuilt between 1178-83),

Richard I (1210),

John I (1211),

Henry III (1236).

In 1252 further alterations were cancelled, and only routine repairs were carried out until the time of Edward I (1272). Under Edward II (1313) it was granted to Richard Arundel for life, but the buildings were found to be in a ruinous condition. Repairs were ordered in 1315 and 1316 but in 1317 Arundel died and the Manor was granted to Sir Richard Lovell. Royal interest in the house then ceased.

Elaine Lovell.

BRIDGES AND BAKER

The entries for Silverstone in, first, Bridges (published 1791) and, second, Baker (a 19th century work) are given here, but readers should beware of the moderate standards of scholarship in local history at the time of their writing. Much of the information given above is repeated here, but it may be valuable to have access to these rare texts. The way in which the letter "S" is shown in type, looking like an "f" may confuse at first, but will soon be mastered if the text is read carefully.

SILVESTON.

*S*ILVESTON, or *SELVESTON*, and by contraction ufually called *Silfon*, is an hamlet belonging to the parifh of *Greene's-Norton*, but appendent to the townfhip of *Whittlebury*.

Within the liberties of *Silvefton* was antiently a lodge or manfion houfe, [*] the refidence of our Kings when they came into this part of their dominions. In 1194, *Richard* I. was lodged here in the fifth year of his reign, when *William* King of *Scotland* came to make his complaints, for the affront he had received from the bifhop of *Durham* at *Brackley*, [b] who denied him admittance into his inn, and feized on the provifions that were preparing for the King's table. There are now no remains nor tradition of any royal houfe in the Lordfhip of *Silvefton*. But about a mile and half fouth weft of the town, and about a quarter of a mile north eaft of *Sirefham*, in the midway between *Sirefham* and *Whittlebury* foreft, are fome grounds which have the name of *King's-hill-grounds*. In the middle of thefe inclofures is a fmall pleafant eminence, on which about thirty years ago was built an houfe called *King's-hill-lodge*. On the fouth fide of it is an inclofed piece of ground called the *Old Orchard*, containing about three or four acres; and on the weft fide of the lodge is an adjoining clofe, where have been found, in plowing, ftones and foundations of buildings. And there are reports of other large ftones and ruins, that have been difcovered thereabouts. The place is in *Whitfield* parifh, but was formerly included as a part of the foreft.

Upon the limits of this Lordfhip was the priory of *Luffield*; which ftanding at the extremity of both counties was fituate partly in the parifh of *Lillingfton-Dayrell* in the county of *Buckingham*, and partly in *Silvefton* in this county. The greateft part of the manfion, and the offices were in *Buckinghamfhire*, and the church within the diftrict of *Silvefton*. For this reafon the bifhop's mandate for induction of the priors was directed to the archdeacon of *Northampton*, within whofe jurifdiction it is placed by the *Lincoln* regifters. It is now accounted extraparochial. The crofs which divides the counties is cut out on the fite of the church. The chapel hereafter mentioned of St. *Thomas the Martyr* is converted to a dwelling houfe, and ftands on the *Buckinghamſhire* fide. What now remains of this monaftery is only a part of the tower wall.

The Lordſhip of *Silveſton*, at the time of the Conqueror's furvey, was divided amongſt feveral poffeffors. ' One hide was in the hands of the Earl of *Morton :* the arable land was three carucates : in demefne was one carucate with one fervant. It had been rated at x *s.* but was then valued at xx *s.* In King *Edward's* time this had been the freehold of *Leuric.*

' *Gilo* the brother of *Anculf* held half an hide, to whom *Godwin* was under tenant. The arable land was one carucate. There were two villanes and three acres of meadow. There was a wood one mile and an half in length, and a mile in breadth. A fourth part only of the wood belonged to this land. It had been valued at ii *s.* but was then rated at v *s.* Before the Conqueſt it was the freehold of *Siward.*

' *Ernald* held half an hide in *Silveſton* of *Geoffrey de Mandeville.* The arable land was one carucate, with two fervants, one villane and one cottager. The former valuation was x *s.* but it was now rated at xx *s.*

' In the reign of *Henry* II. *Otner* held half an hide in *Silveſton* of the fee of Earl *William :* *William de Keynes* one hide of the fee of *Morton*; and *Henry de Pinkeney* held half an hide. And this divifion of the Lordſhip correfponds exactly with the feveral poffeffions held of the crown in the time of the Conqueror. Earl *William* ' was the fon of *Geoffrey de Mandeville,* who was grandfon to the former *Geoffrey,* and created Earl of *Effex* in the reign of King *Stephen.* ' He fucceeded *Geoffrey* his brother in his inheritance and honour in the fourteenth year of *Henry* II.

' In the nineteenth year of the fame reign, the Manor of *Silveſton* was in the hands of the King; ' and from this time forward was accounted to be held in ancient demefne.

' In the forty fourth year of *Henry* III. *Philip Maynard* and *Nicholas Gerard* were certified to hold each of the King one virgate of land as cuſtomary tenants, by the annual payment of ii *s.* and the performance of certain fervices amounting to the value of ii *s.* ix *d.* ob.

ᵐ In the fecond year of *Edward* I. died *William de Brandeſton* feized of two virgates of land in *Silveſton* which he held of the prior and convent of *Luffield*; and which virgates were given to the convent by the faid *William* in the preceding year. ⁿ In the thirty third year of this reign *Geoffrey de Brandeſton* had the grant of lands in *Silveſton*, which he held of the King *in*

capite, by the fervice of taking cuſtody of the King's wines in his cellar at *Silveſton.*

° By inquifition taken in the thirty fecond year of *Edward* I. it appears that *Edmund* Lord *Mortimer* was poffeffed of one Knight's fee in *Silveſton*, of the yearly rent of c *s.* which was held of him at the time of his death by *Alan la Zouche.*

ᵖ In the feventh year of *Edward* II. the Manor was granted with other Lordſhips, to *Richard de Arundel* for the term of his life; and upon his death in the fucceeding year ' it was taken again into the King's hands, who ' in the ninth year of this reign was certified to be Lord of *Silveſton.*

The next poffeffor that occurs of this Manor is Sir *Richard Lovel.* In the third year of *Edward* III. he ' was required by a writ of *quo Warranto* to fhew caufe why he claimed view of frank-pledge, affize of bread and beer, with other privileges within his Manor of *Silveſton.* In fupport of his pretenfions he urged that the Manor of *Silveſton*, together with the Manor of *Brehul* in *Buckinghamſhire*, was given him by the late King *Edward* in exchange for the Manor of *Bradenache* in the county of *Devon*, and produced the King's deed wherein thefe privileges were acknowledged and confirmed.

This Sir *Richard Lovel* ' in the eleventh year of *Edward* III. gave up his right in the Manors of *Brehul* and *Silveſton* to Sir *John Molyns*, ' who in the fame year obtained a grant of them from the King, ʷ and in the year following gave the Manor of *Silveſton* to the convent of *Burnham* in *Buckinghamſhire.* ˣ In the twenty firſt year of this reign Sir *Richard Lovel* releafed to his Majeſty and his fucceffors, all his right in the faid Manors of *Silveſton* and *Brehul.*

The Knight's fee in *Silveſton* which belonged to *Edmund* Lord *Mortimer*, defcended in courfe of fucceffion to *Roger de Mortimer* Earl of *March*, ʸ who died feized of it in the thirty fourth year of *Edward* III. at which time it was held by the heirs of *Alan la Zouche.* ᶻ In the forty third year of the fame reign died Sir *Henry Grecne*, poffeffed of one meffuage and feven virgates of land in *Whittlebury* and *Silveſton*, which were held of the priorefs of *Burnham*, ' and defcended to his pofterity.

John de Brandeſton, a defcendent from *Geoffrey de Brandeſton*, ' died in the forty fifth year of this reign feized of one meffuage, one virgate of arable land, and four acres of meadow, with three cottages in *Silveſton*, which he held of the King by ferjeanty, in tafting the King's wine as often as he ſhould come to refide at his Manor of *Silveſton.* But leaving no children, his father's fifters and their iffue became his heirs. ' By inquifitions taken in the reign of *Richard* II. it appears that this *John de Brandeſton* was further feized of the privileges of *Houfebote* and

Haybote in the foreſt of *Whittlewode*, which privileges upon his death reverted to the King: that he alſo held one cottage in *Silveſton* of the prior of *Luffield*, by the ſervice of ſuit at the prior's court twice in every year; and that he held likewiſe of the King three pieces of paſture, which upon his deceaſe came into the poſſeſſion of the prioreſs and convent of *Burnham*.

' In the eighteenth year of *Henry* VII. died *Thomas Rowland* late prior of the monaſtery of *Luffield* ſeized, in right of the convent, of the priory church, four meſſuages, and a chapel called the chapel of St. *Thomas the Martir*, forty eight acres of paſture, ten acres of meadow, and nineteen acres of wood in *Luffield*; and of three meſſuages, one cottage, three tofts, ſeventy eight acres of arable land, three acres and an half of paſture, with eleven acres of meadow, and a certain annual rent in *Silveſton*. The premiſes were held of the King in frank-almoin.

After the diſſolution of the monaſteries the Lordſhip of *Silveſton* was made a part of the honour of *Grafton*; ' and in the fifth year of *Edward* VI. was granted with the Manor of *Luffield*, the ſite and demeſne lands of the priory, to Sir *Nicholas Throckmorton*. In theſe poſſeſſions he was ſucceeded by Sir *Arthur* his ſon; upon whoſe deceaſe, ' in the year 1626, the Manor of *Silveſton* deſcended to *Mary* Lady *Wotton* his eldeſt daughter; ' who in the eleventh year of *Charles* I. claimed common of paſture in the foreſt of *Whittlewood*, with view of frank-pledge, and weyf, in right of her Manor of *Silveſton*.

' This Lady *Mary* by *Thomas* Lord *Wotton* her huſband had iſſue four daughters; and in the partition of her inheritance after her deceaſe this Manor appears to have been aſſigned to *Anne* her youngeſt daughter, the wife of Sir *Edward Hales*. This gentleman left it to Sir *Edward Hales* his ſon, who ſold it with other poſſeſſions in this County to Sir *Benjamin Bathurſt*, father of *Allen* Lord *Bathurſt* the preſent poſſeſſor of the Manor.

Lord *Bathurſt* keeps here a copyhold court in which the cuſtom is that a *Feme-Covert* may ſurrender without her huſband's conſent.

The priory of St. *Andrew* in *Northampton* had certain lands and poſſeſſions in the Lordſhip of *Silveſton*. ' In the ſixth year of *Edward* VI. theſe in part were granted to *Henry* Duke of *Suffolk*, ' and in part to *Edward* Lord *Clynton* and H. *Hereſon* in exchange for other lands in different Counties. In the time of King *James* I. the premiſes, conſiſting of one piece of paſture called the *Weſt-field*, and a wood of ſixty acres called *Field-grove* or *Monks-wood*, were in the poſſeſſion of *Creſcent Buttrye*, Eſq; ' who died ſeized of them in the tenth year of this reign. Upon his deceaſe they deſcended to *Fulk Buttrye*, Eſq; his ſon, and from him to his poſterity, who now enjoy them. The whole was held of the King as of his Manor of *Eaſt-Greenwich* by fealty only.

Upon the limits of this Lordſhip, as we have already obſerved, was ſituate the priory of *Luffield*; and as the church ſtood wholly in *Northamptonſhire*, ᵐ it hath been generally reckoned amongſt the religious houſes of this County. This priory was founded within the foreſt of *Whittlewood* ⁿ by *Robert Boſſu* Earl of *Leiceſter* in the reign of *Henry* I. to the honour of the Virgin *Mary*. The monks were of the *Benedictine* order. The foundation was confirmed by the charters of King *Henry* I. and of *Maud* his Queen. ° The charter of Earl *Robert*, directed to *Malgerius* the monk, conveys only the ground allotted for the ſite of the manſion-houſe and church. It afterwards received various donations and benefactions from different perſons. ᵖ King *Edward* I. gave to this monaſtery the hermitage of *Flechamſted-wode* in *Warwickſhire*. ᑫ The church of *Dodford* was given it by *Ralph de Keynes*; ʳ and the church of *Thornborough* in *Buckinghamſhire* by *Hamon* the ſon of *Mainfelin*. This donation was confirmed by *William* the ſon of *Hamon* with a grant of the tythes of a mill in *Wolverton*. *Robert Fitz-Nigel* beſtowed on it the chapel, with two parts of the tenths of his demeſnes, in the Manor of *Chaldene*; and the mediety or alternate preſentation to the church of *Bechampton*. ˢ Theſe donations were confirmed by *Alexander* and *Hugh* biſhops of *Lincoln*. ᵗ It received alſo the further benefactions of the chapel of St. *John Baptiſt* in *Lillingſton*, by *Hugh de St. Martin*; of the church of *Water-Stratford*, by *William* ſon of *William de Stratford*; and of the chapel of *Everſhaw*, given by *Hugh de Everſhaw*, and confirmed by *Robert* archdeacon of *Buckingham*. Theſe reſpective benefactions, with lands belonging to the priory in *Langeport*, *Wavendune*, *Saldene*, *Lechamſtead*, *Weſtbury*, *Bedford*, and *Selveſton*, an houſe in the town of *Northampton*, and other donations, ᵘ were ratified by a bull of Pope *Alexander* III. in the year 1174.

But notwithſtanding theſe gifts and poſſeſſions, the revenues of the priory fell greatly to decay, and at length were inſufficient to maintain the prior and two monks that were left. ᵛ An attempt was therefore made in the reign of *Henry* VI. to unite it to *Magdalen* college in *Oxford*; and upon the deſire of *Henry* VII. ˣ it was ſuppreſſed in 1494, by pope *Alexander* VI. who annexed it with its poſſeſſions to the collegiate church of *Windſor*. The King, however, changing his mind, the monaſtery of *Luffield* was given in 1500, to the abbat and convent of *Weſtminſter*, ʸ and confirmed to them by pope *Julius* II. in the year 1504, and thus it continued as a cell to the abbey of *Weſtminſter*, till the general diſſolution of religious houſes.

Mr. *Camden*, who hath placed *Luffield* monaftery in the County of *Buckingham*, * tells us that the monks here dying all of the plague, the houfe was thereupon deferted. But for this fuggeftion there appears no authority; and the true reafon of its decay, was the infufficiency of its endowment to fupport the buildings and members of the houfe. * The rental of the priory made in the eighth year of *Edward* IV. amounted but to xix *l.* xix *s.* 2 *d.*

In *Silvefton* is a chapel of eafe to the church of *Whittlebury* It confifts of a body and chancel tiled, and almoft of an equal height. At the weft end is a fmall wooden turret in which is one bell. The length of this chapel is thirty nine foot, the breadth of it fixteen foot. Here are no monuments nor infcriptions; the inhabitants of *Silvefton* burying their dead at *Whittlebury.* It is a modern building, and the rector of *Norton* is the minifter, who fupplies it by a curate. The poor have a yearly benefaction of xx *s.* iffuing from Mrs. *Leefon's* charity at *Abthorpe.*

The wake is obferved here on the *Sunday* before *Michaelmas* day.

SILVESTON,

or Silverston, commonly pronounced Silson, is an evident corruption of *silva tone*, or the wood town, which is strikingly characteristic of its situation in the midst of the forest.

It is a parochial chapelry to Greens Norton, and a member of Whittlebury, containing inclusive of old inclosures and the woods formerly part of Hasleborough walk about 1790 acres. The lands "within the liberties or precincts of Silston, otherwise Silverston, otherwise Silveston Burnham," were inclosed under the same act of parliament as Hasleborough walk in 5 Geo. 4 (1824). About 506 acres, including the woodlands, belong to George Henry duke of Grafton, lord of the manor; about 360 acres to Charles lord Southampton; about 180 acres to Mr. Edward Amos; about 140 acres including the Luffield lands, to Richard duke of Buckingham and Chandos, K. G.; and about 127 acres including Monkswood, to John Jackson Blencowe, of Marston St. Lawrence, esq.

Silveston is bounded on the north by Towcester, and north-east by Wood Burcote in the same parish and hundred; east by Whittlebury and the forest, and south-east by the forest and Lillingston Lovell in Oxfordshire; south by the forest and by Luffield and Lillingston Dayrell in Buckinghamshire, and south-west by the portion of Hasleborough walk now disafforested in Whitfield parish and Sutton hundred; west by Abthorp, and north-west by Hanley park in the parish and hundred of Towcester. The soil is in general a strong loam, and except the woodlands, which extend to near 600 acres, the lordship is principally in tillage.

MANORIAL HISTORY. "Silvestone" in the Saxon era, and after the Norman conquest, was compounded of three fees.

MORETON FEE*. The Saxon freehold of *Leuric*† in "Silvestone" rated at 10s. yearly, was doubled in value at the domesday survey, and held by *William* ancestor of Keynes‡ under the earl of Moreton. It contained one hide. The arable land was three carucates, of which one was in demesne with a servant [a].

PINKENEY FEE. The Saxon freehold of *Siward* in "Selvestone," valued only at 2s. yearly, but raised to 5s. at the domesday survey, was then held by one *Godwin* under Ghilo, brother of Ansculf, the ancestor of the Pinkeneys. It contained half a hide. The arable land was one carucate, in the occupation of two villeins. There was three acres of meadow, and a wood eleven quarentines or furlongs long and six wide, but the fourth part of the wood only belonged to this land [b].

MANDEVILLE FEE §. The third Saxon freehold in "Silvestone" belonged to *Asgar* §, the whole of whose possessions were bestowed by the Norman conqueror on Geoffrey de Manneville or Mandeville. His estate in this vill consisted of half a hide, rated at 10s. yearly, but doubled in value at the domesday survey when it was held by *Ernald* under Geoffrey. The arable land was one carucate, with two servants, one villein, and one bordar [c].

In the hydarium of Hen. 2, William de Keynes was certified to hold a hide in Silveston of the fee of Moreton; Henry de Pinkeney half a hide (of the fee of Ansculf); and Otner half a hide of the fee of earl William [d], Mandeville, earl of Essex. These estates correspond with the domesday entries; but the different fees cannot be subsequently identified in the mesne estates; nor can the knight's fee in Silveston held by the Mortimer family [e], be appropriated.

Burnham Abbey Manor. '[f]In the nineteenth year of Henry II. the manor of Silveston was in the hands of the king;[g] and from this time forward was accounted to be held in ancient demesne.' In 6 Ric. (1194) the sheriff of the county rendered an account of £6 for the yearly farm of Silveston[h]. In 7 Joh. (1205) Geoffrey Fitz-Peter, the sheriff, paid into the exchequer £6 for the farm of Silveston for the fourth year of this reign, and the men of Silveston rendered 2 marks (£1. 6s. 8d.) to the tallage set on the king's demesnes[i]. In 1 Hen. 3 (1216-7) the king commanded Fulk de Breant to permit Joudowin de Dou without delay to have the manors of Geddington and Silveston to hold by what farm, or rent they were worth; he had been positively informed that the utmost value of Geddington was £20 yearly, and Silveston £6, but if they were underrated, Fulk was ordered to deliver them to Joudowin, as the king doubted not he would faithfully satisfy him for the overplus[j]; and in 3 Hen. 3 (1218) the barons of the exchequer were directed to allow to the said Fulk amongst other things £6, which Geldewin de Doe had in the manor of Silveston by the king's writ[k]. In 56 Hen. 3 (1271) the treasurer and barons of the exchequer, with the assent of the king's council, committed the manor of Silveston to Thomas del Brok, Henry Wade, and the king's other tenants there, to hold during the king's pleasure, rendering £14 yearly, and the king's houses to be kept in repair at his own proper cost[l]. In 10 Edw. 1 (1282) this manor was placed in the custody of Richard de Holebrok, the steward of the Northamptonshire forests[m]. In 7 Edw. 2 (1313) the king granted the manors of Brehull or Brill in Buckinghamshire, Claverley in Shropshire, Tattenhall in Staffordshire, and Silveston, to

Richard de Arundel for life[n], who, dying the following year[o], they reverted to the crown, and in 9 Edw. 2 (1315) the king was lord of Silveston[p]. In May the succeeding year the king gave this manor, then worth £13 yearly, together with the manor of Brill, to

Sir Richard Lovell and *Muriel* his wife, in exchange for the manor of Bradenach in Devonshire, which he held by grant from the king in part of the value of the manor of Old Rokesburgh [Roxburgh in Scotland] which the king retained for the munition of Rokesburgh castle, and which manors he held at the will of the king until he should make him compensation in lands of equal value[q]. In 3 Edw. 3 (1329) he was summoned by writ of *quo warranto* to shew by what right he claimed view of frank pledge, correction of assize of bread and beer, amerciaments for hue and cry and blodewite, and acknowledgment of pleas of all his tenants by small writs of right according to the custom of the manor, when he pleaded his charter from the king's father. The king's attorney replied, that in the king's grant no mention was made of the privileges claimed. The defendant appealed to the chancery rolls, and the chancellor was directed to examine them. At the day appointed the chancellor reported that the chancery rolls for the 10th of Edw. 2 were in the king's treasury in the tower of London, so that he had not been able to execute the writ, and a further day was given[r]. Muriel, wife of sir Richard Lovell, was daughter of William first earl of Douglas in Scotland[s]. He had the barony of Kary in Somersetshire, and was summoned to parliament from 22 to 24 Edw. 3[s]. He died in Jan. 25 Edw. 3 (1351)[t], but had previously relinquished his interest in this manor, probably in obtaining an equivalent elsewhere. In 11 Edw. 3 (1337) the king granted the manor of Brill by the service of one fee, and the manor of Silveston by the accustomed service, to

Sir John Molins in fee[u]; and the same year sir Richard Lovell released to him all his right in those manors[x]. In 12 Edw. 3 (1338) sir John Molins had a grant in fee of the advowson of Burnham abbey in Buckinghamshire[y], and with the king's licence gave the manor of Silveston to the abbess and convent[z], who the same year obtained an acquittance from tallage for their tenants in Silveston, in Fulmere, Buckinghamshire, and in London[a].

In 43 Edw. 3 (1369) sir Henry Green died seised of a messuage and seven virgates of land in Silveston and Whittlebury held of the abbess of Burnham[b]; and which seven virgates in the inquisition on the death of his son sir Thomas Green are called a carucate of land[c]. The manor of "Silveston Burnham, parcel of the late abbey of Burnham," was, with the manor of Silveston Luffield, granted in 5 Edw. 6 (1551) to

Sir Nicholas Throckmorton[d], of Paulerspury. His son and heir *Sir Arthur Throckmorton* left four daughters and coheiresses, the eldest of whom,

Mary, wife of Thomas lord Wotton, '[e]in the eleventh year of *Charles* I. claimed common of pasture in the forest of *Whittlewood* with view of frank pledge and waiff, in right of her manor of *Silveston*.' On her decease this manor passed to her fourth and youngest daughter and coheiress

Anne, wife of sir Edward Hales, of Woodchurch in Kent, 2d bart. whose son sir Edward Hales, 3d bart. sold it prior to 1687[f] to

Sir Benjamin Bathurst, of Paulerspury, of whose lineal descendant *Henry* 3d earl Bathurst, it was purchased in 1800 by

Augustus Henry 3d duke of Grafton, K. G. father of *George Henry* 4th duke of Grafton, the present proprietor (1834).

A copyhold court is held for this manor, which extends into Whittlebury. A feme covert may surrender without her husband's consent, but free bench or dower does not attach to lands alienated by the husband. The fines payable on alienation are always one year's rent. In all other respects the lands are of the same tenure as freeholds.

Luffield Priory Manor. Richard, son of Elias de Hinton [near Brackley], gave to the monks of Luffield all his lands in Silveston of the fee of Towcester, rendering 9s. yearly, viz. 7s. in his name to the lord of Towcester, and

2s. to Robert de Botlind, which his father Elias gave him in free marriage with his daughter Hucline [g]. Henry de Hinton confirmed his father's grant [h]; and in 29 Hen. 3 (1245) released to William [de Brakele], prior of Luffield, by fine, the service which Warin de Munchensy [lord of Towcester], claimed for lands in Silveston [i]. Henry de Hinton, son of sir Henry de Hinton, added his wood called Hynewood, with land and pasture between the king's wood and the wood of the hospital of Brackley, and abutting on the lawn of Luffield [k]. The above named Richard de

Hinton, patron of the church of that vill, gave to the blessed Mary of Luffield all the tithes of corn of all his demesne of the fee of Mandeville in the territory of Silveston, according to the tenor of a composition made between the monks and the rector of Hinton, by which it was adjudged that they should hold the said tithes from him and his heirs, paying 2s. yearly to the rector for the time being [l]; and strife having arisen between the rector and the monks respecting this payment, the prior gave the rector two marks for good peace, and the rector for himself and his successors renounced all right to the said 2s. yearly [m]. Emma de Selveleia gave all her land in Silveston, rendering 11s. yearly [n]; and William de Selveleia, for the souls of Emma his mother, Eustachius his father, and earl Geoffrey (de Mandeville), gave all his lands there [o]. William de Mandeville, earl of Essex, confirmed the donations from the Selveleias [p]; and by another deed confirmed all the land of his fee which ought to render the service of one knight's fee, quit from all service [p]. The prior of Luffield in plea to a *quo warranto* in 3 Edw. 3 (1329) claimed by prescription, view of frank pledge and assize of bread and beer of all his tenants in Silveston; but it appearing that he punished offenders against the assize by amerciament of 40d. instead of the legal punishment of pillory and tumbril, the view was forfeited, but restored again for a fine of half a mark [q]. In 50 Edw. 3 (1376) the prior and convent demised the moiety of their manor of Monksbarne to Joan Hancock for life, saving 6s. 8d. for a heriot at her death, and suit at their court of *Silveston* [r]. This priory was, in the reign of Henry VII. annexed to the abbey of Westminster, to which it continued a cell till the final suppression of monastic establishments.

The possessions of the late priory of Luffield, parcel of the late abbey of Westminster, including the manor of " Silveston alias Silston," were granted in 5 Edw. 6 (1551) to

Sir Nicholas Throckmorton [s], of PAULERSPURY, and this manor became " the inheritance of *Anne* viscountess dowager of Baltinglass in Ireland," [t] daughter and heiress of *dame Anne Temple* *, second daughter and coheiress of sir Arthur Throckmorton.

On a partition in 1698 between *sir Richard Temple*, bart. (afterwards viscount Cobham) " the right heir of the said viscountess Baltinglass on her father's side," and *Thomas* earl of Sussex, grandson and heir of Elizabeth, third daughter and coheiress of sir Arthur, the manor of Silveston Luffield was conveyed to the earl; who in May 1703 sold it to

Sir Benjamin Bathurst [t], of PAULERSPURY, from which time it has descended with Silveston Burnham manor down to *George Henry* 4th duke of Grafton, the present proprietor (1834.) A court is occasionally held for this manor, but there are no copyholds attached to it.

St. ANDREW's PRIORY, NORTHAMPTON, had lands and woods in Silveston, but by whom given is not recorded in the cartulary. They were partly granted in 6 Edw. 6 (1551-2) to Henry (Brandon), duke of Suffolk [u], and Monkswood was the same year granted (int. al.) to Edward lord Clinton (afterwards earl of Lincoln) and Henry Herdson in exchange for lands in other counties [x]. In 10 Jac. 1 (1612) Crescent Botry, esq. of MARSTON ST. LAWRENCE †, died seised of a pasture called the Westfield, and a wood, grove, and land called Fieldgrove and Foxhall alias Monkswood in Silveston, parcel of the late abbey of St. Andrew in Northampton [y]. They remained in the family of Botry at the time of Bridges [z]; but were afterwards alienated to the *Blencowes* of MARSTON ST. LAWRENCE, and are now vested in John Jackson Blencowe, esq.

SILVESTON was the residence of our early monarchs when they resorted to the forest of Whittlewood to enjoy the pleasures of the chase. A mandate from king Henry II. for the monks of Bordesley in Staffordshire to have all the villeins and fugitives belonging to their lands, was dated at Selveston [a]. King Richard in a personal conference with William king of Scotland, at Northampton in April 1194, delivered to him a special charter whereby he regulated the ceremonial and covenanted to bear the expences of the Scotch in coming, staying, and returning, when he was summoned to attend the great councils of England. From Northampton, Richard proceeded to Silveston in his way to Winchester on the 12th of that month. Hubert (Walter), archbishop of Canterbury, and Hugh (Pudsey), bishop of Durham, went as far as Brackley, and took possession of the inn which the bishop had occupied thirty years before. The servants of the king of Scotland surprised them there, and attempted to eject the bishops' servants, but were not able. They nevertheless purchased provision for the king, and dressed it for the table. When the bishop came he boldly entered the inn, and ordered the meal to be served, but the archbishop resigned his pretensions and retired. On the return of the Scotch king from hunting—probably with Richard—he refused to go there, and commanding what was provided to be given to the poor, he went to Silveston to complain of the bishop to the king, who was exceedingly angry, and warmly reprimanded him. The next day the two monarchs advanced to Woodstock, and on the 15th, Richard was solemnly crowned at Winchester [b]. King John was frequently here. On the 3d of Jan. 1200 he dated from hence the grant of Medmenham in Buckinghamshire to Woburn abbey [c]. He was here from the 2d to the 5th of Sept. 1204, and from the 10th to the 12th of Feb. 1204-5 [d]; on the 24th and 25th May 1205, and 15th Mar. 1206-7 [e]; on the 8th and 9th of Aug., and the 5th and 6th of Nov. 1207, and 17th of Jan. 1207-8 [f]; from the 6th to the 9th of Aug. 1212 [g]; from the 16th to the 18th Feb. 1214-5 [h]; and from the 4th to the 6th of Mar. 1215-6, during which three days he issued more than twenty orders and grants, principally of the forfeited lands of the adherents of the barons [i]. King Henry III. was here on the 16th of June 1224 [k]. A grant from him to the university of Oxford bears date at *Silveston* 6 Feb. 1235-6 [l]; and in Aug. 1258 whilst staying here, he gave the monks of Luffield a charter placing them under his special protection [m]. King Edward I. was at Silveston 22 Dec. 1274 [n]. From the circumstance of his placing an oblation of 7s. on the great altar in the church of Luffield priory on the 9th of Aug. 1290 [o], it may be fairly presumed that he was then living here, and this is the last notice which I have been able to trace of royal residence at Silveston.

Geoffrey Fitz-Peter the sheriff, in rendering an accompt of the farm of the county of Northampton for the first half year of 6 Ric. 1 (1194) deducted 20s. and Simon de Pateshull for the other half year deducted £6. for the repairs of the king's houses in Silveston [p]. In 6 Joh. (1204) the sheriff of the county was commanded by view of legal men to do the necessary repairs of the king's houses and walls in Silveston without delay before winter, and it should be accounted to him at the exchequer [q]. In the following year Robert de la Saucei and Henry Fitz-Peter the custodes or sheriffs, in rendering their accompt for the first half year, deducted £9. 5s. for the repair of the king's houses in Silveston by the king's writ, and by view of William de Silveston and Henry Clerk; and Peter de Stokes, custos or sheriff for the other half year, deducted 116s. 8d. by view of William and Henry de Silveston [r]; and a writ issued to the barons of the exchequer to account with the sheriff for what he had expended in the reparation of the king's houses in Northampton and Silveston [s]. In the succeeding year a writ issued to the barons to account with Peter de Stokes for what he had expended by writ and view of legal men in the repairs of the king's castle and houses in Northampton, and houses in Silveston, so that it should all be accounted to, or deducted from, his farm of the county of Northampton if sufficient, but if not, that it should be accounted to him out of the issues of the Norman lands in his custody, and for which he ought to answer to the exchequer [t]. In 17 Joh. (1215) the sheriff was commanded, if the men of Silveston had repaired, or were willing peacefully to repair, the pond there, to let them have 60s. which he should otherwise require from them for their farm, which Simon son of Walter took [u]; and the barons of the exchequer were directed to allow the sheriff 49s. 2d. which he had expended on the king's house at Silveston [x]. Similar orders were issued in 3 Hen. 3 (1218) [y]. In 5 Hen. 3 (1221) the sheriff was commanded without delay to repair the king's pond and the walls round the king's houses at Silveston as they were accustomed to do in the times of king Henry the grandfather, Richard the uncle, and John the father of the present king [z]; and in 6 Hen. 3 (1222) [a] and 8 Hen. 3 (1224) [b] orders were again issued to the sheriff for repairs, and the expense would be allowed at the exchequer. In 34 Hen. 3 (1251) the sheriff certified that timber for the king's works at Silveston could not be found in the forest of Whittlewood, without the woods of Pokesley and Hanley, and a mandate issued for him to take the timber where it would be to the least damage [c]; and in 38 Hen. 3 (1255) the sheriff rendered an account of the completion of the works begun by Simon de Thorp at Geddington and Silveston [d].

Several entries of wine sent for the supply of the royal table here occur in the Close Rolls. "The king to the sheriff of the county of Northampton, greeting. Know ye that we have commanded W. de Wrotham to purchase wine for our use at the fairs of Hoyland to the value of £100, and to cause the same to be sent to Jakesley [Yaxley], and to let you know when it should arrive there; wherefore we command you when he has apprised you thereof, to cause three casks of the said wine to be sent to Clive [Cliffe Regis], six to Geidington, and four to *Selveston*, and all the remainder to Northampton, and to appoint some trusty person to take care that it shall not be injured in the carriage, and you shall be accounted with at the exchequer. 24 June 7 Joh. (1205) [e]." In Nov. 16 Joh. (1214) the chancellor was commanded to purchase five casks of the best wine which could be found in London, and send one to Clive, one to Geddington, one to Rockingham, one to *Selveston*, and one to Salcey, in good casks, for which purpose he might if necessary use the king's casks, and moreover provide sufficient wine for use in each of the said places [f]; and in Jan. following, another order issued to the chancellor to send without delay four tons of red wine to Wallingford, three to Bruhull [Brill in Buckinghamshire], one to Finemer [in Oxfordshire], two to *Selveston*, and one cask to *Wakefeuld*, and two casks of white wine and ten of red to Northampton, and two tons to Geddington, two to "Salvatu," and four to Rockingham [g]. In 15 Hen. 3 (1251) the sheriff rendered an account of £6. 10s. 6d. for the carriage of four casks of wine from St. Botolph's to Clive, two to Rockingham, fourteen to Northampton, five to Geddington, and four to Selveston [h]. In 2 Edw. 1 (1274) William de Brandeston died seised of a messuage and croft, six cottages and three acres of land, held by the sergeanty of taking charge of the wine in the king's cellars at Silveston [i]. He had other lands in Silveston held of the priory of Luffield, and was succeeded by his brother John de Brandeston, aged sixty years [j]. These lands, with possessions in Braunston and Kirby, remained in the family till the extinction of the male line in 35 Edw. 3 (1361) on the decease of another John de Brandeston [k], whose coheirs have been already given under Kirby in BLAKESLEY *. In the inquisition on his death there was a variation in the terms of the sergeanty; the tenure was *tasting* the king's wines so often as he should reside at his manor of Silveston [k], instead of, or in addition to, simply *taking charge* of it; and the privilege of housebote and haybote in the forest of Whittlewode was also attached to the lands.

A CHAPEL was attached to the royal residence. In 2 Joh. (1200) the sheriff rendered an account of 20s. for the livery or maintenance of the chaplain of Selveston [l]; in 7 Joh. (1205) the same sum for each half year [m]; and in 9 Joh. (1207) the sheriff was commanded to let the king's chaplain at Selveston have hand towels and other necessaries for his chapel to the value of 10s. and it should be allowed at the exchequer [n].

The site of the royal mansion was mistaken by Bridges for King's hill in Whitfield [o], or Siresham †, but there can be no hesitation in assigning the mansion and chapel to King's hill coppice and Chapel coppice, which were within the Haselborough walk of the forest, and in the precincts of Silveston.

THE VILLAGE stands on rising ground, four miles from Towcester on the turnpike road to Brackley. On the 21st of May 1807, between five and six o'clock P. M. a fire broke out here, occasioned by singeing a pig too near some thatch. In an hour and a half nine houses were burnt down, and property destroyed to the amount of upwards of £2000 [p]. By the census of 1801 it contained 138 houses and 586 inhabitants; by that of 1811, 161 houses and 696 inhabitants; by that of 1821, 177 houses and 837 inhabitants; and by that of 1831, 202 houses and 947 inhabitants. The annual quota of land tax for this hamlet is £79. 7s. at 4s. in the £. The estimated value of real property as assessed to the property tax of 10 *per cent.* for the year ending April 1815, amounted to £1,106. The poor's rates for the year ending Easter 1832, raised £730. 2s. 6d. at 9s. in the £. The wake is held on the Sunday before Michaelmas day.

THE CHAPEL. ' [q] In Silveston,' says Bridges, 'is a chapel of ease to the church of *Whittlebury*. It consists of a body and chancel tiled, and almost of an equal height. At the west end is a small wooden turret, in which is one bell. The length of this chapel is thirty-nine foot, the breadth of it sixteen foot. Here are no monuments nor inscriptions; the inhabitants of *Silveston* burying their dead at *Whittlebury*. It is a modern building, and the rector of Norton is the minister, who supplies it by a curate.' The present chapel is a plain neat building of stone, 59 ft. 9 in. long by 39 ft. wide.

A separate register was first kept at Silveston in 1831, and marriages began to be celebrated at the chapel.

THE WESLEYAN METHODISTS in 1811 erected a chapel here, 34 ft. long by 37 ft. wide.

BENEFACTIONS (vide p. 2). LEESON'S CHARITY *. The sum of 20s. *per annum*, received under this charity, is given away in bread, money, or linen, among poor people selected at a township meeting.

SAUNDER'S CHARITY †. Eight poor children from Silveston are admitted under this donation into the national school at Whittlebury, and gratuitously instructed in reading, writing, and arithmetic.

POOR'S LAND. The commissioners for inclosing Hasleborough walk and Silveston, allotted eight acres in trust for the poor of Silveston in lieu of their right to sere and broken wood in Whittlebury forest. This allotment is now let in small portions to the poor.

LUFFIELD PRIORY.

Luffield, according to the etymology of Browne Willis, " *Ager amabilis* or *Lovelyfield* from its situation [r]," is a secluded spot within the forest of Whittlewood, or Whittlebury. Here, at the junction of the two counties of Buckingham and Northampton, the conventual buildings and offices being principally in the parish of Lillingston Dayrell in the former county, and the church wholly in the precincts of Silveston, stood a small priory of the Benedictine order, dedicated to the Virgin Mary. It was founded in the reign of Henry I. by Robert Bossu, earl of Leicester, who, for the souls of William king of England and queen Matilda, and Roger de Bellamont and Adeliza his wife ‡, and Robert his father, and for the health of the souls of himself and Waleran his brother, gave in alms to Malger the monk, the servant of God, a small laund between " Lunbricodam & Cepieleiam " for mansions or dwellings, and to make an oratory there, and also as much of the other land of "Cerveleia" as with the advice of his friends he should consider sufficient for building. The charter is headed, " the foundation of the monastery of the blessed Mary of Luffield in the county of Northampton within the forest of Whittelwode;" Waleran earl of Mellent is the first, and Osulf the forester the last witness to it; and it was made by the advice and approbation of the earl Warren, Nigel de Albini, and the grantor's brother Waleran earl of Mellent [s]. King Henry I. commanded R. Basset, A. de Vere, and Hugh de Chalian, and all his foresters of "Whitleword," to permit the prior and monks of Luffield to have, as they were accustomed, all convenient accommodation in his forest without waste, and to protect them from all injury and contumely so long as they were under his patronage ˢ. The empress M. daughter of king Henry, issued a similar command, though rather differently expressed ˢ; and by another charter in which she styled herself queen Matilda, directed Vitalis Engaine and William de Lusoris or Lizures—the foresters, though not so designated—as they valued her love, to maintain Malger the monk, and his [" servientes "] servants in the peaceable enjoyment of what the king had granted to them ˢ. King Henry III. in the 42d year of his reign (1258) by a charter dated at "Selveston" took into his special protection and defence all the men, lands, and other possessions of the prior and convent of Luffield, whose church was of his foundation ᵗ—or more correctly, patronage; and in the 55th year of his reign, acquitted them of the twentieths for their natives, which they had certified to him and his eldest son Edward ᵗ. The donations to this priory in Dodford *, Heyford †, Maidford ‡, Greens Norton §, Silveston ‖, and Whittlebury ¶, have been already detailed, and in Challock, Cosgrave, Eltington, Milton Malsor, Northampton, Paulerspury, Slapton, and Towcester remain to be noticed as they respectively arise.

In Buckinghamshire the monks of Luffield had considerable possessions. Hamon, son of Meinfelin de Wolverton, with the consent of Hamon his son gave them the tithes of the bread of his house wheresoever it might be on his land, and the church of Thornborough ᵘ; and William son of Hamon de Wolverton confirmed the church of Thornborough, and gave them 10s. yearly rent for ever out of his west mill in Wolverton, in lieu of the tithes of the bread of his house, which they had of the gift of his ancestor ᵘ. Sir John, son of sir Alan de Wolverton, released to them all the lands which they had of his fee in Thornborough, free from all service ˣ; and John, son of John lord of Wolverton, ratified the donation which John, son of Alan de Wolverton, his father, made of the homage and service of William de Fraxino, but saving to himself and his heirs the proportion of hidage, scutage, and castleward to Northampton castle due from those lands; and at the same time granted them all the lands and tenements which belonged to Robert de Fraxino of Thornborough the day he was hanged for felony ʸ, and which had escheated to him as chief lord. Robert de Aerial or Dayrell, with Ralph his son, gave them the place in his wood of Lillingston, in which was built the chapel of St. Thomas (a Becket) the archbishop and martyr ᶻ; to which Ralph afterwards added all his wood in width from the king's way to Westbury wood, and in length from St. Thomas's chapel to great Holebeck ᶻ; and Hugh de St. Martin gave them the chapel of St. John the Baptist in his court of Lillingston ᵃ. Hugh de Chastellon gave half a virgate in Leckhampstead ᵇ. William de Westbury "Vicecomes de Dumard," confirmed to them all the land in Westbury of the gift of his father ᶜ. Simon de St. Liz gave them part of his wood there between the woods of Richard de Castillon and the prior of Brackley ᵈ; and Ralph de Hareng gave them all the wood between Kenpad and their own wood in width, and from the trench cut from the rivulet of Holebeck to Pickering cross in length ᵈ. Ralph, son of Ralph Hareng gave them a messuage with a croft and half a virgate of land in Chakemore ᵉ. Robert de Langeport bestowed on them half his land at Langport or Lamport near Stowe, which his son Jordan confirmed by the description of five virgates of land ᶠ. Pagan de Beauchamp confirmed to them that hide of land in Evershaw, which Ralph the son of Richard held of him, and had granted to them ᵍ. Ralph lord of Evershaw gave them half a hide of his land there, and the chapel of the said vill ʰ, which half hide prior John released for 4s. 8d. yearly to Hugh de Evershaw, son of William, who confirmed the grant of the chapel ʰ, probably in consideration of the easy terms on which the land was surrendered to him. William Baynell gave the monks a virgate of land in "Saldeston ⁱ" or Shalston. William Baynell, son of William, presented to them the tithes of bread at his house there; and sir William Baynell, son of sir William Baynell, lord of Shalston, assured to them all the lands which they then held or might hereafter acquire of his fee. Another William Baynell confirmed to them the land there called "Aldwic ⁱ." Richard, son of Nigel de Bechampton, gave them a moiety of the church of Bechampton, and half a virgate of land in "Salden," which his father Nigell gave them, and two parts of the tithe of his demesne there ʲ. Sir William Bechampton gave them half a virgate, and Henry Kyneman a virgate and a half in Bechampton ᵏ. William, son of William de Stratford, gave them the church of Water Stratford ˡ, and they had two messuages in Buckingham ᵐ, and small rentcharges in other places. King Edward I. gave them the hermitage which Gerald the monk made in the wood of Flechampsted in Warwickshire ⁿ, but afterwards transferred it to the knights templars.

Pope Alexander III. by a bull in 1174 (20 Hen. 2) confirmed to Ralph prior of St. Mary of Luffield, all the possessions of the convent, including the site of the convent, the church of Dodford, the chapel of St. Thomas the martyr, Fleckhamstede, Charley (qu. where?), Bradwell, the vill called Eversaw, lands in Langeport, Wavendon, and Salden, with two parts of the tithe of the demesne lands in Leckhampsted, Westbury, and Bedford with a certain manse before the archdeacon's gate, lands in Silveston, the tithes of bread from the houses of Hamon, son of Meinfelin, William de Brun, William de Plumpton, and William de Lillingston, and a house in Northampton ᵒ.

The annual rental of this priory in 17 Edw. 1 (1289) as entered in the cartulary, was " in rents from divers tenants £1. 4s. 11d., in Eversaw [co. Bucks] £1. 12s. 2d., in Buckingham 7s. 6d., in Chalkmore 1s. 4d., in Langport 9s. 8d., in Acle one pound of wax, in Leckhampsted 5s., in Lillingston (Dayrell) 9s. 8d., in Bechampton £1. 11s. 10d., in Stoni Stratford 2s., in Wolverton 10s.. in Salden 2s. 6d., in Thornborough £6. 11. 5½d., in Shaldeston £2. 15. 1½., in Boicote 12d., in Bedford 3s., in Lillingston major [Lovell, co. Oxon] 13s. 8d., in Braklee [co. Northt.] 4s., in Silveston 4s. 2d., in Wittlebury 9s. 1d., in Towcester 12s. 5d., in Blacovesle 9s., in Middleton 12d., in Brockhole one pound of pepper, in

Dodford £2. 16s. 10½d., in Heyford £1. 1s. 4d.,   Total £22. 6s. 10½d." There were also then paid by their tenants in these places thirty capons and seventy-seven hens [P].

TAXATIO ECCLESIASTICA P. NICHOLAI IV. A.D. 1291 (20 EDW. 1).

LUFFELD PRIORAT'.

DIOC. LINC.				li.	s.	d.						li.	s.	d.
(BUCK.)							in Luffeld in tĩis & redd'	-	-	-	i	xi	ij	
Porc' in Ecctia de Murescle	-	-	i				ibid. in fruct' greg' & aïal'	-	-	-		x		
in Schalden in redd'	-	-	-	-	ii	vi	in Westbur' in redd'	-	-	-		iij		
in Eveshawe, Schaldeston, Eldewyk, } in tĩis redd' cur'	-	-	-	ij	xij	v	in W'loston [Wolverton] de redd'	-	x					
ibid. in fruct' greg' & aïl'	-	-	-		vj	viij	(OXON.)							
							in Lulingston in redd'	-	-	-		xiij	viij	
in Bukynghm	-	-	-	-		iv	(NORTHT.)							
in Thornb'we in tĩis redd' p'tis cur' } fruct' aïal'	-	-	-	vij	xiv	xi	in Dodeford de redd'	-	-	-	-	ij	iij	
in Bechmpton in tĩis p'tis deduct' } deducend'	-	-	-			v	in Westcote & Helmeden & Schol- } delak [Challok] in tĩis & redd'	ij	xv	xiob.				
							ibid. in fruct' greg' & aïal'	-	-	-	v	vij	iv
							[Summa xxvli. xixs. viiob.]							

A comparison of these two valuations made at an interval of only three years will discover many discrepancies which it is impossible now to account for, or reconcile.   Whittlebury, Silveston, and other places are wholly omitted in the latter.   Both, however, agree in the exility of its income; and it is rather remarkable that a religious establishment which originated under such favorable auspices, founded by a powerful earl, sanctioned and seconded by royal charters, and patronised by the neighbouring lords, should, after struggling with poverty for centuries, be compelled to resign its independence.   It was sunk so low in the reign of Edward III. that a licence was obtained to endow it further for its better support, and enable it to receive £10 *per ann.* to pray for the king's good estate while living, and for his soul when dead, and for the soul of sir John Grey [q], probably the donor of this augmentation.   This well-intentioned effort to raise its fortunes was unavailing, and in 1457 (35 Hen. 6) the president of St. Mary Magdalen hall in Oxford procured the royal licence for purchasing the site and possessions of Luffield priory [r].   This hall had been founded in 1448 by Waynfleet, bishop of Winchester, who now proposed increasing its endowment, but obtaining St. John's hospital at Oxford, he altered his purpose, and the hall was merged in his new foundation of Magdalen college.   A short respite of the fate of Luffield intervened till at the suggestion of Henry VII. pope Alexander VI. in 1494 (10 Hen. 7) issued a bull for appropriating it to founding a chapel and chantry to the Virgin Mary in the royal collegiate church of St. George at Windsor [s]; but the king subsequently abandoned the design, and in 1500 (15 Hen. 7) obtained another bull from the same pope reciting the former disposition of it, and settling it with Motisfont priory in Hampshire on the foundation of a chapel to the virgin Mary in Westminster abbey [t]; which grant, however, did not take effect during the life of prior Thomas Rowland, who died in 1503 (18 Hen. 7) seised of the church, the chapel of St. Thomas the martyr, four messuages, forty-eight acres of pasture, ten acres of meadow, and nineteen acres of wood in Luffield, and the other possessions of the priory held of the king in pure and perpetual alms [u].   In June the following year pope Julius II. by bull confirmed the annexation of this priory with the royal chapel of St. Martin Magnus in Tickhill castle in Yorkshire, to king Henry the Seventh's chapel in Westminster abbey [x]; and it continued a cell to that splendid establishment till the general dissolution of the monasteries.

Camden places Luffield in Buckinghamshire, and says, " by reason that the Monkes were all consumed with the plague, the house was utterly left desolate."   No authority is given for this assertion; and in truth, irremediable penury was " the plague" from which they suffered, the inadequacy of the funds of the priory to support a prior and two monks being the reason assigned for its suppression in 1494 [y].   One principal cause of its poverty—and which is equally applicable to many of the minor priories—was the improvident demises of lands in fee at small reserved rents which remained stationary whilst money was progressively advancing in value.

ADVOWSON.   On the extinction of the Norman line of the earls of Leicester, the patronage of this monastery appears to have been claimed by the king, and was henceforward exercised by the crown to the exclusion of the representatives of the original founder.

A CARTULARY of this religious house is amongst the muniments of the dean and chapter of Westminster, to whom it was given by John Batteley, esq., in the time of queen Anne.   It contains 240 leaves or 480 pages, and is probably the same volume which is mentioned by Tanner as belonging to a person of the name of Okeley in 1649.   Collectanea by Francis Thinne, concerning the foundation of Luffield, occur in the Cotton. MSS. Cleop. C. 3, art. 26 ; and excerpts from the register are preserved in the Ashmolean museum at Oxford, Dugdale MSS. vol. 39, fo. 131.   Among the ancient charters in the Harleian collection in the British Museum, 84 F. 35 & 36, relate to this priory; and in Nasmith's edition of Tanner's Notitia Monastica are numerous references to public records.

FAIR. In 14 Hen. 3 (1230) the king for the souls of himself, his ancestors, and heirs, granted to the prior and monks a charter for a yearly fair at Luffield on the eve, the day, and the morrow of the exaltation of the holy cross [h]. The time for holding the fair was a very unusual deviation, at so early a period from the general custom of having the wake or fair on the anniversary of the patron saint, which in the present case would have been on the assumption of the virgin Mary. This fair was confirmed to the monks on plea to a writ of *quo warranto* in 3 Edw. 3 (1329) [i], and again by exemplification in 15 Ric. 2 (1391) [k]. No mention is made of it in the inquisition after the death of prior Thomas Rowland in 18 Hen. 7 (1503) [l], and it may therefore be inferred that it had fallen into disuse.

THE PRESENT STATE of Luffield corresponds with the description given a century ago by Willis, who says [m], " when I visited this place, I was informed it was extraparochial, and belonged to *Westminster abbey*, and that on the Division of the Bounds of the Counties, the greatest part was included in *Silveston* parish, co. *Northampton*, and the rest in *Lillingston Dayrell*. Here was then nothing remaining whatsoever of the Priory Edifices, except a Piece of the wall of the Tower. I measured from this Tower ruins, the supposed Dimensions of the Church, which appeared to be about 80 Foot in Length, and 30 in Breadth ; they informed me, that by Tradition there were five Bells in the Tower, and that they were carried to *Paulers Perry*, on the first Bell of which Church I met with this inscription, Sancta Maria Ora pro nobis; and so it might possibly have been brought from hence."

" At some Distance on the *Northamptonshire* Side, is a Tenant's House, and on the *Buckinghamshire* Side, an old Chapel turned into a Dwelling House, which was the Chapel of *St. Thomas Becket*, given by the *Dayrell* Family aforespoken of n *Lillingston*. It is assessed to the Land Tax, and all other Parish Rates, with the Lords of *Stow's* Demesnes, as they are proprietors of this Estate; whose Tenants, in digging about this old Tower in the year 1732, they there found (which was shewn me *Oct.* 11, 1733) an old Grave-stone like the Lid of a Stone Coffin, in the middle of which was a Cross of Brass Flory infixed, and these Arms engraven, víz. *Two Bars, in Chief, three Martlets*. Here were Letters round the Verge, enchased in Brass, which being pickt out, and lying dispersedly, nothing could be made out or conjectured from those loose Letters who it belonged it to; but I suppose it was laid over one of the Priors, probably Prior *William Horewood*, in whose Time the Choir of this Church was new roofed and leaded about the year 1380, or Prior *John Horwood's* Time, who was admitted a Monk of this Convent *Anno* 1367, and died Prior thereof 1419." The cross which divides the counties of Buckingham and Northampton is cut out on the site of the conventual church; and there are between fifty and sixty acres of Luffield within the parish or liberties of Silveston, but, being reputed extraparochial, they were not exonerated from tithe under the act for inclosing Silveston.

THE SITE and demesne lands of the late priory of Luffield, parcel of the late abbey of Westminster, were granted in 5 Edw. 6 (1551) to *sir Nicholas Throckmorton* [n], of PAULERSPURY. *Anne*, the second of the four daughters and coheiresses of his eldest son sir Arthur Throckmorton, was the first wife of sir Peter Temple, bart. of Stowe in Buckinghamshire *, by whom she had an only child, Anne, who married Thomas Roper, viscount Baltinglass in Ireland. In 1698, after her decease s. p. a partition was made between Thomas earl of Sussex, grandson of Elizabeth, the third daughter and coheiress of sir Arthur Throckmorton, and sir Richard Temple, bart. (afterwards viscount Cobham) " the right heir of the said viscountess Baltinglass on her father's side [o]," when Luffield was assigned to the latter, and has attended the inheritance of the other Temple estates down to *Richard Nugent Temple Bridges Chandos, duke of Buckingham and Chandos, K. G.* the present proprietor (1834).

THE KING'S HOUSES 1066-1485

Silverston, Northamptonshire

Silverston is a village in Whittlebury Forest where there was a royal hunting lodge which was frequently visited by the Angevin kings. Henry I dated a charter here some time between 1121 and 1130, but there is no direct evidence that there was a royal house at Silverston until the reign of Henry II. It is mentioned in 1164, and between 1178 and 1183 it was evidently rebuilt, for during those years over £280 were spent on *"the work of the king's houses of Silverston"*. The buildings specifically mentioned are the hall and the cellar. There was also a fishpond fed by a spring. Both house and pond were regularly repaired during the reigns of Richard I and John, and in 1210-11 the latter built a new chamber and a stable. In 1236 Henry III had *"long and beautiful windows"* inserted in the walls of the king's and queen's chambers, and in 1247-50 he built a new chapel and wardrobe for the queen. At the same time repairs and alterations were effected to the king's chapel, the king's *"new chamber"* (to which a porch was added), the kitchen, the wall round the courtyard, and the bridge before the gate entrance. An order for further alterations in 1252 was subsequently cancelled, and only routine repairs were carried out until 1271, when the kitchen was found to be so decayed that it had to be entirely rebuilt. Further repairs are recorded in the reign of Edward I, but when Edward II granted the manor to Richard of Arundel for life in 1313, the buildings were found to be in a ruinous condition. An inquiry was held, and evidence was given by local people. According to them the decay had begun in the time of Henry III and had been pulled down by Elias de Hauville, custodian in the reign of Edward I, and the accumulated dilapidations were assessed at £164 3s. 4d. Repairs were ordered in 1315 and 1316, but in 1317, Arundel having died, the manor was granted to Sir Richard Lovel, and royal interest in the buildings ceased. The site of the house is uncertain. According to Bridges it was in the neighbouring parish of Syresham, but this seems improbable, and the remains of fishponds immediately to the north of Silverston churchyard suggest that it may have been in that vicinity. (See page 10)

Extract from : History of The King's Works , vol 12, page 1002-3

KINGS OF THE FOREST

We are privileged to live here in Silverstone, in this forest land that was the haunt of kings and courtiers. The hunting lodge and two manors echoed with the Norman shouts, and calls of merriment from men well-pleased with hunting the fat deer that roamed in fair Whittlewood.
By contrast, was it the strong local men of Anglo-Saxon blood who had to carry back the Norman prey? Who had to fell the trees to supply wood for fires and roasting venison, while their conquerors relaxed and drank wine from French vineyards. As the Normans tried to speak the words of these proud country men,

was their accent reminiscent of mine, with rolling "Rs" and clear-cut vowels? ..... Maybe!

So few acres remain of the huge forests of Northamptonshire, where the nightingale sang all night, to charm the ears of Norman lords. Some of those riches still remain. We today, can ride where the kings once rode.

We can see the glory of Silverstone in the bluebells that grow in profuse and breathtaking beauty in the copse named after Bold King Richard. Why is that spot named after him? Did he and his men follow a Silverstone verderer on some moonlit night to watch the badgers at their play among tall oaks in the verges? Or was it their sole desire to hunt the hart and hind with arrows keen and sharp?

The kings and their horsemen returned time and again, in Winter and high Summer, to find refreshment and new strength in the green cool of deep forest, their ears filled with strains of song from thrush and robin, chiff-chaff, wren and blackbird.

We, who inherit these acres, are as privileged as they, for we too, can walk free and at ease, to renew our harrased minds, and to breathe in the fresh beauty and fragrance of the forest ways. No longer hunting the fallow deer of their high regard. We are armed, nonetheless, not with sharp arrows of pain and death, but with our boxes of magic that catch on film or tape, the creatures fleeting past, or lying still in a patch of dappled shade. We can have their charms and sound at our command. We can cast these scenes upon our screens, and add the sounds of birds and beast, whenever we wish within our warm sheltered homes.
Yes, we are as privileged as Kings!
Ruth Denney (born in the Channel Islands).

SILVERSTONE FIELDS FARM.

This is a brief history of the farm now known as Silverstone Fields Farm, looking back through time to uncover the evolution and to reveal the changes that have occurred. The earliest record appears in 1299 when the land comprised part of

Whittlewood Forest. The boundary ran to Watling Street, including parts of Towcester and contained around 20,000 acres. The forest law enforced the preservation of red deer, fallow deer, roe and wild boar. Royal status was accorded to the forest in 1527 when Henry VIII exchanged some of his land holdings for land within the Grafton and Hartwell Estates. In 1600 the area now containing Silverstone Fields Farm was known as Silson Common. At this time the land would all have been largely forested but changes were to occur during the seventeenth century.

On 31st July 1628, Lord President Marlborough gave warrant for the Earl of Northampton to cut down woods and to convert the land to arable in return for a payment of £5,000 and £10 rent. This would have represented a substantial sum of money at that time. By 1629 Charles I was in need of money and gave consent for further de-forestation whilst at the same time extending Salcey and Whittlewood Forests. This continued throughout the century with a record from 1670 showing that there were 7,000 oaks in Whittlewood Forest fit for plank, needed to provide timber to the Royal Navy.

On 21st June 1673, the use of the land passed to the Duke of Grafton although he was only entitled to the profit from the sale of underwoods. The swapping of land occurred frequently and the records indicate that the Dukes of Grafton and Southampton appear as regular owners. A map showing Swinney Field from 1714 includes the present land area. The Swinney is the name of the brook at the bottom of the farm. Swinney Fields is by then shown as open ground where trees and underwood of forest lands had been grubbed up to clear the land and convert to arable and pasture. Almost inevitably, because of the effect of de-forestation, by 1772 there was reported to be a shortage of timber in Whittlewood and substantial fines were imposed for any timber supplied to the East India Company.

The wood should be made available for the Royal Navy. By the end of the century, Whittlewood Forest comprised 5,424 acres of which 3,476 acres were in the ownership of the Duke of Grafton.

The enclosure of the land continued through the 1800s. By 1826 one of the enclosure areas was Swinney Fields. The area was divided into allotments for Samuel Sheppard, John Sheppard, Richard Gardiner of London, the Duke of Grafton, John Malsbury Kirby, and Edward Amos. By 1831 the ownership was shared between the Earl of Pomfret, Duke of Southampton and the Reverend Sanders. On 11th October of that year they granted a tenancy of the land only to Mr Franklin. Franklin was a Towcester grocer. In September 1832 a barn was built at Kingsmore which cost a total of £79 8s 7d, of which the landlord paid 50% and the tenant 50%. Franklin also agreed to do all the carting free of charge. Over the period of his occupancy, Franklin built all of the hovels and cowhouse at his own expense and was allowed to take them away when he left or to sell them on to the next tenant or to the landlord.

In January 1836, Franklin commenced construction of the house, then known as Swinney Ford, for a total cost of £103 16s 9d. The census of 1851 identified the property as Fields Farm and showed the tenant as Edward Ridge, Henry Ridge (his brother), Mary Smith (a servant) and John Scott (a servant). They farmed using 9 labourers in addition to the servants. They farmed both Fields Farm and the land now known as Shacks Barn Farm.

By 1861 Edward Ridge had married Susanna and they had produced a daughter, Penelope Eliza (11 months old). He farmed without his brother and was helped by 6 men, 2 boys, and 3 servants within the house. Edward and Susanna produced a son, George, who is shown as being 8 years old in the 1871 census. By this time the daughter was known as Nellie. Robert Loder acquired the whole of Lord

Southampton's estates in Northamptonshire in 1874. Edward Ridge continued to farm the land effectively on a year to year tenancy.

"A choice residential and agricultural property having 127a 2r 6p of excellent grass and arable land situate in the Parish of Silverstone. There is a brook on the

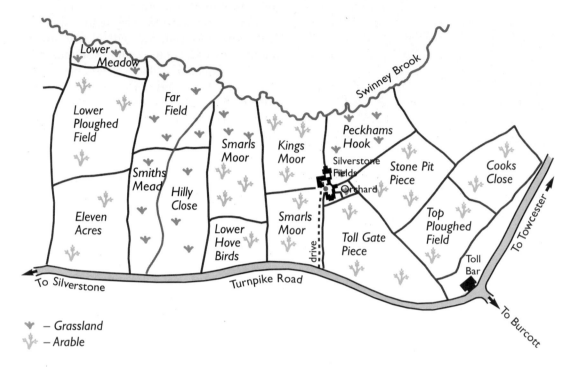

Silverstone Fields Farm; a map with field names taken from the 1875 valuation list.

- Grassland
- Arable

A valuation list was produced in 1875 and shows that the land holding included the present area and also part of Shacks Barn Farm. There does not appear to be any record of when Edward Ridge left the farm, but by 1903 Ellis Clark was the tenant at Silverstone Fields Farm. As well as a farmer he was a threshing machine operator.

At the start of The Great War, the ownership remained in the Loder family, now being owned by Sir Edmund Giles Loder Bt. and farmed by Arthur Edwin Southam. On 7th July 1914 Silverstone Fields Farm was sold at auction, and bought by Ellis Clark for £3,960 4s. The auction was conducted by Messrs. Farebrother, Ellis & Co. at the Pomfret Arms, Towcester, commencing at 4.30 p.m. Silverstone Fields Farm was lot 26. The catalogue describes the lot as:

Western boundary and the farm has over 3,000 feet frontage to the Towcester road. The stone built residence is substantial, stands well back from the road and is most pleasantly situated with a Front Garden and Lawn and Orchards."

There is then a description of the various rooms.

"The outbuildings comprise Wash-house or Brew-house, Coal and Wood Hovels, Store House etc. The Farm Buildings are stone, brick, and timber built, in good condition, conveniently arranged close to the house, and comprise: Coach-house, Saddle Room, Fowl House, Piggeries, Five-stalled Stable and Fodder Stall with Hay Loft over, Two-bayed Cart Shed, Range of Seven Open Cattle Sheds with Fodder Loft and Two Loose Boxes, a Return Range of Six Open-bayed Cattle

Sheds with Cattle Yard, a Four-bayed Wagon and Implement Shed, a Four-bayed Barn, a Two-bayed Cattle Shed and Rick Yard".

In 1970 the farm was bought by Northamptonshire County Council for £23,600. They had previously acquired Shacks Barn Farm in 1919 and Rookery Farm in 1953. These farms formed the Silverstone Estate. The aim of the development of these holdings was to provide units that could be run by one man, with help at peak periods. The improved holdings were to give the tenant a good living, make a significant contribution to agricultural output and provide the tenant with the opportunity to amass sufficient capital to enable him to compete for the tenancy of a larger farm.

Peter Tyrell was the farmer in 1972 and he was followed by Andrew Diment, who farmed up to 1999. Little had changed to most of the buildings in his time. Modernisation had taken place inside the house. Some of the farm buildings remained. The Coach House now garaged a Rover 214 and the Saddle Room is where Lucy, the collie dog, lived. Other buildings were used as a workshop-cum-garage for an ageing Landrover, and Jenny, another collie dog. The Two-bayed cart shed was home to baby calves. The fields were no longer known by their individual names. There was no arable, just grass and maize grown for fodder. There were 70 Friesian dairy cows milked in a 10/10 Herringbone Parlour and the milk was collected every other day for use either as cheese or liquid milk. There was a Hereford Bull, 20 bulling heifers, 10 steers, 10 beef calves and 25 dairy calf replacements.

All of the work on the farm was done by one man, using contractors for tasks such as silage making, hedging, and cattle transport. A relief milker visited on Sundays to allow Andrew Diment to lie in until 7 a.m. How things in 1999 had changed since 1851 when the Ridge family had 9 labourers working outside and 2 servants in the house!

The Council sold their holdings with both Shacks Barn Farm and Pits Farm having been bought by their tenants. Silverstone Fields Farm was the last farm in the area owned by the County Council and it was sold in 2000. The proposed Silverstone by-pass is planned to go through the field near the roadside, previously known, appropriately, as Toll Gate Piece.

Rachel Diment.

HAZELBOROUGH FOREST

Whittlewood, formerly known as *"WYTLEBY"* situated in the South West of the County is not mentioned in Domesday. The earliest mention is in the foundation Charter of LUFFIELD priory (Silverstone Parish), when Henry I commands *"all Foresters of Whittlewood"* to permit the Prior and Monks to have all convenient easements in the Forest *"without waste"*. A perambulation of 1299 gives the total area as about 20,000 acres. It is interesting that Silverstone, whose timber yards still rely to a great extent on Hazelborough Forest, has always been a village of some importance. The King's wine cellars used to be here in 1274 and the derivation of Silverstone is thought to be Silatone or *"wood town"*. A perambulation by Edward VI defined the limits of Whittlewood after these limits had been extended by King John 300 years earlier. In 1639, Charles I again added to the forest area after perambulation, but these new limits were rendered ineffective by Parliament in 1641, which confined the forests to the limits as at the 20th year of the preceding reign. The wood and underwood and timber of 7 coppices belonged to the Earl of Bathurst at this time and the produce from 62 others belonged to the Crown until the reign of Charles II, when

Salcey as well as Whittlewood were settled on Queen Catherine for life as part of her jointure. In 25 years of the same reign after the Queen's death, the coppices in both forests were granted to Lord Arlington for life, with the remainder to the Duke of Grafton and other (illegitimate) sons of the King. By a grant in the reign of Queen Anne, the Duke of Grafton was appointed Lord

called *"A Survey of Whittlewood Forest taken in the year 1787"* by Richard Davis gives information about both the deer and the timber and underwood of those days. Although much information about the deer is available, it is sometimes difficult to find references of much value about sylvicultural conditions. As in Rockingham, Whittlewood was mainly a Royal Hunting

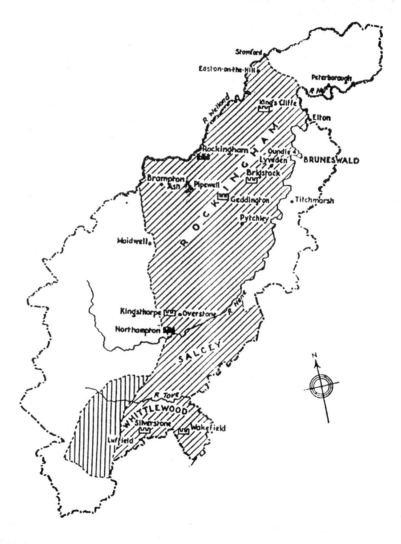

A map of the Royal Forests of Northamptonshire in the 13th century, after M. L. Bazeley (1921). Diagonal shading indicates the Royal Forests and vertical lines show the area added by the Inquisition of 15 Edward I. Royal castles are shown with a solid symbol and royal houses with an outline symbol.

Warden or Master Forester, which gave him possession of the chief lodge (Wakefield Lodge) with 117 acres of Forest and 245 acres of enclosed lawn.

An interesting and revealing manuscript

Forest and much of the records refer to the rights of venison and the management of deer. In 1787 the forest was divided into five Walks:

Sholbrook Walk

Hazleburrow Walk

Wakefield Walk

Hanger Walk

Shrob Walk

and the keepers to each Walk were appointed by the Duke of Grafton. Two verderers were also appointed. This appointment was drawn from the landowners in the District.

At about this time the constitution of the forest was as follows:-

3,895 acres - 69 coppices, timber and underwood

887 acres - open lawns and ridings, never enclosed

312 acres - enclosed meadow and pasture

329 acres - enclosed lawns for use of deer and cattle

_____

5,423 acres.

It was the practice until about 1800 to cut the coppice in a 21 year rotation and for 9 years after the cutting the area from which it was cut was fenced at the expense of the Duke of Grafton to exclude the deer and cattle. How it was fenced there is no mention, but they must have been substantial fences to exclude deer. Amongst the underwood oak were interspersed with ash, which were reserved for the Crown. It would appear that the ash were not regarded as of much value, as they were nearly always pollarded for the deer. Davis mentions that in 1787 an annual supply of timber might be raised here and suggests that acorn planting and saplings should be resorted to in places to augment the natural seedlings. His object was to aim at about 30 trees per acre or more if available. Trees called *"Browse Trees"* (trees pollarded for deer) were selected by an "inquisition" and

it is the complaint that too many have, in the past, been left to the detriment of the coppice. It is, however, on record that between 1705 and 1786, 480 loads of timber were taken from the forest for the building of Blenheim Palace. The first fall of Naval timber was in 1772 when it is known that the stocking of the coppices in timber trees was only three per acre and that this number included *"browse trees"*. It is small wonder that Davis's report suggested a more comprehensive programme of regeneration. A survey in 1608 gives the value of Whittlewood Oak as £25,755 and, as a result of the fellings between 1705/86 the income was £37,026.15.6d. It seems that by the time of Davis's report the forest had been seriously overcut and that his job was to find a remedy. As well as sales to the Navy, the Lieutenant of the Forest, 22 Yeoman keepers and 11 Page Keepers were paid in timber from the forest, a method of payment approved by the Treasury.

The present main block of Hazelborough Forest stands on what was the Hazleburrow Walk and it is recorded that this walk contained 10 coppices in the parish of Whitfield.

It appears that in the forest of Whittlewood it was the practice to plough some of the ridings and sow corn. The population of deer in 1810 is given as about 1800 head, and the number killed annually as 138 buck and 100 does. The whole forest, apart from the 9 year close time of the coppices, was open to grazing. The keepers kept cattle and many occupiers of land in adjoining villages were entitled to graze horses and cows *"to the number as can be maintained on their respective farms in the winter"*. Up to 1800 the 5,424 acres were fenced completely to prevent the deer and cattle straying from the forest.

Whittlewood was completely surrounded by a *"ring mound"* which defined the boundary, and had done for many generations. It is interesting that no mention is made of any maintenance

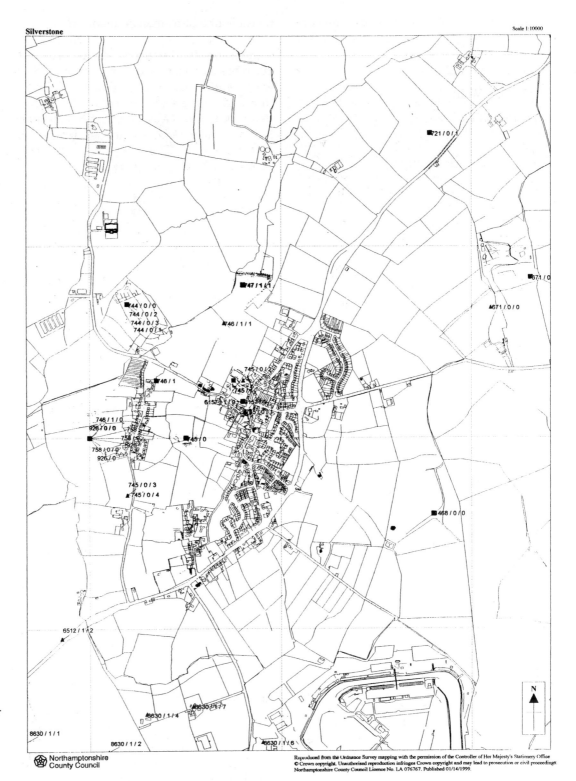

Silverstone   Scale 1:10000

The map from the Northamptonshire Heritage Sites and Monuments Report. The sites of every official archaeological dig are shown with their reference numbers. (Northamptonshire County Council)

Northamptonshire County Council

whatever to the growing trees and nowhere in Davis's comprehensive survey is there mention of drainage which must have been of some consequence. Rabbits and hares do not seem to be regarded as any kind of a menace to the timber or coppice and, as ash coppice was of value, there could not have been many in the woods. The Walk of Hazelburrow was deforested in 1824 (V.C.H.) but the remains of the rest of Whittlewood was not deforested until 1853. It is recorded that the deer were destroyed, the officers discharged and the Commissioners of Woods and Forests were empowered to lease the remaining Crown Lands in 1851.

One of the first operations undertaken by the Crown Lands was to plant with Oak/Spruce-Pine mixture. Thinnings of these crops were started in 1853 and continued at 5 yearly intervals up to 1903. It appears that these thinnings were often to the detriment of the crop as immediate financial return was the main object. This system ceased in 1903 and one of clear cutting and replanting was undertaken. In some cases up to 1916 Spruce-Pine and Elm-Lime were still used but most of the conifers were removed 10 years after planting.

The main block of Hazelborough was transferred to the Forestry Commission in 1924, 487 acres in all.

Note: From internal evidence this essay appears to date from the period 1940-1950. Its authorship is unknown.

ARCHAEOLOGICAL SITES

Sites and Monuments Catalogue

The reference numbers relate to the map on the facing page.

Amphora: 721/0/0/1. Neck and handles of large amphora, also animal bones, ashes and pot shards. Romano-British (43-410), possible site of Roman settlement?

Church: 6157/1-6157/1/0. Present church is 1884, but graves in graveyard are older. Site of much older church.

Deer Park: 926/-926/0. Some obscure 13th century reference to a deer park in Silverstone. Mediaeval (1066-1500). Landscape feature (earthwork).

Fish Pond (small): 745/02. N. of churchyard, possibly related to hunting lodge. Probably breeding tanks supplying pond 746/1/1. Mediaeval. Small rectangular ponds 2.5m deep, dam 3m high forms NW and NE sides. Second dam 2m high and damaged divides ponds.

Fish Pond (large): 746/1/1. Associated with Royal Residence, 1227 sheriff of Northampton ordered to repair the King's ponds at Silverstone. Mid 13th century references to activities of "William - King's Fisherman". AD 13th century mediaeval (1066-1500).

House: 745/0. House site 1. Pot shards.. Mediaeval, boulder clay and stone area.

Houses: 745/03-745/04. Scatter of stone rubble marks sites of at least four houses shown in 1600. Buildings gone by 1827. Mediaeval building stones and 13th and 18th century pottery.

Military sites: 8630/1-1/7, 8630/1, /1/1, /1/2, /1/4, /1/6, /1/7. Airfield and associated sites and buildings. World War II, opened 20 March 1943.

Royal Hunting Lodge: 745/1. Area known as Hall Garth is where present church now stands. Mediaeval (1066-1500). The vegetation there grows oddly and is especially short in the middle of the area.

Royal Residence: 746/1/0. Overlooking the

grand fishponds, evidence of King's and Queen's chambers, hall, kitchen, stable, etc., all hint at substantial manorial complex. Perhaps even with a substantial garden to border the ornamental lake. Mediaeval (1121-30), rebuilt and altered several times before 1317 when it was abandoned. Residence possibly moated.

Stocks: 745/0/1. Silverstone village stocks stood on open space "Stocks Hill", near church. Post-mediaeval. Precise site of stocks not determined. Removed 1866.

Watermill: 747/1/1. Large linear bank across terrace of small stream and breached by stream. Mediaeval mill dam, also large marshy depression at east end of dam and feed by leat may be mill.

Map of Silverstone of about 1640. Housing is dense along West End, on the left, and continues along Church Street to Stocks Hill and Little London. Running down from there, High Street connects with Green Lane to give the main thoroughfare, joining Cattle End, the fourth concentration of housing. A single house stands in Cockshoot End, which became the continuation of High Street. (Northamptonshire Records Office, #4210)

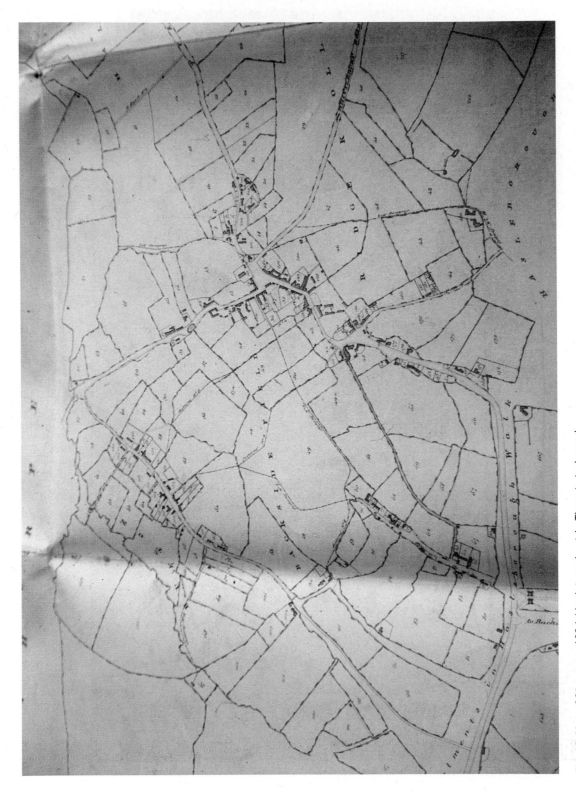

Plate 2: Map of Silverstone, 1824. North is to the right. The principal growth, not substantial in 200 years, has been along the High Street rather than Green Lane. The Church and the Chapel are clearly seen. Note the footpaths. (Northamptonshire Record Office # 2996)

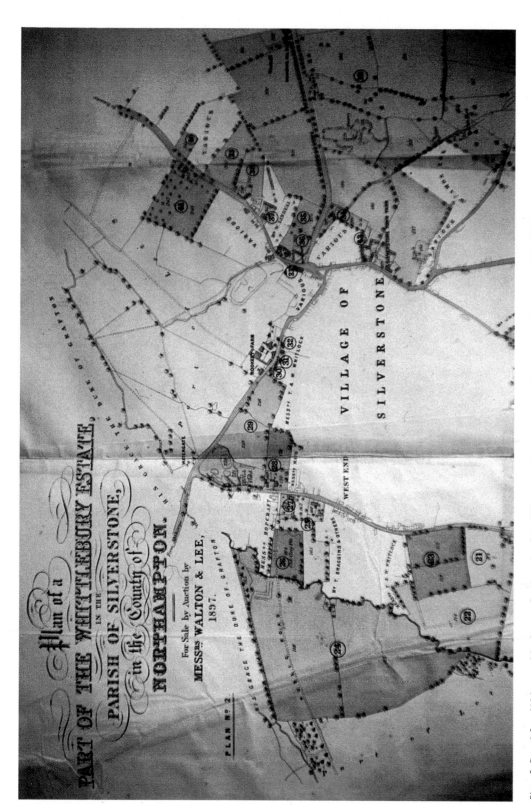

Plate 3: Detail from Walton and Lee's map for the sale of the Whittlebury Estate in 1897. Wm Rush's cottage and garden (No. 27) had a rental value of £6.13s.0d and the "accommodation holding" of the brickyard (28), occupied by Wm Miller, was valued at £17.1s.3d. Joseph Linnell's meadow land (29) had a value of £11 and the school and residence (33) £15. The market garden and dwelling house (41) occupied by Thomas John Whitlock had a rental value of £20, Silverstone Town Farm (11) of Jno. Webb Jnr & others £103.7s.0d. and Mrs Rebecca Mayo's pasture paddock (35) £2. (Courtesy Bernard and Pam Smith)

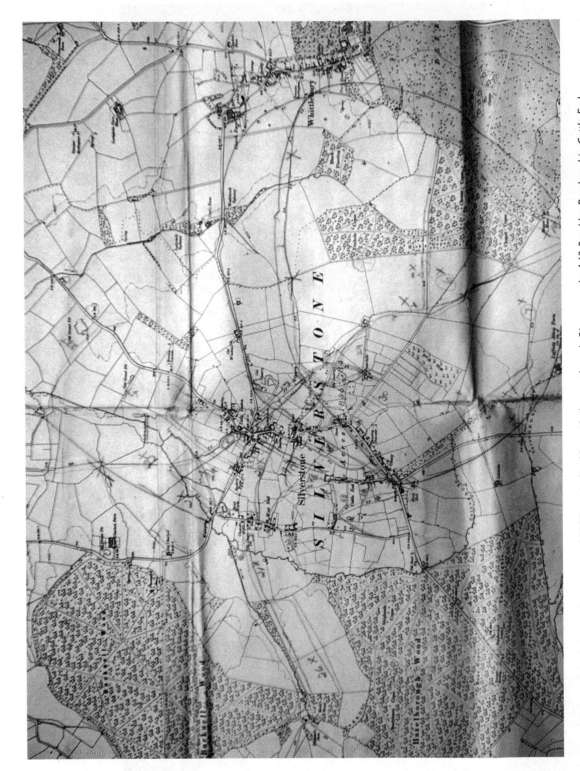

Plate 4: A copy of the Ordnance Survey map of 1900 marked in blue with the footpaths and the official numbers still in use a century later. The main development of the village has been in the former Hasleborough Walk, through Olney, now the A43 Brackley Road, and in Cattle End. (Northamptonshire Record Office # SPR 68)

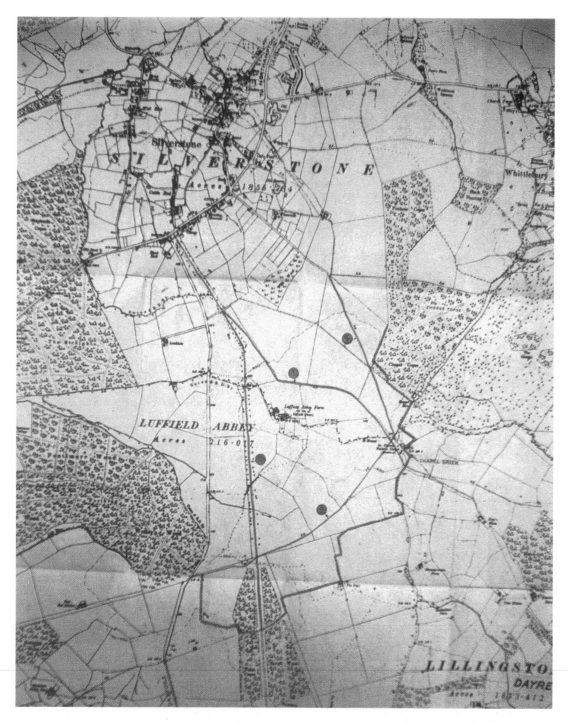

Plate 5: The Ministry of Transport map RLA 28/20 of 9 October 1963 showing the re-routing of the old paths or highways, shown in red, and the establishment of their replacements, shown in blue. The airfield, which had by then become the racing circuit, was crossed by the former paths, necessitating the change, but the circuit is not shown! The by-pass built in the 1930s can be seen. (Northamptonshire Record Office # SPR 75)

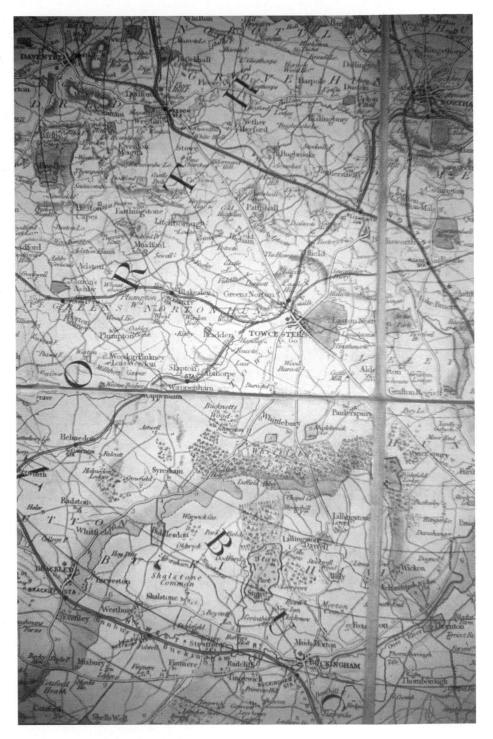

Plate 6: Map of South Northamptonshire in the early 20th century, with distances from Northampton indicated. The road and railway network shows clearly. There are some curious spellings. (Courtesy Gwen Cox)

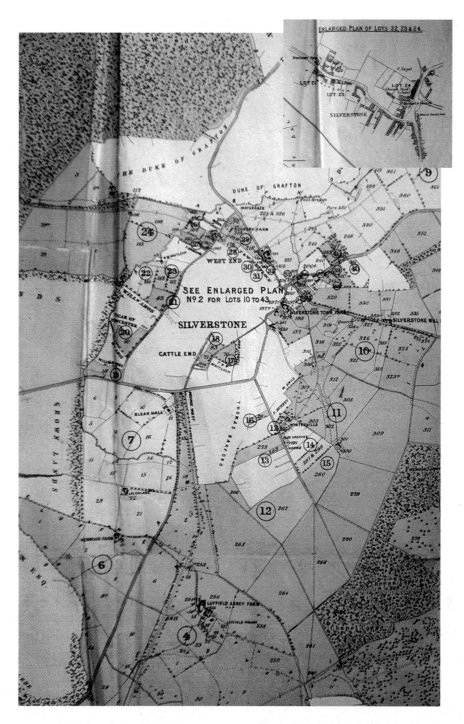

Plate 7: The Farebrother and Ellis map for the next sale of the Whittlebury Estate in 1914, with, inset, a detail of the village centre. The eight cottages in Gravel Walk, now demolished, can be seen along the path immediately left off Church Street when coming from Stocks Hill. (Courtesy Bernard and Pam Smith)

Plate 8: The Ordnance Survey map of 1884.
(Northamptonshire Record Office # SPR 132)

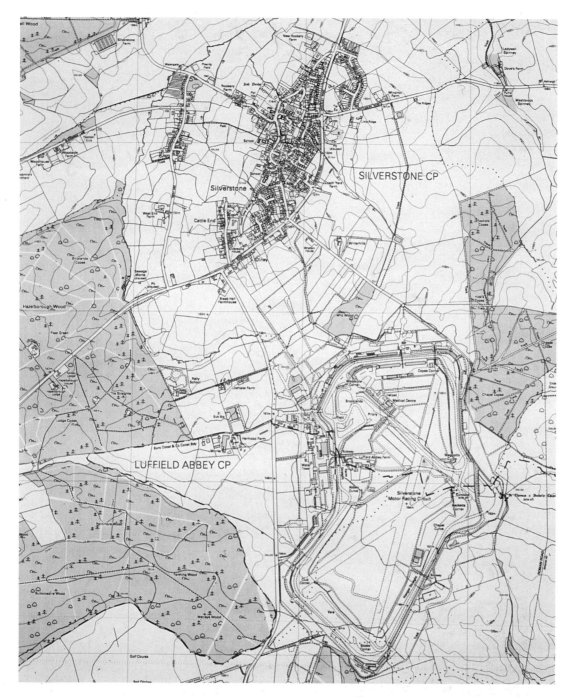

Plate 9: The Ordnance Survey map of 1999, from 1:10000 sheet SP64SE, by permission of Ordnance Survey on behalf of the Controller of Her Majesty's Stationery Office. Crown Copyright MC 013836. Cat's or Catch Yard Farm is wrongly shown as Coach Yard Farm and the Towcester Road is shown as Brackley Road north of the junction with Whittlebury Road. Public footpaths are not shown on mapping at this scale.

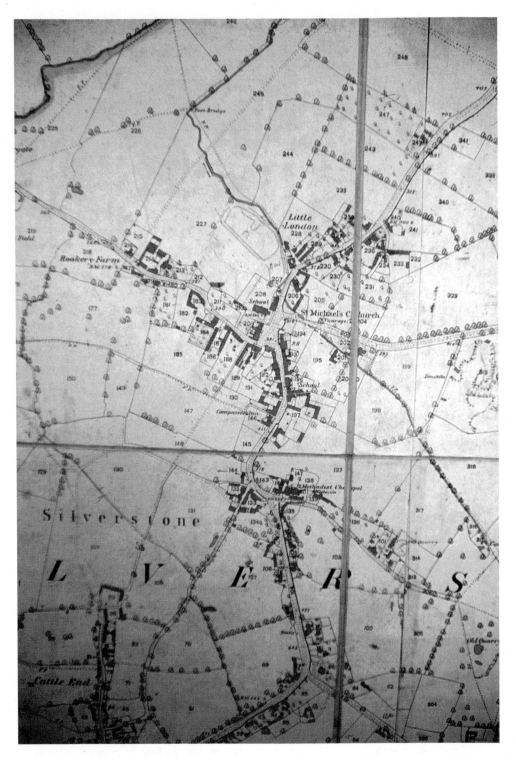

Plate 10: Detail from the 1884 OS map. Barrack Row, at the end of Cattle End, can be seen. Its *foundations can be felt underfoot in the field today.*

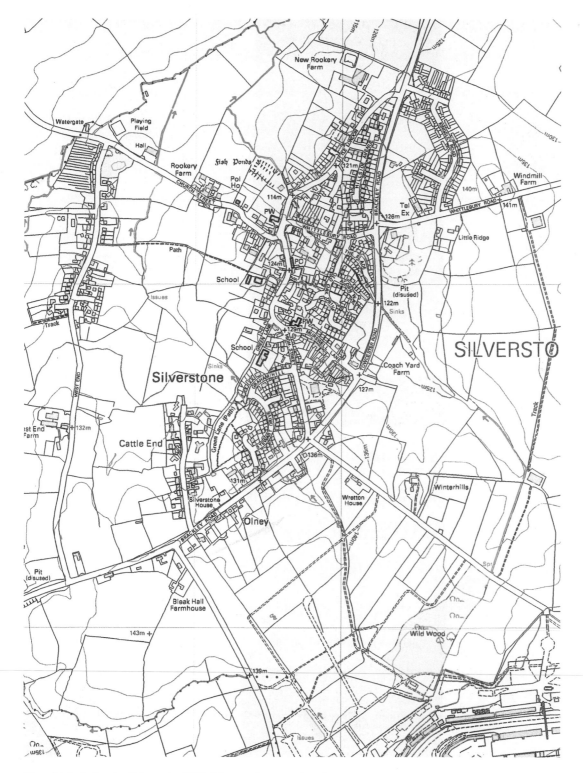

Plate 11: A similar detail from the 1999 OS map shown in plate 9

*Plate 12: The abstract of title of the manor of
Silverstone dated 17 October 1800 but including
papers dating back to 12 November 1685.
(Northamptonshire Record Office # G4198)*

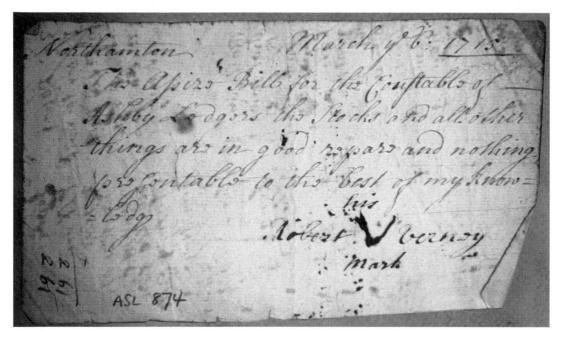

Northampton   March y⁶: 1715.

This Assizes Bill for the Constable of
Ashby Ledgers the Stocks and all other
things are in good repair and nothing
presentable to the best of my know=
=ledg

                                        his
                        Robert V Verney
                                       Mark

ASL 874

Plate 13: On 6 March 1715 Robert Varney certified the stocks at Ashby St Ledgers (north of Daventry) were in sound condition and signed the document with his mark. (Northamptonshire Record Office # ASL 874)

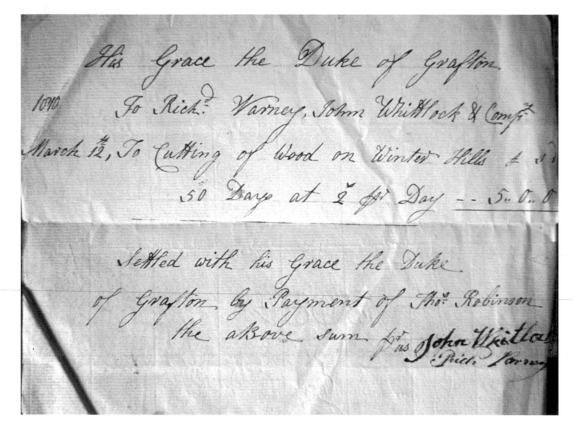

His Grace the Duke of Grafton
        To Rich.ᵈ Varney, John Whitlock & Comp.ᵃ
March 12, To Cutting of Wood on Winter Hills
        50 Days at 2ˢ ⅌ Day -- 5.. 0.. 0

Settled with his Grace the Duke
of Grafton by Payment of Thos Robinson
the above sum ⅌ us John Whitlock
                                    Rich. Varney

Plate 14: A remittance advice note made out by Thos Robinson on behalf of the Duke of Grafton for payment to Richard Varney, John Whitlock and company of £5 on 12 March 1810. (Northamptonshire Record Office # G 4075)

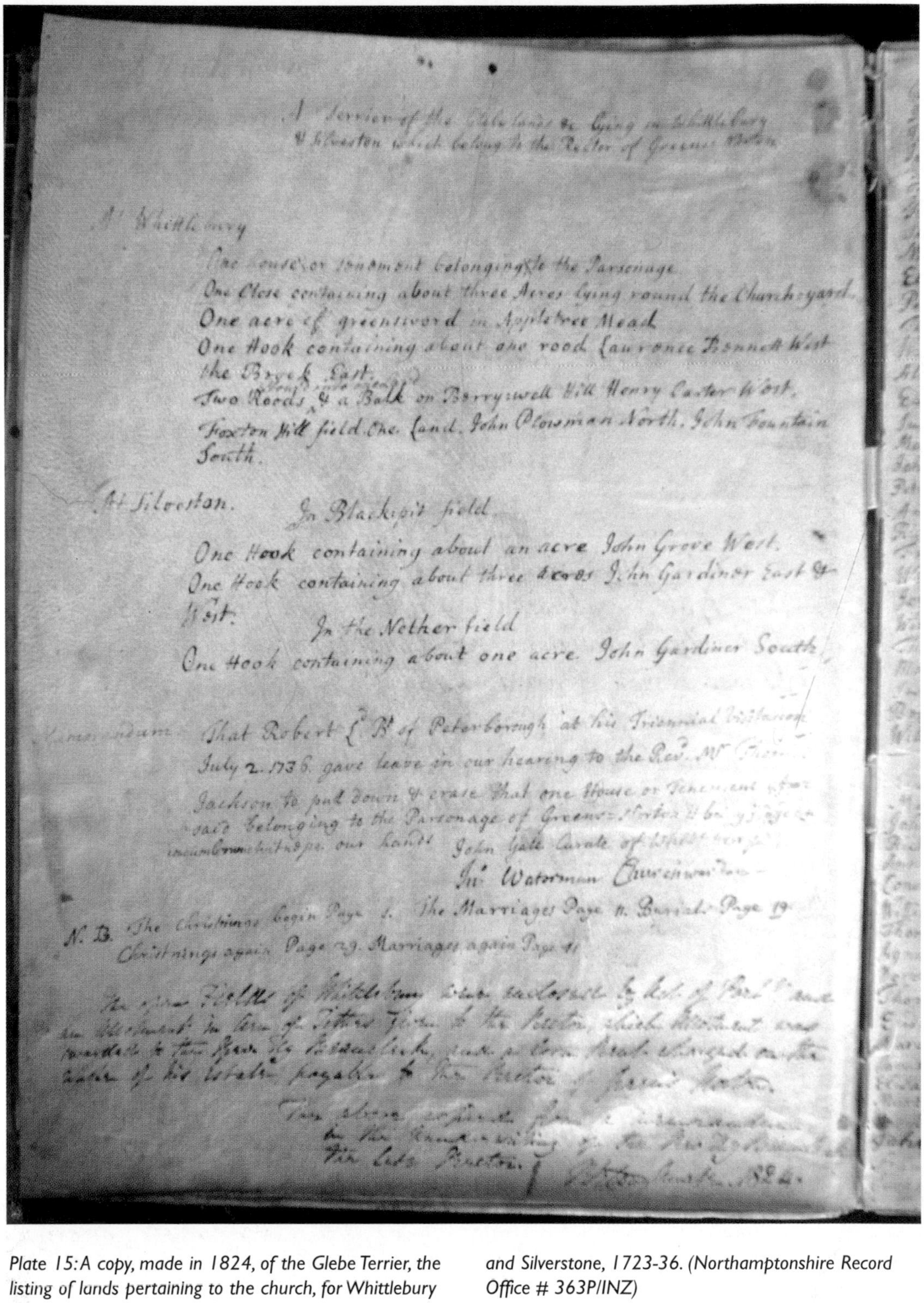

A Terrier of the Glebe lands &c lying in Whittlebury
& Silverston which belong to the Rector of Greens Norton

At Whittlebury

One house or tenement belonging to the Parsonage.
One Close containing about three Acres lying round the Churchyard.
One acre of greensword in Appletree Mead.
One Hook containing about one rood. Laurence Bennett West
the Brook East.
Two Roods & a Balk on Berrywell Hill Henry Carter West.
Foxton Hill field One Land. John Plowman North. John Fountain
South.

At Silverston.   In Blackpit field

One Hook containing about an acre John Grove West.
One Hook containing about three acres John Gardiner East &
West.   In the Nether field
One Hook containing about one acre. John Gardiner South.

Memorandum   That Robert Lord Bp of Peterborough at his Triennial Visitation
July 2. 1736. gave leave in our hearing to the Revd Mr Thomas
Jackson to pull down & erase that one House or Tenement afore
said belonging to the Parsonage of Greens Norton & be ...
incumbrance to us out of our hands. John Gate Curate of Whittlebury
Jnᵒ Waterman Churchwarden

N. B. The Christnings begin Page 1. The Marriages Page 11. Burials Page 19
Christnings again Page 29 Marriages again Page 41

The open Fields of Whittlebury were enclosed by act of Parliament and
an allotment in lieu of Tithes given to the Rector, which allotment was
...

Plate 15: A copy, made in 1824, of the Glebe Terrier, the
listing of lands pertaining to the church, for Whittlebury
and Silverstone, 1723-36. (Northamptonshire Record
Office # 363P/INZ)

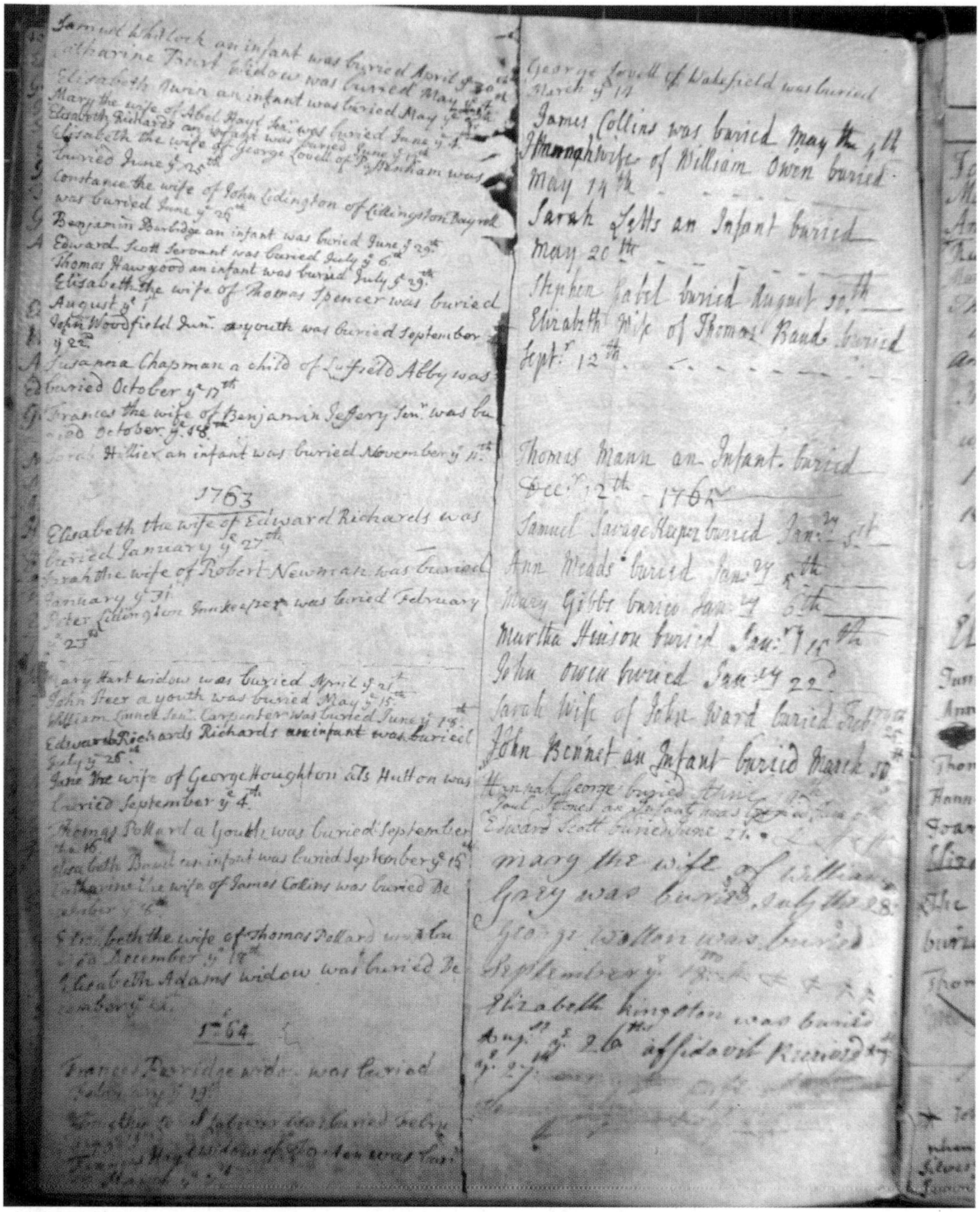

Plate 16: A page from the Parish Register, 1762-64, kept by John Yate. The Reverend John Yate became curate of Whittlebury on 4 October 1711 and was buried at the same place in October 1766. It was written of him that he continued curate 55 years of one parish, and died without having ever obtained any preferment whatever.

He was a man of great integrity and simplicity of heart and a most pious Christian. He did constant duty in the Church till within two years of his death when his eyesight gradually failing, he at last became totally blind. (Northamptonshire Record Office)

Plate 17: Hall End (High Street), Silverstone, with Stocks Hill and the church in the distance. On the right is the Post Office, now a private house, and the cottages on the left have gone, although part of the raised pavement in front of them survives. From a hand-tinted postcard.

REET, SILVERSTONE.

Plate 18: Little London, Silverstone. Edna James (later Dodwell) with her mother and father at the door of the house and Arthur Bounds on the bicycle. Beyond Arthur are the water pump and the paraffin store. From a hand-tinted postcard, 1935.

ITTLE LONDON, SILVERSTONE.

PART 3 The Age of the Landlords

POACHERS AND HIGHWAYMEN

When the old turnpike road was being widened during the 1700s, (it is now the A43 between Silverstone and Towcester), attention was paid to the trees that lined it and a space of 50 yards was made between each one. This was in order to aid the detection of highwaymen. Dick Turpin was thought to have had sympathisers among the villagers, and he was known to frequent the area. In a report from the Northamptonshire Mercury of 22nd October 1744, *"A highwayman was taken in bed at Silston"*. To give a clearer picture of what life was like in those days, here is an extract from *"Old Oak"*, a book written by the Rev. J. E. Linnell who was brought up in this forest village.

The Forest Laws

The forest laws were severe. A deerslip (deerskin) found in a cottage down to the time of Waterloo secured for its tenant a six months lodging in the county gaol. A forest buck discovered on the *"lusty shoulders"* of some Silson poacher meant twelve months and a day in the same fever-ridden abode. The theft of a park deer meant death. They knew they were taking their lives in their hands, those Silson men, Adams and Tyrell, when one night somewhere about the year of our Grace 1748 they turned for their venison to Stowe Park. Why they forsook the Forest I have never heard. All one knows is that the Kingdom was in a very exhausted condition during the years that followed the victorious campaigns of the great Duke of Marlborough on the continent, and men were driven by the sight of hungry women and children to dare and do what they never would have attempted under happier circumstances. Herded in a more confined space, perhaps the park deer offered an easier chance for securing the meat they sought than did the King's, which had the run of many square miles. Be that as it may, they went, brought down their buck, and were carrying him away, when they fell into an ambush of keepers and were made prisoners.

Poor fellows! They doubtless put up a desperate resistance, but they might just as well have fought it out to a finish there on the sward, for their doom was sealed from the moment of their surrender. They were marched off, in the first place I believe, to Stowe House, and thence to the county gaol. The Assizes were close at hand. The trial, verdict, and sentence followed each other like the events of some short-lived dream, and nothing was left for them but to die. Short was the shrift of a condemned felon in those days, and, before either of them could have well realised what had happened, a heavy cart was driven up to the door of the prison with two coffins for its seats, and their last earthly journey had begun, with the gallows as its end. They were drawn through the town streets to a neighbouring common, and there done to death amid the yelling of an execution mob that had gathered to feast its eyes on the sight of their agony. But their wives, what of them that wintery night? The faggot that stood in the chimney corner grew less and less, as they used its brands to feed the fire on the hearth, till not a stick remained. Ever and anon they went out into the night and listened, if haply they might hear the distant footfalls of the returning men. At last the dawn showed itself through the cottage window, and then cold despair fastened on the soul of poor Mary Adams, a mere girl and but recently married. If Joe had not come he would never come now. A little later her worst fears were confirmed. Ill news travels fast. A messenger from Stowe came to tell of the night's happenings, and before noon all Silson folk knew that Joe Adams and Jim Tyrell had been caught stealing park deer.

Yet hope returned. The fate of the men they loved was virtually in the hands of old Lord Cobham, owner of Stowe House, a very distinguished soldier under the Great Duke, a patron of the poet Pope, and a man of many parts. By happy chance he was in residence. They started off in haste, craved and gained an audience, and tearfully implored him to use his great influence on behalf of their unfortunate husbands. He received them with apparent sympathy, and the interview ended with his promising that they should have them home for certain on a day he mentioned in the following week. His influence, however, which was possibly almost as great as they believed, was only used to hasten on the hangings. When the day arrived and they, poor simple folk, were joyfully awaiting the fulfilment of the promise, a cart containing two coffins lumbered down Silson street and halted at Mary Adams'door, for the driver to descend, enter the house, and ask what he was to do with his gruesome luggage; he also brought a special message from Lord Cobham to remind her that he had kept his word.

The law of the land, cruel as it was, had been satisfied when the deer-stealers had been hanged, but not this grim old man. He had life-sized figures of them cast in lead, one with a buck on his shoulders, and placed them among other groups of statuary in his gardens. He himself died soon after and, like a certain king of Judah, *"departed without being desired."* The gardens were some of the finest in Europe. Temples, like those of ancient Greece, rose up from among the trees; winding, gravelled paths ran for miles through plantations of the choicest shrubs or skirted the edges of little artificial lakes, while the glory of the flowers alone made the place a veritable paradise. Royalty itself loved to resort thither, so famous was their beauty. But years went by, and a blight fell on all this loveliness; the gardens were robbed of their treasures, the temples were given over to decay, the park was despoiled of its timber, the costly furniture of the mansion was sold by public auction, and the house itself left bare and tenantless; where there had been so much to charm the eye and ravish the senses, ruin was written for all the world to read. It may be the idlest of fancies, but I have often wondered if perchance there could have been any connection between this reign of desolation and the curse of a brokenhearted girl.

In justice to Lord Cobham's memory, I would say that what I have written is the tradition I received, when a child, from old people whose parents were living at the time; moreover, my own sister, many years older than myself, could actually remember seeing Mary Adams, who lived for over eighty years after the tragedy, and so I cannot but think that the story is true in every particular. She never married again, and never really recovered from the shock of the day when they raised the coffin-lid and she looked down on the swollen and discoloured features of her newlywed husband. Never again did she taste venison, though she might have had plenty of it. All through the eighty long years of her widowhood she wore one white apron, resisting its wear and tear with her darning-needle, till scarcely a thread of the original tissue was left. Its history was ever held a secret. It might have been a love-gift from Joe in their sweet-hearting days, or she may have worn it on her wedding morn; at any rate, there must have been some sacred memory connected with it, and her neighbours did well to put it into her coffin and bury it with her.

It was a shame that anything of a ludicrous nature should have attached itself to the memory of such a woman; and yet it did. She was a hundred and two when she died. In those days when poor folk were buried it was the custom to tack on the coffin lid the initials and age of the deceased in tinsel. My father, who was present at the funeral, looked down into the grave and was amazed to see her age given as a thousand and two. Turning to the village coffin-maker who stood alongside proudly viewing his handywork, he whispered, *"You've made her a thousand and two, you old fool!" "I know I ahnt,"* replied the other hotly; *"one an' two nowts make a hunderd, dooan't they? and two ma-akes a hunderd an' two!"*

There was one consolation: few of those who took a last farewell at the end of the service would see anything amiss.

The life size statues of Joe Adams and Jim Tyrell, which were cast in lead by order of the ruthless Lord Cobham, stood for years within the grounds of Stowe House. As time went on, Stowe House fell into disuse and many of its assets were sold, among them garden features such as statues. It is our fervent hope that, somewhere, someone knows the whereabouts of these monuments to hardship in past times, assuming that they were not sold abroad or, the worst fear of all, melted down. It would be a more fitting end if they could be found and brought back to Silverstone where they belong. They could then perhaps stand on Stocks Hill as heroes, rather than as villains, who have at last come home.

E.Lovell.

The Great Silson Fire of 1807

In May 1807, the Northampton Mercury carried the following report of a tragedy that was to alter the look of what is now Silverstone High Street.

It was reported that on the 21st of May 1807 between 5 and 6 o'clock at night, fire broke out caused by singeing a pig too near to some thatch. In one and a half hours nine houses were burnt down. The fire swept down the High Street and reached at least as far as the White Horse.

It appears from the closeness of the houses that they must have been rebuilt by the 1830s.

SILVERSTONE CHARITIES

The first charity was founded by Mrs Jane Leeson's 1648 will: the share payable to the Parish of Silverstone consists of a yearly sum of £1 out of the rents and profits of an estate at Abthorpe.

The Silverstone Poor's Allotment Charity was formed in 1826 at the time of the Enclosure Award. The following is an extract of the award which is held at Northamptonshire Record Office.

"By the award 29 June 1826 they did allot unto and for the use of the poor inhabitants of the said parish, in lieu of all rights of sere and broken wood, within the walk of Hazelborough, one plot or parcel of land situate on Winter Hills containing eight acres".

The two fields were six acres and two acres respectively.

Prior to the Enclosure Award the land was part of the forest to which certain poor inhabitants of Silverstone claimed a right to gather sere and broken wood two days in the week in every year. The soil was peculiarly well suited to the growth and cultivation of timber. After the timber had been cleared, it was decided the land could not be economically improved for the benefit of the Crown and was therefore allotted to the poor of Silverstone, the rents and profits to be used for the relief of poverty and all rights to sere and broken wood, all right of common etc., should cease and be forever annulled.

From the beginning of the charity until 1908 no records of income and expenditure can be found. In 1908 100 plots of allotment ground were leased at 2s 6d (12½p) giving an annual income of £12 10s 0d (£12.50). Expenditure to deserving cases was 2s 6d (12½p) each to 32 widows and 1s 1d (6p) each to 151 householders. The rents were unchanged until 1921 when they were increased to 3s 0d (15p) per plot, only to be reduced to 2s.6p. (12½p) in 1924, continuing at this level until the 1970s. 100 plots were let every year from 1908 until the mid 1930s. The number of cultivated plots declined from 60 in 1938 to only four in the early 1960s. During this period the number of people receiving payment from the charity each year varied between 34 and 60.

In 1957 the six acre field was let to Mr E. Hinton. Later as very few allotments were cultivated, Mr. Hinton rented the smaller field too. Although the soil was heavy clay, the two fields were used for growing corn and in a wet season it was difficult to complete the harvest. This arrangement continued until 1974.

By now the larger field was grassland and until 1981 was let as grass keep or hay rights. By this time some 50 elderly people were receiving £1 each at Christmas. In 1981 the trustees decided, owing to the poor state of the land in Winter Hills and to the low demand for allotments, to vandalism and damage by rabbits and pigeons due to the remote location, a better income for the charity would be available if the land were sold. After twelve months of negotiation and a visit by some of the trustees to the Charity Commissioners, permission to sell was granted and the land was sold by auction in March 1982. It realised £10,200 and was bought by Silverstone Circuits.

The trustees sought to replace the Winter Hills land with something more accessible and with better soil. The district council were approached concerning the land behind the flats they built in Little London known as The Limes. They decided to sell the land by public auction. The Charity Commissioners reluctantly gave the trustees permission to bid for this land, although in their view it was not making the best use of the charity money nor was it the responsibility of the charity to provide allotments for the inhabitants of Silverstone as a whole. The maximum allowed for the purchase of the land was £6,500. This was easily exceeded at the auction. After expenses the money was invested in a fourteen day notice account with Lombard as it was not used to purchase land.

At the meeting in London with the Charity Commissioners, the trustees were told very forcibly that the charity funds were not being properly used and that the mass distribution of £2 each at Christmas time to about 40 elderly people must end. Money should only be paid to people who made individual applications while any state benefits, help from Social Services and/or the Department of Social Security should be taken into account before any payment was made. This new system works very well as help can be targeted and larger payments can be made where necessary. It has been the policy of the trustees to use some of the interest earned each year to make payments. This allows the capital to increase in order that more and possibly larger payments may be made in the future. This policy seems to have been successful as the £9,000 invested with Lombard in 1982 had grown 16 years later to over £21,000.

In conclusion, from the beginning of the charity the changes in personal circumstances of people have been well reflected. The funds distributed have proved to be beneficial and it is hoped distributions will continue for many years.

Whereas years ago people used allotments to grow food for their families mainly because of low incomes, today as living standards have improved, it may be more economic to buy the food instead. The keeping of allotments today may be seen rather as a recreational activity rather than a practical necessity.

John Tustian.

STOCKS HILL

It is natural to assume that Stocks Hill is the place at which the village stocks stood, but while that may be true, the name itself more probably derives from the selling of livestock in this nice, wide place at the centre of the village.

There are records of stocks on Stocks Hill. They were removed as late as 1866, six years after the stocks at Whittlebury had gone. A drawing exists of similar stocks, showing them to be equipped with four leg holes, that is for two people sitting side by side, with a whipping post at one end. It has been said, mistakenly, that there never were stocks here, but that miscreants were punished by pillory.

That Stocks Hill was also a market is well recorded. Silverstone did not stand on a drove road, as those were principally north to south in their orientation in west Northamptonshire and the Whittlewood

The stocks at Little Houghton, said to be identical in design to those that stood on Stocks Hill.

Forest on the south of the village blocked such a route. The main markets for cattle, in and around London, were supplied by drovers working down from the north, from Wales or from Derbyshire and Yorkshire. Banbury was a major market, but for the London trade the Vale of Aylesbury was the great fattening ground. Drove roads from Banbury went past Buckingham and Winslow to the great market at Aylesbury, and driving from Buckingham to Aylesbury takes you along a drove road. It does not pass through the centre of the villages, but round the outside; no one wants a massive herd of cows defiling the high street! A drove road came round the side of Abthorpe, where the road does not go close to the church even today and much of the housing, except for what was a drovers' pub, on the main road is relatively modern. Some overspill from the main droving routes probably came through Silverstone, though quite which way is not clear as even on the 1640 map a route that avoids the village centre cannot be seen. Numbers must, therefore, have been small and local beasts the principal offering. Like most villages, Silverstone had its own abbatoir or slaughterhouse. There was one in the Old Post Office, next to the White Horse, where some of the old carcase hooks were, until recently, still attached to the beams, and the stone floor beneath was so constructed as to provide a blood drain. Though these relics have now been moved, they have been preserved on the premises. Later, beasts were killed at what is still the butcher's shop on Brackley Road.

ST MICHAEL AND ALL ANGELS

This history of St. Michael's Church was written by a member of the Church Council, Colin Hughes. Colin and his wife, Sara, together served the community for many years, not only through the church but as owners of the Top Shop at the top (south) of Silverstone High Street. They sold the shop in the 1970s. Sara then ran the local church Mums and Tots group, a valuable asset to the new generation, and fast becoming a tradition. Sadly Colin is no longer with us, but he will go down in village history for this record of our Church's past and various other written contributions that he and Sara have made to this book.

The Rebuilding of St.Michael and All Angels' Church, Silverstone 1884

An early place of worship in Silverstone was a chapel attached to the royal hunting lodge, built in about 1200. This is later referred to as *"a chapel of ease to the church at Whittlebury"*.

The chapel was replaced by a small church in 1780. This building was described by Bishop Magee as *"a barn"*, and by Mr R. Loder as *"about the most uncomely edifice ever denominated by the respected name of church"*. The Rev J. E. Linell, in his book Old Oak, refers to *"the scornful utterances of wicked wags with regard to Silson Church"*. The church was dedicated to St Michael, but somehow it became known as St Anne's and its name is printed as such in some county histories. Two photographs of this plain building still hang at the back of the present church.

In 1882 Robert Loder Esq, MP for Shoreham, of Whittlebury Lodge, was seen examining the building. At that time the Rev John Fallon was the resident curate living at The Walnuts. He *"had quickly won the hearts of all his parishioners"* but was considering leaving because of the depressing atmosphere of the church in which he had to work. Seeing Mr Loder's interest in the church building, the villagers drew up a memorandum, referring to the

"desire which we have long entertained to see our parish possessed of a more

suitable edifice for the purposes of divine worship" but *"the greatness of the work seems to make the undertaking quite beyond our means".* It goes on to say that

was done entirely by local Silverstone and Whittlebury men. Mr St Aubyn said, *"One and all took the greatest possible interest in the building, and did the work to the best of*

An engraving said to be of the original Silverstone Chapel.

"the fact that you have been lately seen examining the building seems to revive our hopes" and *"...that you will be disposed to give us your advice and generous help in so great an undertaking".*

Mr Loder responded cautiously, willing to finance the work but only on condition that he should *"be free to act as I think best and only answerable to my Bishop or to his Archdeacon".* This was accepted by the Vestry meeting on April 27th 1882.

The new church was built on the old foundations, but with a larger vestry and the addition of a porch. The new seating was to accomodate 262 people. The design was by Mr Piers St Aubyn of London, and the work

their skill and knowledge".

The pulpit and reading desk were carved by Mr Wrighton Linnell. James Adams, stonemason, (grandfather of Mrs Holton, whose husband is the present organist) carved stone taken from Mr Loder's quarries, where Clare House now stands. Another stonemason, Mr Lepper, carved the window surrounds and Mr Osborne, (grandfather of Mr Leon Blackwell who was still living in the village at the time of writing and father-in-law to Mrs G. Osborne), was the stonemason who made the font.

Born in 1880, Lettie Liddington lived at the Mill on the Whittlebury Road. She would sometimes take a can of tea to her brother,

Frederick, who was working on the church around 1883-4. Throughout her life she could remember walking up the church aisle, on the neatly levelled sand, before the laying of the floor tiles. Later she became

Church and Village, Silverstone

Mrs Jack Webb of The Limes in Little London, and was the mother of Mrs Violet Potter and Mrs Mildred Varney.

During the rebuilding of the church, Mr Thomas Barford, Church Warden, of Home Farm, allowed one of his barns to be used for worship. It was a barn situated alongside Green Lane. A faculty was granted *"to celebrate Divine Service"* but *"on no account to solemnise marriages"*.

The first marriage in the new church was that of James Whitlock, a baker, age 23, and Mary Ann Linnell, age 22, on August 4th 1884. The bride was the aunt of Messrs. Jim, Sim, and Vic Linnell and of Mrs Doris Hinton.

The bellcote of the new church held three bells, which at that time were rung by Edward Reeve, a shoemaker and maternal grandfather of Mrs Marjorie Cracknell. He was much admired by the parishioners for his bell-ringing skills.

Bishop Magee travelled from Peterborough to Whittlebury Lodge on Saturday September 27th 1884 to spend the weekend with Mr Loder, and together they attended church at Whittlebury on the Sunday morning. The official opening of the new Silverstone church took place on the

morning of Monday September 29th, St Michael's day. This was a great village occasion with at least 500 people present. The workmen would have had a day off work to attend the service. Bishop Magee, Rev.A.J.Street (Rector of Whittlebury), Rev.J.Fallon (Curate of Silverstone), visiting clergy, including Wesleyan Ministers Rev.R.Lickes and Rev.J.Wolfenden, and the choir all processed from the National School, which is now the Church Rooms.

According to the Northampton Mercury the organist and choir rendered the service in *"a creditable manner"*, although the former had to cope with the fact that only 5 out of the 18 organ stops were as yet operational. After the service about 120 guests were entertained to luncheon at Whittlebury Lodge by Mr Loder. He, the Bishop, Mr St Aubyn, and Rev. J. Fallon all made speeches, with many *"hear-hear's"* and occasional laughter. The Peterborough party all headed off for home by the 4.10pm train from Towcester.

During the same afternoon, the members of the choir and the Silverstone Sunday school teachers were entertained to tea in the Riding School at Whittlebury Lodge. Amongst the latter would have been Martha Julia Linnell, whose memorial tablet can be seen in the church behind the font. That evening there was a service in the new church at which the vicar of Brackley delivered the sermon.

Colin Hughes

Sources: County Record Office, Delapre Abbey; Record Library, Abington Street, Northampton; Whittlebury Church; House of Commons Library.

REVIEW OF OLD OAK

This is an extract from The Northampton County Magazine of 1932 reviewing Old Oak which was published in that year. Old Oak (ISBN O 953288307) was reprinted in 1988 by Ivor Floyd of Little London.

OLD SILVERSTONE.

TALES OF A GRANDFATHER.

Old Oak : The Story of an English Forest Village by the late Rev. J. E. Linnell. London : Constable & Co., Ltd., 1932. 8vo. cloth gilt, pp xxxiii., 195 illustrations and map. 7/6 net.

THIS is one of the most delightful books of the year. It is a remarkable collection of anecdotes of Silverstone, mainly of the first half of the last century, and as such is of special interest to Northamptonshire readers. They are told with a natural raciness which makes every page a treat to read. The writer of most of them and the relator of the remainder, the Rev. J. E. Linnell, rector of Pavenham in Bedfordshire, belongs to the S i l v e r s t o n e family of the name and was brought up in the village. He was an exceedingly interesting personality, as is shown in the memoir written by one of his sons. The gift of writing seems hereditary in the family. Mr. Linnell, a most loveable man, is presented to us like the wind of the East coast, strong, exhilarating and engaging. Seldom has a writer so successfully shown the man in a character sketch of only a score small pages.

With respect to the rest of the book there is positively not a dull sentence. Every line is quotable. Story after story is told—stories handed down and stories of the writer's own time—and every one is of interest. Many of them are dramatic and historic. Silverstone being a forest village with the inhabitants poachers almost to a man, it is obvious that life did not proceed quite so placidly

SIMON AND JOSEPH LINNELL.
(About 1864.)

as in most other Northamptonshire places. The people, necessarily, are more than usually robust in physique and action. When the episodes occurring in such a village are recounted by a generous sympathiser the telling is usually good.

For instance, the reader enters with spirit into the nutting excursions into the woods, made in mass because there was no telling how many " watchers " there might be to drive them off. " Silson " people of course took care to be the more numerous. The next night both sides are strengthened, and the next, until every man and woman are in it. By this time the reader is on the side of the Silson people, and is downright sorry at their discomfiture and rejoices when they triumph. Silverstone is a chapelry attached to Greens Norton. Greens Norton rector was a landowner and therefore game preserver, and a magistrate. He was seldom seen at Silverstone and his curate not often. There are amusing stories of encounters between priest, or rather squarson as he is called in these pages, and people. Here is a story of another " squarson " of the neighbourhood, selected merely because it is short enough to quote :

Entering his church one cold and snowy Christmas morning he found a congregation of exactly two—both men—awaiting him. The place was chill as a vault, and his heart failed him.

" I think it'd be far wiser," he said, " if, instead of my holding a service, you two men went across to the house and drank a pint of ale apiece by the kitchen fire."

" Thank you, sir, very kindly," said one. " That'll suit me very well, I'm sure."

" Oh no," said the other, " I bean't a-gooin' to do no such thing; I come here for a sarvice, an' a sarvice I be a-gooin' to have!"

In spite of all arguments he remained obdurate, and at last squarson gave up trying to persuade him. " If he demands a service," he said resignedly, " he must have one, I suppose," and turned towards the vestry.

" Try him wi' a quart, sir," suggested the clerk, who had hitherto remained silent.

" Well, my man," said the squarson, " what do you say to a quart?"

" Now you be a-talkin', sir," replied the other, and there was no service.

Silson church, or chapel, which was very old, going back to " Nooah's Flood " according to Simon the sexton, was demolished in the period of these stories, and a Georgian structure put in its place. There is a delightful account of Old Kelly and the strange way funds for the new building were obtained, how fox hunting was strengthened and Kelly given eminence in the new structure which he was commissioned to build. It was all one intricate transaction. The new church was a deplorable structure with a flat roof on which Morris dancers gave a performance on the day and as part of the dedication of the church. This building was replaced by a handsome edifice built in 1884 by Sir Robert Loder.

On the death of their father, Joseph and Simon Linnell became clerk and sexton respectively. During the greater part of Simon's sextonship the church was served by a curate who rode over every Sunday from Whittlebury. He would jump off his pony at the gate and turn the animal free into the churchyard. After service : If he had pleased Simon, the pony was caught and brought up to the church door; if he hadn't, it was " Catch him yourself, if you want him; I wun't!"

The accounts of the church choir and band and Sunday School are exceedingly humorous. Some of the stories are almost unbelievable but they all fit in with the Silson charcter. The Sunday School was held in the church.

" Two teachers would choose an epistle and then see which class could get through it first. Bad readers on these occasions were bidden to keep silent, good ones advised to skip as many verses as they safely could, and great was the

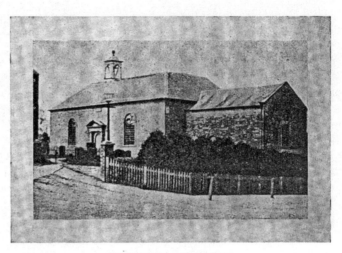

SILVERSTONE OLD CHURCH
(as it was in 1870.)

glee of the winners when their last verse had been read."

Silson was great on cricket. Cricket matches frequently ended in racial fights, even if sometimes they were not arranged for the purpose. Indeed though Silson was notorious for the ardour and violence of its politics the cricket match was superior from the point of view of pugilistic encounters. And pugilism next to poaching was the chief delight. The story is told of a fight between Old Brag and Pat Tooley for the title of " Best Man of the Village." When the two met at the appointed place there was mutual chaff in which Pat's wife joined :—" An' here I be to carry hum his bwuns if he keeunt beeat you!"

The coming of the Methodists and the visitation of cholera provide many anecdotes. But we must hold. Everyone who likes Northamptonshire should read the book from beginning to end. It will be of great interest, it shows what sturdy folk we have, it reveals the soul of a countryside.

IN A TIME OF CHOLERA

The feud between church and chapel was once, though only once, nearly forgotten. There used to be a long line of graves in our churchyard that was known as the *"Cholera Row."* In 1854 the dread disease struck the village, and so many were its victims that at one time it seemed as if the awful experiences of the people of Eyam in the year of the Plague of London were to be repeated at Silson. A young maidservant returned from her situation in a distant town to visit her widowed mother. Full of health and strength to all appearances one afternoon, she was a corpse before the next morning. She had scarcely been laid in her grave before another fell, and then another. The people were terror-stricken, and with good reason. Farmer, the butcher of nutting memory, who had been one of the strongest men in the shire, succumbed. My own dear mother had to go, and my father was brought to death's door. The bodies of those who died were taken to the churchyard in a cart, only the outdoor part of the burial service was read, and the mourners stood at a distance from the grave to avoid infection. Still the pestilence pursued its baleful course, and one day it was whispered that the doctor was down. Then the whole neighbourhood was stunned. One of the finest men - physically, mentally, and professionally - in the whole kingdom was Dr Lett. Six feet three in his stockings and broad in proportion, not a man in Trinity College, Dublin, was his match with the gloves, and, despite his size, was so light on his feet that he could jump twenty-one feet either way on the greensward. He was an absolute enthusiast in his profession, and though, on his first coming to the village, he raised up enemies through refusing to be humbugged by anyone, rich or poor, he turned them into friends later, and made such headway in the district that all the surrounding gentry became anxious to secure his services. He had been very successful in his treatment of typhoid fever, then very prevalent through the country, and was longing for an opportunity to grapple with the cholera. It came, and he fought it night and day, testing the theory he had previously formed that many of the stricken could be saved by keeping them warm by artificial means.

Alas he fell in the struggle.

Dr Lett's gravestone is in the corner of the churchyard opposite the church porch against a red brick wall, near that of his young daughter.

"Martha," he said to my sister, who nursed him devotedly throughout his short illness, *"what colour are my hands?"*

"Blue," she replied.

"Then God have mercy on my poor wife and children", he murmured. A little later he asked her to read to him the second chapter of St. Paul's Epistle to the Ephesians, after which he commended his soul to his Maker and passed on.

The young curate of the parish, Mr. Delafons, providentially an exception to the general run of our clergy, had just gone away for his first holiday for five or six years. He had never seen her who was to be his wife during the whole of that, yet without the slightest demur he returned to his post of duty as soon as he heard of what was happening and, contemptuous of danger, was constant in his attendance on the sick and dying. The leader of the

Methodists, *"Tailor"* Coleman, gave himself with equal devotion to the same task.

Old churchmen of the Simon type attended prayer-meetings in the chapel, and stiff dissenters, who classed churches and theatres together as being equally godless, forgot for a few weeks their bitterness towards the Establishment and joined in its services. *"At a time like this,"* remarked Simon, *"I dooan't think us ought to be as us ha'bin."* The truce, however, lasted only as long as the terror, and then matters were just as they had been before.

Envy, hatred, and malice, and all uncharitableness still divide the Christian bodies in this our England. Will there have to be further plagues and pestilences to unite us?

God have mercy on us all!

From Old Oak

SILVERSTONE METHODIST CHAPEL

Methodism began in the middle of the eighteenth century as a movement for renewal within the Church of England. Its leaders, John and Charles Wesley, were Anglican clergymen, concerned to take the Christian message to people and places as yet unreached by the Gospel and to see people deepen their knowledge and experience of God. To this end, the early Methodists used open-air preaching to proclaim their message and gathered those who were interested in Christianity into groups where they could worship and learn together. At first the Methodist societies met in private homes, but gradually increased and chapels were built. In the meantime, relations between the parent Church of England and the Methodists became strained, and there was a gradual separation which left Methodism as an independent Christian Church.

Methodism did best in areas neglected by the traditional Churches. From the early days, moreover, the movement gave lay people plenty of scope for involvement in leadership in their local society. This may help to explain why Methodism made a significant impact on the independent forest villagers of Silverstone. John Wesley preached in the village, in a cottage near the present chapel. The chapel itself was begun in 1811, twenty years after Wesley's death, and is the oldest church building in the village. The original rectangular chapel was extended towards Murswell Lane about ten years later, with the addition of a gallery, and other buildings were gradually added over the next century. The size of the property - seating for several hundred people in the chapel itself and extensive

The Methodist Chapel and No. I Murswell Lane.

ancillary halls - bears witness to the strength of Silverstone Methodism in the nineteenth and early twentieth centuries. Silverstone was the strongest church in the former Towcester Circuit, with a Methodist minister based in the village. The chapel was home to a busy programme of activities through the week, as well as crowded Sunday services, and the premises were used for a day school.

Rev. Dr Martin Wellings

WHITTLEBURY ESTATE

The following material refers to a sale of 1873. It gives some insight into the nature of land holdings in the late 19th century. Blackmires is part of the property, a corruption of the old name of Black Friars, the name of the religious order which occupied the land in mediaeval times. The Benedictine monks were at Luffield Abbey. The Blackfriars were a medical order and the ancient building that used to stand where the farm house is now would have been a hospital. Monks wood which is attached to the Blackmires property is the burial place of the monks.

Whittlebury Estate

Manorial and Residential domain will be sold by auction by Mssrs. Moston, Teist & Watney, at the Auction Mast, Token House Yard, Near the Bank of England. On Firday the 2nd day of May 1873. By the direction of the trustees under the will of the late Lord Southampton.

Blackmires Farm

Adjoins Bucknells Wood, Wappenham Lodge Farm and Estate of the Duke of Grafton and consists of a Farm House, now used as Labourers Cottage with gardens containing together: Three rooms up, two down, pantry, wood sheds and the outbuildings comprise, Eight horse stable, hay and chaff house, barn and four horse stable, cow hovel and enclosed yard. Also some capital farm buildings known as Blackmires ... comprising, a large barn, Cow hovel, bullock shed, and enclosed yard together with several enclosures of arable and pasture land, containing together an area of about Two Hundred and Ninety Four acres. Let to Mr Frances Montgomery on a yearly Lady-Day tenancy at the annual rent of £322 12s. 4d.

Wappenham Lodge Farm

Is bounded by Bucknells Wood, Blackmires Farm and Priesthay Wood Farm and comprises of The Homested consisting of a comfortable farm house with six bedrooms, two sitting rooms, pantry, kitchen and scullery. The outbuildings include, pigsty, wood house, four horse stable, chaff house, cow hovel, calf pen, implement shed, cast hovel with enclosed yards. At a short distance from the above is another homestead known as Pot Ash, a capital labourers cottage of seven rooms with hen house, chaff house, barn and cow house also a barn, cow hovel and yard, The whole containing about 230 acres, 2 roods, 36 Perches, of arable and pasture land ... The above is held by the executors of the late Mr R Jones on a yearly tenancy at the annual rent of £276 8s. 10d.

A Dwelling House

Situated in the village of Silverstone and comprising of: Five Rooms, Kitchen, Cellar, Wood and Tool Shed, Greenhouse, Garden and Orchard, Barn, Piggery, Cart Hovel and Nag Stable with loft overhead and whole containing about four acres, Two roods and five perches ... Let to Emanuel Adkins on a yearly Michaelmas tenancy at the annual rent of £27 0s. 0d.

An Enclosure of Meadow Land

Situate adjoining Bucknells Wood and known as Cottage Close and Riding. It ... contains an area of about 8 Acres, 1 Rood, 1 Perch. It is held on a yearly Lady-Day tenancy by Mr Thomas Gibbins at the annual rent of £9 3s. 0d.

Two Enclosures of Arable and Pasture Land

Situate in the village of Silverstone containing about, 7 acres & 1 Rood. Held by Mr Thomas Braggins on a yearly Lady-Day tenancy at the annual rent of £18 14s. 0d.

Three Enclosures of Arable and Pasture Land

Situated in Silverstone Village and containing about, 10 Acres, 2 Roods, 13 Perches. Let to Mr Thomas Linnell at the annual rent of £22 0s. 0d. [Part] being a Lady-Day tenancy and the remainder a Michaelmas tenancy.

An Enclosure of Meadow Land

Known as Three Corner Close, situate in the village of Silverstone and containing 22 acres, 2 roods, 20 Pole. Let to Mr William Wake on a yearly tenancy at the annual rent of £9 9s. 0d.

An Enclosure of Arable Land

Close to the village of Silverstone and containing, an area of about, one acre and twenty three perches. Let to Sarah Baud on a yearly Lady-Day tenancy at the annual rent of £2 10s. 0d.

An Enclosure of Arable Land

Known as Winter Hills Close, close to the village of Silverstone and containing One acre and Nineteen Perches (or thereabouts). Let on a yearly Lady-Day tenancy to Mr Alexander Kirby at the annual rent of £3 0s. 0d.

A Capital Dwelling House and Premises

Situate close to Silverstone village and containing, Four Bedrooms, Landing, Entrance Hall, Three Sitting Rooms, Two Stair Cases, Kitchen, Scullery, Larder, Beer and Wine Cellars, Pump House (with force pump to supply house and tool shed). Two Stall Stable. Flower and large kitchen garden; One rood, or thereabouts. Thirty Six Perches, let to the Rev. Alan Broderick, a yearly Christmas tenant at the annual rent of £15 0s. 0d.

Two Enclosures of Arable Land with Barn

Situated in Silverstone village containing Two acres and Seventeen perches ... The above is held by Mr Edmund Linnell on a yearly and Michaelmas tenancy at the annual rent of £6 15s. 0d.

A Dwelling House, in Silverstone Village

Containing, Four Bedrooms, Sitting Room, Kitchen, Pantry, Cellar, Woodshed, With Garden and Orchard. One acre and Three perches Let to Mr W.J.Wake on a yearly Lady-Day tenancy at the annual rent of £11 0s. 0d.

An Enclosure of Arable and Pasture Land

In Silverstone Village and containing about Two acres, Two roods and Sixteen perches. In the occupation of Mr John Varney on a yearly tenancy at the annual rent of £6 10s. 0d.

A Homestead

Situated near Silverstone Village and known as Winter Hills comprising of A Dwelling House, consisting of: An Attic, Four Bedrooms, Two Sitting Rooms, Kitchen, Pantry, Cellar and Garden.

The Outbuildings consist of: Pigsty, Boiling House, Three Horse Stable, Chaff House, Cow House, Barn and enclosed Yard. Also Several enclosures of Arable and Pasture land embracing an area of 33 acres, 1 rood and 31 perches or thereabouts ... The above is in the occupation of Thomas Rush on a yearly Michaelmas tenancy at the annual rent of £56 7s. 4d.

Several Enclosures of Capital Pasture Land

Situated near Silverstone Village, together with some farm Buildings known as Butteridge and consisting of Cow House, Open Hovel. The whole occupying an area of about: 32 acres and 17 perches ... The above is held on a yearly Michaelmas tenancy by Messrs Coleman and Richardson at the annual rent of £64 4s. 6d.

An Enclosure of Meadow Land

Situated close to village of Silverstone and containing as area of about Three roods and Thirty Seven perches. Let on a yearly Michaelmas tenancy to Mr Thomas Adams at the annual rent of £3 15s. 0d.

A Brickfield

Situated close to the village of Silverstone

with several sheds thereon containing about, Two acres, One rood and Ten perches. In the occupation of Mr William Foxley, a yearly Lady-Day tenancy at the annual rent of £20 0s. 0d.

Several Enclosures of Pasture and Arable Land

Situated close to the village of Silverstone, together with a Timber Yard and a long range of Workshops and sheds, also, a Cow Shed, Pigsty, Enclosed Yard. The whole embracing an area of about 11 acres and 3 roods ... The above is held on a yearly Michaelmas tenancy by George Adams at the annual rent of £33 0s. 0d.

Two Dwelling Houses

Situated in the village of Silverstone and containing; Several Rooms, Wash House, Hog Room, the other five rooms, Pantry, with Outbuildings that consist of, Ranges of Pigsties, Cast Hovel, Large Barn, Two horse stable, Butchers Shop, Enclosed Yard, Garden and Paddock containing an area of about One acre and Twenty Two Perches ... The above is held by John Coleman on a yearly Michaelmas tenancy at the annual rent of £16 0s. 0d.

Silverstone Mill and Land

Situated near the village of Silverstone and consisting of: A Capital Windmill in good working order and driving three pair of stones. A Dwelling House with Three bedrooms, Two Sitting Rooms, Cellar, Wash House and Back Room, with Outbuildings comprising of: Nag Stables, Cart Hovel, Woodshed, Barn, Piggery, and Stack Yard. Garden and Three enclosures of Pasture land ... Total Acres, A.08. R.02. P.28. The above is in the occupation of Mr Charles Higham on a yearly Michaelmas tenancy at the annual rent of £55 0s. 0d.

Bleak Hall Farm

Is situated close to the village of Silverstone, and is bounded by the Brackley Turnpike Road, The Dadford and Buckingham Road, and lands belonging to the Court. The Farm House, which is close to the road, contains the following accommodation: Two Attics, Three Bedrooms, Parlour, Sitting Room, Kitchen Pantry, Dairy, Cellar, Woodshed, Garden with Cow house and Calf Pen. Also in field No. 248 on plan, A capital Barn, Cowshed, Nag Stable, another Cowshed and Yard. At some little distance and known as Litchgate is another little homestead. A Labourers Cottage of Five Rooms, Pantry and Coal Cellar, with Outbuildings comprising of Barn, Two Cowsheds, Nag Stable, Three Horse Stable and Chaff House together with several enclosures of arable and pasture land containing as area of about 127 acres. The above is held by Mr Thomas Adams on a yearly Lady-Day tenancy at the annual rent of £169 1s. 10d.

Priesthay Wood Farm

Adjoins Priesthay Wood and Wappenham Lodge Farms. A set of farm buildings consisting of, barn, cow shed, four horse stable, chaff and hay house. The whole contains an area of about 80 acres, 0 Roods, 28 Perches of arable and pasture land ... The above is held by a Mr William Farmer on a yearly Lady-Day tenancy at the annual rent of £94 13s. 0d.

C.N. WHIGHT'S DIRECTORY 1881

Silverstone is a considerable parish and scattered village in the southern division of the county, hundred of Greens Norton, union and County Court district of Towcester, rural deanery of Brackley No.2, and archdeaconry of Northampton, 4 miles S.W. from Towcester, 6 N.E. from Brackley, and 60 from London. The village is on the road from Towcester to Brackley, and occupies a very uneven site at the foot of and on the slopes of several hills. The

Church, dedicated to St.Michael, has been restored and partly rebuilt at the cost of R. Loder, Esq; M.P., of Whittlebury Lodge. The chancel has been rebuilt, a new organ chamber, vestry, and south porch erected, new roofs and arcades added, and all the windows filled with new tracery; and new open seats of stained pine and other fittings placed in the interior. The architect is Mr St. Aubyn of London and it is estimated that the expense will be more than £3,000. The Register dates from 1780. The living is a vicarage, annexed to Whittlebury, of the joint yearly value of £376. with residence, in the gift of the Crown, and held by the Rev. A. J. Street, B.A., of Whittlebury, assisted by a resident curate. There is a National school, towards the support of which £11 a year is paid by the Vicar out of Slapton's charity. There is a Wesleyan Chapel with resident minister and day school. The principal trade of the place seems to be that of making wooden hurdles. Area, 2110 acres, rateable value, £4090; Population in 1881, 1153.

St. Michael's Church. Services, Sunday 10.30 and 6. Communion first Sunday in month at midday. Rector. Rev. A. J. Street, B.A. (Whittlebury); Curate in charge, Rev. John Fallon; Wardens, Messrs. T. Linnell and T. Barford; Organist, Mr G. Powell; Clerk, - Linnell. Hymns A. and M.

Wesleyan Chapel. Services, Sunday 10.30 and 6. Wednesday 6.30. Rev. W. J. Evans; Chapel keeper, Mrs Markham.

Post and Money Order Office. Mrs M. A. Cartwright, sub-postmistress. Letters through Towcester arrive at 8 a.m. Box cleared 5.30 weekdays, 10 a.m. on Sunday. The nearest Telegraph office is at Whittlebury (1 1/2miles).

Adams, James: stone mason
Adkins, Emanuel: market gardener
Barber, Mrs Anna: lacemaker
Bradbury, George: brick & tile maker
Braggins, Mr. Thomas: brick & tile maker
Buckingham, Joseph: blacksmith
Coleman, John: bricklayer & builder
Coleman, William: tailor

Denney, John: master of Wesleyan Day school
Fallon, Rev. John: curate-in-charge
Hinton, Peter: of P Hinton & Son, and beer retailer.
Hinton, P. & Son (Leonard): brick-layers and builders
Hinton, Mr. William
Jeffrey, James: butcher
Linnell, Miss Martha Julia: Needles &
Linnell, Joseph, threshing machine owners
Phillips, John: sawyer
Pollard, Edward: carpenter & wheelwright
Powell, George: master National school
Rush, George: beer retailer and timber merchant
Sewell, William: sawyer
Varney, Richard: carpenter & wheelwright
Wake, Mrs: The Rookery
Weir, James Brownlee: surgeon and union medical officer
Whitlock, Frederick: rate collector
Whitlock, Thomas: butcher & timber dealer
Williams, Jeremiah: gamekeeper to Mr. West

BAKERS
Clark, Francis; Markham, Thomas; Wake, Thomas

BOOTMAKERS
Hawkins, John; Reeve, Edward; Scott, William

CARPENTERS
Rogers, Henry, and shopkeeper; Rush, William; Sewell, William Joseph

DRESSMAKERS
Braggins, Mrs. Elizabeth; Hawkins, Miss Harriet; Whitlock, Miss Ada

FARMERS AND GRAZIERS
Barford, Thomas James; Clark, Francis, & saddler & shopkeeper; Higham, Charles, and miller; Liddington, Valentine, and beer retailer and timber merchant; Linnell, Thomas; Rush, John, and beer retailer and timber merchant; Rush, Thomas, & timber merchant, Winter hills; West, George, and timber merchant; Whitlock, Thomas, and butcher; Whitlock, Thomas, & William & timber merchants; Wood, Thomas

GROCERS AND SHOPKEEPERS

Amos, Mrs.Harriett; Cartwright, Mrs. Mary Ann, P.O.; Clark, Thomas, & farmer & saddler; Kirby, Alexander; Peach, James B.; Richardson, George; Rogers, Henry, and carpenter; West, Mrs Esther; Whitlock, Thomas
HURDLE MAKERS
Chapman, Henry; Hayle, John; Spencer, John; Spencer, Joseph; Spencer, Thomas; Spencer, William
PUBLICANS
Fisher, King, v, White Horse; Heath, Thomas Henry, Tailor, and v, Compasses; Liddington, Valentine, beer retailer; Linnell, Joseph, v, Royal Oak; Mayo, George, bhs, Woodmen's Arms; Rush, John, farmer, timber dealer, and beer retailer
CARRIERS
Peach, James B., to Towcester M, Tu, W, F, S, & to Northampton W, S.

THE NATURAL HISTORY OF HAZELBOROUGH FOREST IN THE 20TH CENTURY

Hazelborough Forest is part of the old Royal Forest of Whittlewood (Whittlebury Forest) and as such has certainly been woodland ever since the days of William the Conqueror. This does not mean that it has been left in a purely natural state untouched by the hand of man. Woodland was extremely important from an economic point of view before coal came into general use, the main products of these woods being oak and "underwood." The plants which grow here are as close as one can get to the native flora of this part of the country - modified only by their adaptability to the coppicing cycle i.e. years of growing under a close canopy in deep shade, alternating with sudden exposure every 21 years when cutting operations took place above them. Insects and other fauna would obviously be subject to the same conditions.

The other factor determining which plants are to be found here is the type of soil present. In Bucknell Wood itself the first feature is a layer of vegetable mould, which has lain so long that there are quite sizeable roots in it. It is unusual to find such a sudden transition from leaf mould to the soil below. This soil varies from a golden sand to a medium loam. One side of the wood becomes clayey with some gravel in it and a trace of glacial material. All samples tested were acid (pH 5.0 - pH 5.5) and this accounts for the arrested decay and the sudden change between leaves and soil.

Hazelborough Forest is rich in plant species which are particularly characteristic of very old woodlands . These include a variety of ferns, e.g. the Lady Fern (Athyrium filix-femina) and the Broad-leaved Buckler Fern (Dryopteris dilatata) as well as the commoner Male fern (Dryopteris filix-mas). Sweet Woodruff (Asperula odorata) is plentiful especially in Bucknell Wood, although usually a very uncommon plant, and so too are the Hairy Woodrush Luzula pilosa and Melica uniflora, a very pretty woodland Broad-leaved Helleborine (Epipactis helleborine) Twayblade (Listera ovata) Spotted Orchis (Dactylorchis fuchsii) Early Purple Orchis (Orchis masculata) Greater Butterfly Orchis (Platanthera chlorantha) and Bird's Nest Orchis (Neottia nidus-avis). Among the rarities in this part of the country are two members of the pea family, Narrow - leaved Everlasting Pea (Lathyrus sylvestris and Bitter Vetch (Lathyrus montanus), an indicator of the acid soil. A good list of fungi has been recorded by the Northamptonshire Natural History Society.

Many of our rarer butterflies such as the Purple Emperor, White Admiral, Silver Washed Fritillary and Marsh Fritillary have been recorded in the Hazelborough woods but have not been seen in recent years. The Wood White is probably the rarest species which still survives.

The bird life of Hazelborough is full of variety both for winter residents and a very good selection of summer visitors including attractive species such as the nightingale. A large number of the birds given in the list were in fact seen on one visit to the way-marked walk.

There is a wide selection of our common mammals. The tracks of muntjac and fallow deer are very evident and a badger sett is recorded. One mammal of rarity has also been seen here, the dormouse.

Grass snakes and the much less common slowworm, or legless lizard also live in Hazelborough Forest. Both these reptiles are harmless.

The Northamptonshire Naturalists' Trust Ltd.

PART 4 🚗 People and Places

The principal legacy of Joy Townsend is the collection of interviews she made in the 1970s and 1980s. All her work is included in this section, together with more recent material. Some of the interviews have been edited and shortened to remove repetition and to clarify statements where possible, but as little change as was vital has been made. The full texts of these interviews have been deposited in the Northamptonshire County Archives at Wootton Hall.

AUBREY LINNELL

(A digest by Elaine Lovell of an 1974 talk recorded by Joy Townsend).

The landmarks that delineate Silverstone boundaries are a series of brooks. There is a brook at a place known as *"The Swinnies"*, a mile to the Silverstone side of Towcester. Another boundary is a brook at the *"Crown Lands"* of Hazelborough Woods on the way to Buckingham, just past the Tustian Farm [Bleak Hall] before the *"aerodrome"* (or the racing circuit as it is now). The other boundary is at the *"Watergate"* near West End and this completes the Silverstone parish.

In the Domesday Book, Silson (Silverstone) was referred to as *"The Hamlet in the Wood"*. A hamlet is a settlement without a church. The first church was built by King John and it stood near to the spot where the war memorial stands today. It was constructed from timber and was burnt down long ago.

At that time Greens Norton housed the *"Mother Church"* whereas today Whittlebury holds that honour. The vicar would live at Greens Norton and he would have 2 curates, one to serve Whittlebury and the other to serve Silverstone.

A second church was constructed on the same site and this also burnt down, so the third and present church was built on the present site, although it has gone through many changes to create the building we enjoy today.

The Woods that run either side of the road to Brackley were always known as The Crown Lands. Now called Hazelborough Woods, they were common land and the Silson people were allowed to use it for grazing cattle, picking fire wood, harvesting nuts, and for what ever they liked. Then came the Enclosure Act of 1825, and all that was stopped, so for compensation the villagers were given allotments at Winter Hills. The Crown Lands had been planted with Oak trees the year after Waterloo, 1815. Hazelborough is in the Parish of Syresham, whereas Bucknells, once part of the 600 acres of Silson, is now in the parish of Abthorpe.

Silverstone was one of the few villages where everyone was self employed. The forestry made a mistake, they cut the oaks down when they were growing pea sticks for bean poles, and ash poles for making hurdles, and for making baskets and such like. Instead of planting oak, they planted conifers, which killed all of the undergrowth so nothing new grew, thus putting a lot of Silson people out of work. They did however plant oak at Bucknells Wood, but when the trees were 25 years old they were poisoned because the Forestry Commission decided that the oaks were taking too long to grow and not giving a quick enough turnover, as a good oak has to be a hundred years in the making before it can be felled. So conifers were planted because they only take 25 years to mature. Aubrey Linnell was so disgusted by this incompetent act of mismanagement, that in 1967 he wrote a damning article about it in the Readers Digest. Aubrey thinks that it must have done some good, as not long afterwards the Commission started to re-plant oak, and Silverstone was the only place to make a profit as a result.

In the Crown Lands there is a portion of the woods known as King Richard's Copse, which contains the finest crop of timber that you could wish to see, but it is all useless, because when it is felled it's all chaffy and can't be made into posts or fencing. Now here, the mistake was reversed, oak had been planted but the soil was too gravelly for oak; here is where they should have planted conifers.

The present church was rebuilt by Sir Robert Loder who is buried at Whittlebury church. His grave has an iron railing all around it. About twenty years ago, Whittlebury church council wrote to Sir Robert Loder's grandson asking if he would like to contribute to the upkeep of the grave. The grandson wrote back saying

"My grandfather spent a great deal of money on looking after Whittlebury and Silverstone, so I think it should be your turn to look after him."

The oldest building is the once thatched farmhouse which stands on the first corner of Puddledock (now Church Street). Further down the road, Rookery Farm with 1659 inscribed on it was built a year later. There was a murder committed in the field behind the older farm. It was said that a burglar had tried to rob Home Farm on Chapel Hill. The robber was chased over the fields to the back of the barns that lie between the old farm and Rookery Farm, where he was shot dead. Tradition has it that on the anniversary of that desperate chase the sounds of someone running, out of breath, and panting can be heard.

Silverstone used to be quite self supporting, there were two bakers, two butchers, a shop at the lower end of Little London, and there was also a bakery and a shop where Crofts Stores now stand. The big white house on Stocks Hill used to be a drapery shop owned by Miss Richardson (who also owned other properties in Silverstone). There was Townsend's General Stores and Post Office (as it still is, but now under new ownership). Further up the High Street on the right hand side, just beyond the chapel, stood the village bake house which was demolished in Autumn 1967. Older residents of the village can remember taking the Sunday Yorkshire puddings and meat joints up to the bake house on their way to Sunday school or Church and collecting the finished cooked meal on their way home. Carry on up to the top of the High Street and on the left hand side is what used to be another general store known as the Top Shop. Today it is a private house. Opposite there on the junction of the main road, where some bungalows now stand, there was a row of old cottages and, a little way behind them was another row of three cottages and a shop.

Cattle End was also self sufficient. There were two shops and a row of six cottages known as Barrack Row. In West End, opposite Pyghtle, was a shop, and a *"bottle shop"* called the Woodmans Arms, then further on down West End was another pub called the Chequers, all of these premises are now private houses.

The Compasses was one of the oldest and largest public buildings in Silverstone, its full title on its sign board outside was, The Lord Encompasseth Thee, and the monks of Luffield Abbey used to call in there for refreshments on their way to Blackmires. Once refreshed they would walk along the Pyghtle path to Blackmires and this is what gave Pyghtle its name, for it means *"prayer way"* in Latin.

The monks would also come down to

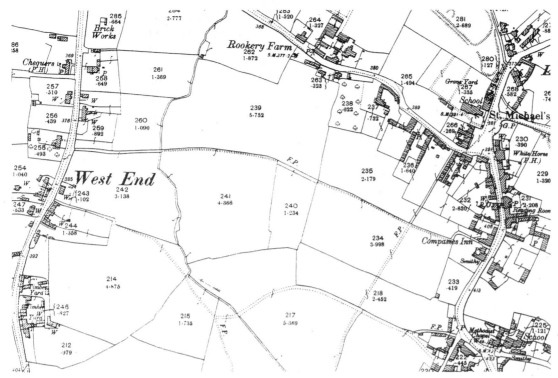

Detail from the Ordnance Survey map of 1900 showing the footpath called The Pyghtle running west from The Compasses.

fish at Fish Waters, which in those days was about 5 acres of managed fishing grounds where West End meets Church Street (Puddledock). We know the ground today as the recreation area and sports pavilion. You can still see the high banks to the South of the area which once formed a dam.

In winter time the streets of Silverstone were unwalkable because of the mud and slush. Every so often the County Council would send *"the brush"* to come and sweep it. The streets were also unlit. On Sunday nights when Chapel and the Church were coming out, it was *"quite a do"* to get past in the dark and muddy slush.

Before the 1914 war there used to be a band in Silverstone, and they used to play either in the warehouse of the post office or in the barn that's alongside it. The band had broken away from the Chapel. It would parade through the village up to Cattle End where they would have an open air service and then parade back. The normal practice

in those days was for people to have their Sunday tea and then walk right around the village going down West End and back up and then finish up at Church or Chapel. As there were no cars in those days it did not matter that many people were walking in the middle of the road, they could do so at their leisure and in complete safety.

The Towcester to Brackley by-pass was opened just before the second world war. Also Kingsley Road was just being built. They had got as far as building but not quite completing ninety cottages, when the government commandeered them to billet their soldiers in at the start of the 1939 war. The R.A.F. were billeted up by the aerodrome. It was at this time that Aubrey became a special constable. Aubrey remembers how worried Silson people were about letting a light show at night in case they were bombed, but the soldiers up at Kingsley were not so bothered and used to let lights show all the time which used to worry the village folk very much, but whenever Aubrey in his capacity as special constable would try to find someone in authority up at Kingsley to sort the men out, there was never anyone there to be accountable. Thankfully despite the villagers' worries not one bomb was dropped on Silson soil.

Back in the time before the 1914-18 war Silson was a rough and ready place. Each family had on average six or more children and the average wage was about 12 shillings a week if you were lucky. So most families had to resort to poaching, mostly rabbits. Some fellows even turned to attempting robbery.

There was a parson called John, who one evening was on his way back from visiting and had got as far as Challock Farm, which lies on the Abthorpe to Silverstone road and is situated just opposite Bucknell Wood, when two men approached him and asked for the time. The parson pulled out his gold watch and told them it was 10 o'clock to which one man replied: *"We're going to have that watch now"*. *"Oh, are you?"* said the parson, and then proceeded to give the two men a good thrashing. Afterwards he made them both get down on their knees with him and say the Lord's prayer!

Canon Brittain lived at Whittlebury vicarage. He used to ride a three wheeled bike to and from Silverstone, with his son always walking beside him so that the latter could push the bike up hills and the Canon could ride down them. One day, leaving Silverstone after a service he and his son were returning along the Whittlebury road, when the bike got a puncture. The Canon told his son to fix the bike and he would walk on and his son could catch up with him later. The Canon got as far as the old windmill on the Whittlebury road when he met a Romany who lived there, and he could hear him swearing and cursing at his lawn mower that would not start. *"Here, here, my good man,"* he said to the Romany, *"that's*

no way to carry on, cursing and swearing won't get you anywhere. What you should do is to get down on your knees and give a little prayer to the good Lord to help you". The two of them got down on their knees and prayed, and when they had finished praying, the Romany tried once more to start his mower. It fired first time, and the Canon is reputed to have remarked, *"Well I'm buggered"*.

From before the 1914 war 'til just after, there used to be two butchers who visited the village. One was Harry Walker or Norris and one from nearby Greens Norton. They both used to come to the village on Tuesdays and Saturdays, so with all the other local produce, the village was quite

Billy Baud's team hauling timber at Dadford.

self sufficient. The only thing the village did not have was a Fishmonger.

On the odd occasion if the women needed to go into Towcester, they would hitch a ride on the regularly passing horse drawn timber carts. These timber carriages had four cart wheels with a long pole through the middle which over hung the back by 6 to 8 feet, and this is where the women used to ride. As there were no bus routes to Silson in those days, catching a passing timber cart was the best and most reliable mode of transport, especially when you had to catch a train from the local station at Towcester, there was always a local *'Timber Express'* going to the station.

To visit Northampton, one could hitch a ride with the *'Carrier'*. These were the men who would visit the local farms for eggs and butter to sell at the Northampton market on Wednesdays and Saturdays for the farmers. There was a Mr Peach from West End and a Mr Rush who were the carriers for the church school and in between time they went to Towcester for the Tuesday Market. Aubrey remembers going to Northampton on the carriers cart, it was in 1911, and they started off on the journey at 8 am and arrived in the town at about 12 noon.

The church school in Green Lane was built by Canon Brittain with money from India and at no cost to the parish or county. Canon Brittain was the Canon of Madras and he obtained the money from the Indian Princes. Until this time there were only two very small schools, one was located just in front of the church, now known as the church rooms in Little London, the other was run by the chapel in their attached hall. The pupils numbered as many as 100 in each. The chapel was the first to provide a school in 1811 and it was a little while before the penny dropped with the Church of England when they realised that the Sunday School attendances were getting very low. This was because the villagers were attending the chapel so they could send their children to school there.

The church school was set up about three years later, although there was a pay-to-go school in between, this was known as *'The Mission Rooms'* and the pupils had to pay 2d a week to attend. This was a lot of money to those who were only earning about 12 shillings a week, or less in some cases. If you had the misfortune of being the school dunce, the headmaster would pay you a half penny to stay away when the school inspector was due to visit the school. The mission rooms were where the post office is today, in the High Street, and before it was a school it was the reading rooms as far back as the 1600's.

The only Grammar School for older children was in Towcester. This is now Sponne School founded by Sir William Sponne and one of the oldest schools in the county, dating back to 1492.

Aubrey went to this school in 1914 and there were only 21 pupils then as opposed to the some 1300 or more that attend today. Aubrey recalls his school days. In particular, two sons from another timber family by the name of Whitlock who were sent to public school (believed to be neighbouring Stowe) in an effort to better themselves in preparation for taking over the family business. This backfired on the Whitlocks however, as, when the sons left school they did not want to work, but led the lives of gentlemen like their fellow pupils. This was not to be, as there weren't the funds to support this life-style. Eventually, one son ended up in the work house and later died there, while the other went away and was never heard of again.

As we know, Aubrey went to Grammar School, for which the fee was £2-3 per term, a lot of money in those days. The best way for him to travel to Towcester was to cycle, however if it was snowing, then he would walk, taking him about an hour to do so. When Aubrey left school, he joked, *"All I could spell was, "Ash, Oak and Elm"*.

In those days the pupils were excused Summer school to help with the farming and harvesting or to take lunch and refreshments to the men working the fields. Most children left school at twelve years old, although it was gradually raised to 13 and then 14. All of the boys would have jobs to go to. In the summer months lads helping the farmers would work from 7am 'til 5pm for 6d a week.

Aubrey remembers one farmer called Arthur, who lived in the High Street, and one day Arthur called to his boy worker and said *"I'm gonna pay you an extra 3d a week, but you got a come in twice on Sunday"*. Most boys when at school, would save up and buy a *'Shut Knife'*; these were like a large pen knife with two blades and one of

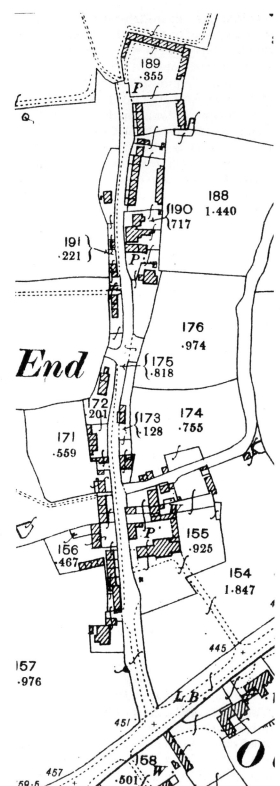

Detail from the 1900 Ordnance Survey map, showing Cattle End. Barrack Row is the terrace at the north, the foundations of which can be found in the field, next to the footpath.

their main purposes was to eat their dinner with, which usually consisted of bread, meat and cheese. Another essential item to be bought would be a pocket watch and this would cost around 5 shillings.

Bread was the main food for the workers on the farm, and one family alone would order 13 loaves on a Saturday afternoon just to see the men folk through to Monday when the baker would open again.

The men would go off to the fields at 6 in the morning and not return until 6 at night, so they would need to take two loads of food with them. Tobacco was another essential aid to keep them going through the long day and this would be smoked through a clay pipe.

There was a shop in Cattle End that sold tobacco and this would open at 5:30 in the morning so they could catch the men on their way to work. For 1d you could buy a box of matches, a clay pipe and a ha'penny of tobacco. Aubrey recalled one day when a man went to buy his *'Bacca'*, and the nice old lady who owned the shop said *"I can't sell you any just yet 'cos I 'avn't watered it"*, the purpose of watering it was to make it heavier on the scales and therefore she could sell less tobacco for more money.

The clay pipes were very delicate and easy to break. Although they were cheap enough to buy, the men would try to keep them as long as possible because the more dirty and sooty they became, the sweeter the smoke.

Aubrey tells us of a *'Silson Bloke'* that never bathed after he was three years old, and this became typical of this chap, when he had a new pair of socks they would never be taken off until they fell off through rotting on his feet, this was when it was time for a new pair. This same chap lived to be 86 years old and he drank and smoked as much as he could. He married and fathered 6 children, and never had a doctor to him in his life, he was as tough as old boots. This old man always attributed his good health to

The shop in Cattle End.

never bathing.

The cottages that the people lived in were quite small, usually two rooms over one. The parents would be in one room and anything from six to eight children would be sleeping *'head to toe'* in the other. The wife would usually take in washing to assist with the family income.

Before the 1914 war you could always find Silson folk working in saw mills. One such person by the name of Whitlock, took his own saw bench and engine over to Ireland to work. Even those who did not have work benches and engines would continue to work around the country where ever the demand was, and the method they used was the same as they had always done in the days before engines and benches. The men would dig a hole deep and large enough for two men then they would roll the tree over the pit and using a two handed saw and a man either side, one being on the top side of the tree, they could easily and quite efficiently saw the tree up. At one time there were 35 pair of men travelling the countryside all from Silson, especially in the 1939/45 war these men did nothing else but travel round to fell trees.

There was a tradition among these woodland folk that Towcester people should be grateful to the Silson folk for saving their necks as long ago as the Danish invasions. Apparently when the Danes were approaching Towcester the Silson men went in and moved all the old and young up to

A timber-hauling team pause at the brickworks in West End.

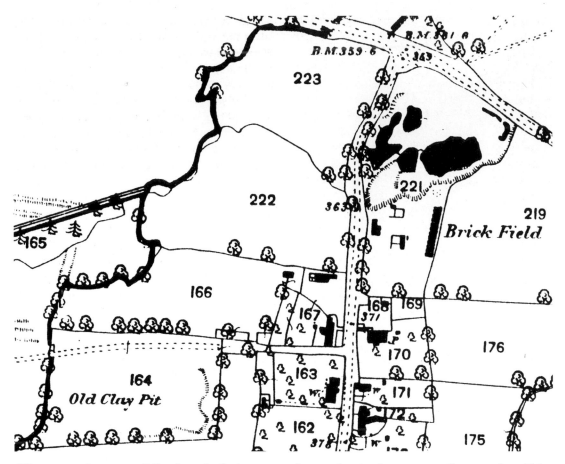

Detail from a 19th-century map showing the northern end of West End and the Brick Field (no. 221). The Chequers is property no. 167.

Silverstone by way of the brook that runs from Towcester to Silverstone. Keeping the men of that town to defend while the Silson men crept around behind the Danes enclosing them in so they could not go forward or backward. Every now and then they liked to remind Towcester of that.

At one time all Silsoners had to go to Towcester to vote, and in the days of Aubrey's father you had to own property in order to vote, so having no property at the time, but owning a sow, and young pigs, he sold these for five pounds and with this money was able to buy a cottage next to the chapel. He, now being a property owner, could vote.

Before the 1914 war we had a heap of saw dust in the woodyard, and when we were shifting all this sawdust an old feller came up to me and said there must have *been about close on a thousand rabbits been hidden in that heap throughout the year. When we came back from poaching late at night we would hide them in there until we could safely collect them the next day.*

These poachers used to have gangs! A kind of a union, a poacher couldn't just do as they pleased. There was a feller down West End and the police arrested him in his bed one morning for thieving the night before. The chap asked if he could get dressed first. He got up and went to a place in the room where he had a hidden trap door and disappeared down the trap into the kitchen below and out the back door before the police knew what was happening and they never did charge him. When Aubrey was a special constable just before the second world war he had to approach a known poacher's wife who he knew used to sell the rabbits and hares that her husband had poached. She wore a long thick black skirt which had many folds held up with a wide belt from which she would hang her ill gotten gains under her skirts. Aubrey was under orders from Towcester to investigate her and find out where she hid them. So being eager to impress his peers, Aubrey went up to Cattle End where he knew she would be. When he caught up with her he confronted her as to where she kept the rabbits and he went to move her skirt out of the way to reveal them. The woman shouted out, *"Now then Aubrey Linnell you've a wife of your own so you can leave me alone."* With that Aubrey was so embarrassed he did no more than to get home as quick as he could.

BRICKHILL OR BRICKLE

After the site of Silverstone's brick clay pit fell into disuse, the pits filled with water. In order to preserve this part of Silverstone's heritage, a project was set up by the residents for the site to be bought for the village as a whole and to be turned into a Pocket Park. In this way the memory of the village brickworks could be preserved in an environment favourable to wildlife. The scheme was brought to fruition in the late 1990s and visitors to the park may well find fragments of brick in the undergrowth, perhaps still bearing the wire cutter marks made when the wet brick was scraped off the turning out board before being dried. The site of the brickworks itself with its kilns is now built over with housing.

There was a time when houses in Silson were very hard to sell. There was no piped water or sewers. Even the nice large houses up on the main road would only sell for around £600. There used to be a well opposite the row of cottages in Little London and that would serve all the residents there. Further up Little London to the right in Tinkers Lane there was another.

Then coming down Little London and turning left up Whittlebury road there was a stream that runs from behind Frog Hall through the very end of the White Horse car park and across under Whittlebury road to the bottom of the garden of No. 4 Little London under that road up Water Lane where it emerges again and goes on a journey across the fields. Up the top of the High Street just before Green Lane was a timber yard owned by the Wests and just in front of it was the village pump. Running along side of the yard was a foot path call Pump Lane. Cattle End could also boast its own pump to serve the people there whose comunity was bigger than it is now. West End had a very old well called Black Well and was not far from Blackmires farm. There is also one of the houses in West End that had two wells one in the back and one

George Rush's mobile timber yard went where it was wanted.

in the front, they must have felt very privileged.

Silverstone used to be made up of many timber yards, starting at the top of Little London and walking our way down the first yard we come to is Webb's just along side of the Limes farm. Moving just a little way down on the right hand side is Tinkers Lane. Up there was the Little White Horse pub and that had a coal and timber yard. Coming back out of Tinkers Lane and continuing back down Little London, right on the corner where it meets Whittlebury Road, now stands a doctors surgery but before then it was George Lovell's timber yard.

Move on up to the top of the High Street on the left hand side Stan Linnell's yard, the only remaining timber yard left in Silverstone. Further on across the main road there was yet another yard.

Other yards could be found in Cattle End and Mayo's timber at West End.

Newcomers

Joy, herself a relative newcomer to the village, asked Aubrey Linnell about his feelings on the subject.

Tell me Mr Linnell what did the people of Silverstone think when all these new houses started being built here? An honest opinion.

AL Well they didn't think much to it and they didn't think much of the people who came. I can't understand you "Silverstone people". You're Silverstone people, I'm a Silston man. Now if I go up the village and see a Silston person it's "Good morning!" "Good morning!" but none of you ever look at us, just pass us by.

I was very surprised when we moved here how friendly the original Silverstone people were, and what they used to keep saying was "I hope you're happy in our village."

AL We Silston people, we like to speak to everyone, we're very friendly. I hope after this, you'll know me now, shan't you? Everyone calls me Aubrey in the village, I don't like Mr. Silston people will shout out "How are you?" But the people who've come in they won't look at you. Don't know why because the old Silston people are a very friendly lot. Do anything for anyone.

How long do you have to live here before you're a local?

AL You who have come out since the '39 war are Silverstone people. But we who were here before the '39 war are Silston people. We like to mix with you but you won't mix with us.

Don't you think the barriers are coming down now?

AL It doesn't matter whether you're new or old, it's what sort of person you are. That's right.

Not many villages accept outsiders

AL You've come to live in the best village in England.

SAVE OUR LANGUAGE

In 1988, an appeal was launched in the NEWS & VIEWS by Neal Lovell. This is an extract from that appeal.

Save Our Language Appeal.

Over the past few years, a disturbing trend has been noticed. As old families leave and new ones arrive, the native Silson tongue has been spoken less and less. Don't let our language suffer the same fate as Manx or Cornish.

In a slender hope to slow down the vanishing, please make more use of the words listed below, they make conversation so much more colourful.

Ommackin abait: *Moving in an annoying, loud and clumsy manner.*
Wollurin: *Lounging around and being of no use.*
Slummuck(ing): *To walk in a slouched and sluggardly manner.*
Mar'uz, tai'uz an' pays: *Tomatoes, Potatoes and Peas.*
Goo furra mooch: *To take a slow stroll.*
Dunt attoo: *Don't Have To.*
Dunt wonoo: *Don't Want To.*
Ent gunoo: *Not Going To.*
Cays, Dugs, Uggs: *Cows, Dogs, Pigs.*
Uggish: *Greedy or selfish (piggish).*
Sebbum, Lebbum, Twowve: *Seven, Eleven,*

Twelve.
Leyzee (Lousy): *Slovenly and Dishevelled.*
Aglin an'a caglin: *Arguing over trivia for arguments sake.*
Frez: *Froze or frozen.*
Werdunt: *Were not or Was not.*
Teyn: *Town (meaning Northampton).*
Gret: *Great or large and cumbersome.*
Wow: *Well (as in "Well, I never did!).*
Shallus Goo?: *Shall we go.*
Mozy on back up eir eyse: *Go back up to our house.*
Ud, Udden: *Wood or wooden (Goo up the uds, go up Bucknells Woods)*
Betternus: *Had we not ought to, should we not.*
Kaylide: *Under the influence of alcohol.*
Up Muzzell: *Up Murswell Lane.*
Dain Fishugs: *Down Fishwaters.*
Keych: *Couch or sofa.*
Chopsin: *Talking.*

These words are only the tip of the iceberg, our language takes a lifetime to perfect, and the accent is even more elusive. Don't be tempted to use the Towcester tongue. Although it is similar, it's a little more raucous. In addition to the above vocabulary, remember a few (but oh, so difficult to get right) rules. Never pronounce the T at the end of words and *"on"* replaces *"of"*, e.g. *"He were a top on it"* i.e. *"he was on top of it"*, *"in the middle on it"* etc. We don't say *"is not"*, we say *"ent"*. Practice these daily and you might just pass for a villager..., eventually.
Happy Chopsin!

LINNELL BROTHERS' TIMBERYARD.

The firm Linnell Bros Ltd, Timber Merchants, was founded by two brothers, Arthur and Brum Linnell in approximately 1890. The two brothers parted after a few years and Arthur started his own timber business at Winter Hills, Silverstone. Timber purchased was small, most of it split for cleft rails and post.

During these years, Arthur married a local girl, Rebecca Mayo, combining timber work with being landlord of the Royal Oak pub.

From left to right, Jim, Aubrey, Simm and Vic Linnell.

Times were very hard, but by using a pit saw and later a circular saw, business progressed. Thus more space was required. So in 1918, the present site in High Street was purchased and the equipment moved. Horses were used for hauling timber from local woods, thus land was needed for them to graze. This resulted in the present farm being obtained and the family, now four boys and two girls, moving from the Royal Oak. The boys, Jim, Aubrey, Sim and Vic were now working in the business. In 1930 a band saw was purchased from France enabling larger trees to be converted into planks, beams and coffin boards. To provide power for running these machines, a steam engine was acquired. The trees were now getting too big for horses to haul, so contractors with road running steam engines were hired.

In the late 1930s Arthur retired and the business was run by the four sons who purchased a large band-mill and crane which were electrically powered. Timber was now purchased within a radius of 40 miles, using motor powered haulage.

During the war timber was in great demand, oak being cut for building of mine sweepers; ash for the aircraft industry; various hard and softwoods for coal mines;

The Farm, Church Street, property of the Linnell family.

oak and elm for railway trucks. To produce these items, larger updated machines were required.

With advancing years the four sons handed over the running of the business to their sons Ken, Bryan, Barry, Edmund and Don. During the coming years to move with changing times, machines were changed and replaced with the latest electrical and hydraulic machines and a treatment plant installed, to cope with rising demands for treated softwood for building and farming requirements.

Round timber for conversion now comes from all parts of England and softwood for treatment is obtained from various places in Europe.

In 1998, the time of this writing, the company held large stocks of produced and purchased soft and hard woods and was run by Barry, Edmund and Don Linnell with their sons working in the business too.

LITTLE LONDON.

Little London has changed much over the years. It was once a very close and thriving community in its own right. It was not just the long road leading up to the Towcester road that we all know today, with houses on either side. Little London was a large cluster of cottages to be found between what is now No 5 (Lake Grange) and No 7 situated at the back and running the length of the row in front.

The people who built these cottages were refugees from the plague in London around 1665 or the Great Fire of 1666. The cottages start to appear on maps from the mid 1700s. On subsequent maps from the mid 1800s right up to the present day you will see the gradual decline of the community. Where cottages once stood there are now the gardens of the front row that runs up the main road of Little London. Gone too are the cottages at the side of No. 5 and in front of the house beside Water Lane (the public footpath by the stream). Between these cottages, on what is now the garden of No. 5) was one of the village's two (possibly three) Pounds. The Pounds were used as places of detention for roaming deer, cows, or sheep that quite often would wander into the village. The Londoners had built their little group of houses in the same cramped fashion as the streets of London at the time of their leaving. Perhaps they knew no other way of doing things or perhaps simply wanted to recreate their lost homes, and so made tight rows of cottages and little alleyways.

Edna Dodwell was interviewed in 1998 and again in 1999. Edna and her husband Dennis (known to all as Doddy), ran a newsagents and tobacconist shop in Little London. She wore many hats during her service to the community, one being as writer and director of the W.I.'s drama group. She was also a clever poet, as well as writing occasional articles for the News and Views, some of which are in this book.

Memories of Edna Dodwell

Edna was born at Laurel Cottage, on the

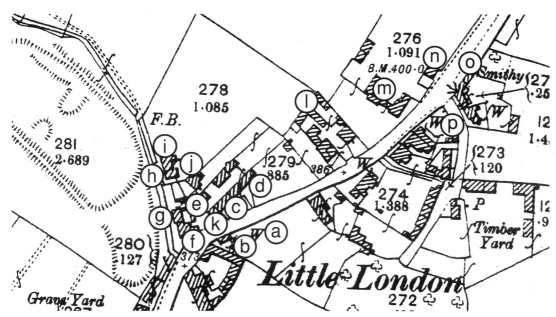

Detail from the Ordnance Survey map, showing Little London. The places spoken of by Edna Dodwell are marked as follows: A pump & well. B red brick building for paraffin. C Edna's cottages. D Ginny (the witch's) house. E Mrs Harrison with her 3 children. F No.5 The shop run by Mr & Mrs Lovell. G Mr & Mrs Cox and four children. H Mrs Linnel and her drunken husband. I Mrs Champman. J The couple with six children. K Poll Spencer (wobble) + 22 children. L The Laurels (Edna's grandparents). M The Limes farm. N Red brick building that residents tried to save. O the Blacksmith's forge. P Tinkers Lane. The row of houses behind Edna's was a terrace.

western side of the hill up from the stream, in 1920. Her great-grandfather was the first in the family to have the cottage. He was a shoe maker named William Scott. When Edna's great-grandparents died her mother took over Laurel Cottage shortly after getting married. One part of the cottage at the back (which is now an extended kitchen) was the work shop, and the furthest part (which is now a granny annexe) was the wash house and lodgers bed-sitting room, occupied by a disabled man who was a very clever wood carver and herbalist. His potions were used by most of the people in the village. At Christmas time he would make toys for the village children.

The first house at the north of Little London belonged to the Whitmore family. This is on the right hand side as you are coming into Little London from Towcester. They also had a timber yard next to the house and then there was a paddock. Next to the paddock was a red brick building

which was used as a blacksmiths and was part of the property belonging to a beautiful, large, old farm-house called The Limes. Both buildings were very lovely and, in the 1960s, when the last occupant of each died the Council bought up the properties and land then demolished them. They had come up against great opposition as the village would have liked, at least, to have had the old red brick building to become a village club house. The council would not hear of it and built the council flats instead. Opposite the house, on the left hand side, were fields all the way down through what is now Hillside Avenue, up to Tinkers Lane. The house on the corner of Tinkers Lane was owned by Mr and Mrs Betts, the sheds adjoining the house were a workshop where cane furniture and wicker baskets were made, but at one time long ago these too were a blacksmith's forge. Further up Tinkers Lane we come to Farm cottage. This for a long time had been a public house called the Little White Horse, probably decommissioned just after the First World War. It then became a farm house with yard and also a coal merchant's. The cottage next to it is the Berries and at one time it was a wash house which had a very large copper inside it. Further on was Orchard Cottage so named because it was surrounded by an

At the rear of the Laurels sometime between 1906 and 1910, from left to right, Will Farmer (cousin to the Scotts), Grandma Scott, Margaret Edna Linnell (later James, Edna Dodwell's mother) and William Scott, (Grandfather).

orchard. The other cottages in the lane were mostly farm hands' cottages.

Coming out of the lane and carrying on down Little London, we come to a red brick building called Ginger Bread Cottage, this used to be two cottages but has now been merged into one, and was named Ginger Bread Cottage in the 1980s. Next door are two grey stone cottages, the end one having an alley-way running along side of it which takes you up and round to Tinkers Lane. Next, there are two other houses set up on the bank. Opposite those is a fairly large grey stone house which is sideways on and looks down the hill to face the rest of Little London. At one time, a Sunday school teacher from the Chapel lived here and would hold school sessions there. After this house there were large gardens that went all the way to Lantern Cottage which was owned by Edna's father.

There is a little cottage between Edna's and the archway. This used to belong to old Ginny Coleson. Most older residents of Silson remember Ginny when they were children because they thought she was a

witch. Poor old Ginny was a little woman and wore a black leather patch over her nose. The children were told that she lost her nose through taking too much snuff and one day she had sneezed and blew it off. She did not like children much either, can you blame her, she must have been teased rotten! The cottage next to that was also owned by Edna's father, but, before he bought it, the cottage belonged to the Tailor of the village and he could be seen sitting cross-legged in the window sewing away at his cloth. In the bottom house was a Mrs Harrison who lived with her three children. Across from there was a red brick building which is no longer there [but can be seen in Plate 18] and that used to house the paraffin which supplied the whole village, in the days before electricity. The village was not connected to the gas main so the only lighting was paraffin or candles. Paraffin was used for heating too. The village was not connected to mains electricity until 1942. Opposite where the red brick building was, is No. 5, a pebbledash building, and this used to be a general store and was bigger than it is now. Where their garage is now was once a little red brick cottage (two up and two down) belonging to a Mr and Mrs Cox and their four children. Opposite Mrs Cox was a very small cottage and in it lived a very big women named Poll Spencer who had twenty-two children and who (according to one old resident) wobbled like a jelly when she laughed. Children, being what they are, used to throw stones at her door and call out names just to make her come running out of the house, at first a bit cross but, seeing the funny side of the chidren's cheek, she would soon end up laughing and wobbling which is what the children were after. On one occasion their joke went a bit too far when on a winter's day they threw a snowball down poor Poll's chimney and put out her fire, sending smoke billowing through her house. On that occasion she came running out of the house wobbling with anger.

Further on behind there was another cottage and another couple with six children, behind that, running alongside and in front of Mrs Chapmans house, was a cottage split into two and rented out to two different families. These cottages were very old, in one half there were two rooms down stairs (one was really a pantry) and one large room up stairs divided by a partition, there was one window at the front and one at the back. Mr and Mrs Liddle or Linnell used to live there with their seven children. Mr Linnell was a drunkard and kept his family poor by his selfishness. Edna remembers, as a child, going up the stairs to see her little friend who was sick. Although the room was spotlessly clean it was so sparse, the windows had little leaded diamond-shaped panes of glass and at least four of these were out and stuffed with old bits of cloth. The large bed in which all the children slept was bare with just one ragged old army blanket and lots of old coats huddled on the bed. When Edna's mother found out, she called the doctor then went round to Mrs Linnell with sheets and blankets for the bed, which she had just taken off her own, and a night gown. She helped Mrs Linnell put the little girl in the night gown, and then made the bed. She did all this to save Mrs Linnell from embarrassment in front of the doctor, although I wonder if it might have been better if the doctor had seen just what poverty her husband had kept them in.

Opposite No. 5 and a little way up was a well which produced lovely fresh sparkling drinking water. One day Mrs Linnell, who was nine months pregnant at the time, went to the well to draw two buckets of water, when she saw her husband come staggering down the road from the White Horse and collapse by her feet on the grass in a drunken stupor. Edna's mother saw this and went up to Mrs Linnell and said, *"Don't you dare carry those,"* and she picked up the buckets and took them in for her. Once Mrs Linnell was inside, Edna's mother came back out and told Mr Linnell how he should be ashamed of himself, *"How can you be so selfish?"* to which the man hung his head and said, *"You're right. I am sorry."* To which she replied *"It is not me who you must be sorry to, but your poor wife and children."* He then went home with his tail between his legs. The well was later replaced by a pump and later still, in 1947, when mains water was introduced, it was sealed up but it can still be recognised by a pipe sticking up from the ground.

LITTLE LONDON GENERAL STORES.

The general stores at No.5 Little London was owned by Bill and Ethel Lovell. Ethel ran the shop while Bill worked in the family timber haulage business. Bill was one of four brothers. George Lovell owned the timber yard at the corner of Whittlebury Road and Little London, where the doctors' surgery now stands.

Jack Lovell ran the Compasses pub in the High Street. In the courtyard of the pub was kept an old fire engine with its large wheels on the ladder at the rear, belonging to the Fairweather family. They lived at the old Post Office on the opposite side of the High Street. Also in the courtyard was a large block of stone rumoured to be King John's mounting block. The block is now in the front garden of No.5 Little London, put there by Jack in the late 1950s or early 1960s when Bill's son Sid married Jean Hayle and lived there.

Jim Lovell lived in a cottage by Gravel Walk in Church Street. The cottage was framed by a small orchard that he also owned.

A Tragedy Remembered.

Leonie Yeates is a cousin to Edna Dodwell and was a regular visitor at the James' house when Edna was a young girl. By Leonie's own admission she was a *"thorough snitch"* and a real pain to Edna and her friends. Leonie was one of those youths who would always follow Edna and her chums around, then could not wait to run over to Mrs James (Edna's mother) to snitch on everything that her peers got up to that day.

Leonie and Edna have through the years kept up their visiting to one another, quite often they share a week or a weekend at one or others home. It was on such a visit that Elaine Lovell first met Leonie when interviewing Edna for of this book. It was fortunate that she was there as Leonie often would prompt Edna to remember quite a few tales. Much laughter and many jokes were bandied about, but the mood of the narrative changed when Leonie recounted a sad event that happened in the village which affected everyone at the time.

It was in 1941, I was about 16 years old, Edna was about 21 years. Edna was not here at the time, I was staying with my aunt and uncle Mr & Mrs James (Edna's mother and father). My aunt and uncle were great friends with Mr and Mrs Lovell who ran the general stores at No.5 Little London. Mrs Lovell (Ethel) ran the shop while husband Bill carried on in the family timber haulage business.

Bill and Ethel Lovell had three sons, James who was the eldest followed by Sid and Tony. Jimmy would have been about 14 or 15 years old and helped his father with the haulage business. I will always remember Jimmy, he was very sweet on an evacuee girl from London whom he had been dating for about 12 months. She was the granddaughter of Mr Proston, who always used to smoke a clay pipe. This particular day I shall never forget, it was the first or second week in September 1941. Mr Lovell and Jimmy had been working up at Linnell's timber yard in the morning and came home for their dinner at about 1 o'clock, so it was about 2 o'clock when they got back to the timber yard. The Lovells had been out collecting up felled trees and had a wagonful to unload. The couplings to the cable wire and chains were all on one side

of the wagon and one of the timber hands had begun to undo the chains, but when he came to the wire cables one of the couplings loosened a bit too quickly and sprung over at a mighty speed. No one realised that Jimmy was standing at the other side of the wagon and he took the full force of the cable. It killed Jimmy instantly.

Someone was sent down to fetch Ethel who, on being told, went into shock and became hysterical. Edna's mother was called for as she was the only one at the time who could calm her down. Auntie never left her alone, she stayed at Ethel's side for 24 hours.

I remember the day of the funeral. Auntie used to grow her own roses, her front garden was a sea of roses and very proud of them she was too. On the day of the funeral I was sent up to the haberdashery shop in the big white house on Stocks Hill, to buy some long wide purple ribbon. When I came back Auntie had cut every one of those roses off to make into a wreath that would be tied with the ribbon.

There were forty or more wreaths and bunches of flowers (mostly all hand made as you could not buy them unless you went to Northampton) on and around the grave. The whole village had turned out for the funeral; they always did when a young life had been lost. The grave was so full that we could not get near enough to put our wreath on so we had to climb over the brook along Water Lane and into the field to the hedge just behind the grave. Once there we had to push the flowers through the hedge; while I was doing that, three or four other folk handed me their flowers to push through. That was the day the whole village went in mourning for Jimmy Lovell.

ELSIE CHAPMAN'S MEMORIES IN APRIL 1986

As I turned off the television and reached out to switch on the light, my thoughts drifted back to my childhood days in the early part of this century. They are often referred to as *"The Good Old Days"* and in many aspects they were, but there was also a lot of hard work and poverty. No labour saving devices, no flick of a switch for light, lamps had to be filled with paraffin, wicks trimmed and glass chimneys cleaned before we could lighten our darkness.

I was one of the lucky ones. My father was the village policeman, so we were assured that there was always a living wage coming in to the home. He was a very public-spirited man and was clerk to the parish council for a great many years, and people relied on him to help them in their difficulties, especially legal ones. My early days at school, which I very much enjoyed, were spent in the Church Rooms and later at the Brittain Memorial School (now the junior school), named after the Canon of Madras who lived in Whittlebury and was our local vicar. He was a great favourite with the children, especially as he used to give rides on his tricycle which was his means of transport.

We never had time to be bored in those days. In our leisure time we were encouraged to do something useful: sewing, knitting and pillow lace-making or reading to improve the mind. Of course we had our fun, playing hopscotch, skipping and jumping brooks, the latter often bringing chastisement if one should be unlucky enough to fall in. Then there was the school treat, a tea of bread and butter and cake, no luxuries such as jams or jellies. This was followed by sports, a scrabble for sweets and a currant bun to go home with. Another event that was much looked forward to was the Silson feast in October, a child's delight; wooden horses, swings, coconut shies and all the fun of the fair.

A mission visited the village periodically and set up a marquee in Englands Close, now Linnell's Timber Yard, and the highlight for us was the magic lantern show, depicting Bible stories. Most of our Sundays were spent at a place of worship, and at that time there was much ill feeling and bigotry between church and chapel. How glad I am that today the churches work together. On Good Friday we used to take our baskets up to the woods to gather moss and primroses to decorate the church window sills for Easter Sunday.

There was no health service in those days, and most people mostly cured their ailments themselves with home-made remedies, as they could not afford the doctor's fees. Broken limbs were a different matter. Dr Elphinstone came in his pony and trap, and with the aid of my father, the policeman, set the limb at the person's home, no hospitals and X-rays being available. This misfortune called for a long rest and, unless the patient had been prudent enough and paid into the Oddfellows Club, whereby they would get a small amount of sick pay every week, things were very hard indeed.

During the First World War, there was no rationing, but many things were in short supply, but the village people were better off than most, because they had large gardens and allotments and were able to grow their own vegetables, and often kept poultry and sometimes a pig for killing for household use. We had evening classes for cookery, showing how to make a good meal for very little, lentils and wholemeal flour, which was so brown it looked like pig food, being the main ingredients. There was also a class for those who wished to learn French, which was given by a Belgian refugee.

I could go on for hours, but space is limited. I would like to quote one of the many maxims which we had to write to fill in all the odd spaces in our exercise books at the school, and it is something that stuck with me throughout my life: *"Anything, anyhow, anytime, will not do. Only the best will satisfy."*

SYD HINTON

(A transcription of a talk given possibly to the Women's Institute, probably in the late 1970s, and recorded by Joy Townsend.)

I was talking about the village and its inhabitants - the kind of place we lived in, back in the last 50 years of the last century. And I said to you then, you ought to put out of your heads all ideas of motor cars or traffic or anything like that. We used to walk about at nights arm in arm across the road - I'm sure some of you have done it - arm in arm up and down the main road [Little London, the High Street and Brackley Road]

Well we started up at the mill [Windmill Farm] with Charley Lyon the miller and then you know we came down to the stone pits [the Clare House area] and there were the sand pits, there was the stone and there was the lime for the building in the village. Then down to Frog Hall and there we saw Tailor Coleman - you know his plate's up in the chapel. He's not Taylor Coleman, but William Coleman, but he was called Tailor Coleman because he was the village tailor; then across the road from him where the surgery is now was George, the coal merchant. And then if you went just up Little London, just across up road to get there, there was George Richardson and he was a carrier to Towcester and he also had a shop - you know where Sid Lovell used to live [No 5]- there was a shop there and he also had a wagonette which he used to hire out if someone wanted a day out and you

Stocks Hill in the 1930s.

and nobody interrupted us because there was no traffic about then so it was all very quiet.

had to hire a wagonette to go in. And then further up we saw William Scott, Baggy Scott's uncle, Mrs Edna Dodwell's brother and he was a shoe maker. He used to sit in the choir seats here. Then we came back down to Stocks Hill. There of course was saddler Clarke. Francis Clarke his name was. He was the father of Ashley Clarke, whom some of you will remember. And he not only was a saddler but he had a grocery and bakery business also on the corner [No 6/7], and then later on Ashley Clarke took over the grocery and the bakery, and Mr Ted West, when Saddler Clarke died, he took over the saddlery business [No 9]. Do you remember Ted West being killed that Sunday night coming home from preaching at Tiffield, coming out on the main road and getting knocked over by a motor car - killed instantly? I remember the Sunday night. Oh dear. What a to-do. We came out of the chapel. We got the news. Ted West has been killed. Well on the organ in the chapel, I don't know if you know this as it's faded now, but there's a frame there and that's in loving memory of Ted West.

Across the road was butcher Whitlock, [5 Stocks Hill] round where Mr Jefferies used to live. At one time butcher Whitlock used to play the organ, in the old days when they had an old organ. He was father to Mr Frederick, who used to live at the parsonage [4 Whittlebury Rd].

Well now, we've got to the big house [2 Stocks Hill] that faces down the hill, that was a draper's shop. Miss Ann Richardson - oh dear, I can just remember her - very prim and proper she was and I can just remember in the shop. It was quite a big shop and all bales of cloth all round and a counter full of rolls of ribbons and laces and buttons and so on. You see you could go to Miss Ann and buy your cloth and go to Tailor Coleman and have it made - very handy that was. And Miss Ann Richardson she's on those photographs in the vestry. The third in the second row down. She was, as I say, very prim and proper. There was a story that attached to her, I suppose. Her sister, this is only what I've been told, I don't know. Her sister had married Peach, who was a carrier

down West End, and his first wife was Ann Richardson's sister. Now there was some scandal connected with her death. Some way they blamed Peach for her death, and I remember them coming home from chapel one Sunday morning and saying that Miss Ann had set about Peach with her parasol and had sent him off down the road poking him on the back with her parasol, getting her own back on him.

And if we come on up the street, of course, we come to the Post Office which was in the house [where 4 High St. stands] opposite Mr Townsend's [No 5], not as you'll remember it, in the house [No 1] next to the White Horse, and of course that was Gilly Cartwright and Arthur Cartwright. Of course you don't really want a post office like in those days. Nothing was very private. If you had a telegram coming, you could

Hall End, now High Street, in 1949. The raised pavement, resulting from the lowering of the road surface to ease the passage of horse-drawn timber, can be seen. (RCHM BB88/1183)

hear the contents of the telegram before you got it sometimes, you know.

Then we come on to the old Rush. He was a carrier, used to go to Northampton Wednesdays and Saturdays and Towcester Tuesdays and Thursdays. Now none of you have had the pleasure of going to Northampton with the carrier's cart have you? I remember from our one. He used to come round at about half past eight for orders you know. Then if you wanted to go to town, you had to walk up to the top of Little London to get on his carrier's cart. You could ride to Northampton in about two hours and then you'd got to come out again at about half past four. If he was very well loaded and you came to a hill, you'd have to get off and walk. And the same at Blisworth Hill and the same at Whittlebury Hill, just that last bit to give the horse a bit of a break. Well Bill Rush was a Sunday School Superintendent as well, I'll always remember. He always used to wear a rose in his buttonhole.

And now we're up to the Meeting Hill, not the Chapel Hill. I know it's called Chapel Hill because the chapel's there, but in the old days it was the Meeting Hill for meetings of course, and just on the corner where Mr West's house is now was the Blacksmith's shop [19 High Street] and that used to be quite a pleasure you know, to see the sparks fly at night, when he was making his sparks fly. There used to be another blacksmith's shop down where Carroll has her garage [14 High Street]. That was a blacksmith's shop as well. The last one to be there was a Mr Becket. And then just behind the school [Green Lane] there was Markham's bake house - oh and you know, when we were in school in the morning, around ten o'clock, there used to be that lovely smell of new baked bread coming into the school - I can smell it now, you know when they were drying the loaves out. Well as we go up the village and in that house that's painted a horrible red now [33 High Street], next to the Timber Yard, Sam Edwards used to live. Sam Edwards was a shoemaker as well. He was also an exalter. What we called exalters in those days, you know - a local preacher. I should have mentioned while I was there, because I've mentioned all these people, George Payne - he was a Sunday School Superintendent as well. I can remember George, he was the last one I can remember to shout out Alleluia right there in the hall, when something struck him that the Parson was saying.

In the house where Wests live now [19 Brackley Road], there used to be a shop there. There used to be a window and a door at the end there. That used to be a shop. And old Esther West, as we used to call her, used to sell odd bits of grocery, like sweets and that.

So we've got to go down Cattle End, and where Mr Coleman [Colbourne] lives now [No 6], lived Billie Richardson and that was a shop - he used to sell various bits of grocery, sweets and so on. Course he was Alf Whitlock's wife's father. Well just down below where Mrs Peaks lives there lived Tom Waite's father and mother and they had a shop in the back kitchen there and they used to sell odd bits. And then you went next door and he had a shop, an outdoor beer house, and then next door to that, Linnells lived there, years and years ago and they had a shop [No 10]. So just down Cattle End you had four shops. I know they weren't what you'd call well stocked shops, but they stocked odds and ends, bits and pieces of groceries. I suppose it was very handy you see - because in those days people very often liked to have a bit of trust and what they used to call *set it up* you know, and you see you could go to the one shop and set it up, but you couldn't go the second time to set it up, you'd got to go to another shop. So you see when you could pay off what you'd set up in the different shops, you could go back again. You could work it - it was a very good idea really. I think that accounted for all the shops really. You must remember that Cattle End was well inhabited then. There were sixteen cottages there and they'd all got big families in, apart from all the other housing occupancy. That about brings me to the end of that part of the story. I know many years ago there used to be another blacksmith's shop at Forest House [33 Brackley Road], on the corner of Buckingham Road and Natty Coleman kept that - Harriet Coleman's father.

Now I'm going to tell you about the village life. In those days, Christmas used to come about the last fortnight in December - now of course it comes in the middle of July! We lads never thought about

Christmas till the last fortnight. And I'm certain that Christmas was enjoyed much more because it came at the end there. The women used to be busy in the home making the plum puddings and mince pies for the fortnight. Well of course Christmas was a good holiday, always spent at home. We always used to hang our stockings up - stockings not pillow cases or bags or things like that, and we always had an apple and an orange, a sugar pig, a sugar father Christmas and a few things like that and we really enjoyed those. In the morning that was the first thing in your stocking. Just marvellous weren't they? You didn t get a bicycle about 3 months before Christmas as your Christmas box. And I'm certain that it was much more enjoyable.

Then we went on to Easter. Of course Easter was always the Towcester Race Day, when we had traffic coming through and they used to go up to the Crown Lands and gather some bunches of primroses, and as the brakes came by, the wagonettes - and there used to be an old-fashioned coach come through from Brackley as well with the postillion on the back blowing his horn - they used to pick these bunches of primroses and throw them up into these coaches as they went by, hoping they'd get a penny thrown back for the bunch of primroses. Course they very often did.

You know Whitsuntide was really the big holiday - now they've cut it out altogether more or less. And it was always the Sunday School Anniversary. And for six weeks we'd all been learning new hymns. We always used to have a special set of hymns, ten hymns, we always used to learn them six weeks beforehand. And we all used to sit up in the gallery and they used to have a little harmonium in that little window which somebody could play. And of course the gallery used to be crowded. And the girls always had new frocks. It was the day when they came out in their new finery. There was one lady who had two children, two girls, a widow, and she was a

dressmaker - I think she made clothes anyway. She's made her two daughters a new dress for the Sunday School Anniversary and she was having Parish Money - I dare say she was having about a shilling [5p] a week. And one Parish Councillor thought, if she can afford to get her children new frocks just to go to an anniversary, she can do without the Parish Money. And they took it away from her. Well that was the Sunday School Anniversary.

Now it was also always the pubs holidays. Now each public house used to run a club. I don't know what sort of a club they were. But I remember that on Whit Monday, they always used to parade the village with a band. And they'd go to each pub and have a drink and then they'd go to each pub and have a dinner and spent the afternoon just lolling about or something like that. That was always on Whit Monday.

The great treat of the year for us was the Sunday School Treat. We always used to look forward to it. I should explain what this is - it's a log book of the old day school, John Denney's log book and it starts when he came to be headmaster here and it finishes when he retired. We get some glimpses of what it was like in reading these minutes. I just want to give you what it says here about the school treat: *Thursday afternoon and evening, there was no school on account of the children, about 270, having their tea in the three rooms.* This was in January this one, and they had a Christmas tree. 270 children. This was in August 1877: *There was no school on Tuesday, on account of the school treat, when about 300 children and teachers sat down to tea.* I hope I'm not boring you with this. It just gives a glimpse of what the past was like. Here's another one. This was the next year 78 . *The annual children's treat took place in Mr Whitlock's field. Near upon 300 children and teachers took tea and during the evening 500 children and friends passed a pleasant evening.* There were some other references as well. I think they had a band to play as well. The School Treat was a great day for us. You took your cup and saucer wrapped up in your handkerchief. Tea wasn't till about 4 o'clock. It was always up at the Elms. There was no cut bread in those days. The teachers had to cut enough for about 300 children. The children used to play games amongst themselves until teatime. For tea we had bread and butter and we had cake - that was all it consisted of. I don't know that we ever had anything else. Course there were no tomatoes in use in those days you know. They used to come round with the clothes baskets full as we sat round in a circle. After tea it was each teacher's job to run races for his class. They each had their own class and they organised races with a penny or tuppence [2d=1p] as a prize. And then we used to mix up all together, adults and children, and play games. You know the sort of games: twos and threes, a hunting we will go, all that sort of thing, kiss in the ring, and we played until the evening - until it got dusk and then we all used to gather - there was a boarded fence all round the garden and we all used to stand round there and they gave us a bun each to go home with. Then Old Rush used to strike up: *There is a land of pure delight where saints in* .... Do you know how it goes on? (all sing). It was a beautiful conclusion to a marvellous day.

And of course the other great holiday in the village was the village feast, when we used to expect roundabouts. They used to come in on the Friday and go round on the Saturday, never on the Sunday and then on the Monday and then the Feast. We used to save our pennies until the lights were on. It was so much more thrilling to go on the roundabouts when the lights were on. The field used to get very crowded. You had a job to get on the horses. You had to stand up sometimes but it was marvellous specially at night, and they used to stop for about two or three days and that was always in October. They were some of the things we used to enjoy.

I was only reminded the other day but there used to be a man come round from Brackley, walking, pushing a pram, just selling oranges. Brackley Jack we used to call him. Every Saturday he used to come - he'd walk all the way from Brackley and walk back again afterwards. And then of course we used to get the scissor grinder come round. Some other attractions were the street piano. There used to be a man come down from Northampton pretty regularly and he used to play us all the latest songs on the street piano with a monkey on top, and I remember once we had a man with a bear come round, quite a big bear it was, I can just remember him. He had a pole and he used to sing and the bear used to dance. The dancing bear.

Quoting from John Denney's Day Book, he says *"The school's very thin today, all the children have gone nutting"* , and that carried on for two or three days and that was quite a business. People used to go nutting, get them in sacks. Then they used to club together and they used to take them to Northampton Market and they used to sit on the market and sell them. A penny a pint or if they were slip nuts they were tuppence a pint. They used to do that every year.

And then again he used to say *"The school's very thin today because the children have gone gleaning."* Most people used to go gleaning you know in the fields in those days and then they used to take it up to the mill when they'd got any amount and have it ground into flour.

Course there are tragedies here as well, but I didn't want to end on a tragic note. But I'll tell you this, because it must have hit the village very much. It concerns the vicar, the rector of Whittlebury. His two sons were drowned in the Avon at Stratford on Avon. I could just imagine that they'd gone for a day's outing. If you wanted to go to Stratford on Avon, you went to Towcester Station. But six months later it records the death of their father. You could read quite a story there. I would imagine that these boys went there for a days outing, fell in the river and that affected their father. That must have affected the village for John Denney to record it. There are other things like that but I won't go into them.

Syd Hinton Awarded B.E.M.

It was with great delight that the first Silverstone Boys' Brigade Company heard the wonderful news on January 1st, that Syd Hinton had been awarded the British Empire Medal in the Queen's New Years Honours List for his service to the 1st Silverstone B.B. Company.

For those who may not know the facts, Syd, his cousin Walt and the minister of the time, the Rev. Rowton Lee, founded the 1st Silverstone Company in 1929. A few years later Syd became captain, a post he continued to hold until 1979 when he retired from the post in his 50th year with the company.

During those 50 years, Syd devoted a tremendous amount of time and effort to running the company and providing the lads of the village with something to do. The majority of the village lads joined the company and Syd organised football and other games for them as well as taking them on summer camps each year - without which many of them would never have gone on holiday.

In more recent years under Syd's leadership, one lad, John Harris, gained the highest award in the brigade, the Queen's Award, and no less than eleven lads have been to Buckingham Palace to receive Duke of Edinburgh Gold Awards. This again shows Syd's success at guiding the company and, although no longer captain, he continues to play a very active part as well as being President of the Boys' Brigade Old Boys' Association.

As well as the current company members, there will be many old boys who will remember Syd's influence on them during their time in the company and no doubt they, along with other villagers, will want to join us in offering Syd our warmest congratulations on his award. There surely cannot be a more deserving person.

When questioned about his award and the ceremony, *"I wish they'd have sent it in the post"* was the comment expressed by Mr Sydney Hinton B.E.M. when he heard that the Queen's representative was to present him with his medal personally.

Nevertheless, the Queen's representative in the person of the Lord Lieutenant of the County, Lt-Col John Chandos-Pole (medals, sword and all) arrived at the Chapel last Monday evening and Mr Hinton, much moved by all the fuss, was duly presented with his British Empire Medal for outstanding service to the community, the Boys' Brigade and the Methodist Church in particular. [See Plate 29]

The bright silver medal on a broad red ribbon was much admired, as also was the personal letter from Her Majesty thanking him for his service. There were many familiar faces, family and friends from the village who later congratulated him and sang *"For he's a jolly good fellow"*.
Congratulations Syd!

Silverstone News & Views, 1 February 1982

THE END OF AN ERA

Regulars at the Post Office may have noticed a change there since Christmas. For Mrs May Hinton, for so long the friendly supplier of pensions, postal orders and postage stamps has decided to retire.

She came to Silverstone in 1921 as the wife of Walt Hinton of Hinton Bros, Builders. The couple met in Newark, May's home town, at a Chapel social in 1916, when Walt was stationed in barracks there. When she first came to the village the couple lived in Little London and then later moved to Stocks Hill, to the house next to the shop (in those days Ashley Clarke's bakery).

Life was very different then, there was no piped water, every drop was drawn from a well in the garden or fetched from the pump. Not every house had electricity and much time was spent in getting in the firing, boiling washing in the copper, trimming and filling oil lamps and cooking hearty meals for the menfolk. The village was smaller then and the community very closeknit. A non-villager was considered a stranger, so it was not surprising that the young bride was addressed on Stocks Hill one day thus: *"You must be Walt Hinton's missus."* Pause ..... while she was looked over from top to toe. Then, scornfully: *"I heard he'd married a foreigner!"* End of conversation.

However Mrs Hinton soon became involved, through her husband, in life in the village. Walt was a local preacher and parish clerk, and co-founder with his cousin, Syd, of the Silverstone Boys' Brigade. Mrs Hinton was not only a member of the Ladies Guild, but President and Treasurer for many years. She remains a faithful attender of both the Guild and the Wesley Guild. Her talents as a dressmaker and seamstress raised much money for village and chapel funds.

In 1948, Mrs Hinton went to help Mrs Bound at the Post Office, mornings only. She stayed on to help Mrs Ledger after Mrs Bound's death. Then in 1950, Walt died. His premature death was a shock to all. Mrs Hinton left her house and moved to the High Street where she still lives [lived].

In 1966, the old Post Office was sold and Mrs Hinton did retire for a short time. But in early 1967, the Townsends, who had come to the village the previous year, asked her to help for a few months. That was 15 years ago! (at time of this article). She helped out to such good effect, that she has become almost a part of the family and things cannot be the same without her.

She will not, however, be idle. Work for the chapel, her home and garden, her many friends, her daughter, Sheila, her grandchildren and great grandchilden will all keep her exceedingly busy. All her many friends and relatives will want to wish her a long, happy, healthy and active retirement.

Joy Townsend, News & Views, 1 February 1982.

DAN HINTON

(Abridged from two interviews with Joy Townsend in 1976-7)

Dan Hinton was born on July 22nd 1896. He was related on his mother's side to Sir Hereward Wake and hence to Hereward the Wake.

He relates a typical day, fifty years ago, of two timber carters, who arrive at the stables at 5.00 a.m. to feed and water their five horses before going on a journey, 14 miles each way, to pick up oak trees which had been felled previously and were ready to be carted to the Silverstone sawmills. The care of the horses was religiously maintained by the carters. They used to talk to them and humour them like human beings.

So here is an imaginary conversation between the carters Bill and Jack:

Bill: I think I shall have Old Star Filler today and Old Captain Forest. I reckon she sits back in the bridging better than Old Captain. Which one will you have?

Jack: I shall stick to Old Flower. Old Jack hummocks about too much. We'll give them a brush down and a bucket of water. Boss will be down soon.

The boss arrives: *Good Morning. You've got to go up to Salcey Forest today. Three trees you've got to get on Bill and two on you Jack. All right? You know where the trees are.*

So off they go with their teams: Bill three and Jack two. In about three hours they arrive at Salcey and find the trees.

Bill: They lay a bit awkward Jack. Let's lay your'n up first. I'll get the chains on the first one and then hook on your

Forest. All right, now for the next one. Steady. Now for t'other. Chain 'em all on and all draw out. Yours now Jack.

The two load up and feed the horses.

Jack: Us'll put the nose bags on and have a bit of grub.

During the food break they talk about the gardens, how the tatters are turning out. Jack tells Bill how the boys (the young snots) whacked a stone through his window. If he'd a cot them, he'd a throttled em.

Bill: That'll be the same party because they hummocked all over my green stuff and tatters.

Ready then Jack? You'll take the nose bags off and I'll go first and get off back. We don't want to be late.

So off they came with their loads back to Silverstone, humouring and talking to the horses all the way. And then unloaded, groomed and fed and watered the horses before they even thought of going home and having a meal for themselves.

In a team of three horses the Forest was the first horse, the lead horse. The next one was the middle horse and the third was the filler. The filler was the one that steadied the load going down the hill like a brake with a wide leather strap, which was part of her harness hooked onto the shaft so that when the load went forward, she'd back into it to hold it back.

Dan explained the word hummock: There was a preacher, preaching in the Methodist Church here about how Pharaoh beat the Israelite slaves down, and he said: *You know my friends, it says in the Bible that the children of Israel were downtrodden. They were worse than that, they were hummocked down.*

When Dan was two years of age, he remembers how he and a brother nicked some pears off a tree that grew up to the gable window of the attic bedroom of the house where he lived. When he was coming down, Grandfather Hinton stood on the landing. He could see what they'd got in their hands and he caught Dan and flung him down the stairs. He cut his tongue - practically severed it. His mother nursed him for 12 hours, so his tongue knitted together. It didn t affected his speaking. She somehow contrived to hold his tongue in warm milk.

He also remembers the first day he went to school: *'My eldest sister she was a teacher at the school. The headmaster was a renowned gentleman name of John Denney, who incidentally was the first schoolmaster at the place which we have as a workshop now, next to Mr Townsend s the grocer and post office'* [bought by the Townsends in the late 1970s to be the main Post Office shop]. *'My eldest brother and my eldest sister they went to school in the workshop. The rest of us went up to the Methodist School, the new one by the chapel. It was built before 1900. So my sister took me to school on the first day, and John Denney stood in the doorway. He said "Hello, Miss Hinton, have you brought another one along?" She said "Yes sir!" He said "What's his name?" "Wilfrid." "Never in your life," he said. "It's Dan Hinton all over again. It's got to be Dan now." and that was how I came to be know as Dan Hinton.'* [Mr Denney had taught the older Dan Hinton, his uncle.]

'This John Denney the headmaster at the workshop school, besides scholars from Silverstone, he used to have some come from Abthorpe, Whittlebury, Syresham and he d got two that came from Paulerspury. He was very strict on time: nine o'clock school opened. Twelve o'clock close for lunch that was it. Start again at half past one, and half past one it had to be and four o'clock. Well the two lads who were coming from Pury, it had been a very deep snow overnight and they started off early, but they never arrived at school till ten

Schoolmaster John Denney, left, and his assistants flank their pupils.

minutes to ten. When they came in Denney asked them where they had been. They said they were sorry sir, but they'd been held up by the snow. So he flogged them for being late. But good heavens he did make you learn. You were too frightened to do anything but learn. He did a lot of flogging to me, but he never did enough. I should have been a better man if he'd flogged me more. One of the favourite ways of corporal punishment in my days was in the infants room. If you did not do as you were told, the teacher made you clench your fist and then she'd thrash your knuckles with the edge of a ruler - not the flat. That was a very common punishment.'

Originally all the buildings at the back of what is now the Post Office [5 high St.] were used as part of the school. The Hintons workshop was the old chapel school with a classroom in the gallery, two classes in the big room. The door opened into another room and farther on was a studio where Miss Burton taught the Infants. The garden was the school playground. There were 60-70 children.

The Church School was going on at the same time in the Church Rooms, but there was no playground there, so the children played in the road. When Dan's mother and dad first started school, they were in the workshop. They used to pay either a penny or tuppence a week. Some children could not pay one week, so they stayed away. When they had got the money they would go again. That was before 1870 when elementary education was made compulsory and free.

The Hintons as builders was originally started by Dan's grandfather Hinton who came as an apprentice stone layer from Steeple Claydon and worked with a man by the name of Braggins. He fell in love with Braggins' daughter. They were about the same age and the Braggins tried to stop it. So Dan's Grandfather made arrangements with his Grandmother to leave the bedroom window open. He put his ladder against the window and his Grandmother came down and they eloped. They were forgiven because they came back to Silverstone and he took over the business. They had four sons: Dan's father, Uncle Dan, who he was named after, Uncle William and Uncle George.

Dan started work at about 11 with his father after he left school, but then his father changed his mind. He thought that Dan was more knowledgeable than he had taken him to be and sent him back to school. After another 18 months at school he sat an exam. He got through that with flying colours, but failed the oral, because *'I never answered the questions properly. I remember one question distinctly. Name two islands in the Mediterranean. I gave 8 or 9 and that was all wrong. That went against me. I'd only got to answer 2. And another question they asked me. How many milestones did I pass going from Silverstone to Towcester, and you know I just couldn't remember. So I went to work on a farm - Webb's in Silverstone with old Jack. The farm in those days was about 150 to 200 acres. I was driving plough for them at 3 bob a week. That was 1910.'*

Dan then worked for John Ashley Clark, who had the grocer's on Stocks Hill. He paid Dan eight shillings [40p] every fortnight, but he never took any money from Clark. His mother had it all in groceries. He helped with everything, grocery, bakery, pigs, horses, the lot. Eventually Dan got the sack and went to Leamington to an uncle for whom he worked for about 3 months, before going into a job at a Kenilworth bakery. Then he got a baker's job at the Stony Stratford Co-operative Society. He was there until he joined the army in 1915. 131 from Silverstone from a population of about 900 joined up.

Dan relates his wartime experiences: *'They marched us off to Aldershot. It was the first time I had been to London and the first time I saw the sea, I couldn't see anything else but sea, cos we were in the middle of the Channel. When I got down to Southampton, I'd got tuppence [2d = 1p] in my pocket. I bought a penny postcard and a penny stamp and sent the postcard to my parents. When I came back after 3 years and nine months, when I got to Le Havre I'd got exactly tuppence in my pocket and I had two cups of cocoa with the two pennies at the canteen, so I went out of the country with nothing and I came back with nothing. I didn't have anything until we got to the demobilisation centre. We had to go to about 12 different departments. You handed your rifle in at one place, your haversack in at another place, your equipment at another place. The last but one, there were three parsons of 3 different denominations sat at the table to ask you what religion you were. But the best of all was the last. They gave you a voucher to get home with and two pounds - I'd never had so much in my life. Two pound notes - that was until I got my demobilisation money through. Course it would take me too long to tell you what happened in between time - about going through France and Italy overland, down to Milan, Pisa, Rome. I think I'm the only one in the near vicinity that's been blessed by the Pope - we had three days in Rome and they took us round the Vatican, the Sistine Chapel and then we came across from Naples to Brindisi, then from Brindisi across the Adriatic, which at that time was infested with mines, German and Austrian submarines. I was very lucky I was not sent to Flanders. As a matter of fact it used to be a joke in our mob. They'd say ten years after you get home when you've got married and got a family and one of the kids would say "What did you do in the Great War Daddy?" You'll be able to tell them: I was on one of those magnificent Cooks tours.'*

Dan goes on to describe old Silverstone: *'Stocks Hill gets its name because thats where the stocks used to be. Where the war* memorial is now, there used to be a pond, Frog Hall pond. The timber people used to take the horses there to wash the mud off their hooves. Of course, nearly at the bottom of Little London as the brook comes through Torrs [2A - 2D Whittlebury Road], under the road, through the gardens and under the road again - that's just below the Church Hall now, that used to be a ford back in the very early 1800's. Stocks Hill in those days was very steep. So they took the top of the hill off down by where Potters live now [1 High Street] and on the opposite side, you'll see there's a platform there. And the buildings which are on Stocks Hill, on the left hand side [2 Stocks Hill], you'll see where the foundations of the houses are all exposed. One of the village monuments was just at the bottom of the church steps. It used to be the village lamp there, an old fashioned lamp post with a lantern on the top. That was a big hefty thing, put there by Sir Robert Loder, when he rebuilt the church. And that's where the kids used to play. They used to climb up it. I remember the time it was taken down, but I don't know why. It was an oil lamp. Where the war memorial is, Sir Robert Loder wanted to put a fountain there and the village wouldn't have it. My father could remember the stocks and the ducking stool in Hall pond.'

Joy Townsend adds: 'I've heard that where those three houses [7 - 9 Stocks Hill] are next to the church, which was only a little chapel then, there was a big house, Silverstone Hall. The lower part of the High Street was called Hall End. When it was demolished, the stones from it were used to build those three houses and that's why they're not Silverstone stone like the rest, because the stones were brought from somewhere else to build this hall because it was special. It's a reddish stone - more like you see at Blakesley or Blisworth than you see round here.'

Dan continues: 'I can remember when there were 4 butchers shops: One where Mrs Potter lives [1 High Street], there was a hook and a big wooden wheel to pull the sides of beef up, there was one on Stocks Hill [No 5] run by Mr Jack Jeffrey and then De Groot, another one at Hughes shop

John Barrett's butchers shop in Brackley Road in the 1930s.

[Top Shop, 39 High St] - name of Heritage. and another one where Mr Blencowe is [11 Brackley Road]. And grocers shops I remember 7. One at the bottom of Little

The interior of Barrett's butchers shop.

London [No 5], one on Stocks Hill [No 7], at the post office now [5 High St.], the name was Brooks, one at Hughes, which was Heritage, two down Cattle End, one where Ken Linnell is [No 10], and one next door and one down West End [No 60, Pyghtle Cottage]. That was Tom Waite.

There was a saddlers shop on Stocks Hill [No 9]. Clark, then Ted West was the

The shop in West End, now Pyghtle Cottage.

the first motor vehicle came through the village. It belonged to a gentleman, name of Ashby from Towcester. I must tell you one incident regarding a motor, which is rather funny. My Grandfather, Tom Wake, used to be the local baker. There were 3 bakers in the village - Tom Wake, Markham and Clark. As we went to school, we used to help him up the street. He hadn't got a horse and cart, he'd got a hand truck.. He baked in Little London where Rodney Hinton lives [No 14]. And the oven was fired by wooden faggots, not by coal. And of course, on the Saturdays we used to have to go right round the village with him. There was a small grocer s shop on the Brackley Road [No. 17], and Grandfather used to leave as many as two or three dozen loaves

local saddler. They used to come from a radius of three to four miles and bring all the harnesses in. I've been in the shop when you couldn't get through to the back door because they'd got sets of harness,

In Cockshoot End (at what is now 42 High Street), from left to right, Nance Dunkley (Mrs Burnley), Violet Reeve and Rose Crowley.

piled on top of each other which they'd got to mend.

It wasn't till about 1908 or 1909, when

there for them to sell. And he'd gone into the shop, taken the bread there and had a glass of beer; I used to have a glass of *lemonade. We went to start off with the truck and this motor vehicle came down. And the motor only just touched him. He put the truck handles down and he said "My poor leg, my poor leg." Incidentally, he was as deaf as a stone. So the car pulled up and the chauffeur came across. And gramp said "Oh, my poor leg what shall I do?" So the chauffeur went across to the gentleman and said "I think it's hurt him, sir" So the gentleman went over to Gramp and asked him "Are you hurt very much?" and of course Gramp just kept on "My poor leg, my poor leg." So the gentleman put his hand in his pocket and pulled out a golden sovereign and gave it to Gramp He was still rubbing his leg when the car went off. As soon as he saw it had gone, he turned round to me and said "That's better."*

I can remember Brooks baking at the Post Office [5 High St.]. You know where the gallery is in the workshop well the ovens are under there - they are still there. The oven was too big for Brooks, so he got inside the oven and built a partition across it to make it smaller, because that too was wood-fired. and he used to bake bread twice a week and then he used to make a batch of buns and he had a son named Edie, and Edie used to have these two baskets of buns and walk round the village.

There was another shop on Stocks Hill [No 2], which was haberdashery, ribbons, laces, calico, drapery. I'm going back now to about 1908. It belonged to Miss Richardson. Of course you know, Silverstone is renowned for nicknames, Miss Richardson was called Nannybun.

Dan then lists some of the cottages that have been demolished: four in Tinkers Lane opposite No 26; four where No 6 High Street stands now; five on Chapel Hill (known then as Cockshoot End) where the bungalows Nos 11-17 are; on the corner where No 19 High St is there used to be a blacksmith s shop and house and three other dwellings.

The blacksmith Owen Coles owned two others at 8 and 14 High Street. When they were demolished the Forestry Commission had the stones to make roads with. Others were demolished in the area now occupied by 26 and 28 High St. Going farther up the High Street three cottages went just before Graham Hill [Nos 38 and 40] and a further four just after; opposite Winterhills Road the four terrace houses were demolished, as were the six one-up-one-down along Gravel Walk, where the bricked up doorways can still be seen in the wall.

Dan expresses his opinion of the wholesale demolition: *'It was bureaucracy gone mad. There were beautiful old houses in Silverstone which never should have been demolished. It was just before the last war. The local medical officer of health came round with certain members of the Towcester District Council and they never asked permission. The Council and the doctor, they'd stand outside a property and they'd say Is this worth saving or is it not? We'll go and have a look and they'd go and knock on the door and ask if they might come in and they'd come out and perhaps the doctor might say I don't think it's fit for human habitation and that was that. On the other hand, houses which they thought could be modernised, they made a note of that. The owners were notified by post that there would be a meeting in the Town Hall at Towcester and anyone that owned property, providing they hadn't been condemned previously by the medical officer of health, if they attended this meeting at Towcester Town Hall, each application would receive a hearing and they would put the proposals in front of the Council and the representative from the Ministry of Health in London would either give the OK in conjunction with the Council and the medical officer of health or he'd put an order on the property to demolish it. When the meeting eventually came to Towcester, no one turned up. The owners of the properties said "It's no use* taking notice of that. They can't do this - it's our property." But they found out they were wrong. The law had been changed. So when the ministry came down to Towcester to attend the meeting and found no applicants there they said "Right" and put the blue pencil through the lot and thats why we had so many condemned houses in the village. Then the Council notified the occupants what had happened. If one of the cottages became vacant, they were not under any circumstances to relet it. So when the war broke out there was anything from two to three dozen houses empty in the village and no one could do anything about it. They were condemned you see, but they hadn't served a demolition order on them, only on some of them. Once they served the demolition order on them then that was that. We owned the cottages which were pulled down opposite the Post Office [4 High St]. The council gave permission that anyone who felt so disposed could let the condemned property to the evacuees, coming from London. Which we did. Well then, after the war, the owners of the property they sold some of them, and done some of the work to them themselves and the Council was closing their eyes to it. And in the course of time the whole thing was washed out. You've got four down Church Street [Nos 1-5], which could be made into two very good houses. The Council wouldn't say anything if anyone submitted plans to bring those up to date - they'd welcome it.

In those days you know, there was no drainage to the village and - here's another story for you. There was a gentleman in the timber trade who used to ride his bicycle to Banbury Market. He used to go to the timber yard to see if everything was all right, then he'd go back home, wash and change and get on his bicycle and away to Banbury Market. As I said, there was no drainage then, and the great idea was to wash up on the table and then when you'd washed and dried you took your enamel bowl and threw the water out of the front door onto the road. And this good lady - her name was Betsy Bazeley, she did the washing up one morning and she happened to throw the washing up water out onto the road, just as our friend, all dressed up, was going to Banbury Market. She didn't look to see if anyone was coming, so he had to go back home and change.

We don't come to any more demolitions until we come to Olney. Next to Joan West [17 Brackley Rd] were six cottages, which I bought in 1952. Again we come to condemned property. I bought them at the auction for £100 and we were building the council bungalows on Chapel Hill. We had a deputation come round from the Council one day, because they'd been told that they were the best built bungalows that the Council had. Now the gentleman who was Chairman came to me and said "You've made a good job of that - there's quite a few sites that we could develop like this. We should like to develop them." So another councillor he had with him said "You've got a site, haven't you?" I said "yes." They said "Would you be willing to sell it?" I said "Yes, if the figure's all right." So we all went and viewed the Olney site. They were all of the same opinion that it would be an ideal spot for old people's bungalows. About a fortnight later someone came with paperwork for me to sign to say that I was willing to sell to the Council, but I still hadn't been told what they were prepared to pay. So next time I was in Towcester I called in to the office and said "I hope theres nothing going on behind my back - I can't get from anyone the price they are prepared to pay for the site." He said "You'll hear about that later on." I said "What will happen if I'm not prepared to accept the price?" He said "We'll have to put a Compulsory Purchase Order on it." "Thank you VERY MUCH!!" Anyhow after a lot of letter writing and me attending meetings at Towcester, I was to demolish

Looking north down West End. On the right is part of Mission Row.

A Photograph taken in 1999 looking down West End from approximately the same place. Mission Row has been replaced with 20th century housing, but other buildings survive.

the houses. I could have all the stone and debris, clear the site ready for building operations and after I'd done that they'd give me the sum of £25. I protested most violently about it and said under no circumstances would I accept it. They said it was based on the District Valuers Report. I went to see the local representative of the Council and I went to see two fictitious customers, getting them to ask me to build them each a fictitious house on the site. They were happy to do it. I got the plans drawn up in just over 24 hours. I gave it to the local representative and said, "You know the Council want to compulsory purchase and you know they've offered me £25, and I gave £100 before all this started." He promised to put the plans in front of the meeting. There were such heated arguments over it that they had to put it to the vote. They put it to the vote and it was even. I just got it through by the Chairman giving his casting vote.

There were a lot of demolitions too down Cattle End. It was a slum. The first was down by [No 17]. There was a single house there which was demolished before the war. It was never condemned - it just fell down. And then, down below where Ken Linnell lives [NO 10], there's a row of 6 brick-built cottages which were demolished. Opposite was another little single cottage and beyond the six cottages was a single stone built cottage, beyond that there was a row of four and then running L-shaped to it there was a row of six cottages called Barrack Row. Barrack Row was infamous. It's all barbed wired off now but the site's still there [in the field north of The Woodlands]. No one seems to know who that belongs to.

You see in those days people were very poor, even the owners of property. They hadn't the money to spend on the property to make them into good comfortable homes.

Carrying on with the demolitions, we come to West End. The first demolition where Kate Picket's is [Monkswood], that's

only just been done. There were some [at No 72]. There was a pair of stone-built cottages there, on the left hand side. On the right hand side going down, there were two and then there was what they called the Mission Row. The two cottages were parallel to the road and the Mission Row went off at right angles to it, [along the footpath beside No 51]. I've heard them preaching down at the Mission Row. They used one of the cottages. I've been to several Harvest Festivals down there with the Methodists. It was for West End people. It was such a long way to come to the Chapel.

At the bottom of West End when you get to the T road [next to the playing field], there were two cottages there. Then coming up towards Church Street the next demolition was opposite the Rookery. A couple of three-storey cottages [between the farm at No 11 and No 13] were condemned and demolished. The nine houses in Paradise were condemned, so they applied for them to be used for agricultural purposes. It was a sacrilege that we needed such a large council estate to house all the families. There's no doubt about it. Kingsley was a colossal mistake. The bypass [A43] had already been built and then they built on the other side of the bypass.'

BILLY & ADA BAUD

(A digest of a 1981 News & Views article and a 1982 interview by Joy Townsend)

Billy Baud was born in 1895, the second of eight children, in Bluebottle Row, Murswell Lane now to the east of the A43. His father worked in the timber, making gates and cattle cribs for John Webb, the father of Jack Webb. As the family grew, they moved to Terrace Hill at the top of the High Street on the right and then to a house opposite the Post Office Stores. All the houses have since disappeared.

Billy went to the Church School on

Stocks Hill, when Mr Ainsworth was the schoolmaster, leaving at the age of 13 to start work at the Elms (Silverstone House) as a driver. After that, at the age of 14 or 15,

Billy Baud with his horses in the field at the southern end of West End.

he recalls '*I went off to Liddingtons up at the mill, hauling with horses, fetching coke in wheelbarrows for the church and the big houses up there. I took loads of gravel up there, when they made that road up to Blackmires - loads and loads of gravel. I got about 3 shillings [15p] a week and had to give most of it to my mum. I used to have about thruppence to myself. I used to go to the shop and buy some sweets and things like that and I was finished then. Hadn't got no money.*

I went down to Lillingstone after I'd finished with Mr Liddington. Me and Harry Rush used to walk across those fields there and back six days a week. We used to get home on Saturday at 5 o clock at night and had to be there at 7 in the morning for 3/6 (17½p) a week. And then when I left there I went to Mr Charlie Linnell on the timber. And that's when I started timbering. And I went with 2 horses then and we used to drive 5 horses. 3 and 2. I had to drive these horses and another man was with me took the three. We went everywhere, wherever the timber was. Then I went to Wests - took home a bit more money. 21 shillings [£1.05] a week. Took 3 horses on there. We used to ride up to Salcey Forest and back, fetching timber.

We used to start at about 7 in the morning and you got home about 6 at night. Then you've got your horses to look after when you come home. I remember one Saturday I went to Salcey Forest. I got the horses laid out on Whittlebury Road, where those new houses are now round about 5 o'clock that morning. Set out for Salcey Forest round about 7 o'clock. It was a Saturday and I wanted to get back home quick. When I went through Shutlanger, it started raining and it poured with rain all day. I went down the woods and put the load of timber on and then I couldn't get out with that, so I had to throw some off and go back down this road and load them up again. When I got back into Hartwell, it was about 5 o'clock at night. Out of Ashton I couldn't get up the hill. An old chap there had just put his horses away, a coal merchant with two horses. He said "I'll fetch my horses in too and that'll get you there." So he took his horses out of the field, put them in front of mine. We got to the top of the hill and I was all right then. I could come home. I was wet through. By the time I got to Towcester it was dark. I borrowed two candle lamps off of a farmer. I got home round about 1 o'clock Sunday morning. That was the worst day I ever had in my life, timbering. I took the horses back into the field . I went up Tommy's for a pint of beer on the Sunday morning and he said "Where the hell did you get to last night?" I said, "You ought to have been there and seen." He said, "You ought to have been quicker than that. It's only a short way." I said "I've put the horses in that field and I'm not taking them out ever again. I'm finished." He came up to me afterwards and he said he'll give me a weeks notice. I said "You can do what you like."

On the Monday I went down to Towcester to join up. The office was down on the market square. It was run by Old West, Sergeant West. He said, "What regiment do you want to go in?" I said, "Northamptonshire Yeomanry." He said, "You can't get in that because it's full up. They don't want any more." So I said, "Well give me a ticket, I'll go to Northampton and I'll try to get on there." So I went up to Northampton and went to the Royal School, which was the headquarters of the Yeomanry and they asked if I was used to horses. And I said I'd been used to them all my life, so I got on there. I came back to Towcester with the Yeomanry and then we moved out of Towcester. We went to Luton, then to Bury St Edmunds, Knaresborough, Scarborough, Tedworth, Salisbury Plain and then Tedworth and that's where I went out to France, from there.

I can remember a lot of places we were: Calais, Dunkirk, Ypres, Armentieres. Whenever they were wanted, we had to go, in the middle of the night. Take all the horses into the valleys and the woods, out of sight. It was awful out there - I tell you. Never see a bed from one 12 month's end to another. Night time we had to dig - cover the horses up in these valleys. Peg the horses down to the ground, then you had to sleep back of your own horse. We used to dig us a little grave, lay in that all night, because of these spring bombs. They'd drop these bombs on us. They'd shoot out and do the horses an injury - the horses' legs and things like that. To save that we had to dig ourselves in at the back of our own horse at night. I was out there just over 3 years. I were glad to come home and glad that I didn't have to go back.

I went back into the timber. Me Dad worked for Burbidge you see felling the timber - that's when I started timbering. Had three men employed under him, including myself.

So I went and worked with Burbidge at Linford and that was when I took up with Ada. [Ada had gone into domestic service at the age of 13, doing such chores as scrubbing floors and black-leading old fire

grates. They married in 1921.]

That doesn't feel long ago. When Burbidge went bankrupt, we came back to Silverstone and lived at West End.

Billy Baud in uniform during the First World War.

I worked for Mr George Varney, down West End for a long while. I got knocked over once in Dadford, while I worked for Mr Varney. You know Dadford. There's a school on the right hand side and just past that there are two big banks. I'd got 4 horses going to fetch a big elm from Water Stratford. We'd got a new horse in. A lovely chestnut. When I got to the school they started singing. It upset this horse. They all went galloping away. Wouldn't stop for anybody. I couldn't get after them. I were done. You know Sid Hutchings. He used to do a bit of faggot hawking at that time of day. He was down by the cemetery. He could hear these horses come galloping along. He guessed whose horses they were and he took a load of faggots and drew a load across the road and that stopped them. There was another chap coming up. If he hadn't stopped them it would have smashed them up. I kept on with the horses but not long after that. That horse never did another day's work in its life. I took it down to the farm, they couldn't do anything with it. They had to shoot it. I was in hospital for some time. It's still crooked, but it never hurts me much now, just itches a bit in the night. It was then that I started gardening, first at the Chantry for 12 years and then at the Green Man for 25 years.'

When the Second World War started Land Army girls were billeted in the Baud household, and it says a lot for the home comforts, when one hears that these same girls still keep in touch with their erstwhile hosts.

Billy was proud to say that until he retired a few years ago, he was never out of work, and Ada loved to chat about the 15 years that she spent as a cook in the local school canteen.

When asked the ingredients for a happy marriage, they both agreed that it was good living and being content with one s lot. They had never had a serious quarrel, only little arguments with no bad feelings, Billy stating the old adage, "The woman always has the last word!" and Ada chipping in with a chuckle, "Not with Billy Baud around!"

The couple lived out their lives in their snug little cottage, Billy taking a great pride in his garden, tending his flowers with loving care, leaving Ada to entertain their many visitors and to enjoy her whist drives. They celebrated their Diamond Wedding in 1981. [See Plate 28]

MRS FLOSS WHITLOCK

(Excerpts from an interview with Joy Townsend in 1976)

Mrs Whitlock was born in 1901 in Banbury and came to Silverstone in 1918:

I wondered where I was coming to. I met my hubby up at the ammunition works at Banbury. He was discharged out of the army through wounds. He got a job as a policeman up at the works - that's where we met. So he was going to bring me home to see his mum. There were no buses - we'd either got to come by train to Wappenham and then walk here or we'd got to bike. So we came on bicycles. When we got to the top of the Old Riding, I wondered where he'd brought me to. It were not a proper road. It had two big gullies where the wheels of the timber carriages had gone. It were clear in the middle where the horses walked. We courted for some time and then - I was seventeen - we got married and came straight on here. We had to come to Wappenham station and walk from there to Silverstone. We stopped with his mother for ten days. We got a little house, but it wanted doing up very bad. And Mrs Twists helped me do it up beautiful. Then we moved into it. We had to fetch our furniture from Banbury on a timber cart with a flat top. My husband and his brother Bill had 6 horses.

Mrs Whitlock continues: *Nellie Day [No.72] had a new house built. They would have been 3 lovely houses for old folks - massive bedrooms. And we'd got a big pantry - big enough to salt a pig in. Lovely big garden. We fed our own pigs. They'd have been lovely for old folks now - there was only one bedroom.*

I used to bike it both ways myself to Banbury to do a bit of shopping and go and see Mum. And then when the boy got big enough - at just over 5, we bought him a new bicycle, learned him to ride it and we all three used to ride. Stop the weekend. I loved my bike.

The boy were took very ill once, when he was about 18 months old. Dr Cornwell, the old doctor, he were on holiday and he got a young doctor to carry on while he were away. He came to see the boy and I said "What do you think is the matter with him doctor, I'm getting terrified." "Well," he said, "I don't know what's the matter with him. Whether he's got a twisted gut or something. You've got to get him into hospital." So I come down and told my hubby's mother. I said I can t afford it We only had 30 shilling a week. To hire a car.

Somebody at Whittlebury used to hire out. He came and took us. Mother said, "I shall have to pay till Saturday then, if you haven't got it." I said, "I haven't." He charged a shilling each mile there and back. And we stopped till the doctor come in. He said, "Who sent this child into hospital?" So I said, "It wasn't Doctor Cornwell. He's on holiday. But it's the young one doing it while he's away." So he said, "What did he say was the matter with him?" I said, "He said something about a twisted gut." "Twisted gut, be damned" he said "This child shouldn't have been brought out. He's got double pneumonia. You've got to stop in Northampton to see how he goes on." Well we both wanted to stop, but they'd only allow one. I said to my hubby "I'm going to stop." He said he shouldn't let me. I were knocked up. Doctor come in. He said, "What's the matter?" My hubby said, "I want to stop. My wife's nearly knocked up. She can go down to Aunty's and have a rest." "Well" he said, "It's only natural that the mother should want to stop - I think you should let her. You go down to your Aunty's." I was in a room with someone who was getting up and walking about. Yelling. I never had no sleep. They wouldn't let you stop in the ward with the kiddies then. The nurse came in in the morning and I asked her "How is my little boy?" She said: "Don't tell the doctor I told you but I really think he's changed for the better. I've brought you a cup of tea, drink this and then you can go in and see him." And I went in. He put his arms up. "Mummy!" he said. The first he'd spoke. He stayed in about 3 weeks. Then when we did fetch him home, course there were no buses, no ambulances. So I said to my hubby I don't know how we're going to get him home. We can't afford that 24 shilling again. Your mum stopped that all out of your 30 shilling. I don't know what we lived on that week. And he said, "Well, Jack Jeffrey - he were the butcher - I'll go round and ask him if you can go to

Towcester in his trap." So he said "Yes you can go." I went and got up and it was everso high up. And when we got towards the Bull at Towcester, the public house, someone name of Roberson kept it. She were everso nice. And she looked and see us acoming and she knew the boy was in hospital and she pointed to Northampton. A drink lorry stood there. So when us got there, we stopped. She said they said they'll take you. I said, "Will you really?" They said, "Yes. Come on get in. We're going to Northampton and we shall be there about an hour." They'd come from Brackley. They run me right up to the hospital and they said, "How long do you think you'll be?" So I said "I don't know. The doctor will have to pass him out, I dare say." So he said "We'll come back in an hour - see if you can get out in that hour." I did. They brought me right home and came right round here and put me down at his Gran's. They wouldn't take a penny. So at night when we got home, I was getting him ready for bed. Oh what a pantomime. He wasn't going to go to bed. Not in this house, he said. "I want to go home." My hubby had to go and fetch his mother before we could persuade him to go to bed. I had to go with him. Otherwise he would have come back down.

Joe (Arthur) Webb and his horse Charlie outside the Post Office in the High Street.

A bomb dropped up Abthorpe Road, up agin the Hays. And a splinter of something flew and hit this man. He had his back to *it. He sat down in that little paddock hours and hours after he'd been hit, bathing it. He couldn't cure it. That was the only thing that we heard that happened. We heard it fell in the rickyard. So nobody didn't get hurt. It was a land mine. I won't forget the nights they were over Coventry. They came over here. We could see London when they were burning it. We stood outside. The bombers were coming over the top of us. During one raid I just couldn't go indoors. My hubby said If we don t go in and go to bed, I shan't go into work in the morning. So we went in and went to bed. He fell straight off to sleep. I stuck it till one o'clock, then I got up again. Made the fire up and put the kettle at the side and the guard in front. And I twisted the big chair round in front because it were cold and sat down in it and fell off to sleep. I were clappered when I woke up. I put a bit of coal on and the kettle at the side, pushed the chair back and went and got back into bed everso quiet. My hubby got up, thought he'd got to light the fire and boil the kettle. He hollered up the stairs: "You been up again?" I said, "No." He said, "You liar you. There's a lovely fire. The kettle's aboiling." One of his Aunty's sons was bombed out. They came back to Banbury.*

There were several evacuees here. Mission Row where we lived then, two others were set to evacuees. Tustian's old houses, opposite Day's. [72 West End] They're all pulled down now.

THE VILLAGE OF NICKNAMES

SILSON SPEAK

For the uninitiated, old Silson's language, sometimes even heard today, is spoken as it is written. Fust and Cussed meant First and Cursed. Pla'us and Pa'us was Place and Pace, Na'um and Ga'um, Name and Game.

'Um on its own meant Home.

"When us fust saw the 'Silverstun News 'n Vews', which were published on Aprul the fust,

Us spirits o' Silsoners long passed on - looked deyn from our 'eavun an cussed,

The darn fool folk who'd thought up that trash 'bout the Silson o'long days o' yore

E'en Pastor Linnell 'ud never 'eard the likes o' before, an' if he adn't no one else 'ad f' sure.

Now about this thing called an Abattoir, there ain't never bin such a pl'us,

Our ven'son an rabbits w' killed in the woods an smuggled 'um at a rattlin' good pa'us.

A stock market wus held in the front o' the White 'orse an' that's 'ow the hill got its na'um.

Nay, o'course stocks w'there, as us rightly knew.

Drovers did pass thru' wi' gret 'erds o' beasts, but that were mostly durin' the day

'cus all they blokes knew that in Silson at night some beasts might well go astray.

Our descendants all know that this tale were false, or t'wud a a'bin their own Old Oak book,

And are ponderin' why, after all these years Silson's 'istory should get a new look.

Now you lot deyn there, who wrote that silly tripe, must apologise t' the new Silson folk,

'cus us old'uns will haunt y ya 'till ya confess t'was your Aprul fool's joke.

THE WOODMEN OF OLD SILSON

My Granddad was called Bill Pepper, as most of Silson know,

A Varney lived up Little London who was known as Bow,

I had an Uncle Charlie, but they called him Waggy,

He also had a brother, but his nickname was Taggy,

My father was called Bumble, another Uncle Lucky,

Although the villagers always knew his mother as Poll Mucky.

There was a Forty Linnell, his brother known as Brummy,

No one thought in any way that these names were funny,

Cherry, Wab and Betty, Frizzle, Noah, Boggy,

Sankey, Scrumpy, Fidget, Nilf and Tidler, Snoddy,

Shady, Sharper, Struddy, Fumpty, Shoppy, Bogey,

Ickle, Pal and Debbie and old Owen Toby,

Hikey, Flash and Tucker, Sparks,Wacky and Paff,

Dinkey, Notes and Dokey, some might make you laugh,

Shaddocks, Smarry, Jolly, Stitcher, Henny, Wink,

To go back to all these names you really have to think,

Saddler, Lork and Monty, Guy and Shunt and Trimmer,

Some were jolly fat men, others tall and slimmer.

Flitty, Shirt and Mousey, Siggy, Killer, Natty,

Billyeye and Fawkey, Coddy, Flim and Catty,

Jimson, Bush and Crusty, Donny, Tiggy, Shet,

Names that most old Silson folk will never once forget,

Most of them are gone now, but no grave bears their name,

Yet those left in Silson, remember just the same..

So be it Linnell, Mayo, Whitlock, Hayle, Dunkley, Rush,

The nicknames are always sacred in that village just for us.

And so the church gave us the names, to see us through the Pearly Gates,

The ones we carry all our life, are the Nicknames from our mates,

And the Christian ones that came from books, they gave all at the start,

The names our childhood friends gave, were given from the heart.

P.S. Now I dedicate their names to them, every one was such a cracker,

For all my life I've been proud to be known to all as Backer,

I am sorry if I have left some out, I did not do it for a Japer,

But as you see when you read this, I have run out of paper...

NEWS AND VIEWS

The News & Views has been a source of village information chronicling news and events of our village community since 1979. News & Views was the brain child of J. Plummer, D. Harris, J. Firth, L. Gates, P. Baker, J. Turton, E. Craven, K. Kedros and P. Byng, who collaborated on the launch of the first issue. The realisation of how important this regular news letter is, became more apparent as our research for the latter part of this book progressed. Looking through the back issues of News &

Views revealed a fascinating array of interesting characters volunteering interviews, anecdotes and features. A wealth of information that has turned out to be precious in the recording of village history, it has immortalised the ways, lives, memories and dialect of a community that was strong in traditions and a way of life. In reproducing a selection from News & Views, we can stand back and let the people of Silson speak. Thank you News & Views and all the subsequent N & V teams of which Peter Byng is still a valued member.

TWENTY YEARS ON

The summer of 1966 in Silverstone. Villagers mourned the sudden passing of Miss Ledger at the Post Office, and there were some new people coming to the shop next door. Mr and Mrs Archer were at the Top Shop, Jack Whitehead ran the Bottom Shop, Mrs Hinton sold up the remaining goods at Miss Ledger's, Mrs Roberts kept the stores on Kingsley Road [see Plate 31], and Dodwells were the Newsagents in Little London [plate 18].

Mr Blencowe supplied meat and conversation from his shop on the main road and Don de Groot from his on Stocks Hill, until he sold it to John Newman to become the new Post Office. The Co-op butcher called and Ron Parker too, with fruit, flowers and veg. The fish man came, a travelling grocer and the chip van were all weekly visitors.

Markhams baked and delivered bread all round the village from their bakery in High Street and Tustians took their own milk round each day, including Sundays [Plate 30].

Jack and Gwen Adams were at the Royal Oak, Jack Lovell at the Compasses, Sid and Flora Webb at the White Horse [Plate 24]. It was only the previous year that Becky Smith had retired from the Chequers

in West End, and the premises were delicensed.

Son James ran the garage next to his home on Brackley Road and did some timber-hauling and taxi work in his spare time. There were plenty of timber yards, Linnells, Lovells, Hutchings, Dunkleys, Mayos, Varneys, Whitmores, Wests; some felling and sawing or making fencing, hurdles, and gates; supplying poles and beansticks, coffin boards and colliery posts. Dan Hinton's workshop was in the old Chapel School next to The Shop, and Jack Webb rode in his float, pulled by his old horse, also Jack, to tend his sheep *"up Wet Leys"*.

Hutchings's timberyard was opposite the Royal Oak in Brackley Road. From left to right, C. Dunkley, A. Hayle, G. Whitlock and S. Hutchings.

The Headmaster of the three class Junior School was Mr Roy Jones, who lived in Church Street. The Headmistress of the two-class Infant School was Mrs Whitehead, who lived at the top of the High Street. The other teachers were Mrs Davies and Mrs Linnell at the Juniors and Mrs Middleton at the Infants.

Mrs Lamb lived at Silverstone House, looked after by two ladies, who lived in the cottage next to Blencowes. As president of the W.I. she entertained all the members to a strawberry supper at the July meeting.

The population of the village was 1,080. Many were related to each other, if not by blood, then by marriage. There had been very little new housing, apart from council development, since the war, as the sewerage works were small and old. So Hillside Avenue, the Slade, Graham Hill, Stewart Drive, Brabham Close, The Willows, the Woodlands, Frog Hall and Walnut Close did not exist. New houses in Whittlebury Road, West End and Cattle End were yet to come. The British Legion Hut stood at the bottom of Little London next to the Churchyard. The Football Club played on Penn's field, as there was no village playing field or Pavilion.

There was no Silson Surgery, nor a Towcester Health Centre, but Dr Newton could be consulted twice a week in Alice Mayo's front room up the High Street, and Dr Lewis visited twice a week, holding his surgery in Torr's sitting room at the Old Parsonage. Once a month, the baby clinic was held at the Chapel Room, with a doctor and Nurse Mowbray or Nurse Liddington in attendance. Mrs Tustian and Mrs Prentice weighed the babies and distributed National Dried Milk. There would be tea and biscuits for the mums, welfare orange for the

An aerial photograph of Silverstone when The Limes was still standing; lower left. Stocks Hill is in the centre of the picture, and the small fish ponds, below the church, have not yet been built on.

There were eight buses a day to and from Towcester and Northampton, with George Lovell, District Councillor and Parish Council Chairman as one of the drivers, but there was no Play Group, Toddlers Group, Age Concern, Silverstone Housewives Register, Brownies or Guides, no Cricket Club, no Badminton, no Playscheme or School Associations.

toddlers and a busload came down each month from Whittlebury and Paulerspury to join in the fun.

There were very few strangers in Silverstone then, so the new folk at The Shop were a bit of a novelty for a day or two. Helpful customers soon told them where to find items among the varied stock held on their cramped premises and they soon adjusted to the pace of village life. Over the years there have been changes in their shop, their family and most of all in Silverstone itself. They mark twenty years of shopkeeping at the beginning of July 1986, now the longest established retail proprietors in the village, Tony and Joy Townsend.

News & Views 1986

THE LIMES

Silson bay-windows and rickety gate,
Walls of stone and roof of slate,
A smithy, an orchard, a stable for one,
A lean-to shed; now has all gone.

Dick Webb was once the master there,
Farmyard, garden, everywhere,
A family home that was built to last,
But sadly now a thing of the past.

It was sad to see the old house go,
But the planners said it must be so,
New blocks of flats will fill the space,
When they've razed this homely place.

The limes would not be felled, they said,
Needless to say, one day they were laid,
The apples and walnuts were cut down too,
Out with the old, prepare for the new.

From gravel, sand, bricks and mortar,
Mullock, mud, cement and water,
The walls shot up, the roofs went on,
Inside work was then begun.

Prospective tenants patiently waited,
There's a lot to be done, the builders stated,
Electrics, plumbing, paint and plaster,
It's a well known fact, we cannot work faster.

At last came the day when they gave the all clear,
Get ready to move, the keys are all here,
You can have this one, you can have that,

If you can't manage stairs, have a ground floor flat.

There are sixteen homes where once there was one,
The planning was good and the work well done,
So, don't look back on "The Limes" with sorrow,
Far better that people have homes for tomorrow.

G.J.Cox, 1981

STOWE LODGE HOUSES

Early in the 19th century, before 1814, the Marquis of Buckingham wanted to create an avenue from Stowe as far as Silverstone for the carriages arriving from the Northampton area, an imposing avenue similar to the one to Buckingham. A straight avenue would have placed the lodge houses at Winterhills, but he was unable to aquire the necessary land, so the avenue had to take a bend at Luffield Abbey which is now part of the race track.

The Marquis, buying and exchanging parcels of land from the commoners of Silverstone, and from Thomas Barford, farmer and landowner, was able to acquire a narrow strip of land all the way to Stowe wide enough for a carriageway bordered by trees. This avenue of trees survived until the aerodrome was built during the second world war.

The lodge houses were built in the same style as those on the outskirts of Buckingham, with flat roofs and balustrades. The high roofs and and attic rooms were added at the end of the 19th century, as we see them today. The foundations of the gate posts can still be seen between the lodges. They were sold to the Keniston family who farmed at Luffield. They are now owned by Mr Churchill and Mrs Lovell.

Plate 19: Aerial view of Silverstone from the north, October 1978. The Limes farm has been demolished and flats are in the process of construction on the site. The white house in the centre overlooks Stocks Hill and the Chapel backs onto the field upper left. (Gerald Lovell)

Plate 20: Aerial view from the south, looking up Green Lane and High Street to Stocks Hill and Little London. (Gerald Lovell, 1978)

Plate 21: Aerial view of Stocks Hill, the church and, left foreground, the mediaeval fishponds. (Gerald Lovell, 1978)

Plate 22: Aerial view of Linnell's woodyard with the Top Shop and the petrol pumps in the foreground and Murswell Lane beyond. (Courtesy Sara Hughes)

Plate 23: Facsimile of the first Grand Prix programme cover produced to celebrate the 50th anniversary.

Plate 24: Racing driver Graham Hill, centre, at the door of the White Horse with Edna Dodwell and the landlord Sid Webb. The three men to the right are visitors whose identities are not known.

Plate 25: Elizabeth II's Jubilee, 1977. A commemorative tree is planted at the playing fields. From left to right: Brian Linnell, Chairman of the Jubilee Committee; Geoff Lidgard, Chairman of the Silverstone Recreation Association; Syd Hinton, representing his sister who was the oldest person in the village but was too infirm to attend; Helen Odell carrying her son Jonathan, the youngest citizen. (Gerald Lovell)

Plate 26: The Kingsley Road street party, one of a number held to celebrate the marriage of Prince Charles and Lady Diana Spencer in 1981. (Gerald Lovell)

Plate 27: The celebration of the Golden Jubilee of the Silverstone Company, The Boys' Brigade in 1979. Arthur Payne leads the march down High Street. Home Farm in the background. (Gerald Lovell)

Plate 28: Billy and Ada Baud of Rose Cottage, High Street with the telegram received from Buckingham Palace to mark their Diamond Wedding, 1981. (Gerald Lovell)

Plate 29: Syd Hinton being presented with the British Empire Medal by the Lord Lieutenant of Northamptonshire, Lt-Col. John Chandos-Pole, in the chapel rooms in 1982. (Gerald Lovell)

Plate 30: Jess and Daphne Tustian delivering the milk in Kingsley Road, 1975. The shop is concealed by the cab of the vehicle. (Gerald Lovell)

Plate 31: Hilda Roberts, who kept the shop at 26 Kingsley Road, with her husband. (Gerald Lovell)

Plate 32: The new front of Matthew Croft's Stores on Stocks Hill made in 1996.

Plate 33: The former frontage before a vehicle damaged it. (Courtesy Matthew Croft)

Plate 34: The Post Office in the 1970s, before it moved into the old Reading Rooms next door, at this time Dan Hinton's workshop. (Courtesy Catherine Townsend)

Plate 35: A snapshot of Joy and Tony Townsend in the Post Office. (Courtesy Catherine Townsend)

Plate 36: Elizabeth Whitehead, cashier at Hughes Stores, serving the postlady, Dorothy Smith in 1977. (Gerald Lovell)

Plate 37: Hughes Stores - the Top Shop, High Street, with petrol pumps, in the days before safety regulations put small traders out of business. (Gerald Lovell)

Plate 38: Stocks Hill, January 1982. (Gerald Lovell)

Plate 39: The inn-sign of the Compasses taken down when the pub closed and became a private house. (Courtesy Geoff Blackwell)

*Plate 40: Les and Bill West at their woodyard on the
corner of High Street and Green Lane in 1976.
(Gerald Lovell)*

Plate 41: A lot of Linnells! From left to right: Roger (sitting), Barry, Vic, Don, Brian and Ken at their woodyard in 1977. (Gerald Lovell)

Plate 42: The Grafton hunt meeting at the Windmill in March 1978. From left to right: James Sanders (now of Richmond Court, Towcester); huntsman Tommy Normington; Bill (Cecil) Webb; Marion Webb; John Blackwell with Ralph Webb on his shoulders. The windmill was converted to a house in 1999 and Marion moved in. (Gerald Lovell)

Plates 43 and 44: Rookery Farm, presently owned by John & Sue Rudland, is one of the oldest houses in Silverstone, with a date mark of 1659. Only a little way up Church Street stands a house completed in October 2000 for Mr N. Hayes of Cosworth Engineering which uses a number of architectural features in common with Rookery Farm and with the farm illustrated on page 60. Photos by Joe da Casa

In times when many of the women of Silverstone made lace, they delivered it to the lodge house where Mrs Lovell now lives, and it was then dispatched to the markets.

Colin Hughes., News & Views, August 1982

RECOLLECTIONS OF MAY ADAMS

May Adams has been part of life in Silverstone for 78 years, joining in many village activities. She was a W.I. member for many years, and is now a stalwart of Age Concern, keeping them laughing with her great sense of humour. She has been a staunch Chapel member all her life, and she and husband Percy were married there nearly 59 years ago, having grown up as neighbours. May was born in a house in Gravel Walk, the lane between Stocks Hill and the Infants' School (all the cottages have been demolished, but the fronts can be distinguished in the line of the wall).

Her family (Varney) moved to West End when she was four years old. She lived there for over fifty years. When quite young, she took the tea to the harvest workers in the fields and later joined the potato pickers and did other agricultural jobs in the various seasons.

In her own home, all the cooking was done on an open fire, and the Sunday roast was taken along to the Bakehouse (Markhams in the High Street, next to No.34, now demolished) to be cooked.

Her brother, Shet, would collect the tin with the cooked joint and Yorkshire pudding, covered with a cloth, when he came out of Chapel, and run across Crarves footpath back to West End, where his family, and the vegetables, were waiting!

Eventually, electricity arrived (but not till after the Second World War) and the Electricity Company rented out stoves. She was in service with the Mayo family for Five years - she remembers lots of scrubbing and polishing, and after that time continued to do all sorts of jobs in other peoples homes. In the days of home confinements, she helped the mothers with new-born babies, and she and her mother were often called in to 'lay out' the dead when necessary. At that time West End was a self contained little community with quite a large population, and its own shop and pub. There was no National Health Service, of course, and Doctor's visits had to be paid for.

After the war, before the first Grand Prix, Jimmy Brown came to see her to ask if she could find some ladies to clean up the Nissen huts, officer's quarters and control tower for the airfield's new role. One Sunday Jimmy called to ask for litter pickers for the very next day. May found 22 ladies. The ladies formed a line across and swept the runways with brooms ready for the racing. May and Percy went up after club meetings throughout the season to clean up. When the first banks were built around the race track, the womenfolk laid the grass turf, a heavy job.

For sixteen years May worked at Plessey on the production line, at Woodburcote Road, Towcester. Mrs Edrich, the Personnel Manager, suggested to May that she should pay a full insurance stamp, but she said "No, I'm not going to work here until I'm 60!" - but in fact she did. The hours were originally 8am till 6pm, until eventually a union was formed and got the hours reduced.

Percy and May moved to Murswell Close and have lived there for 17 years. They have 2 daughters, 2 grandsons and 2 great granddaughters.

Colin Hughes, News & Views

IN MEMORIAM: DAN HINTON, LOU VARNEY AND HARRY RUSH

It is with regret that we mark the passing of three people who represented the best of

Silverstone.

Dan Hinton, craftsman builder, who literally kept our roofs over our heads, taught us much, and whose conversation and advice will long be treasured.

Lou Varney, noted as a hard worker, was generous with her appreciation of the efforts of others, a shining example of

The Varney's steam engine with Lou Varney in attendance. She often helped with jobs in the timber yard.

sturdy independence.

Harry Rush fought, and was wounded, in some of the earliest battles of the 1914 war, returning to a quiet Silverstone life, working in the timber trade, and enjoying the tranquil pleasures of family life and of dominoes at the White Horse. The Rev. Fred Smith, talking as a friend about friends, rather than giving formal sermons, made the service moments of real consolation for their relatives and friends. We are grateful to him, and thankful also to have met, and known three such as these.

News & Views, 1979

IN MEMORIAM: BILLY BAUD

With great sadness we record the passing of Billy Baud, who died in mid-November, two months after his 90th birthday. Billy was born and raised in Silverstone, and his talk of past times in the village, times of hardship often enough, was fascinating to hear. Mainly, he worked in the timber trade, driving the team of horses that fetched timber to Silverstone from miles around. When Billy served in the First World War, one of those who did return from Flanders Field, there too he worked with horses, looking after the cavalry animals.

Billy was a man who had a great fondness for all animal life, unless it was pests attacking his vegetable plot! He was noted for his green fingers and many years of triumph in growing champion plants. Since the death of his wife Ada three years ago nearly, the support and caring comfort of his family helped him reach an independent old age. His departure is a loss, not only to his family, but to his many friends, young and old, in this village which has changed so much during his ninety years here.

P. Baker, News & Views, 1985

GHOSTS

A Ghostly Tale from the Top Shop

The closure of "top shop" reminded one of the News and Views team of a story, told many years ago, by an elderly resident, now sadly no longer with us.

As a young man he worked as errand boy at the Silverstone Supply Stores. In those days, of course, they worked much longer hours than we do now and I think he slept at the shop sometimes. Certainly they were pretty busy and in the days before Christmas he became very tired. On Christmas Eve he would go to the midnight service at church and would then walk back to the shop for a well-earned night's sleep. One particular Christmas it was especially cold and frosty. *"The stars were out and sparkling"*, he said, *"It was bright enough to see your way back up the street without a light, there were no street lights then! I was just going across the yard when I heard a sound, like a footstep, then a thud. Of course, I turned around quickly but no-one was there. The noise had come from over by the well, so I went to have a look, but no-one was there. I knew what it was though and I got into the shop as quickly as I could! It was that poor chap that drowned himself in the well. The thump was when he lifted up the well cover before he jumped down. Folks had said he came back each year, and I'd never believed it, but I did after that!"*

There is no well visible now in the shop yard, but who knows? On a Christmas morning very early, you might just hear the footstep and the thud as the unhappy spirit comes back yet again.

The Top Shop with, left to right, Les Potter, John Potter, Alice Potter and George Mayo [?].

Village tradition has it that one Christmas Eve in the late nineteenth century, the storekeeper Mr Burbidge and a friend were drinking together to celebrate the festive season. It was approaching midnight when Mr Burbidge went out to the privy down the garden, and did not return. His friend eventually went in search, and he was finally found drowned in the well. His ghost is said to have been seen at midnight on many Christmas Eves.

A Ghostly Tale

Have you heard galloping hooves in the middle of the night? There is an old story that the ghost of Old Barford can be heard in the fields around Green Lane, the Pyghtle and around Cattle End. Mr Barford lived at the farmhouse at the bottom of Green Lane and farmed the land thereabouts, and was known always to ride a white horse around his farm. After he died, many folk said he used to come back at nights and gallop all over his meadows. Many old Silverstone people said they had seen him, some only heard the hooves. When children were going out in the evening they were always reminded *"mind old Barford don't come tonight"* by their parents. He doesn't seem to have been heard for a long time, so perhaps he has been laid to rest - or is traffic noise and the new street lighting putting him off his nocturnal wanderings?

News and Views

The Winter Hills Ghost

The Winter Hills ghost was a lady in grey,
She haunted the house, or so people say,
She peeped through the windows and rattled the doors,
Moaned through the keyholes and tapped on the floors.
She became such a tiresome spiritual force,
That the house was left empty as a matter of course.

The owner was worried and sent for the Cleric,
Who will please exorcise this spectral relic;
With lighted rush candle, Good Book and Bell,

The villagers followed him all round the well,
He seized the ghost, threw her into the water,
"In peace rest you now, for ever after".

On Winter nights when the wind is high,
Strange sounds are heard, the ghost of a sigh!
Now is she at rest?
Or again does she walk?
It's hard to be sure, but the old folks still talk.

The Compasses' Ghost

In the house where I live there is supposed to be a ghost, though none of the family have experienced any manifestations. One of the bedrooms is known as *"King John's Room"*. On some nights of the year it is claimed that the door inexplicably springs open and a sudden chill is felt. That colourful village personage, the late Mr Dodwell, recounted to me that he had seen those particular happenings. And, moreover, whenever the open door and chill occurred, a fellow-lodger found his bed covers snatched off. Apparently, it was in that room that a mistress of King John was murdered, by Royal appointment. Well, it's a good story. But when our doors spring open, it's because the cat is trying to batter his way in. The house, as it stands, did not exist in King John's time, so any legend must refer to an earlier building.

P. Baker, News & Views, 1992

Old Ridings Cottage

It is thought that in the sixteenth century Old Ridings Cottage was a stone, two-up, two-down gamekeeper's cottage. In the eighteenth century it was extended in local red brick to accommodate a dairy with a chicken loft above. By the early twentieth century it belonged to the Varneys, who operated the timber yard on which Hazelwood is now built. Indeed Mary Varney was born in this cottage in 1902, moving later to 73 West End. In those days the cottage was served by a 20 foot deep, brick-lined well. Between the wars Aunty Clara and Aunty Tilly (Matilda) Varney lived here, running a small market garden and selling flowers. Access to the cottage was originally through the garden of number 73, but the development of Hazelwood allowed a drive to be put through from there.

Between Old Riding Cottage and the West End road stands 71 West End, a red brick house, a former public house, which is semi-detached to number 73. In early 1999 it was in a parlous, dilapidated state, but a year later it had been restored and rebuilt. It was formerly the property of the Mayo family, whose woodyard was situated across West End in what is now Monkswood. It also had its well in the garden. Until 1998 Doll Picketts lived there.

Bernard and Pam Smith, the present owners of Old Ridings Cottage, tell how a visitor, one Pauline, a stranger to Silverstone, felt a presence in the house and described a lady of dark complexion with her hair in a bun, who was wearing a brown dress and carrying a bunch of daffodils in her arms. Pauline said this lady gave flowers to people she liked and was welcoming the Smiths, who had not long moved into the house. Pauline added that her name began with "M", but that she was not called by her proper name, but by a name beginning with "T".

This meant nothing to the Smiths, who passed on the details to Doll Picketts, who recognised at once a description of Tilly Varney, who used to sell daffodils at 6d a bunch, but gave them away to people she liked and was always worried that her sister Clara should find out.

Other odd things have happened: Bernard Smith was certain he had put a ring that had belonged to his father on a shelf behind his bed. Next morning the ring had disappeared. Pam and Bernard searched

everywhere, even taking the bed apart, but could not find the ring. Some days later, however, there lay the ring exactly where Bernard thought he had left it. The cleaning lady also tells how she once left dusters and cleaning stuff on a downstairs table, while she went upstairs. When she came down everything had disappeared, only to reappear again after she had searched the house. Doors open for no apparent reason, things disappear, but Tilly's ghost is in no way a threatening or unpleasant presence; rather she is friendly, as she was in real life.

Welcome to The Wilderness

When we moved into The Wilderness, 3 Murswell Lane, in the early 1990s, it was high summer, clear and sunny, warm and welcoming. I work from home and a room was chosen to be the workplace. It used to be, I guess, the scullery, built on to the back,

the Northern side, of the old stone house in solid Victorian brick, with a door knocked through the thick stone wall to connect it to what was once the kitchen but is now the dining room.

Shortly after we arrived I was sitting at my work-table when I became aware of something coming between me and the sunlight flooding into the dining room. I looked up and there, through the door, her head turned to look over her right shoulder, was a lady. She was dressed in a full-skirted, floor-length grey dress with some sort of shawl or kerchief about the shoulders. Her hair was worn up, neat and close to the head. I could not make out her face against the brightness behind her.

I felt no threat, but obviously this was no ordinary visitor. There seemed to be an atmosphere of mutual mild surprise, each to find the other person there. I felt obliged to explain myself. "My name is Martin Marix

Evans," I told her. She moved away to the right and I have not seen her since.

VERSE AND WORSE

THE OLD WOODMEN

They rose from beds before the dawn,
From fields fetched horses, gave them corn.
Had a quick breakfast, to get early start,
Then hitched horses up to timber cart.

As first light appeared, it was join the road,
To bring in the trees, load after load,
On old bicycles fellers travelled afar,
Axes and crosscuts tied to crossbar,

From daylight till dusk, in the yards whirred the saws,
No set hours, no union laws,
No paid holidays, no pension, how good,
The only perk, a sack of firewood,

No money if ill, they had to keep fit,
Wrinkled chapped hands, softened by their own spit,
Gateposts and planks, were put in large stacks,
A continuos stream, came off the racks,

Sheep hurdles, field gates were also made,
This was their lifem this was the trade.
Six days a week, no time to flag,
With a drop of cold tea, a pipeful of shag.

With aching backs, and sweating brow,
How many young men would want this job now,
But now goods are made with plastic not wood,
New houses are there, where the yards stood.

These men are at rest now, beneath yew trees now lay,
Yet still in our memory day after day,

Stroll through the churchyard, look on stones at a name,
'ard udd was their living, 'ard udd was their game.

Note:" 'ard udd" is "hard wood"

WIVES OF THE WOODMEN

They could not leave the village to earn an extra dime,
For what they did inside the home took up all their time,
Most had many children, life was one long toil,
No running hot water then, a pot they had to boil,
At day break on Monday mornings, as their husbands left to do their bit,
Those women were in the wash-house, the old copper to be lit,
With reddened hands they scrubbed the clothes, 'til they were gleaming white,
Then up the garden on the lines, they dried in the sunlight,
Then get the children's breakfast, see them to school slowly wend,
A quick trip to the local shop, a few shillings just to spend,
Back home again to stoke the fire, scrub floors on bended knees,
And like their men these women, had no time for ease,
Then they would prepare the dinners, which were never late,
Though cooked upon an open fire, inside a black leaded grate,
Pots of good old rabbit stew, dumplings and bacon clangers,
Or a plate of peas and mash, to go with the bangers,
Fetch the children back from school, give them all their tea,
Dish up husbands dinner, feed baby on her knee,
Wash up all the crockery, and neatly stack in place,
Put the children in their beds, with a well

scrubbed face,
Bring in the clean washing, take a flat iron from the hob,
No electric ones in those days, it was a tiresome job,
Place in the airing cupboard, all folded flat and creased so neat,
Around sixteen hours had passed by now, that she'd been on her feet,
She would drag her body up the stairs, sometimes racked with pain,
But never once did you ever, hear these women then complain,
No holidays for them in Spain, or on the Isle of Sark,
Perhaps a day out once a year, to nearby Wicksteed Park,
Baby sitters were not heard of, in those years gone by,
Wherever poor old mum went then, their children went also,
This was their whole life time, like a plotted course,
And however hard that lifetime, seldom was a divorce.
Now younger ones around today, seem a sorrier lot,
They are in an Eldorado, with the help that they have got,
Machines they have for everything, every little chore,
Could it be so much spare time, will make life such a bore,
And at todays weddings, as they make vows from their heart,
Why do these newly married, so quickly drift apart?

A TRUE SILSON NURSERY RHYME

Two little blackbirds, without a feather to their name,
Crept into a fruit cage, scrumping raspberries was their aim.
Along came a lady, before they'd had many pecks,
And grabbed the two young rascals, by the scruff of their little necks.

She marched them to her homestead, put them under lock and key.
Then sent for their parents to dole out the penalty.
What happened to those blackbirds, is a fate that's still not known,
So be warned, if you like raspberries, make sure you grow your own!

WHERE HAVE ALL THE SPOTTED DICKS GONE?

(A letter to News and Views, December 1985)
Dear Madam Editor (no slight intended),
I would like to use your worthy newsletter to search out one of the rare breed, namely the Spotted Dick. (Capitals to be used at all times for the noble Spotted Dick).

I am of sound mind and of Silverstone blood (not a contradiction). I would like to ask the question: "Where have all the suet puddings gone? I, like my contemporaries, was brought up on a galaxy of treats like beef pudding, bacon and onion roll (made in a cloth), jam roly-poly, plum duff, treacle pudding and last, but by no means least, the immortal Spotted Dick.

Is it coincidental that the decline in the Spotted Dick and the emergence of the "newfangled woman" (no capitals) one sees walking the streets of Silverstone have occurred simultaneously? There are no longer cooks regrettably, merely good warmer-uppers of Birds Eye This and Mr Kipling That. They probably use microwaves.

Suet puddings have, over the centuries, made Silverstone Man the pride of his country. Alas, with the decline in living standards everywhere, it has hit us right where it really hurts; in our stomachs.

The change in diet of Silverstone Man is completely against his will. And as for those "wholesome light sweets" they wouldn't fill the stomach of a two-year-old, let alone a man who's done a hard day's graft.

The Spotted Dick, covered in oodles of

steaming custard makes a meal fit for a king. (Spotted Dick was named after King Richard the Lionheart). And as for these stupid people who say that suet is bad for you - all I can say is "Poppycock and Balderdash".

To put Britain back on its feet calls for the re-establishment of the great Silverstone Spotted Dick. Don't allow it to die like the poor Crowfield Clanger. If my letters are answered, Father Christmas will bring me a gift-wrapped, cloth-bound, steaming four pounder of Spotted Dick and he can then have my turkey and cranberry mullock.

Comments from the Silverstone "newfangled women" in your next edition would be welcomed, especially those newcomers who think they know better.
Yours,
Iam A. Glutton.
P.S. Silverstone men have Yorkshire pudding with every Sunday lunch, and not just with roast beef.

February 1986
The letter in the last issue of News and Views (December 1985) caused quite a stir. Mr Iam. A. Glutton bemoaned the lack of decent puddings nowadays, and asked for support in his campaign to bring back boiled suet into the local diet;
Now read on...........
To Mr Iam A. Glutton:
I hope you have rediscovered the taste of Spotted Dick during the Christmas period. I am sorry it was left on the doorstep, but I was very busy on Christmas Eve.

I agree with your theory that Silson seems to be filling up with new-fangled woman "warmer-uppers". It may be a good idea to have a Spotted Dick competition at the Village Show.

I must take umbrage at your claim to be Silson born and bred, as I have it on good authority that your birth was in an ambulance on Towcester humpback bridge.

I hope you don't have to write for a Spotted Dick next Christmas, as your new wife will no longer be a "warmer- upper".
Yours faithfully,
S. Claus

Dear Editor,
I cannot understand why there is so much fuss about the disappearance of Spotted Dick.

Every proper Silson person knows that the staple food of this area is CLANGER and that it has now become almost extinct. In years gone by, a tasty bacon and onion clanger, boiled well in a pillow case, has kept many a working man going in field and forest. The best ones had bacon in one end and jam in the other, so you had dinner and afters in one handful, as you might say.

But nowadays wives can only pack up crackers and cheese, or cold meatpaste sandwiches, there's no body in that, or encouragement for man to keep working on a cold Winter's day.

So never mind Spotted Dick, bring back clangers, I say.
Yours faithfully,
I. B. Thynne

April 1986
Mr Glutton seems to have had some support in his plea for the revival of Spotted Dick.

This warming addition to local menus has been a great comfort during freezing February. We forecast an increase in the numbers of joggers and keep-fit ladies now that Spring is here, all trying to shift the extra weight that has accumulated.

Dear Editor,
The Spotted Dick has been sighted.

Have a guess what I had for Christmas, a lovely Spotted Dick.

The gem of culinary delight was found cloth-bound on my doorstep at midnight on Christmas Eve. Having read the interesting article by Iam A. Glutton in your last edition, it would appear that Father Christmas had delivered the beautiful Spotted Dick to the wrong house.

Not wishing to waste good food, I asked Carolyn, my wife of 9 weeks and 4 days, to cook this cloth-bound gem as instructed on the accompanying card. This she dutifully did, much to the delight of all assembled.

Three hours produced a corker. It was tremendous and satisfied the hungry onlookers. Carolyn's father, David, had not eaten one in 40 years.

Since then both treacle pudding and another Spotted Dick have been beautifully cooked, which indicates a thriving suet industry.

Iam's article has done the trick in several Silverstone homes. Not having seen him since we were together in Mrs Middleton's class (a lovely teacher), it would give me great delight to bump into him once more and thank the lad personally for his help in saving the Silverstone Spotted Dick.
Yours,
Gerald Lovell.

Dear Editor,
The Local History Society thought your readers would be interested in the origins of that local delicacy, the Spotted Dick.

In the early nineteenth century, outbreaks of tribal warfare between Silverstone and other villages were frequent in the Summer, and were called "Cricket Matches". Those of you who have read "Old Oak" will know that I do not exaggerate when I describe this sport as an excuse for violent encounters. Feuding with Syresham was particularly bitter; the more so since the Silverstone team were better fighters, but the men of Syresham were usually victorious with the cricket.

In the mid 1860s Syresham hosted a match against Silverstone. We know from the account books and extant committee minutes that on this occasion, they decided to provide a lunch that would sedate, if not actually paralyse, the Silverstone team.

At this point the Spotted Dick was concocted, the most lethal gastronomic weapon ever devised.

Alas, the plan failed! The Silverstone men ate heartily, even calling for seconds, complimented the cook, strode onto the pitch and beat Syresham at cricket for the first time that century.

They then indulged in the usual fisticuffs. Clearly the Spotted Dick was ineffective against such forceful players!
Yours etc.,
A. J. Yoke

PART 5 ✈ The Twentieth Century

PUBS

The Royal Oak: John James's Memories 1940s/50s

I moved into the Royal Oak in 1947. I was ten years old, with my mother, father and sister Carol, who was seven. It was one of the village's four pubs and some way from the centre on the Brackley Road, so the catchment was somewhat limited by its position. However, it had its regulars, supplemented by one or two old faithfuls from Dadford which had no hostelry.

Little were we to know that within a year the whole complexion of the village was to change with the British Grand Prix starting in 1948. This very much put the Oak on the map and the Brackley Road became the main artery to hundreds of thousands of enthusiasts from all over the country and the world. Thus this sleepy little English pub became transformed.

Another minor but equally important event for the Oak was the establishment of Cody Circus's winter quarters in Winter Hills. This brought another type of clientele such as Darty and Pluto who were not to be outdone by the elephant that occasionally came down for a pint.

I was 10 years old and new to the pub business, but my Mum soon established her credit control system, the slate. Depending on your ability to pay, and your status, you were allowed a maximum of two pints (2s 4d - two shillings & four pence) or one pint (1s 2d) on tick at any one time. My Dad, who ran the garage attached to the pub, occasionally overrode my Mum without her knowing and made his own much more lenient rules.

The village was the centre of the timber industry and the people working out in the woods, felling etc. were very dependent on the weather. If it rained they didn't work, but came to the pub for the day and even all night sessions. Many was the time I would get off the school bus at Archer's shop some 100 yards from the pub at 4 p.m. to hear the singing from the bar. On arriving home I would admonish Mum, telling her that the policeman (then on a bike) would close us down if she was caught selling after hours. Her comment as usual was *"How will they know boy? I've drawn the curtains"*. I couldn't convince her that you could nearly hear the singing on Stocks Hill. It was then my duty at night to help get the clientele home, falling in the hedge with them and occasionally getting to their front door with the irate wife waiting with all her little ones. This was not something to be relished.

My enterprising Auntie Edna and Uncle Den decided to go into the fish and chip business and bought the necessary wagon which was sometimes placed in the Oak car park or my Dad's garage yard for the after hours drinkers. Things went well until one day my sister Carol had to call the fire brigade to put out the burnt-out chip van, so another business ended.

The bar room was typical of a village pub with open fire, chairs, benches and tables, the latter being used mainly for domino playing and occasionally crib. The games room consisted of a few more tables and chairs, plus darts, table skittles and the piano, which was used on Friday and Saturday nights, if you could persuade anyone to play. Skittles was probably the favourite Oak game, and I arranged a championship every year, culminating in the final being played at Christmas time for a first prize of a bottle of whisky. We had some great players, but probably the best was Bert "Shirt" Dunkley. Bert could make the cheeses talk and floorers (all nine pins down with one cheese) was the order of the day.

On getting off the school bus at Archers stop one day, I walked down the Brackley Road to home along the short stretch by Dillows. Every 15 yards I found a dead mackerel. One of our regulars, who shall remain nameless, had come from Towcester, where he'd bought the mackerel in a brown carrier bag and proceeded under the influence to the Oak. The blood from the mackerel had dampened and finally split the bag and the mackerel dropped out at regular intervals. I carried them home and Mum did no more than wash them and return them to the original owner.

left to right: Son James, Mr James and Edna (Dodwell).

The Compasses Inn

Hard though it is to imagine, until the 1930s the village High Street was the main road to Oxford. Thirsty travellers stopped at The Compasses, which ceased to be a pub in 1970, and was sold as a private house in 1971. [See Plate 39]

According to legend, King John stayed at The Compasses on his hunting visits, and one bedroom is said to be haunted by the ghost of his murdered mistress. As a result the door inexplicably springs open and a sudden chill is felt. Yes, the old country door-latch tends to spring open unless fastened carefully, but no sign of haunting has occurred in the decades we have lived here. Mr Dodwell, lodging here many years ago, told me he had seen those particular happenings and a fellow-lodger found his bed covers snatched off. The worst we have ever seen is teenager messiness. If King John ever stayed, it could only have been in an earlier building.

When the High Street was dug up a few years ago to lay gas pipes, signs of earlier construction were visible about three feet below the current road surface. Large blocks of dressed Northampton stone, forming some sort of a wall, lie buried beneath the road. Some earlier, substantial building or its boundary wall, once stood on the High Street, stretching towards Stocks Hill. Similar blocks of dressed stone lie beneath the path that runs alongside The Compasses towards the Infants' School.

As well as being an inn, The Compasses has also been a farm, but we have no maps old enough to show the extent. The pig sties were large enough for at least four pigs, and the old winnowing barn, converted in 1986, was large enough for a good sized farm. In some parts of the garden foundations of outbuildings have rotted, leaving rubble deep below our onion patch. We often dig up cobble stones in some parts.

In the nineteenth century, there were no dustbin collections, and household rubbish was usually buried on boundaries. We spent one busy Easter excavating such a rubbish dump, finding countless earthenware jars, mustard pots, cider jars and pop bottles, some still intact with their marble closures in place.

The Old Oak book relates how The Compasses and its paddock was a centre for social gatherings such as the Sunday School picnic. Here the cricket team assembled before matches, here "The Blues" waved their flags, gave ale to their supporters and started their voting processions to Towcester.

Dan Hinton told me that, when he was a lad, he saw the travelling theatre perform Shakespeare plays in the yard of The Compasses. The actors would erect a canvas wall, so no-one could watch the play without paying. In 1973 the tradition was revived when Fair Exchange, a travelling theatre group, presented a Jacobean farce and, the following summer, a Pierrot show, both of which drew appreciative audiences. The yard has also been used for two street parties in the seventies, to celebrate the Queen's Jubilee, and later the wedding of the Prince of Wales to Diana Spencer.

The Compasses paddock was also used for games. I still dig up metal circles, the rusting remnants of quoits matches. In one room of the pub was an old table for the traditional Northamptonshire form of skittles, with even some of the cheeses surviving, but too worm-eaten to be restored.

Gradually, some of the old features have vanished. The pump is no longer used, the outside loo, of uncertain rusticity and dodgy hygiene, has been dismantled, as have the more modern sparge pipes of what was once the Gents, and the bare earth floor of the stables has become a kitchen floor. Other features have been recovered. Unpleasant 1930s tiled fireplaces concealed the old inglenook fires, and the oak beams were buried under many layers of paint and paper, including a wood-grain effect number.

Patricia Baker, 6 June 2000.

VILLAGE LIFE

Welsh Brides in Silverstone

Bert Dunkley was one of a family of 9 who lived in a cottage in the High Street. When he was still a school boy he worked for Markham's bakery, and delivered the bread to Lillingstone and Stowe. He then worked for about 17 years felling timber for Linnell's yard. The timber fellers would set off for the Oxford area, about 40 miles away, early on Monday morning with crosscut saws and axes tied to their bicycles, take lodgings during the week and cycle home on Friday night. There was not so much felling in the summer months when the sap was up the trees, but some of the time was spent in cutting off the bark of fallen trees to be used in the Northampton tanneries.

In 1930 they were felling in Wales, which led to two Welsh brides in Silverstone, Mrs Bignall and Mrs Dunkley, from Ruthin in North Wales. Bert and Maggie were both 17 when they met. Bert was lodging in a house a few doors away from Maggie's home, but his washing was not done by his landlady, so Maggie's mother stepped in to help.

When the timber fellers moved away from Wales, Maggie went to work in service in Northampton. She was one of a family of six so she had to leave school young. She had hoped to train as a nurse, but was not accepted and worked for a family at Hunsbury Hill in Northampton, where she had to wash the dog and bath the canary. Once she thought she had drowned it so stuck a needle in it and it soon came to life! Sometimes when walking the dog she would call to see a cousin at Far Cotton; the dog got a shorter walk. She was not very happy with this family so the next job was with an auctioneer at Canal House, Blisworth. They had a married daughter who was a model. At that time narrow boats on the canal was still carrying coal, but the families on the boats were very poor. Maggie saved the scraps of bread, cake etc. from the house and visited the boats spotlessly clean and gaily painted. She knew the canal families really well.

When she was ill and returned home to recover, Bert cycled all the way to Wales to see her. They were married in 1933 in the Registry Office in Towcester with Maggie wearing a red dress and red hat. Her family did not approve of her marrying an English man and outside the Welsh Church.

Their first home was a cottage in Cattle End for 2s 6d (12 ½p) rent a week. She had been used to tap water and gas lighting in Wales and found Silverstone very rural, but very friendly. They moved after less than a year to a cottage at the top of High Street owned by Mr Heritage, the shopkeeper of the Top Shop, for the same rent.

They have been at Kingsley Road since 1947 in a house built before the war, but occupied by the Army during the war. This house is said to have been the NAAFI Canteen for the King's Royal Rifles. After 61 years living in Silverstone, Maggie still thinks of herself as a newcomer.

Colin Hughes.

Percy Adams, Jack of all Trades

Mr & Mrs Percy Adams have lived virtually all their lives in Silverstone, but Percy mostly worked away from the village. He came here when he was about eight years old. By the age of thirteen he was working with a threshing gang at Silverstone Fields Farm, starting at 7am, with the farmer watching out of the window to see if he was a minute late. If so, he lost a penny from his six shillings a week.

At fourteen he worked for Mr Burbidge, a contractor from Blisworth. They drove to Barsley, and Percy drove a Fowler steam engine all the way back to the estate of the Duke of Buccleugh at Boughton House.

For some time he worked near Reading

with steam engines, hauling timber. It was a long journey by racing bicycle on Monday morning, and sometimes when he was courting he would return to Silverstone on Wednesday night, loaded with rabbits. He would distribute these to the homes of his mates and their wives would make rabbit pies for their men. In the morning he collected the rabbit pies and other food for the return journey to the camp. He worked for Burbidge for about fifteen years.

When returning to West End with a steam engine he would give three blasts on the whistle and May would know that he was coming. He drove steam engines to

Steam traction engine in the car park of The White Horse, 1994.

Northampton to have them tested, rather like an M.O.T. for insurance purposes. Eventually Burbidge went bankrupt, and Percy passed a test to drive double decker buses, and drove at weekends. Then he joined and worked for London Brick Co. at Calvert for thirty-eight years as a driver. One very severe winter, Bill James, who was a fitter at Calvert, got stuck in the snow at Dadford in his little car on the way to work. He knew Percy would be along soon, so he waited, but dozed off and a lot more snow fell. By the time Percy arrived, the car was almost invisible, but Percy spotted it, so it was a lucky escape for Bill.

During the war, the Calvert lorries and drivers were requisitioned, so Percy was driving all over the country, through air raids, staying in lousy lodgings sometimes. One load was 22ft long containing a Kittyhawk fighter aircraft, another was 16 tons of shell casings to take to Salisbury. When a railway station was bombed, Percy took a load of steel to rebuild it. He retired in 1973, and he and May moved to Murswell Close in 1975.

FARMS

Bleak Hall Farm

The 129 acres of Bleak Hall Farm lie to the south of the Dadford Road and stretch from the A43 to the county boundary with Buckinghamshire and from the Dadford Road to Hazelborough Wood. Jesse Tustian has lived on the farm since 1918, when at the age of two he came to Silverstone with his family from Bloxham. He took over the farm in the early 1940s when his father died. It was a mixed farm with something of everything. They kept 15-16 milking cows, a bull, calves, bullocks, sheep, pigs and chickens (with 25 cockerels at Christmas) and grew wheat,. barley and oats, manglewurzels and swedes.

During the Second World War the farm fetched the milk from Buckingham station from the 6.00 a.m. milk train for the 2000 service men and women on the airfield, delivering it in churns. The unpasteurised milk produced on the farm was delivered to the village, in the late 30s in cartons imported from Sweden, then, with supplies

of cartons cut off because of the war, in churns and later in bottles, which were sterilised on the farm and had at first cardboard tops and only later aluminium caps.

The farm employed two hands: Jack Roberts who lives in Kingsley and Edgar Swinford. Both joined the farm at the age of fourteen in the early 40s and retired in 1987, at which point Jesse Tustian also retired. During the war they were helped with the hay-making by those on the RAF base and also by prisoners of war, one German and two Italians, all three very grateful to be out of the war. The Italians were very different from one another: one was fair and a wine merchant from Northern Italy, while the other from the South was dark and temperamental. Their camp is now the kennels at the cross-roads between Stowe School and Water Stratford. Mrs Daphne Tustian came to the farm as a land girl.

Farming was, of course, much more physically demanding in those days, many jobs being done by hand, such as the thatching of straw ricks. Nowadays it is the paperwork that is demanding: each animal has to be tagged and its progress through life recorded in a passport-like document, and much work has to be done for the tax and VAT men. Gone are the days when Johnny Barratt the butcher, a bit short of meat, owing to being too generous with the meat rations, nipped up to Blackmires Farm which had been rented by the Tustians since 1929, to slaughter a sheep or two, unknown to the authorities. Gone too the days, thank goodness, when Jesse spent the night with three others in the Home Guard on top of the Windmill at Windmill Farm on observation duty. Fortunately no bombs were ever dropped on Silverstone, but bombers did pass overhead on their way to Coventry.

(Tustian recollections continue on page 113)

WHICH WAY FOR —

Silverstone

DICK CHATBURN and SANDRA LEY
tour our County Villages

Silverstone is, of course, internationally known for its motor racing track. Above James Hunt, winner of the Graham Hill Memorial Trophy in April this year, is seen with Mrs. Bette Hill, widow of the popular driver.

Below Hunt is seen with the Duke of Kent at last year's John Player Grand Prix. (Photos by Fred Taylor)

Not much of the village can be seen as one drives along the main Brackley road (above). The Royal Oak and a few houses give little indication of the sizeable village which the road has bypassed and which is seen below—a view down Stocks Hill.

Touring our county villages we usually start talking to people by announcing that we are from the "Independent". The rest of the interview follows quite naturally. In Silverstone, however, Sandra Ley and I received a classic conversation-stopper when our quarry replied "Independent, are you? Well, we're all independent here!"

This is, in fact, the keynote of Silverstone. Since the Middle Ages there has not been a Lord of the Manor here and nobody owed allegiance to anybody. Anciently the place was a settlement in the forest of Whittlewood, owned in part by the priory of Luffield and peopled by woodsmen and cottars. Time left Silverstone immune from the kind of progress that made or broke many other villages and the vigorous individuality of these comparatively free people remained. Though the local "characters" of yore have gone they have left their legacy of independence of spirit not only in their grand-children but also to be absorbed by the new-comers of recent times.

From the main Towcester to Brackley road there is little to be seen of the village proper. Before the bypass was made travellers had to go through Silverstone and it is hard to visualise those village roads, particularly Little London, as

30

part of a fairly busy highway. But they were. Certainly, from a glance at some old maps the place seemed more compact in the last century; it would have been easier for our purpose then. Now the several component parts must be sought — we sought them and found them with a few surprises thrown in. We met a hurdle-maker who plays (expertly) the electronic organ. We learned some gems of dialect that we couldn't possibly spell out for you. And more than a couple of firms of international repute.

Any account of Silverstone must include the Racing Circuit which has grown from a modest adaptation of a Second World War airfield into the fastest and most sophisticated track in Europe. Though the B.B.C. and some of the world's Press still seem unable to make up their minds where it is — "near Buckingham", "Oxfordshire" or "at Towcester" — the Circuit has seen in its short history most of the greatest names in auto and motor-cycle racing. Two years ago Peter Carrick wrote a lively and eminently readable book, "Silverstone — the story of Britain's Fastest Track", in which the author takes his reader curve by curve through some of the most spectacular races of the Track's colourful past and provides some entertaining glimpses of its equally colourful characters. The Circuit is now an integral part of the village although it was regarded initially with mixed reactions. Much of the adverse opinion remains but it hasn't prevented many scores of people from moving into the new properties built in the locality in recent years and making their homes within the sound of engines and tyres being tried to their limits. It was while a light easterly breeze brought the distant sounds of track tests across the village that I talked to "Torr of Silverstone" at his studio at the Parsonage and heard his story of his company's rise to international recognition.

Alfred Torr set up business here as a lithographic plate maker in the December of 1965. For the uninitiated, this is a photographic process in which pictures, photographs and drawings are transferred to metal sheets so that they can be printed in books and other publications. The Torr products are of the highest possible quality, this being the object of the firm since its beginning and printed reproductions of pictures proudly displayed on Mr. Torr's office walls, some by one of our county's best-known artists, Peter Newcombe, bear witness to this claim. The daunting days of the firm's early struggles, however, might well have spelt disaster a dozen times. Looking back from his modern, temperature-controlled studio fitted with every conceivable facility Alfred Torr pointed to the wooden shack where he started 10 years ago and recalled the mornings when he used to make up the boiler at 6.0 a.m., those mornings when the pipes were frozen solid and those other days when it was too hot to work in there by 2.0 p.m. But such hardships brought their own reward because their very modest resources forced them to make a lot of their own equipment, designed to their exacting requirements and in due course that same equipment was so much admired by other workers in the trade that the House of Torr formed a separate division to manufacture it. A branch in Leicester deals with distribution which is made to many parts of the world. Now Mr. Torr and two of his sons are beginning to reap the harvest of their decade in this highly specialised technical field,

while maintaining the same standards of the best attainable quality with which they began. While normal business profit must not be ignored the prime motive of everyone involved in Alfred Torr's garden studio is job-satisfaction.

In Silverstone technology turns up in the unlikeliest places. Opposite the main entrance to the Circuit a gravel lane leads to some old Air Ministry buildings and cattle graze on either side. In those old hangars, barely visible from the main road, there is an industry which is rapidly growing out of its pioneering stages into what may well be an essential process of the future. As everyone knows, steel rusts, copper corrodes and things made of metal cannot last for ever. As the world grows more aware of the need for conservation and as the supply of raw metal becomes more difficult and expensive, ways must be found to preserve whatever we have left of it. Acalor International have most of the answers to the problem. Eleven years ago they rented the old Air Link training area here and built themselves up to their present state of maximum activity. For seven days of every week they work on grit-blasting and coating virtually anything you can name from an oil-well tower destined for Abu Dhabi in the Persian Gulf to a Victorian coach for a private collection. Girders and reinforcing bars for motorway bridges, power stations and tower blocks — any size and shape can be sealed against the ravages of rust and corrosion, thus extending the life and usefulness of metallic structures for many times their former expected life-span. Most of their work comes from London and Birmingham but as a steadily growing concern Acalor is drawing business from an ever-widening field. Sooner or later, no doubt, the treatments will be applied to metals as a legal requirement — imagine a car chassis capable of lasting a hundred years or so!

In the next field Michael Tate works on the reconditioning of light aircraft engines while sheep graze around the old H.Q. Nissen hut which is now a well-fitted workshop shared with his partner Mr. Claude Humphrey. This is a business which opened its doors in 1962 and never suffers a slack moment. "Too busy" is an encouraging thing to hear in these days. Messrs. Humphrey and Tate accept as much as they can do, their subjects being mainly German, Czech or Rolls Royce engines and practically always "wanted yesterday". It's exacting work, precision to very fine limits, and obviously has to be completely reliable. Engines of another kind are tuned in the next-door hut by a gentleman whose name will be well-known to followers of racing history — Bill Lacey, ex-Brooklands racing champ. Now a senior citizen, he gives the experience and expertise of a long lifetime to the tuning of racing engines within sound of "Britain's fastest Circuit".

Absorbed as I was in the thriving industry of Silverstone I was almost forgetting my usual preoccupation with history. On the Circuit I looked in vain for the remains of Luffield Priory near "Abbey Curve" but the archaeological work that has been done here has been carefully concealed and the site is grassed over. "Chapel Curve", too, takes its name from the site of a medieval church but although some flooring is still there the turf is shrouding what little can be seen. Back in the village there are several old buildings, some protected by preservation orders and others by private owners who care. The Anglican church, built in the last century, is

Silverstone's "Doddy"—Mr. Dennis Dodwell and his wife Edna, newsagents in the village for 25 years.

The Post Office is run by Joy and Tony Townsend.

Mr. and Mrs. Alfred Torr, of The Parsonage. He is a lithographic plate maker who has extended into the manufacture of equipment. Mrs. (Elsie) Torr is president of the W.I.

Mr. Roy Humphries, sprayer with Acalor International a firm operating in former aircraft hangars and doing battle with the great enemy of metal—rust. Pictured below right are, Mr. William Bliss (fork lift driver), Mr. Len Lovell (production manager) and Mr. Holland (manager),

Mr. Norman Smith took time off from his work of making gates to give us an organ recital at his home while Dorothy, his wife, provided iced orange drink.

faithfully Gothic in style and well kept by devoted hands. Inside the church I found a panel outlining some of the village history and repeating a common mistake in supposing the origin of the village's name to be derived from "Silva" — a wood whereas it is "Sigewulf's Tun" — the farmstead of Sigwulf, a Saxon. Another error has crept into some accounts of the local history concerning the Priory of Luffield which some writers said was wiped out by the Black Death. In fact, though the plague certainly hit hard in the desperate years between 1340 and 1350 the Priory survived, the last Prior, Thomas Rowland, being instituted in 1488.

More to the point of Silverstone's history is the forestry and timber trade which continues vigorously as it has done for many centuries. In West End the sounds of a high-powered saw caused us to seek out the source; we found Ron Mayo and his colleague working in a shed and coaxed them out for a photograph. We sat on stacks of planks and talked about timber, Ascot and the dying elms.

Elms stricken by the Dutch Elm disease are to be seen all over Silverstone and there's no doubt that the blight has had its effect on the timber trade. Ron Mayo went down to Ascot this year to indulge his fancy at the races and was shocked by the ravaged trees he saw on the journey. "Much worse than round here" he declared. We asked him what uses could be made of the dead elms. "If they're left for a year or so they will be no good at all" he said "but if they can be salvaged in time they mostly go for props in the mines". Timber for this yard comes from "all over the place — Stratford on Avon, Wales or wherever there is any" whereas the Silverstone businesses used to rely on local supplies which have now mainly dried up. Ron Mayo was born here at West End — 65 years ago — and has two sons, both of whom are farmers, one at Cosgrove and the other at Maidford. "Do you plan to retire now?" I asked. "Not really" he said "I've got 50 acres of (farm land) back here". The screaming saw had started up again and he said something I completely missed. "What did you say?" I asked. He repeated "I like living here. It's a nice quiet country lane".

A bit further along this nice quiet country lane the sounds of a hammer and chisel led us to another workshop. A man was in there making a

In the timber trade—William Pickett and his employer Ron Mayo.

gate. Introductions over, Norman Smith began to tell us how unimportant and unambitious his job seemed to him and was somewhat taken aback when I sailed in with a strong defence of it. "You might have spent your life passing bits of paper from one file to another in some Government Department and ended up in the Honours List" I told him. "But as it is your gates may well be safeguarding and beautifying the countryside for generations yet unborn!" He accepted my point and we talked on. "My real enjoyment comes in playing the organ," he confessed. At that point his wife came up the path and we managed to talk them both into posing with one of Norman's gates in the light of the afternoon sun. The sun was hot, too, that day and when Mrs. Smith invited us home for a drink of iced orange we jumped at the offer.

The half-hour that followed was sheer delight as Norman Smith regaled us with selections from light opera on his electronic organ. I shall never again see a new five-barred-gate without the music of "The Desert Song" running through my head.

Over to Sandra Ley

Whilst Dick had been chatting to Mr. Alf Torr I had meandered off in the direction of the Torrs' beautiful garden where I had been told I would find Mrs. Elsie Torr, Mr. Torr's wife and President of the W.I.

We sat in the shade of trees as Mrs. Torr told me a little about the W.I. As with most things in Silverstone the Institute seems to be flourishing. "We have some 70 members, many of them young ones. We meet the second Tuesday in the month in the Church Hall. We have a drama group, a craft group and a music group. One of our Drama Group's most successful ventures quite recently was a play called 'Venison and Vengeance' taken from a book called 'Old Oak', which is about the village. The music group holds music evenings and joins in other music evenings and our craft group sent something to the East of England Show this year."

How long had the W.I. been going and who was the founder? "Marie Curie was our founder and I believe the group has been going for 41 years in Silverstone," Mrs. Torr who has been a member for some years told me, "We help with the village fete every year and hold various other events. The members are very good, we always make a joint effort out of things".

What about new members? "We encourage them of course, we love to have newcomers, if we hear of anyone new one of the Committee usually invites them along. And we are always pleased to have visitors."

In Mrs. Torr's absence there are two vice-Presidents Dorothy Brown and Jenny Tero who help to keep things running.

At this point Dick was preparing to leave and we bade our farewells to the Torrs.

The noise from the Silverstone circuit buzzed in my ears as I was greeted by Mr. Robert Fearnall who was so helpful to Dick and me during our visits. He is the Press and Promotions Officer

Mr. Sid Hinton—when you had to walk for water.

Mrs. Mary Denney—"We are very independent at Silverstone".

Mr. Michael Tate — reconditions light aircraft engines.

Mr. Dan Hinton—remembers Silverstone's first car.

at the track and it was from him that I heard of the new safety measures and other developments which have been going on in the last few years.

"Some £100,000 has been spent on safety measures in the last six years" he told me, "a total new pit complex was built recently, and we are now supposed to be one of the best if not the best circuit for motor racing in the world, which is a big compliment for a private organisation."

I was curious to know more of the marshals whom you see in profusion at meetings. "We have up to 1,000 marshals for Grand Prix days," Mr. Fearnall explained, "They are trained by the British Motor Racing Marshals Club, and I believe we are the only circuit in the country to have marshals on test days."

The last serious accident was in 1973.

"Recently our fastest bend, Woodcote Corner was slowed down a little by incorporating an 'S' bend but we are still the fastest circuit in the country. Obviously motor racing is to a certain extent a dangerous sport."

As I left Mr. Fearnall he gave me some tickets for the next Sunday's meet. I went along to this and watched as the cars roared around the track. I must admit I don't enjoy motor racing now as much as I did a few years ago, but the atmosphere still continues to fascinate me.

Walking up one of the village streets I noticed a sign reading "Dodwell's Newsagents and General Store". Apart from the sign you would hardly have recognised it as a store from the road. Mrs. Edna Dodwell chatted to Dick and me about the village and told us that they had been the newsagents in Silverstone for some 25 years. "Have you been selling the Independent that long in the village?" I asked. "Almost, we started selling the Independent when we began the evening papers," Mrs. Dodwell told me. At this point Mr. Dennis Dodwell appeared, better known to the locals as "Doddy". Dick decided a picture was appropriate and I bade my farewells and moved on.

At 23 Brackley Road lives Mr. Sid Hinton who has always lived in Silverstone where he now lives with his sister Mrs. Mary Denney. When I called on them and I asked them what life in Silverstone used to be like in years gone by Mr. Hinton told me, "Well I remember a time when you used to know more or less everyone you met in the street, but now of course you don't know most people. There are many newcomers. The water shortage too, reminds me of when we used to have to walk all the way

to Cattle End for our water—there was no running water in those days."

Mrs. Denney told us that many things have changed. "Before the bypass Silverstone used to be more like one long straight street from Towcester end. Although it has always been a bit of a straggling village. There has never been any squire, we are very independent, and Silverstone was at one point, well known for its poachers."

It was from Sid's cousin Dan Hinton that I learnt much more of Sid's activities. He was organist at the Chapel for over 60 years and has run the Boys' Brigade for as many as 50 years and still goes to camp with them.

One could almost say the cousins are on opposite sides of the fence for Dan Hinton was organist too, not at the Chapel but at the church in Silverstone fo 18 years and he recalled to me with a smile his most embarrassing moment. "I was sitting at the organ playing for a wedding which was supposed to have taken place at 2 p.m.," he explained, "well I ended up playing until nearly 2.30 and still no wedding was taking place. The vicar kept asking me to carrry on and I was getting really embarrassed. Finally it was discovered that the bridegroom who was from Towcester had not had his banns published and the whole thing was called off until the following Saturday, but it was a performance! The bride's mother was in tears."

He went on to tell me of one of the first cars he saw in Silverstone which belonged to a Mr. Ashby of Towcester. "Just after the 1914-18 war I don't think there was more than three cars in Silverstone, we were never a wealthy village. Everyone used to make a living but not much more. I think there were eight timber merchants in those days and each had a team of horses. They used to start really early in the morning. There were no steam engines and in the saw pit it was one man above and one below. I remember one of the people from the saw pit was taken ill once and the Doctor went to see him and asked him if he drank beer? 'Only about 16 pints a day', he told the doctor. '16 pints!' was the Doctor's reply. 'Well what is that for a man?', the sawer replied."

Leaving Dan Hinton I made my way to what must be one of the liveliest centres of any village, the Post Office. In Silverstone, Tony and Joy Townsend maintain a store of widely varied stock and in the course of each working week probably see almost everyone in the locality.

Sipping coffee in the garden behind the "Stores" with Joy, leaving Tony behind the counter, I listened to some highly amusing tales. One time chairman and now vice-chairman of the Parish Council, Joy takes a vital interest in the Silverstone people amongst whom she and her husband have lived with their three children for the past 10 years.

"Tony and I love some of the older customers," Joy told me, "and particularly when we first came here you could almost set your clock by them especially on Monday mornings. And the Silverstone accent! Well, one old gentleman who used to come in I couldn't understand a word he said, but he was a really pleasant man and fortunately for me used to have exactly the same purchase each time he came. Then there was Jack Webb who used to farm and some of the acres he farmed, were up near the track called Wet Leys, and I think everyone remembers the day of the big race at Silverstone when Jack set out as usual to feed his livestock at Wet Leys and trotted up the A45 at about five miles an hour with his old horse and cart, with the feed on the back leaving a queue of traffic going to the track for miles after him. He had been using that track for years to feed his livestock and no amount of hooting and disturbance was going to make any difference to his usual routine. He sauntered on oblivious to the jam he was causing. He was over 90 when he passed on. Silverstone folk, particularly the elder generation, are very independent and do everything for themselves."

Joy told me about the playing fields they have just managed to purchase. "It comprises about seven-and-a-half acres", she told me, "and it means that now the children have somewhere to go and play. They have a cricket square and a football pitch. This is run by a management committee which has representatives from all the other various village enterprises. For myself I just like to see that the children have all the opportunities they can."

And indeed they have ample facilities for the children of Silverstone which I will tell you more of next month. As Dick appeared and managed to catch Tony in a spare moment to take his picture with his wife, we left promising to call again and find out more about the playschool, keep fit group and have a word with some of the many people in the village we had still not seen.

Next month we will tell you about those people, and a little about "Old Oak" to which so many of the villagers referred.

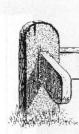

WHICH WAY FOR —

Silverstone

DICK CHATBURN and SANDRA LEY
tour our County Villages

We conclude our look at Silverstone which is best known as the home of international motor racing, but where a great deal more than that is going on. It's a place with an independent spirit and can boast its share of "characters", such as the Victorian John Denney, (right) schoolmaster, county councillor, Methodist preacher, village patriarch and protector of the poor; and Aubrey Linnell (far right), member of a timber firm in the village who told us: "It's a bad business with these elms" (like those in the vicinity pictured below) "We can't get all the elm that needs cutting into the yard and when they're gone a great deal of our livelihood will go with them." In the inset picture he is seen measuring timber.

Stocks Hill, seen from the car park of one of the two public houses in the village, the White Horse.

In those distant days which I call my youth I read all that H. V. Morton wrote "In Search of England", "In Search of Wales", "In the Steps of Saint Paul" and the rest. Later, in the steps of H. V. Morton I visited places he had described and I was often disappointed to find my idol had failed to mention so much of what I found fascinating about them. While the great Morton had provided a colourful picture of towns and people on his travels there was a good deal he had apparently missed. Eventually I realised Mr. Morton had set himself the impossible task of describing a huge tract of country in some 280 pages where a ten-volume work would have been barely enough. And this is our problem in making our word-sketches of Northamptonshire villages— Sandra Ley and I have to be content with presenting our impressions in a few pages and quite a lot of people and things are inevitably left out. Silverstone proved to be another example of the unattainable and we must satisfy ourselves with a sincere but inadequate sketch. There is a lot of Silverstone.

Look at the industry, for example. While we found a fair proportion of it and did our best to give an account of it we learned of many more people who are beavering away in odd corners doing all sorts of fascinating jobs. They must forgive us. We can't fit them all in. There are many of the older inhabitants who can tell some wonderful stories of the village of days long past but they must be given the detailed chronicle they deserve. Silverstone is not without its chroniclers. Peter Carrick's "Story of Britain's Fastest Circuit" specialises in that one aspect of the place while the village of a century ago is treated faithfully and sympathetically in the classic work by the Rev. John E. Linnell entitled "Old Oak". John Linnell died in the March of 1919 but his papers were collected by his son and published in 1932 in the form of this book which is a unique study of the personalities of this unique village. In reading "Old Oak" one gets the same kind of sensation engendered by Cobbett's "Rural Rides"—John Linnell's life began when Cobbett's ended and continued with something of that author's forthright vitality. Both were big men, both were power-

Jack and Gwen Adams have been at the Royal Oak for 20 years.

Mrs. Pauline Hawkins and Mrs. Joy Lee (licensee) are at the White Horse.

Butchers in the village and in the surrounding area are Mr. Brian Beagin and Mr. Barry Tapp.

ful orators and shared a profound love of their fellow men and a savage hatred of pomp and humbug. There must be some kindred spirit of John Linnell now in Silverstone who is ready to write "Old Oak Re-visited"—the time is ripe. After all, only a few miles down the road from here is the country of "Lark Rise" and "Candleford" immortalised by Flora Thompson in her beautiful portrayals of English village life of 80 years ago. Will Silverstone's contemporary John Linnell or Flora Thompson please stand up?

Meanwhile, something of the sort is being done. Gerald Lovell, a young man with the right idea is building up a library of colour photographs. A few hundred slides recording the local scenes and people of today are already stored in Mr. Lovell's collection; his skill with the camera combined with a lively interest in his environment make him Silverstone's pictorial historian of the present. Being far from an expert photographer myself I have a profound admiration for that very exacting art.

In the home of Dan Hinton I stood enthralled by a small collection of old studio photographs of Silverstonians of the past; one of his mother, in particular, is an exquisite example of the superb photography of those days when the model had to stand quite still for maybe half-a-minute. Another treasured photograph which we reproduce here was lent to us by Sid Hinton and is a portrait of one of Silverstone's most notable men of the last century. John Denney, schoolmaster, County Councillor, eloquent Methodist preacher and protector of the poor was to this village a tower of strength whose influence reaches into the present day. Writing of him in 1893 W. Ryland D. Adkins said "On the Council he has been a distinct figure. He is gifted with a voice which can do everything but whisper and when he is roused to utterance, no-one is likely to sleep under his remarks". The same author remarked that John Denney "seems to unite for his beloved

village the power of an Irish priest and a French **maire**". Certainly it seems no secret amongst the older villagers that Mr. Denney, being so well endowed with a personality of forceful persuasion, was frequently called upon by local poachers to use his influence on their behalf—let us hope that his labour didn't go unrewarded and that he occasionally found a pheasant or a hare on his doorstep! Mr. Sid Hinton showed me a precious piece of parchment which records John Denney's examination in 1861 at the Westminster Wesleyan Training College and his subsequent appointment to Silverstone Wesleyan School. The annual reports by the Government Inspectors acknowledge his teaching ability and continue through to 1883. One entry was made by the great Matthew Arnold, the educational reformer and poet who visited John Denney's village school on December 3, 1867.

Poaching was perhaps a fine art and a minor local industry in Silverstone's history. "Old Oak" begins with a legendary story of two young newly married men, Adams and Tyrell,

who went into Stowe Park for venison and were unlucky enough to be caught in the act. In their time, 1748, the penalty for such a crime was death and their wives, in mortal fear for their husband's fate, made the journey to Stowe House to plead for mercy from the then owner, Lord Cobham. His Lordship heard them out and promised them the return of their men one day of the following week. The women went happily home, prepared a welcome and waited. Punctually on the appointed day the men were brought to their homes, in their coffins, judicially hanged. It was said that one of the widows never re-married and lived to be over a hundred, understandably somewhat mentally deranged by the bitter and tragic experience of her youth.

"Old Oak" is an essential background for the proper study of Silverstone, its temperament and the sturdy independence of its people. I'd guess the spirit is still there in the modern village where conversation is to the point and a straight question is met by a straight answer.

Work goes on in large or small units and

The remains of Silverstone's windmill, on the Whittlebury Road.

One of the village's more picturesque thatched cottages is Rookery Cottage, on the way to West End.

At this point there was formerly an access point to Stowe Park from the Oxford Road. There is also a tradition here of a tunnel used by medieval monks. Presumably gatehouses to the estate the two cottages are now in private possession.

evidently thrives. I literally stumbled upon several of the workshops: one of them behind Mr. Collins' garage in Little London is almost totally concealed but houses a group of sophisticated machine tools, instantly recognisable as the best of their kind. Here Martin Hart and Chuck Salmons engage in the precision engineering of parts for light industry—as busy as they want to be and selective regarding the work they do. Martin Hart, whose business it is, began here about five or six years ago and has made steady progress ever since. Nearer the road Mr. Collins conducts his garage and motor engineering concern which again is as self-sufficient as possible, every kind of repair being within his scope. Up a lane off the A43 is yet another enterprise-Churchhill's, whose business is in tractors and plant hire. Just about everyone we met in the district has had dealings with Churchill's who provide an essential and efficient service far beyond the bounds of Silverstone.

At the far end of the village, on the Brackley side, hurdle-making is the occupation of a team of men led by Mr. Ron. Hutchings who continue a trade which must be one of the oldest in the district. Convinced I would never reach the end of Silverstone's industry I took a snapshot of Ron Hutchings and Stan West by a mountain of hurdles that were destined for one of the big agricultural shows and travelled back to another rendezvous with Sandra Ley.

At the White Horse on Stocks Hill she was talking to Pauline Hawkins who was dividing her time between the lounge, the public bar and the kitchens. It was lunch time and our opportunity to confer. Settling down to an unusually palatable pub-grub meal we sorted out our notes and then had a chat with Joy Lee. Joy is the licensee of the White Horse and shares with the Royal Oak the custom of the village and the Circuit. Race days mean busy times for the two pubs—Joy and Pauline know full well what it means to be run off their legs when faced with a crowd from all parts of the country. The story of a recent Motor Cycle Grand Prix weekend when an unpleasant incident occurred was fresh news when we were having this conversation and

we asked how the racegoers behaved down here in the village. "They were marvellous" said Joy. "The whole of Stocks Hill and the car park was crowded with youngsters, all of them good-humoured and courteous even though they had to wait some time to be served. There was absolutely no indication of the stupid behaviour that happened up at the Track—20 to 30 were involved in that affair and the total number of spectators was about 40,000! Let's keep the thing in perspective. There is always a group of trouble-makers in any activity. At the risk of repeating a well-worn thing I say it's wrong to suppose that owning a motor-bike and wearing a leather jacket automatically makes a young man a hooligan. And I hope you'll print that!"

Of the two doctors who practise in Silverstone one lives here and the other in Towcester. Dr. Lewis has his home and headquarters with his partners in Towcester and holds a surgery at the Old Parsonage in Silverstone. Just across the road at the bottom of Stocks Hill is the surgery and dispensary of Dr. Frank Newton who has lived here at Cattle End for the past eight years. Dr. Newton is at present the chairman of the Parish Council but it was learning of his activities with the British Olympic team that impelled us to seek him out. To do that we had to go to Towcester where he attends at the Health Centre—interviewing a busy doctor is rather like trying to chat to an Olympic runner in action! Dr. Newton's recent globetrot to Kingston, Ontario, with our Yachting team was an episode in his official duties as a member of the British Olympic Association Medical Panel. A lifetime's interest in the medical welfare of athletes and sportsmen has led him to this very enjoyable though exacting role, led him in 1972 to Kiel, this year to Canada and will see him in 1980 with the Yachting Team at Tallinn in the U.S.S.R. As official doctor to the Yachting team he sees his responsibilities to advise and direct them through their training and almost their whole way of life with success in the events as a natural conclusion. "It has been accepted in the past that we are traditionally best at sailing and riding" he told us "but unless we maintain

our teams at better than best continually there may come a time when we could be overtaken." We got the clear impression from this athletic G.P. that if 'golds' pass us by it will not be due to any lack of effort by the medical and physical training people behind the teams.

Over to Sandra Ley

Silverstone is simply crammed with activity, particularly and especially for the young. I visited as many of the organisers, secretaries and other people who run them as I could, but am very much afraid I have barely touched the surface of just what does happen in Silverstone.

One interesting scheme is of activities for the children and in many cases the mothers too during the long summer holidays. "It ran from July 28 to August 26 this year and we were so well supported it was really very successful. We organised days out in the forest, trips to the swimming baths and many other trips," Mrs. Anne Weldon, secretary of the scheme, told me. "I think everyone including the mothers enjoyed themselves thoroughly. We were taking as many as 80 at a time swimming. To round the whole thing off we organised a big party for the children."

On Thursday evenings the Junior School is a hive of activity. The Brownies are in occupation from 6 until 7.30, and no sooner are they out than the Guides take over until 9. Mrs. Carole Flynn told me: "The group has been going for some four years. We have members from other villages, including Wappenham, Abthorpe, and Greens Norton. We have quite a few members and the children all seem to enjoy coming." For just over a year Mrs. Carole Walker has been helping to run the Guides and she told me it now has some 21 members.

Among other groups in the village are the Girls Brigade run by Mrs. Christine Wilson and Mrs. Janet Wilson, which is held at the Chapel, and the Boys Brigade. There are no scouts or cubs in Silverstone, but any children who wish to attend these may do so at Whittlebury which is the nearest place that they are held.

For the ladies there is a weekly keep fit group

43

run by Mrs. Rita King, which involves sports, talks on health and beauty, as well as what we used to call "physical jerks".

A Playgroup of which Mrs. Joy Townsend, now chairman, was one of the co-founders in 1970 has gone from strength to strength ever since. Held on Mondays, Wednesday and Friday mornings from 9.15 to 11.45 a.m., each session is attended not only by a supervisor and assistant but by the mothers themselves. "This is worked on a rota system", Joy told me, "and it seems to work very well. All the mothers take part, and seem to thoroughly enjoy doing so. It seems to work very satisfactorily, and serves the purpose of not only giving the mothers a break, but helps the children to adjust for the time when they will be going to school." All the mothers I spoke to on my travels around the village seemed to think the Playgroup was an exceptionally good idea. There is also a mother toddler group which meets once a week in the afternoon, and this too would seem to be proving a success. It gives all the mothers and their youngsters the chance to get out and meet other mothers and the children love it too.

Joy also told me a little about the School Association in which interested parents and friends raise money for school equipment. "We had a fete quite recently and raised about £100, which was a great help," she told me.

"There are thriving Sunday Schools here too", she continued. "There are about 40 children on the Church register. We are trying to think of something to do to celebrate the church's centenary in 1981 too."

Joy's husband Tony is the only practising bee keeper in Silverstone.

Jack and Gwen Adams have been at the Royal Oak for some 20 years, moving there from a pub in Lillingstone Dayrell. Mr. Adams has in fact been in the trade all his life, he was born at The Goat at Towcester which is no longer in existence. The Adams share the trade from the track with the other pub in the

Mr. Martin Hart (top left) is in precision engineering of parts for light industry, running his own business in Little London, where Mr. Rex Collins (lower left) has his garage. On right a hurdle mountain at Hutchings' yard—Stan West and his employer Ron Hutchings with a stack of hurdles which were on their way to a county show.

village, and most lunchtimes will find someone from the track there supping lager, eating lunch and talking about the morning's activities.

Just down the road from the 'Oak' we found another business which is proving quite successful. Mr. Barry Tapp and Mr. Brian Beagin have been established as butchers in Silverstone for some five years, and not only do they serve the community in Silverstone but also the area for several miles around, where they operate a van. "Butchering in a village is very different from in the town," Mr. Beagin told me, "I never put very much in the window on display because I find people seem to prefer to come in and ask for just what they want, and do in fact know just what they want. But I prefer business here to in the town."

Hughes Stores is another shopping centre in Silverstone. Run by Sara and Colin Hughes it is a small supermarket type shop and also has a petrol pump. There are several other small businesses including Kingsley Road Stores.

Industry seems to thrive in Silverstone, where there are many "one man bands", where people seem to prefer being their own boss or work as a family unit, and Linnells Timber Yard is a prime example of the latter. The Linnells are into their fourth generation at the yard and when we arrived we found Mr. Aubrey Linnell, now retired, talking with his brother Jimmy who is also "retired" but still works a five hour day at 80. Aubrey got out his rule and stood willingly as Dick clicked his camera but Jimmy threatened to lock us in the office at the mention of taking his picture.

"At one time all the wood came from Whittlewood Forest and the Crown lands," Aubrey explained, "Now we go all over the place, but it's a bad business with these elms.

We can't get all the elm that needs cutting into the yard, and when they've gone a great deal of our livelihood will go with them. The way things are going as well there will be too many timber merchants soon. There are for instance many bigger yards than ours in places like Brackley." On this sad note we had to leave as Aubrey's son came in to make an important telephone call and so we took our farewell.

As we left that day I noticed especially the profusion of dead elms in and around Silverstone.

Space has almost run out and there are many things we have not mentioned and many people still not seen. Recently established in Silverstone for instance is a branch of the National Housewives Register.

I must however, correct something written last month. Mrs. Elsie Torr president of the W.I., kindly wrote to me and explained that the Silverstone W.I. was in fact begun by Miss Bouverie of Delapre in 1932, not by Marie Curie as previously stated.

Our tour of Silverstone had to stop somewhere. But where? We looked across the Circuit—we had given it only a paragraph or so and we had made no mention of many other features of Little London, West End and Stocks Hill. We had written nothing of the miles of country lanes and woodland walks, nothing of the history of the Church and Chapel. Out of some 1400 people we had met maybe 40, out of a thousand years of time we had touched on half a dozen events.

Silverstone deserves more—John Linnell's "Old Oak" should be revisited now that his little village of "Silson" (still so called by many local people) has grown to its present size. We turned to go home, leaving some newfound friends in this uniquely independent village.

The presence of the race track has brought international drivers to Silverstone like Stirling Moss and the late Mike Hawthorn pictured at a meeting in July, 1958.

There's More to Jesse than a Pinta

Jesse Tustian, with his familiar milk van, recently replaced by a spanking new version, must notice a fantastic difference between now and the old handcart, measures and waxed cartons of his pioneering days.

His parents had moved from Bloxham to Bleak Hall and they became the local specialists in the production of butter, which sold at one time for 2/- (10p) per pound. The handcart of the 1920s gave way, during the war, to the old cans and measures again because of the rationing of basic materials, and a cart and pony which was inclined to take off at the slightest provocation. The end of the war saw the beginning of bottled milk. This, however, meant an early start, around 5.30am, to go to Buckingham to collect the bottled product. The war years hold extra special memories for the Tustian family. A certain lady (now Mrs. Tustian) was seconded from the Land Army to help with the daily round. She had moved to the area from Norfolk with her family, and finally they too, settled in Silverstone. Milkmen must work quickly, for a spring wedding followed in 1942. A family followed in due course, three fine sons, one of whom, Steve, now helps with the farm and the dairy business.

News & Views 1980.

Jesse Tustian Looks Back

The village was a close-knit community, everybody knowing each other by nicknames, which often caused a bit of bother to newcomers. The layout consisted mainly of rows of cottages, two up, one down with the privy at the bottom of the garden, which meant the use of slop pails for night-time use. This reminds me of an incident when I was bustling around one early morning and the lady of the house must have seen me coming and hid the offending object behind the door. Not knowing this I pushed open the door; over

went the pail spilling its contents all over her clean floor. I think that day I learned a few new words.

Drinking water in those days had to be fetched from various pumps or wells and lovely sparkling water it was too, and it was very rare that the wells ran dry.

When I first started the milk was delivered in cartons, but with the coming of the war we were back to the pony and trap, buckets and measures into customers' jugs - a much slower process but we still got through. It's good to think back on the old times, although it is with regret I realise how few of my original customers are left.

News & Views 1984

Windmill Farm

Windmill Farm straddles the top of the first rise along the Whittlebury Road out of Silverstone. The windmill which gives the farm its name was built there to replace the one at Whittlebury which no longer worked. It has recently been converted into a house, its sails having been disposed of many years ago. It has been the property of the Webb family for over 100 years, since the time when the Loder estate went to auction.

The Webb family concentrates on producing quality meat, primarily lamb and beef, at a time when market conditions and government and EU regulations are making it very difficult for livestock farmers to make a living. The future and the bypass are threatening: the bypass will cut the farm in two, with the cutting 20 metres from the farmhouse.

From an interview with Cecil and Pat Webb

Silverstone Tower Mill

The windmill stands a quarter of a mile east of Silverstone, behind a farmhouse on the Whittlebury road. Now virtually an empty shell, it gives few clues to its varied past, but fortunately, thanks to the owner and other villagers, an unusual tale was pieced together. It was said that this mill was built to supplement or succeed a windmill that existed at Whittlebury. The new mill was constructed of red brick, three storeys high and carried four single-shuttered, anticlockwise patent sails, a dome cap and a fantail. Unfortunately, the year of its erection is unclear as the tower itself bears no clues. It is absent from both the Bryant and Greenwood maps but does appear on the Ordnance Survey of 1833. The miller in 1847 was Mr G. Higham, but within a few years, Mr W. Earle had seemingly taken over. By the late 1860s the mill was once again being worked by the Higham family, although this time it was Charles Higham who was charged with its running.

At some time during the tower mill's life an incident occurred which has become

Silverstone Mill, from a watercolour sketch of 1932

almost folklore. A visitor to the farm was believed to have left his pony and trap on the mill field where the tower mill was working. After a while the grazing animal wandered closer and closer to the mill, until part of the harness was caught by the revolving sails. The horse, complete with trap was snatched from the ground and taken up some feet in the air before the offending strap broke free, sending the unfortunate creature plummeting down. One hopes the pony was merely shaken, but the fate of the animal is unknown.

Grinding at Silverstone came to a halt around the turn of the century. Although disused it remained complete until 1904

when miller Thomas Winkles purchased the four sails for his tower mill at Wootton. In the meantime, Silverstone mill was left to the mercy of the elements. Some time later it was gutted with the exception of the upper machinery, including the windshaft. The cap deteriorated to such an extent that by the 1930s only some framing remained, and it was in this condition that Stanley Freese photographed it in July 1934 and Karl Wood sketched it in April 1939.

Just over a year later the whole country was gripped by war fever, and the fear of German seaborne and airborne landings. Newly formed Home Guard units commandeered weapons, vehicles and buildings in an effort to be ready to repel the potential invaders. Naturally, tall buildings were highly valued as observation posts, and Silverstone mill was earmarked to be used as such. To fit in with defenders' plans the windshaft had to be removed; then the headframe, complete with fan cradle, was rigged up to a tractor and dragged from the tower. Inside, a rickety wooden ladder fixed to the eastern wall led to the dust floor where a makeshift shelter had been constructed for the men on watch. The platoon, under the command of a lieutenant who lived locally, formed part of the 13th Battalion (Towcester District) Home Guard who took responsibility for the security of Silverstone aerodrome.

(from "Windmills of Northamptonshire", ISBN 0 9518557 0 0, by kind permission of the author Trevor L. Stainwright.)

Farming in the 1990s

If you, like a large portion of the village, have been born and bred in a town, it is difficult to appreciate the hard work, long hours and effort that goes into producing the food we all eat. A two mile circle around the village encloses a very mixed bag of farming enterprises.

The north-west side is mainly forest with small green fields dotted between different woods. On the Abthorpe Road we have two very modern chicken farms of a large broiler chicken empire with its headquarters at Brackley. Before the chickens become 'oven-ready' in the supermarkets they have a very good life in centrally heated houses with a warm bed of wood-shavings and plenty of food and water.

Crossing the road we change from feathers to wool. Challock Farm has over 800 sheep which are housed in early winter and after lambing, are turned out to grass in the grass fields running down to the brook at the bottom of the playing field. Crossing over the brook and turning towards Towcester, we find the "milking-mile", made up of four dairy farms with another being built at present. All the dairy farms run large herds of Friesian cows with a total population of over 400. (One cow can produce a calf and over 1,000 gallons of milk each year!) The cows graze the fields during the summer but are housed in the winter - feeding on silage, brewers grains and sugar beet pulp for maximum milk production.

On the Whittlebury side of the A43 we have more sheep, beef cattle, and arable crops such as winter wheat and oil seed rape. The rape is harvested in July and sold for its oil content, for making margarine and other oil products.

Completing the circle we have a small pig unit near the race track. Stock from all the farms is sold at local markets at Banbury and Northampton, and milk is tankered to Luton daily. Some of the winter wheat goes to the local flour mill at Bugbrooke. In comparison to other areas, Silverstone parish is well farmed and very productive.

George McNeil

Blackmires Farm and Silverstone Riding School

The farm is about 250 acres (100 hectares) of permanent pasture and is situated between Bucknell and Hazelborough Woods. It is heavy clay loam which is tender and wet in the winter but grows good crops and large quantities of grass.

We moved here in December 1986, but the family has been connected with the area for many generations. My grandparents, Jack and Lily Jeffrey, kept the Chequers pub in West End before moving to Stocks Hill. My mother played in the fields and woods and often spoke of Bill Badger who lived in an old house which, sadly, was pulled down in the 1950s. He was, I believe, a forestry worker. The house was replaced by our present home.

Although the farm is very productive, carrying 500 ewes and 70 suckler cows, in the present economic circumstances it is barely viable. My wife and daughter run a children s riding school with 25 ponies on the farm, which is of great importance to the economics of the place.

D.F. Wesley, 1999

Silverstone Riding School.

We moved the Riding School from Pury Hill, (having previously been at Paulerspury and Heathencote) on a Sunday afternoon in August 1990 after the riders, helpers and pupils rode most of the ponies up to the A5, through Paulerspury, to Whittlebury, across the A43, into Silverstone, and thence to Blackmires Farm. The move went very smoothly.

We are now in our twenty-first year. We are a Children's Riding School. The youngest children at the moment are two years old, and I have excellent boys and girls who help me with the tiny children. We ride in the evenings and Saturday and Sunday mornings. We are only part time, but in the holidays we have extra days: fun days, pony care, gymkhanas, jumping, picnic rides.

We also play Polocross and we hope to

hold competitions in the Summer with other riding schools in the area. We also have a Riding for the Disabled (RDA) group which runs on Monday evenings from April to October and we are always grateful for offers of help. We hold a barbecue in the Summer for them and a Christmas Party, which are enjoyed by all.

Silverstone Riding School.

The Mencap Holiday Scheme bring their children in the Summer and my helpers give up their time to give the children a happy time, riding and playing games. They come for two afternoons.

We are ideally situated for a riding school. The farm is all grass, and the bridle paths lead into Bucknell Woods and over to Abthorpe and the Wappenham Road.

Proprietors Mrs J.A. Wesley and Miss S.M.A. Wesley.

The History of Home Farm Silverstone from 1934

In 1934 Herbert Penn, always known as Bert, his wife and two children Peggy and Bill, came to Silverstone to rent Home Farm from Mr. William Treadwell, who still lived in the farm house at 32 High Street, but had retired from farming.

At the beginning of this century Home Farm was known as the Manor of Silston, otherwise Silverston Burnham, and according to the deeds, there is still

reference to the Manor in 1919.

The Penns lived at 14 High Street. The farm was a mixed farm with a small acreage of arable land, the rest being grazing land for a small dairy herd of Shorthorn and Friesian cows. The farm was only small and divided into two halves: 45 acres in the centre of the village, bounded by Green Lane, Cattle End and West End road and extending as far as the Pyghtle path; the other half was on the right hand side of Winter Hills Lane and comprised six small fields extending to 42 acres.

In the years before the Second World War farmers worked very hard for long hours and very little financial return. In order to supplement the farm income, a milk delivery round was started in Silverstone and later extended to Abthorpe.

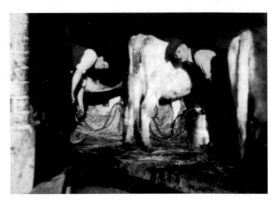

Milking at Home Farm.

Initially this was carried out by a horse called Charlie pulling a milk float. The milk came from the cows which were milked by hand in two cow sheds adjacent to Green Lane. The milk had to be strained and cooled before it was sold. In the 1930s the churns of milk were taken round the village in the milk float, the milk was transferred into a measuring bucket, which was taken to the house door and the milk was measured with a half pint or one pint measure into the housewife's jug. Later the milk was not allowed to be sold direct from the farm, but was collected by the Milk

Marketing Board and taken to a depot to be pasteurised. The Dairyman had to buy in pasteurised milk for retailing.

In the late 1930s a third of a pint of milk was provided to every school child at morning break. The small glass bottle had a cardboard cap with a hole for a drinking straw. At home I remember the filling of these bottles by hand as a very time consuming job, and often my brother and I had to give a hand. At about the same time glass bottles were introduced for the daily milk delivery to every house. These also had to be filled by hand and this was usually my mother's job, as there were no bottling machines in those days for the small dairyman. In 1935 my father bought a brand new Austin 7 van, which speeded up the milk delivery, especially to Abthorpe. A great deal of time was spent on milk production and distribution with other jobs such as looking after the pigs, sheep and poultry, being fitted in around the milking times at 6.30 a.m. and 4.30 p.m.

During the war Silverstone was home to the King's Royal Rifles, who were billeted in Kingsley Road in unoccupied houses built just before the war and requisitioned by the Army. My father supplied milk in bulk to the soldiers there. Also during the war the Silverstone aerodrome was built, and my father had a contract with the Air Ministry to supply milk to the RAF messes which were situated in Hazelborough Wood. By now the milk delivery had become such a big job, my father was unable to cope on his own. The late Marjorie Cracknell (née Dunkley) had worked for my parents in the house, but that was not considered essential war work, so for the duration of the war, Marjorie delivered milk in the village with Charlie and the milk float.

During the war the farm work had to continue, as it was essential to the war effort, and a percentage of every farm had to be ploughed to produce food, mainly cereals and potatoes. In 1941 my father bought his first tractor, a Fordson. This

pulled the plough and towed the binder which cut the corn and tied it into sheaves. There were no combine harvesters in those days, and the sheaves had to be stacked by hand to form stooks which were left to dry in the field for 2-3 weeks. When dry, the sheaves were carted and stacked in a rick where they stayed until the threshing machinery arrived to thresh the corn from the ears. It was an exciting time on the farm, when the threshing tackle arrived and extra hands were needed to help.

When my brother left school in 1945, he went to Moulton Agricultural College to take a one-year course in General Farming and afterwards came back home to farm with my father. At about this time Mr Treadwell and his sister Elizabeth, who lived with him in the farmhouse, died. The farm was put up for sale on 28th February 1946 and my father bought it. In 1961 my husband Peter Sturges came to help my father run the farm and we moved into the farm house, which was quite large enough for my parents and us to live there comfortably. The farming continued to flourish as a mixed farm, centred round the small dairy herd until 1969, when my father, at the age of 70, was ready to retire. At this time the Winter Hills part of the farm was sold to Silverstone Circuits Ltd. The Home Farm land was retained and let out to local farmers as grazing land, and my husband left the farm to work elsewhere. The two families continued to live at Home farm until my father died in February 1980.

Peggy Sturges, 1999.

Shacks Barn Farm

The County Council bought the 96 acres of Shacks Barn Farm in 1921 for £3724, adding a further 25 acres in 1990. Shacks Barn Cottage in Tinkers Lane, Little London was the original farmhouse, the present one just off the A43 being built in 1973/4. The present owner, Mr Andrew Kitchin arrived in

September 1985, eventually buying the farm in March 1998. The farm stretches along the eastern side of the A43 from just short of the Whittlebury turn (A413) to the gardens of the houses at the northern end of Kingsley Road. Its furthest boundary from the A43 is about 500 yards away. The farm got its name from the old barn down in the dip near the stream and narrow road bridge, which belonged at one time to a Mr Shackleton.

Shacks Barn Farm is a dairy farm with 120 cows, which take three hours to milk in the morning and two and a half hours in the afternoon. 50 acres of maize are also grown for fodder, although this has to be supplemented by other feed stuffs to give the cattle a balanced diet.

The calves are sold, heifer calves fetching £10 to £15 now in 1998/9, as against £60 to £80 eighteen months earlier. With bull calves the situation is even worse: they fetch now only £60 to £90, while eighteen months earlier they sold for £150 to £200. In winter the pastures are given over to sheep. Not a lot happens to disrupt the routines of the Kitchins. In summer they have to lock their gates to stop frustrated drivers pulling off the road and into the farm to picnic, while the rest of the time they are the first port of call for motorists seeking help in an emergency, regrettably all too frequently in the past on this notoriously dangerous stretch of road, although with the advent of mobile phones, these requests for aid have decreased. Because the farm lies relatively high, the biggest hazards are low flying aircraft, especially the big double-rotor Chinook helicopters which can cause the cattle to stampede and injure themselves on fences and hedges.

Pits Farm

Pits Farm is situated about a mile from the village centre to the north, bounded by the A43. It is approached by a concrete drive leading to the farmstead in the middle of the fields, overlooking the Silverstone Brook Valley, Bucknells Wood and Handley Park. There are still many mature oak trees, a remnant of the royal forest, the elm trees having had to be felled in 1979 due to Dutch Elm disease, although one remains - a fine specimen. The church spire is visible from the farmstead, and we can hear the bells ringing and the clock striking. We also hear the sounds of the village playing field, which carry along the brook. There is much wildlife - herons, foxes, snipe, woodpeckers, jays, hares and game birds.

Originally part of the Whittlebury estate, the land was divided up when sold around 1919, and bought by Northamptonshire County Council and farmed by various Silverstone men, latterly Mr Owen Betts and Mr Fred Whitlock. After Mr Whitlock retired in 1974, the land was developed into an intensive dairy holding, and a house and buildings added, and called Pits Farm.

We moved to the farm in October 1974 and our two sons Rupert and Tim were born soon afterwards. We established the Silson herd of Pedigree Friesians, with a nucleus of twenty in-calf heifers, which we built up to a herd of eighty cows. Milk was collected each day by the Milk Marketing Board tanker. All heifer calves born were retained for the herd, and bull calves sold at Banbury Market, sadly now closed (1998). Two cuts of grass silage were made each year, and we grew maize, one of the first farms in the locality to do so.

In 1995 we purchased the farm and the farming policy was changed. We now have a Beef Suckler Herd and arable production. Since then there have been many setbacks in the farming world, not least of all the BSE crisis which banned all exports and led to difficult times for farmers.

We have always tried to include the farm in the activities of village life. From 1981-88 the Infants School spent a day at the farm each May taking part in activities and learning all about nature and real farming. The Guides and Scouts camped. The church held various events including the Annual Bonfire Party.

It is essentially a family farm and a way of life, and we are fortunate to be living here, and that our two sons have grown up sharing the exploration and freedom with many friends from the village

Peter, Heather, Rupert and Tim Coles.

Rookery Farm and New Rookery Farm

The Hintons moved into Rookery Farm, which lies to the North of Church Street, in 1952. The farm at that time comprised 75 acres with 12 milk cows, 100 ewes to lamb and 20 acres of corn. In 1974/5 Rookery Farm was amalgamated with the aid of the EEC (now the European Union) Amalgamation Fund with half of some County Council owned land to the north, about 30 acres, which at that time was rented by the Linnell family. This became in 1977 New Rookery Farm under David King, for whom the new farmhouse and outbuildings were built. At the same time the Hinton family bought the Rookery Farm farmhouse, which dates from 1659, together with its outbuildings. In the 1930s/40s Phil Hinton's uncle, Aubrey Webb, shared the farmhouse with another family. In the 1950s and early 1960s Jimmy Brown, who founded and developed the motor racing circuit lived there.

At New Rookery Farm, established in 1977, things were not easy because of the mid-70s drought. Grass leys were sown, but most failed, some taking two resowings before becoming established. Herd numbers were increased each year, until milk quotas were introduced in 1983/4. In 1986 David King decided to retail their own milk, firstly unpasteurised, then all pasteurised, delivering to Northampton and then local villages, trading as Silverking Dairies.

In March 1997, however, milk production was stopped, with the emphasis now on the growing of wheat and forage maize and the grazing of young stock. In 1998 permission was gained to convert redundant farm buildings into office and light industrial units.

TIMBER!

Ken Linnell recalls that in the 1930s the Forestry Commission employed around 30 people in Hazelborough and Bucknells woods, their main activities being thinning growing timber, producing posts, stakes, binders, pea & bean sticks, rustic work, faggots for heating ovens (for bread baking etc), and firewood. They were also, of course, responsible for general maintenance of tracks and drainage ditches, and the replanting of cleared areas.

Still more would be employed on piece work, making gates, hurdles, splitting cleft rails, clearing parts of growing woods to produce stakes and binders, pea and bean sticks, faggots, small ash poles for rails and hurdles, and birch for jumps. The actual felling of mature timber was not done by the Forestry's own employees, because they did not have the heavy equipment needed for that. Instead "stands" of timber would be sold to the trade, usually by auction, and the felling and removal would be organised or undertaken by the buyer. Sometimes the buyer would be an entrepreneur with no facilities at all, but with a buyer for the finished timber already lined up. He would then negotiate with one or more of the local yards to do the actual work. In the forest itself and on the roads the hauling of felled timber was usually done with heavy horses such as Shires or Suffolk Punches, whereas in the closer confines of the timberyards, the smaller but equally sturdy Welsh or English Cobs were popular.

Around 23 years ago (1977), when first I moved to Silverstone, timber and various timber related trades still provided the backbone of the village's economy, alongside livestock farming and the, by then, burgeoning motor racing industry. At every turn and in every small corner there seemed to be a timber yard of one sort or another, large or small. Today there are very few such businesses left. Whereas now our weekend lie-ins are interrupted by the scream of racing car engines being put through their paces at the circuit, only 25 years ago it was more often the whine and

day decided to re-classify timberyards as "industrial", rather than "agricultural" businesses (which latter they had always in the past been). This was part of a programme of regulatory harmonisation with other EEC countries, soon after the UK's accession to that organisation.

One of the first people in the Silverstone area to spot the significance of this change was David Varney, inheritor of a

Linnells Bros timber-yard in 1999, when still processing raw timber.

grind of massive sawbenches which interrupted our early morning slumbers. Those are all silent now, but one way or another Silverstone was never a very quiet spot!

Most of those timberyards, some of them centuries old family businesses, have now been turned into housing developments of one kind or another.

The floodgates for this process were effectively opened in the 1970s, when, in their infinite wisdom, the government of the

fairly large timberyard at the upper end of West End. He realised that applying for planning permission to develop what was now an industrial site into a housing development was a "Planning Gain", whereas, if it had still been regarded as an agricultural site, it would have been a "Planning Loss".

Initially he applied for planning permission to develop the site for housing. This was denied by the local planning authorities. He went to appeal, employing an expert QC to support his argument, and in due course won the case on the basis that the refusal of what amounted to a Planning Gain was unreasonable and against the principles of EEC Law.

Thus started the disappearance of many timber-based businesses, some of which had existed for many hundreds of years, but were already struggling to compete with cheaper imports of both soft and hard timbers. Most of them have since become housing developments, enabling their former owners to retire from an exhausting trade with some degree of comfort.

Before we are too old to remember them all, it might be of interest to take a brief walk around the village and recall

Mr Dunkley with a load of hurdles.

those sites where the village's heritage grew and thrived for so many centuries, most of them long before the arrival of the internal combustion engine. The numbers in

brackets refer to the places marked on the map.

Start at the White Horse pub in the centre of the village, and, having downed whatever fortifier you prefer for the coming pilgrimage, head up the High Street. At the first left hand bend, on your right is the Vicarage, adjacent to which and slightly back from the road was William West's general timberyard (1 on the map), where now stand houses.

A little farther on round the bend, on the left, is Murswell Lane. Go down there and on the left, just before the junction with the A43 main road was another yard (2), belonging to Sid (Sam) Webb who made hurdles and gates.

Turn right out of Murswell Lane onto the A43. Soon you will see on your right, near the top of the slope, the back entrance to the "daddy of them all" in size terms, Linnell Bros Ltd (3). Its front entrance is at the upper end of the High Street. Until very recently its massive steel girder crane dominated the skyline like Silverstone's answer to the Eiffel Tower (See plate 22). Yet even this giant among timber-yards has now found that processing raw timber is no longer an economical proposition. The mainstay of their business is, from now on, going to be the retailing of timber products, such as sheds, trelisses, fencing, and other value-added items.

Having reached the brow of the hill, with Linnell's yard and the top of the High Street on your right, carry on along the A43 main road and soon, on your left, is The Royal Oak Pub, and a few yards on, Mr Blencowe's (now Colin King's) old butcher's shop. Just past the shop and a small cottage is an area of rough ground which was once George West's general timber yard (4). Immediately opposite that, on the right of the road, was another general timber yard (5), W.& S.Hutchings, processing raw timber from the local forest.

Press on up the A43 and at the top of the hill on the right is Cattle End. Down there

The 1900 Ordnance Survey map marked with the timber businesses described, based on information provided by Joe da Casa, Ken Linnell and Robin Berkshire.

was, after a couple of hundred yards or so, another small old yard on the left (6), run by the Varney brothers, Ron and Jack. Their speciality was cut firewood, large logs for open fires, smaller cuts for woodstoves etc, and kindling for anyone who needed it.

When I first knew them they ran an ancient pickup truck for deliveries, but, not so long before, it had all been done with a horse-drawn cart. A few more paces and, still on the left, was Harry Hutchings yard (7), producing hurdles and rails. Next, in what used to be Sid Kingston's small bus depot, is Silverstone's newest timber based business, set up here only 10 years ago, Steven Taylor's joinery and finishing workshop (8). No tree felling for him, but it connects with the village's tradition. Near the bottom of Cattle End, on the right, is a small close of modern houses (9). This also was formerly a timber yard belonging to Dunkley Bros, producing firewood, hurdles and rails.

Return now to the A43, turn right out of Cattle End, and, having passed the Dadford Road junction on the left, approach the right hand turn into West End. On the corner, on the right hand side of the main road was Ron Hutchings yard (10). Ron was a specialist hurdle-maker and horse racecourse jump builder, though he also produced fencing materials and rails if you wanted. There are several sheep farmers known to me still using Ron's hurdles as partitions in lambing sheds or as reinforcing sections in field hedges or fences at least thirty years since they were originally made. Opposite Ron Hutchings's, on the left side of the A43 was Lovell and Dicks yard (11) which specialised in firewood.

Now turn right off the A43 into West End. After a few hundred yards and approaching a narrow high-banked section, on the right is an old track known as The Ridings. Somewhere down there, though nobody now seems to remember exactly where, was Old Shack's timberyard (12) mainly occupied with hurdle-making. Doll Picketts recalls in her West End memories elsewhere in this book, that Old Shacks and his wife died within two days of each other, and were taken to their funeral on a timber wagon. Carry on down West End and you will come to the built up part of that road. On the left is a housing close called Monkswood (13). Before development this was a very old timber yard belonging to the Mayo family (G.& T.A.Mayo). Ron Mayo, the last owner, was one of the first Silsoners who befriended me when I came to live in the village. There was an enormous old

Steve Taylor at his workshop, 1999. The doorway was hinged at the top by the previous occupant so that the bus, too high for the normal entrance, could be garaged here.

sawdust heap in the back of the yard, to which I was invited to help myself if I wanted "some good black stuff to lighten up my garden soil", and poplar planks galore were cheaply forthcoming to line my attic floor. Ron had in fact been born in my house, 51 West End, some eighty years before, and it was he who told me that there was a live well hidden under the kitchen floor.

Almost directly opposite Mayo's timber yard, on the right side of West End (14), was Varney's Yard, the David Varney mentioned above. This was a bigger set-up, occupying the ground which is now known as Hazelwood, another housing estate, and it combined a timber saw yard with a heavy transport business. It was one of the first yards in the area to have a timber preserving tunnel and thus attracted a lot of heavy transports carrying bulk timber for chemical pressure treatment from well outside the immediate catchment area. This heavy traffic was not enormously popular with the locals, bearing in mind that, at that time, West End was still a very narrow backwater.

Carry on down West End until you come to Blackmires Lane on the left. Just up the lane, on the left, was another Varney yard making hurdles (15). This was taken over by the man, Bill Badger, who married the boss's daughter. Immediately past that stands the former pub known as The Chequers. In the ground just beyond the pub, and also owned by the same family as the pub, was Norman Smith's yard (16), now occupied by two red brick houses. His speciality was gate-making and very good sturdy gates he made too. There are many of Norman's gates still hanging in the village and none the worse for wear. His small yard, like so many others, has since been redeveloped for housing, but his son Paul still lives on one part of it at the back of the site, in a traditionally constructed local stone house which he built for himself in the 1990s.

Towards the bottom end of West End, and opposite Coronation Terrace (originally a 1930s council house row) is a small housing close called The Willows. Beyond it is a wooded area now known as Brickle Pocket Park. This was formerly a brickyard, and clay for brick-making was dug from the rear part of it, creating the pond which has now been adapted as a leisure amenity and wildlife sanctuary. On one corner of this area, overlapping with The Willows was W.Whitlock & Sons, Timber Merchants (17). Having reached the end of West End, turn right up Puddledock, and into Church Street at the top of the slope. No timberyards on this stretch, for, as its name implies, it was almost always too wet. But once in the village square, Stocks Hill, turn left past Matthew Croft Stores, down the dip, and enter Little London.

At the beginning of Little London, to the right, and behind a stout stone wall, is the Doctors' surgery. Dr Newton, now retired, records in his account of the building of that surgery, that a deep sawpit and the footings for a (probably steam-powered) saw bench were found during the groundwork preparations for the building. Ken Linnell confirms that this was the remains of an old yard (18) called Lovell & Son.

Onwards up Little London. Towards the

top of the slope, on the left and opposite the entrance to Hillside Avenue is a block of flats called Whitmore Court. They stand on what was formerly a general timber yard (19) run by Vic Lovell. Vic is one of an old family of sawyers, fellers and timber converters. Among other items he made stout farm gates of which I have two, and treated timbers for the building trade. He did not own the ground but rented it from the landowner. Sadly the land was sold by the owner for redevelopment only a few years after he had established himself there, and he had to move out. A little farther on, and still on the left is what is now a motor repair yard. This (20) used to be another timber business, Whitmore's timber merchants.

At the top end of Little London, facing the Kingsley Road housing esate, turn right along the A43 main road towards Brackley. This section of road is, from here to the Winter Hills junction at the top of the High Street a 1930s constructed Silverstone bypass. A few hundred yards along this section is the road crossing with the Whittlebury road, leading back on the right towards Stocks Hill. Down this stretch on the right and standing well back from the road, was Ted Harper's joinery workshop (21), now redeveloped as a small block of flats. Ted was a skilled craftsman and cabinet-maker, and had an excellent line in hand made pine kitchen units and cupboard doors. Outside the workshop there were always large stacks of seasoning cut timber, so his finished doors never cracked or warped. I can vouch for it for I have twelve of them in my own house. Ted is now retired and lives in Towcester.

Well past Ted Harper's place, on the left side, and occupying ground which is now a part of The White Horse pub car park was yet another yard (22), this one belonging to Sid Webb, uncle of the Sid Webb in Murswell Lane. He made firewood, split rails, and hurdles.

That marks the end of our tour, but

since you are now in its car park, what better moment for a quick restorative at The White Horse following your arduous walk? While there, go outside, strain your ears and, if you faintly hear the unmistakeable falling whine of a heavy timber sawbench, I'll lay you a pound to a penny that it's either the drink, or yet another of Silverstone's many ghosts.

Joe da Casa, with invaluable help from Ken Linnell, June 2000.

OLD OAK GOES TO WHITTLEBURY

A fine piece of Silverstone oak was the timber that David Hinton selected to make a cross for the east wall of the newly renovated chapel at Whittlebury.

His father, in charge of the renovation work, gave the task of making the cross to David who, though only fifteen, is a capable wood-worker with a fair bit of experience. He spent some days of his summer holiday making the cross. Now finished, the cross stands 3 foot high, and 2 foot wide, of plain oak, sanded and wax polished.

Though small, the Whittlebury Chapel is a historic one, containing the actual pulpit from which Charles Wesley preached. The people of Whittlebury raised several thousand pounds for the renovations, and David's cross is a fine contribution to the chapel.

News & Views, December 1979

A SILVERSTONE SHOPPING BASKET

Here is a 1930 version of a shopping trip. Or how would you like an evening out for two for 50p (10/-, or ten shillings)? The bus fare to Northampton was 2/6 (two shillings and sixpence) each, cinema 1/6 (one and six), a ¼lb. box of chocolates was 1/3 (one and three) and 10 Players only 6d (about 2 ½p). All that still left a little change from a ten

shilling (50p) note. That, of course, was only about 50 years ago. The bus was a converted World War 1 ambulance run by Mr. Kingston of Cattle End, and very reliable it was too. Groceries for the family were cheap compared with today, best Cheddar cheese 8d (eightpence) a pound (lb), local dairy butter 1/4 to 1/6 per lb. Cake making was reasonable with margarine at 6½d (sixpence hayp'ny or half-penny) per lb and if you fancied a treat for tea, a tin of best John West Salmon at 9½d or a tin of pineapple chunks at 4½d filled the bill very well. Other prices which make one wonder today were: lard at 4½d per lb, sugar 5d for 2lb, jellies at 4½d each, tea 6d to 9d the ¼lb, washing soap 6½d per lb, Saxa salt 2½d, and 1 cwt of potatoes cost 4/6 to 5/-. A gallon of paraffin would cost 8d or 9d and most households bought it as oil lamps were the only lamps we had than. Many people then kept a pig or two in the sty, and the cost of feeding meal was about 6/6d. If they required a finishing meal, that cost 7/6 to 8/- for barley meal. Dances were often held in the Church School up Green Lane, and a man's suit could be bought for those for £2/10/-, a good shirt was 5/6, a tie 1/6 and shoes 8/6. Do these prices make you wish for the old days? It all seems a long way off now but, I think, generally things are much better today. The average wage then in Silverstone was only £1/10/- to £2, and even at these prices there wasn't much money to spare for non-essentials. After-thought!! Marriage licences and dog licences were the same price 7/6 (37½p). There must be a moral there somewhere!

J.L.Potter, News & Views, 1979.

POCKET PARKS

Silverstone is fortunate in having two pocket parks, owned by the Parish Council and maintained as wildlife areas for use by the community for peaceful recreation and as a resource for education.

Olney Meadow is nearly four acres (1.5 hectares) in size. It was formerly part of Hutchings' Timber Yard which was situated opposite the Royal Oak. Most of the yard and the stables, where the yard's Shire horses were kept, are now the new part of Stewart Drive, while on another part of the meadow the Hutchings built in 1939 the two dwellings of Olney Close. About halfway down Green Lane, Hutchings Manger would have been found, supposedly haunted by a ghost.

The meadow is undulating and mainly covered by grass. The dominant grasses are cocksfoot, rough meadow grass, false oat grass, tufted hair grass, crested dogs tail and sweet vernal grass. In 1994 a plant survey recorded about ninety different plants within the grass sward including ladies bedstraw, great burnet, meadow cranesbill, pignut and, a rarity for Northamptonshire, meadow saxifrage.

The hedge on the western boundary along Green Lane was laid early in 1994, as it had become overgrown, although it still displayed the characteristics of a traditionally laid hedge. It is quite rich in tree/shrub species including blackthorn, field maple, hawthorn, ash, elder, hazel and elm. The Eastern hedge which follows the back garden borders of Stewart Drive was planted during 1993/94 with hawthorn, field maple, hazel and ash. In 1992/93/94 two areas were planted with oak, ash, hazel and field maple, some along the Western boundary, while four cherry trees were planted at strategic points. The site was formerly grazed by domestic stock, which would have maintained a grass-dominated site. When grazing ceased, scrub began to encroach, with bramble and blackthorn dominating some areas and individual specimens of hawthorn, goat willow, oak and ash scattered everywhere. The area is maintained by cutting twice a year, in the spring and late summer, which prevents rank grass growth and restricts the spread of scrub. The removal of cuttings protects finer grasses, herbs and wild flowers. A small pond has been created as an additional wildlife habitat. It is fed by the open ditch running along the Northern boundary. A dipping platform is provided, allowing easy and safe sampling of pond life. Water plantain, milfoil, starwort, iris and rush have been introduced and although the water level drops significantly in long dry spells, the pond is full of frogspawn each spring. Vegetation on the hedge side is allowed to grow tall to provide cover for amphibians emerging from the water. As flooding has been a problem, a balancing meadow has been established with culverts on its Northern and Southern sides, through which drainage water flows to the ditch.

Brickle, formerly a brick pit, occupies 1.25 acres (0.5 hectares) at the Northern end of West End on the East side of the road. Clay was dug for about 60 years until 1900. Part of the site was then used as a timber yard until about 1960 and later developed for housing. The remainder was used as a tip for hard-core and soil up to the early 1980s when the site was fenced off for safety. Brickle is predominantly woodland with a number of mature trees, mostly willow, ash and field maple. The hedges on Puddledock (now often called Church Street) and West End were newly planted with hawthorn in the early 80s. The hedge on the Southern boundary is ancient, with bare places and gaps. Otherwise the site is covered with bramble, nettle and snowberry, except in the North-West corner which is poorly drained and supports marsh plants. Muntjac deer and foxes are regular visitors, as are blackbirds, thrushes and tits. Summer visitors include tree creepers and willow warblers. The pond is lifeless owing to lack of oxygen. Tests show no pollution, despite the site's history as a tip, and frogs, toads and great crested newts have been seen.

6 June 2000

GOODBYE TO THE BANK

After at least seventy years in Silverstone, the National Westminster bank will be closing its tills for the last time on December 19th. The once-a-week agency was first sited in Mr Ashley Clarke's premises on Stocks Hill (now Croft's) and was a sub-branch of the National Provincial Bank in Towcester. When Mr Clarke sold his shop and bakery to Mr Titcomb, he moved the agency to his cottage next to the church (now Burrell's). The Friday morning comings-and-goings were watched over by him, and later by Mr and Mrs Crossland. Many villagers will recall transacting their business over a rickety card table in the sitting-room, while the 'security guard' stood by in the hall. When Harrowell cottage was sold, following the deaths of the Crosslands, the bank, by now National Westminster, transferred to the Church Room kitchen and eventually a proper counter and modern security screen were erected. Recently 'Bank day' changed to Wednesday.

Now this long established facility in the village is to be ended, as part of the bank's rationalisation of its operations. It will be difficult for some of its customers to conduct their financial affairs, without transport to Towcester and back, unless they can find some other means of banking. Perhaps we should count ourselves lucky that the service continued for so long.

News & Views, December 1990

WEST END VIEWS

From her sitting room window in West End, Mrs Doll Picketts has a view of a strikingly beautiful pine tree. It has been there as far back as she can remember, and her memories of West End stretch back nearly three quarters of a century . Though the tree remains, much else has changed. The buildings that once clustered around the pine tree have vanished, as have many others, and new houses replace old terraces of cottages and the timber yards.

Imagine, if you will, a grassy riding, rutted with cart tracks, and shaded by huge elm trees. The traffic was horse- drawn, so it was safe for long-skirted, buttoned booted toddlers to play in the 'road' or run errands to neighbours. In winter, not so idyllic, as the lane became churned and muddy. The older children, with boots and pinafores, made their way up the Pyghtle and Green Lane, no fun in winter rain and snow drifts, to reach their schools. Later the road was surfaced, so the errands to and from wells and allotments, was easier going. The road sweeper lived at the bottom of West End, so it was swept almost daily. Later still, Coronation Row was built, with water piped from the springs and ponds of August Grounds. The field behind that was noted for great banks of ant-heaps, until mains water came to Silverstone.

A month before Mrs Picketts was born, a far-off September, 75 years ago, her home ceased to be the Woodman's Arms, leaving just the Chequers pub in West End. At that top end there were two timber yards, with stables, and carts. A huge pile of sawdust was a favourite spot to play. Grass snakes nested in there, and the children used to poke them out. Now two new housing developments stand on the timber yards' site. The fields sloping down the valley were often visited, for there was Blackwell, where water was fetched in heavy iron buckets when the house wells dried up, and Bufton, a field of allotments. After school children had to weed and lift potatoes, for the allotments were essential to help feed families. They must have hurried with their tasks when they heard the hooter that announced that the fair, on the fields behind the new Vicarage, had opened for the evening's fun.

Down a lane on the east side of West End, where today children gather blackberries, was old Shacks timber yard, where they made hurdles. Old Shacks and his wife died within two days of each other, and were taken together for burial on the timber wagon. The cottages of Mission Row, by Day's Orchard, have long since gone, and new houses have filled the gaps. Pyghtle Cottage was a shop, then an artist's studio, before it became a private house. Mrs Waite's grocery shop sold all the essentials, was a newsagency, and a carriers, with a horse and cart to take parcels to and from Northampton. The newspaper, delivered by bike, didn't arrive till lunch time. The pig sties have vanished from the gardens, and The Willows marks the site of yet another lost timber yard and brick yard.

The hard work of earlier days has almost vanished.

News & Views, February 1989

CATTLE END

Jack Roberts has lived in Silverstone all his life. He lived with his parents and two brothers in one of a row of three cottages in Cattle End, now demolished, and his Grandmother was next door. Jack can remember her sitting in her little cottage wearing a man's cloth cap, and taking snuff. As a child he was sent to the shop to get ½oz of snuff and ½ pint of beer for her. The beer was sold out of the barrel, and some of the women took the jug home discreetly under their aprons. She eventually moved to Banbury to a daughter's house and when she died aged eighty-three in 1936, Hintons the builders and undertakers brought her back to Silverstone and made the elm coffin and arranged the funeral, all for £9.16.6d. She had lost three sons in the First World War, and their names are on the War Memorial.

Rabbits were part of the economy, not just for the home pot. Ernie Colbourne had a carrier and coal business in Cattle End, and would pay 9d for a rabbit and maybe sell them for a shilling in Northampton. Jack's father and Sam Whitlock always had a walk up Buckingham Road on a Sunday morning and one day Harry Hutchings's dog followed them. He was a good rabbiter and they got two rabbits from one hole. They sold them to Harry but they didn't tell him that it was his dog that helped to catch them!

C.Hughes, News & Views, 1994.

Jim, Albert and Jack Roberts photographed at school in the 1930s. The Pyghtle is beyond. Albert died in World War II.

NURSES AND DOCTORS, 1945-1999

District Nurse

Gwen Cox is well known in the village for her work with Age Concern and other organisations. She was brought up on a farm in Leicestershire, the youngest of a large family. She was educated in small private schools, there were many such schools run by single ladies after the First World War. There was a lot of work to be done in the farmhouse, so she left school at 14. At 18 she left home to start training as a nurse. Nursing was one of the few opportunities for girls to leave home and gain independence. In those pre-NHS days the probationary nurse was poorly regarded and subject to strict discipline, and paid 26/- (£1.30) per month, rising to about £3.60 per month after 3 years.

There was another year in the same hospital in Derby to get the coveted Nurse's Badge. Nurse Cox was persuaded to take a midwifery course, although at that age she did not like babies. She changed her mind about babies after delivering 200.

The course in England took one year, but Scotland offered a 6 month training course, so she went to Edinburgh. She was paid nothing during her training, in fact she had to pay three pounds towards the cost of the lectures.

The nurses could sometimes get free theatre tickets, and nurse Cox developed a love for the theatre. She recalls seeing Peggy Ashcroft in `Rebecca' but did not like her performance!

On qualifying in July 1939 she was asked to stay on in Edinburgh as a Staff Nurse. Once the war had started and a baby boom was expected, midwives were in a "reserved" occupation and could not move to the other services, so she spent the war years in Scotland.

By December 1945 she felt like moving, and even then it was difficult to get a transfer. She joined the Colonial Nursing Service and she says the journey to East Africa is a story on its own. By flying boat, dressed in full wartime flying suit, with various stages and delays, she travelled from Cairo up the Nile to Khartoum.

She spent many years in East Africa where she met her husband Peter. There were many journeys to and from England, particularly when her son Howard was at boarding school. Many villagers will remember Nurse Cox's years of service to the area as District Nurse until her retirement, and her kindness to new mothers with grizzly babies, as well as to the elderly and infirm for whom she cared in their own homes.

She has many more stories to tell of a most interesting life.

Village GP

It is perhaps convenient that the National Health Service should have come into being only three years into the period covered by the memoirs of this particular family doctor. Up to that time medical care was covered by private care and a system for the less affluent, this tended to divide rural practices into those who catered for the gentry, the land owners and farmers and the tradesmen and those who catered for all others. Class was still distinct. One knew one's place. The practice I joined had its basis amongst those less blessed with the good things of life, and I am not sorry that this was the case.

In 1948 the NHS began and a schoolboy from Shropshire was conscripted into the Royal Army Medical Corps to become a Nursing Orderly in Hong Kong. He thus entered the NHS in its founding year. Eight years later he was released upon an unsuspecting public to learn his trade. After a spell in hospitals and four years in a New Town practice fate took the doctor and his embryo family to Silverstone to become a country doctor. It soon became clear that time had passed the area by. Much was done as it had been before the war. New Town style practices were totally different. Large, impersonal, manned by large groups of doctors, they catered for a young population that had no wish to be on friendly terms with their GP [General Practitioner]. Most were not even relating to their neighbours. How different was Silson, yet in some respects how similar. For it took several years of hunting and refusals from the planners before a site was found for a Silverstone village surgery.

In 1965 I joined Dr Hopkins as junior partner. There were historically two practices based in Towcester which were rivals. The population of the area was fairly stable in the mid sixties. There was thus some serious competition between the two practices, since NHS fees were on a per capita basis at that time. Each held a twice weekly surgery in Silverstone. Dr Guy Lewis would sit at The Parsonage in Whittlebury Road, the home of Torr the printers. We sat at the home of Mrs Alice Mayo (née Potter) at 62 High Street opposite the Top Shop. She was widowed before the war, he catching acute tonsillitis, which in pre-antibiotic days could be fatal. It was. Alice, for a very small fee, had for years provided the back room at 62 as waiting room, the best front parlour being the consulting room for the surgery. I inherited this situation. She would sit in the kitchen between rooms and run the sessions. Afterwards I would invariably be given tea with thin bread and butter and a bowl of tinned fruit salad; whilst Alice brought me up to date with the village news. Then I rushed back to Towcester with the prescriptions. At that time the prescriptions all went to the one chemist in Towcester, Philadelphus Jeyes. If they were there by 4pm the pharmacist would pack those destined for the villages and take them to the Towcester Post Office for sorting. The next morning the postman would deliver bottles and pill boxes at a penny or two pence each whilst on his round, no postage required, a wonderful system reflecting the will of all to service the disadvantaged villagers without a car. Too late back from the round risked missing the post for that evening. We rarely did. At about this time the first prescription charges were levied by the government of the day. We now had to collect money and carry change. The passing over of the scripts was accompanied by the handing over of piles of cash to the chemist, and later by the regular replacement of pocket linings by a dutiful wife.

In, I think, 1972, George Lovell sold me an area at the bottom of Whittlebury Road upon which to build a village surgery. Whilst digging out the footings I had come upon a wide brick culvert that proved to be the area that had been beneath the boiler of a large stationary steam engine, used to power the saw at Lovell's Yard. Adjacent were the remains of a saw pit. Two years after the surgery opened Ron Garner came from Jeyes Chemist in Towcester to be resident pharmacist. We had become a rural dispensing practice. This solved the increasingly difficult problem of getting medicines out to the village. With my spending less time at the new Towcester Health Centre, Dr Sonia Hamer began consulting with me in Silson. She continues to work with Dr Arif Supple, who took over from me in 1989 as a partner in what had become Drs Newton, Sanger and Wallace.

For twenty-two years up to June 1999 I had been fortunate in being entrusted with running the Sports Injuries Clinic at Northampton General Hospital. Fortunately Silson Joggers, which had been founded by me, Gerald Lovell (who has subsequently raised so much in funds for village projects) and John Denney in 1976, did not contribute to my work at NGH. It did, I am sure, contribute in a positive way to the health of those many Silson inhabitants who joined us at times in Bucknells Wood. On one night 107 villagers went jogging. Surely at that time we were in advance of any NHS schemes for the healthy life style.

At that time a wife was a co-partner and essential part of any country practice. At selection the wife was interviewed as closely as the doctor husband. Few single men became rural doctors. Practice duties in the sixties and seventies took over family life. In a two-handed practice one or other of the partners was always on call. At holiday time when one partner was away for the annual two week holiday the other did all surgeries, all regular visits and all emergency calls 24 hours a day for seventeen days. Fetching children from school and doing shopping presented problems, yet we survived. During that early period many of the villages had changed little, estates of executive style housing had yet to come. A request for a home visit to a villager was rarely an abuse of one's limited time. True villagers were supported by parents, relatives and friends. There was a wealth of good common sense and not a little sound knowledge available from round the corner. One's position in society was odd. By tradition the local doctor and vicar are excused the long period of probation to which others are subjected. This convention may come from the days when the pre-NHS doctor would be paid in kind, because many households had no cash to spare. In our case we were amply paid in kindness. This was particularly noticeable when families suffered what seemed an unfair loss. Rarely have I been as moved as when caring for and attending the service for Scott Osborne, a young Silson rascal whom we all loved. The Chapel was packed to overflowing and the village was united in its love for the departed child. Particularly we had noted the offer to share our loss when our own daughter, Victoria, died aged sixteen. She joined our infant son, Peter, who had died whilst we were in Towcester. It is only such support that enables one to keep going at these times.

The local village workplace had been the forest, the timber yard or the farm. Until Luffield Abbey Farm became a motor race track. This has brought with it some employment, just in time since the local timber industry has contracted. Whereas many of my older patients would present with deafness following years of exposure to the tunes of the saw, I anticipate that some of the younger generation may one day present with deafness due to the shriek of the racing engine.

At its modest start the Circuit had to be made to pay by farming the adjacent acres. Jimmy Brown, who did more than any other man to set the infant circuit on its feet, spent many hours working on the feed pellet machine. He was also midwife for the pigs which were destined to become Walls's sausages. During testing on weekdays there were accidents to which I was called. Also shortly after arriving in Silverstone I had become "Alpha 7" working with the County Ambulance service attending road traffic and other accidents in a voluntary capacity. In no time the post-surgery round involved carrying one mobile radio for Ambulance Control, and another from the circuit to whom I responded as "Silverstone 1". Many a house call would be abruptly curtailed as a result of an urgent radio call, the visit having to be completed later. However these radios became a blessing since they also enabled urgent calls to one's patients to be taken during a round. There were many occasions when a distant patient had hardly put the phone down before the doctor knocked at the front door.

During the seventies and eighties the village itself was growing, yet still contained a distinct nucleus of the old Silson families and of those newcomers who had absorbed the village spirit. With the decision to build a village sports hall in 1980 on the playing field, these folk came forth to provide for free their skills.

The family doctor of the period of this history had thus much of the residual best of old Silverstone to enjoy - a blessing diluted by time as the village became almost suburban. In fifty years methods of general practice changed, as patients' expectations changed. Treatments may be expected to change and become more effective, yet we must take care that something significant is not lost in this progress.

In a working lifetime in Silson this particular family doctor gained far more from his flock than he gave. The Boggys, Jacks, Harriets, Scotts and Floras of old Silson, I bless them all. I only hope that the next fifty years gives similar gain to the medical carers who follow on.

Dr Frank Newton

SILVERSTONE METHODIST CHURCH

Craftsmen from Willowbank Joinery of Buckingham check the new frames for the Chapel windows against the old ones, April 1999

Recent decades have brought many changes to the village, and many traditional features of community life have come under strain. The church is no longer the main provider of social activity for a significant section of the population, and fewer people attend services and events than used to be the case. Nonetheless, a busy programme of activities is still maintained. There are two services at the chapel each Sunday (10.45 am and 6.00 pm). The 1st Silverstone Boys' Brigade meets on Monday evenings, keeping up the tradition of one of the oldest B.B. companies in the county. Midweek meetings for church members and friends are provided through the Women's Guild (Tuesdays) and Wesley Guild (Thursdays). Occasions for special celebration in the Church Year are the Harvest Festival in September, Remembrance Sunday, Christmas and Easter.

Two important and beneficial changes have taken place in the last few years. In 1997 a major renovation programme was successfully carried out, marking the biggest alterations to the building in living memory. The main aim of the scheme was to make the chapel and its rooms more accessible and useful to the whole community, and this has been achieved, thanks to the encouragement and support of many people in Silverstone. Then, links between Methodists and Anglicans in the village have become much stronger, and we are working and learning together as we seek to serve the community. The Methodist Church has had a large place in Silverstone's past. It is intended to sustain that role in the present, and develop it for the future.

Reverend Dr Martin Wellings

The Women's Guild

The Women's Guild began in Silverstone in October 1935. The Rev. Jonathan Brown was minister at the Methodist Chapel at that time and he encouraged the women to begin a weekly meeting to share Christian fellowship and to study the Bible. Around 30 women plus children went to the first meeting and the Women's Guild was formed. Each week they sang hymns, prayed together, read the Bible and listened to speakers, and of course a chat was enjoyed over a cup of tea.

The group are very proud that at the time of writing one of their former members, Mrs May Hinton, has just celebrated her 104th birthday. She now lives in a Residential home in Newark and in 1994 the Guild went to visit her to share in her 100th birthday celebrations. They have a birthday secretary so that each member receives a card on her birthday and they usually arrange a Jumble Sale or Coffee Morning as a fund raising event during the year. The Guild always extend a warm welcome to anyone who comes to join in their meeting.

Judith Hodges

Silverstone Boys' Brigade: The First 70 years

The Boys' Brigade in Silverstone had its first meeting on December 16th, 1929. It was set up by the Minister the Rev. Lawton Lee with

strength of the company numbered 24 and ages ranged from 11-18 years.

Syd Hinton was soon to become Captain, a role he performed into his 80s. A typical Company week was organised as follows:

Monday - Drill for 1 hour or more then a tea to finish.

Tuesday - Physical Training for an hour or more.

Friday - Games Evening.

Saturday - Football.

Sunday Afternoons - Bible Class.

The first Silverstone Company camp was held at Cirencester in the summer of 1932 and continued to be held until the outbreak of World War II, during which Boys' Brigade continued to meet as usual. This was made a little more bearable through kind donations of rations of bread

The Boys' Brigade, 1964-65, with Syd Hinton seated, centre, with Arthur Payne on his left.

Sydney and Walt Hinton as Lieutenants and with help from the nearby Northampton Battalion, to which Silverstone would be attached for many years to come. The initial

and cheese which accompanied tea after parade evenings. After the war the Summer camps recommenced with Barmouth being a favourite venue. Syd always enjoyed these. They continued in some shape or form into the late 1980s and 90s, providing unforgettable memories for those who attended them.

During the late 1960s Syd Hinton began a junior section for boys aged 8-11 years. This was run by John and Elizabeth Whitehead, and later by Brian Dale and currently by Andy Payne. Into the 1970s the 1st Silverstone Company left the Northampton Battalion and, with other local companies, formed the South Northants Battalion, which provided competition in inter-company activities not experienced before.

In 1979 Silverstone Boys' Brigade celebrated 50 years in the village with a weekend of celebrations, which was attended by approximately 300 'Old Boys'. The inspection of the Company was made by the then National Boys' Brigade Secretary, Alfred Hudson. During these celebrations a presentation was made to Syd Hinton on his 50 years of service to the company and subsequent handing over of the role of Captain to Arthur Payne. [See Plates 27 and 29]

The Company over the years has produced many fine sporting teams, especially football and table tennis, the latter twice reaching the National Boys' Brigade finals. The company has gained 11 Duke of Edinburgh Gold Awards as well as Silver and Bronze awards. The Gold Award holders on three separate occasions, accompanied by Syd Hinton and their families, travelled to Buckingham Palace to be presented with their awards by HRH Prince Philip the Duke of Edinburgh.

The Gold Award holders were: Graham Blackwell, Terry Blackwell, Nigel Booth, Ronald Dunkley, Hugh Kiddell, Andy Payne, Shaun Rush, Stuart Shepard, Robert Swinford, John Travill, and Steve West. The achievements over the years are due to the efforts of Syd Hinton and officers like Jeff Billingham, Richard Harris, Arthur Payne and Fred Pollard, to mention just a few, all committed to encouraging boys to take part in activities associated with the Brigade. Today the Brigade meet weekly on a Monday evening. Though they are small in number compared with previous years the boys are keen and that makes for an enjoyable evening. This year (1999) will mark 70 years of Boys' Brigade in Silverstone.

Andy Payne.

John James Remembers

I, like tens of other boys at Silverstone, became a member of Silverstone Boys' Brigade, when I was ten years old, in fact my dad Sonny James was the first person enrolled in the Silverstone Boys' Brigade.

In my day we usually met three nights a week, for drill parade, activities, and games night on Fridays. The latter was my favourite and although by today's standards the activities were commonplace, table tennis, snooker (on a one eighth size table), boxing, 5-a-side football with a tennis ball etc., it provided us all with most things. The climax to our year was to go on "camp". For £3.10s (£3.50) and ration books (remember the 2nd World War hadn't long finished) we had 17 days in such places as Preston (near Weymouth), Barmouth and Budleigh Salterton. All our gear was packed in a ruck sack and we usually set off by bus from Chapel Hill with many weeping mothers waving us "bon voyage". My mother was only "allowed" to wave from the Oak window, so that I wouldn't be known as a sissy.

We usually had four bell tents, three for the battalion and the fourth for Syd and his provisions. With some 15-20 boys aged from 11 to 16, you can imagine the food required to sustain us. The thing that survives in the memory is marvellous sunny days with freedom to do as we liked. This was not to say a watchful eye was not kept on us and of course our stomachs dictated returning to base, but we'd go swimming in the sea all day interrupted by games of football and cricket on the beach. The tent could be a little cramped with only a ground sheet to lie on (we hammered the ground with a mallet to level it) and our kit bags for pillows. Six to seven lads slept with feet to the tent pole and all our clothes draped on the same. It was fatal to sleep near the exit-flap, because if anyone wanted to get out at night for the obvious, then there was every chance of being trampled on. Poor John Mayo usually drew the short straw and ended up in this unenviable position.

SAINT MICHAEL AND ALL ANGELS' CHURCH

St Michael's Church, in the centre of the village, dominating Stocks Hill, and surrounded by the churchyard and burial ground for the village, was dedicated in 1884, built on the site of the former church (see Part 3). The church has witnessed the comings and goings of many generations of Silverstone families - baptisms, weddings, funerals. Adjoining the church are the Church Rooms, formerly the National or Church school, and now used for social events and village activities.

Until 1982 St. Michael's was part of the benefice of Whittlebury with Silverstone, with the vicarage being in Whittlebury. In 1983 the Whittlebury Vicarage was sold and a new vicarage was built in the High Street at Silverstone. St Michael's became part of the Benefice of Silverstone, Abthorpe and Slapton, the Rev. D. G. Bond being the first incumbent of the new benefice and vicarage.

Services are held at St Michael's each Sunday - over the years there have been changes to the pattern of worship; until the early 1960's Holy Communion was celebrated at 8am and Evensong at 6pm each Sunday. Now we have Parish Communion at 9am or 11am alternate Sundays. Evensong is held on the third

Sunday at 6pm. Joint benefits service is held on the fifth Sunday. An "All Age Worship Service" without Holy Communion is being introduced for one Sunday each month. Since about 1985, an Open Air Service has been held in Bucknells wood in June each year. Harvest Festival Evensong was always held at the time of the Silverstone Feast in October, the church was packed, chairs having to be brought in from the Church Rooms. This has sadly declined with changing times. The Junior School and Infants take part in special services during the year.

The Sunday School was revived in the early 1950s by Mr and Mrs W.R.Jones, Mr Jones being the Headmaster of the C. of E. Junior School, and held each Sunday at 2.30pm. The younger children were taught in the Church Rooms and the seniors in church. Some sixth form children regularly attended. Sunday school continues but is now called Children's Church and is held during normal service times.

The structure of the church remains much the same as it was in 1884, although some changes have taken place. The Pipe Organ was replaced by an Electronic Organ in 1989 and the vestry enlarged. A children's corner was made at the West end of the church, also providing an area in which to serve coffee after services. New lighting and rewiring was installed as part of the centenary. New oak outer doors were made by a a local craftsman and parishioner in 1992. Stained glass East and West windows were dedicated in 1980 and 1994.

In 1999 St Michael's is supported by its Parochial Church Council and volunteers from the congregation, who help to maintain the church and churchyard and keep both in good heart for the years to come.

Our present incumbent is Rev. Bridget Smith who was inducted in 1995 and whose husband David is Pastoral Assistant.

Heather Coles

St Michael's Church Choir

Apart from a short period in the late 1960s, there has always been a choir at St Michael's, though there have been considerable fluctuations in strength.

Under the leadership of Dr. Ainsworth, Dan Hinton and Ernie Holton, there was a large choir, which led the congregation every Sunday at both morning and evening services. Four-part anthems were sung regularly and for special occasions Mr Potter (senior) from the Top Shop would accompany the choir.

In the 1950s Sybil Linnell and Mrs Partridge used to organise Choir Suppers.

In the late 1960s, numbers dwindled, but after a short spell without a choir, Mr White, the new Head Teacher at the Junior School, was persuaded, with his wife, to re-form it. They only stayed a few years, but then Carroll Hinton took over. Under her guidance, in 1981, members went to sing, for the first time, in Peterborough Cathedral, with choirs from all over the diocese, at the Choral Festival.

Under Jill Bond, we became affiliated to the Royal School of Church Music. This gave new opportunities for training courses etc. It was through the RSCM that Hayley Kuhlke and Amy Prestidge had the chance to sing with the Southern Cathedral Singers at Portsmouth, St. Albans and Guildford Cathedrals and Hayley entered for and obtained her Dean's Award.

Sara Hughes.

Mothers' Union

St. Michael's Church has a small branch of the Mothers' Union, currently 18 members. It is just a tiny cog in a worldwide organization, which meets monthly for Prayer and fellowship and enjoys many good speakers as well as discussion evenings.

The Aim, Purpose and Objects of the Society are important to our membership:

To uphold Christs teaching on marriage.

To encourage parents to bring their children to Church.

To maintain a worldwide fellowship with Christians.

To promote conditions in society favourable to stable family life, and the protection of children.

To help those whose family life has met with adversity.

Here, in Silverstone, the Union runs a Service for Tiny Tots (babies up to school age). Many of the Tots are Baptised which is a great joy. Some go on to join the Junior Church, when they are old enough, and one is now a member of the choir. The next step is Confirmation.

A link has been established with Bungoma, a very poor district in Kenya. So far, introductory letters have been exchanged, so developments are awaited with anticipation. Who knows? The Silverstone M.U. may be able to help the people of Bungoma build their much needed Health Centre.

Finally we thank God for all the good things, and try not to take them for granted.

Victoria Denley-Spencer.

Tiny Tots

The idea of Tiny Tots , a week day service for pre-school children and their carers, was suggested to the Silverstone branch of the Mothers' Union. Joan Smith, the Vicar's wife, led the first session on 19 November 1991, with Gwen Cox at the piano and Mothers' Union members there to give out coffee or squash and biscuits afterwards.

Activities still begin by marching round the church, banging and shaking instruments, and finish by all kneeling at the altar rail. In between, there's a story, singing, prayers and often some kind of activity. Gwen Cox still plays the piano and Judy Berry still comes each week to help with all the extra jobs and clearing up.

Sara Hughes.

Ladies' Bible Study Group

The Ladies' Bible Study Group started in 1984, when some young mums (plus a number of young children) got together to read and discuss passages from the Bible, and to relate what they learnt about God to their everyday lives.

They met weekly in term-time in each other's homes, often taking turns to look after the children. Once a month they held a Bring and Share lunch to which they invited a speaker on a Christian topic. In 1997, St Michael's Church and the Methodist Chapel got together to take part in a nation-wide initiative called Emmaus. These are sessions of Bible-based study and discussion about living everyday lives in relationship with God and encouraging one another in each person's own journey of faith. These are continuing at the moment of writing with an evening and a daytime group, and are not just for women.

Margaret Holland.

Kneeler Group

In October 1988 a project was started by friends of St Michael's to cover the church kneelers and, after ten years of dedicated hard work, 200 kneelers have been completed.

It was decided to use a single tapestry canvas (12 threads to the inch), a deep blue tapestry wool as the background colour which matched the blue floor tiles in church and a dark blue linen fabric as a backing material. The design of the kneeler was left to the individual and consequently there is a very varied and original collection of designs, the only common factor being the deep blue background.

The kneeler designs fall roughly into four categories: those depicting the church, its festivals and traditions; the ones representing various organisations in the village such as the sports clubs, the young people's organisations (Guides, Brownies, Scouts) and the adult clubs; those dedicated to the past and present members of the church and other characters of the village; various businesses and properties in the parish including the world famous motor racing circuit. A catalogue is being prepared which will be kept in the church for reference showing a photograph of every kneeler and the name of the worker together with notes about the subject matter. The group is justly proud of its efforts. The kneelers form an interesting and fascinating talking point for visitors to the church.

Peggy Sturges.

THE OLD PARSONAGE

I think it was in 1947 that we moved into The Old Parsonage. The snow was so deep that we had to dig our way to the door. We had visited it the previous summer when I was three years old, and then it had been the stinging nettles that towered over my head. It was a dauntingly large and damp house, with a garden to match, but my father is a garden optimist on a grand scale, and my mother equally adept at the raising of both plants and children, and they were not to be deterred.

Dominating the front facade was a huge and beautiful lime tree, some seventy or eighty feet tall, a final punctuation point in the avenue of horse chestnuts that curved down from Windmill Hill. Nevertheless it needed considerable imagination to envisage beauty in the rest of the garden. A scraggy overgrown vegetable plot scrambled down a slope to a muddy ditch that severed the house from the orchard. A plank led to the remains of a tennis court, with some gnarled and cankered fruit trees on the slope beyond. Two dilapidated pigsties squatted under the overgrown hedge at the top in a fitting conclusion.

The house itself was based around two small brick cottages knocked into one. There was a stone-built extension, presumably provided for the original parson, containing a large reception room with a marble fireplace and large bay window. The scale of the room was obviously designed to impress parishioners, and we always referred to it as The Big Room. In the hall next to it a mahogany balustraded staircase angled grandly up to the master bedroom above, the original cottage bedrooms being served by suicidally steep steps from the landing. There were further additions, probably also built for the parson's comfort, including a square-brick floored kitchen, a tall, dark pantry with a tiny high window, a lean-to scullery with copper boiler, and assorted outbuildings in various stages of disrepair. When we arrived there was no heating, no food and no furniture. To a small boy it was as cold and uninviting as the snow-filled garden.

I was one of three brothers (soon to be five), my mother was a nurse, and my father worked in Northampton as a photolithographer. We arrived at about the same time as the racetrack, a time of change that was to lead to international fame for the village, and for both of us the process of assimilation was long yet entertaining. For me the roar of racing cars in summer became as natural as the roar of circus tigers in winter. The latter paced around their wheeled cages up at lonely Winterhills during the off-season, as we boys peered at them in terror through the hedge. The circus elephants patrolled the frosty streets with their minders, dropping steaming strawy cannonballs that we rescued for the rose beds. Looking back I realise that this was symptomatic of the changes in society as a whole, for the traditional circus was disbanded, and its cages left to rust, its place taken by more modern entertainment such as the motor racing nearby.

My father set up in business on his own in the so-called coach house in the garden, a wooden shack with double-doors and a corrugated-iron roof that got blisteringly hot in summer. His firm prospered and became quite famous in its own right, for he was an excellent craftsman and innovator in his field. Eventually a new purpose-built studio was erected in place of the original. Visiting commercial representatives and dealers used to time their calls to coincide with mealtimes, and they became friends rather than business acquaintances, to the extent that they often brought their visiting overseas representatives with them for a little taste of England.

Under my father's stern direction the house and garden blossomed over the years, and we boys, and sometimes even visitors, were conscripted as labourers in the realisation of these plans. The gloomy pantry with its ranks of elm shelves curving around three walls was converted into a light and airy conservatory; the kitchen acquired a range, but it proved too small to provide satisfactory central heating and so a coke-hungry boiler was manhandled into the old scullery in place of the big copper laundry bowl on its brick grate. The long, shallow stone sink under the window eventually became a plant holder on the new terrace. For a year or two after moving in we kept pigs in the pigsties, and I remember the old scullery full of villagers helping to cut up and wash the carcass after it had been slaughtered by the local butcher. The smell of chitterlings remains with me to this day. We also used the scullery for extracting honey from the combs from my father's beehives, a very hot and uncomfortable process, and painful if the bees got in. The Victorian toilet suffered less from the changes, perhaps undeservedly. It was an imposing flush lavatory, with a magnificent blue-patterned bowl and a large (parson size?) mahogany seat, with suspect plumbing both above and below. The cistern, located high above the user's head, was made of cast iron, and prone to detach itself from the wall if the chain was pulled with too much force. Proudly emblazoned across its front were the words "The Electric", although anything less electric would be difficult to imagine. It evacuated, rather inefficiently, into a mighty brick cavern of a cesspit in the front garden, which we poor conscripts had to empty with buckets when the necessity arose, which seemed always to occur in hot weather. This usually followed the ritual of "Rodding", where a solid rubbery disc on a chimney sweep's canes was progressively forced down the underground pipeway to relieve the lavatory's congestion so that we could then relieve our own. My father, rather ironically, built a decorative wellhead above the cesspit which elicited much interest from visitors until they found out what really lay beneath.

The stream and the garden were an excellent playground for young boys, though woe betide anyone who noticeably deformed the master plan in their pursuit of boyish things. But eventually we all grew up, and left home, and followed our own paths. I became a graphic designer, but kept in touch with Silverstone through my parents. Some of my earliest commercial work was designing posters for Silverstone Circuits, which were reproduced by my father's firm, a good example of how the circuit looked for ways to put something back into the local community. I felt a little reflected glory recently when some of these were offered for auction at Sotheby's, fetching several hundred pounds each - much more than I was originally paid!

Paul Torr, June 1999

THE CIRCUS

Just after the Second World War wild animals lived at Silverstone, and an ambling elephant was a common sight in the High Street. Cody's Circus had its winter quarters at Winterhills and the cages for the animals were in the paddock and alongside the path from the gate to the house. There were lions, ponies, bears, two elephants (named Rajah and Ranee), and Jacko the chimpanzee.

The villagers got used to seeing the elephants being walked through the village and frequently there would be a pause at The White Horse. The mahout drank his pint inside and another was held out through the open window for the elephant.

The elephants of Cody's Circus. Anita Osborne in control and, from front to rear, Margaret Reeve, Betty Osborne and Reenie Osborne plus an unidentified infant.

One day Abraham the mahout was ambling down the by-pass [Brackley Road] with one of his charges, Ranee. Along comes Son James, then the garage owner, hobbling along after delivering a car to Kingsley Road. The conversation went something like this:

Abraham: What's matter Sonny - you doan look so good.
Son: I'm not, chap, my poor old feet are killing me. I feel I'll never make it to the Oak.
Abe: Youse not used to walking is you? Never mind, you can have a lift on my Ranee.
(Whereon he gave some sort of command, tapped the elephant's knee and down she went, allowing Son to clamber up and settle himself comfortably. Everything proceeded quietly until they almost reached Murswell Lane entrance, then...)
Son: Ye Gods, this'll sind me to sleep. Can't the old girl go any faster, chap?
Abe: Sure thing Sonny - hold on.
(He touched the elephant behind its ear with his stick and, indignant at this kind of treatment it just bolted, straight up the road, turned into Linnell's Timber Yard, out of the other side and didn't come to a halt until it reached the Terrace. Son, hanging on to its ears like grim death and unable to get down had to wait until Abraham, puffing and panting, dark face shining with sweat and concern, arrived on the scene.)
Abe: Ah - puff - dearie me Sonny - puff - you O.K.?
Son: Yes, thank heavens, but I'll tell you one thing, Abraham - the next time, before I mount an elephant, I'll make sure it's got four wheels and a good braking system!

Edna Dodwell spent all the time she could with the circus animals and, of the elephants, preferred Rajah who was very sweet tempered. Edna also got on well with Jacko, the chimpanzee. When first they met at Cody's house, Jacko immediately ran to Edna and put his arms round her. He also made a show of playing the piano and lighting people's cigarettes for them.

"Jacko was such a lovely character," Edna recalls. *"The Codys had him from a baby and he acted just like one of the family. While the Codys were here in Silverstone they had a child. Now then, you'd think Jacko would be jealous of the baby, wouldn't you? But it was just the opposite. He would rock the crib and watch over the child."*

Eventually Jacko got old and bad tempered, bit a stage hand, and had to be put down. Policeman Bill Hart, who came to the village in 1948, remembered being called to Winterhills by Clem Merk, the lion-tamer. A lion had fallen and was apparently injured and unconscious. The RSPCA would not come, and eventually an Army officer from Turweston came with a .303 rifle. Bill, Clem and Marco the Clown agreed which directions they would run if the lion proved to be "foxing", and then the officer shot the beast dead.

Fred Marco, who had ears of different sizes, was not only a clown, but also worked with the elephants and with the lions, and was once bitten by one. He and his wife lived at 67 Kingsley Road with Taffy and Elsie Steenton. Fred and his wife are buried in Silverstone Churchyard.

A SHORT HISTORY OF SILVERSTONE C.E. SCHOOL 1867-1987

Although Lord Southampton helped to set up a Church School in 1847, Thomas Grainger of Loughborough as village schoolmaster reopened the Silverstone National School in what are now the Church Rooms on 1st April 1867 with 35 children, of whom 12 could read moderately, 9 only monosyllables, while 14 did not know all the alphabet. Attendance varied, only absenteeism was regular for various reasons: no money for fees, no shoes, gone to watch Yeoman cavalry at Stowe or sheep shearing or slaughtering, or depending on the season gone to help with hay-making, gleaning, tree-barking, bird-scaring, sloe, acorn, cowslip or dandelion gathering or potato picking, or gone to the Abthorpe or Wappenham Feasts or the Towcester Fair or Circus or to learn pillow lace manufacture or to beg for Valentine Day money. Threatened with punishment or behind with the fees, children simply moved to the rival

Wesleyan School (which was housed in the converted barn behind the present-day Post Office). Attendance declined in winter, when work and money for the fees, low as they were, were scarce. By 1869 Mrs Grainger was holding sewing classes. Average school attendance in 1870 was 53. Mr Grainger started a Night School around 1871/2, replaced by Penny Reading sessions at the insistence of the Vicar, at which Mr Grainger resigned. There followed a quick succession of several Headteachers.

By 1884 fees were 2d (about 1p) a week and average attendance was 90, dropping

new desks were provided. 1901 saw whooping cough shut the school for 4 weeks.

Mr Holden, Head from 1910, worked hard to remove the provincial accent from the children's speech to the ridicule of some parents. Canon Brittain, who was working hard for a new school building, approved the improvement in speech. The old building was now proving increasingly inefficient: in January 1912, freezing temperatures were recorded and in February it fell below freezing. Attendance was consequently poor.

Before the First World War Silverstone had a scout troop, but after that Silson boys had to join the Whittlebury troop.

one day to 13 because of a large auction in the village. In 1894/5 measles killed many pupils and closed the school for months. By 1895 a small extension to the Infants' room was already insufficient, while the gallery where many children spent most of their school life was said to promote only restlessness and inattention. Classes were examined regularly and often, leading the Head to complain about the loss of schooling during the Feast holiday week in October. (Teachers were paid by results at this time).

In 1900 the gallery was removed and

On 11 June 1912 the new Brittain Memorial School (Cannon Brittain had died in the previous autumn) was opened in Green Lane by the Bishop Suffragen of Leicester. Attendance was 112, and in July at 96% the highest in the district. Cottage gardening and elementary science were now on the curriculum for the seniors (11-13 year olds).

On 1st April 1914 Mr W J Rodda arrived as the new Head and was to stay for 37 years except for a brief period of military service. Hygiene, temperance and citizenship now appeared on the curriculum.

In 1931 the School reopened as the Silverstone C.E. Junior School (ages 5-11) with 100 on roll, including 63 from the Council School, which the Seniors (ages 11-13) now attended. Torrential rain in 1939 caused flooding and 45 absences, while in for meals and lectures. In 1949 the two-day Silverstone Feast was revived. 1950 saw a roll of 124 and mains water installed. In 1951 Mr. Rodda retired with an OBE for his services to the School, to the Schools' Athletic Association, to the National Union of Teachers, to the UNESCO Education

A school photograph of about 1948. Back row, (l. to r.): Tim Partridge, Hazel Fields, Ron Parker, Barbara Webb, Lionel Lovell, Daphne Baud, Roger Turnell, Jane Coleman, Audrey Blackwell. Second row: Madeline Hinton, Sheila Osborne, Helen Rogers, Don Spencer, Sheila Dunkley, Tony Whitmore, Winnie Harris, Margaret Reeve, Kathleen Hayle. Third row: Michael Harris, June Linnell, Mr Clarke, Mary Kinsella, Carol James, Colin Metters. Front row: Margaret Potter, Wilfrid Churchill, Barry Linnell, John Harris, Jimmy Harris, Jennifer Linnell.

1940 heavy snow reduced attendance by 25%. Holidays were now staggered with half of the staff available to keep school open so parents could help the war effort. 124 were on roll of whom 32 thanks to the Blitz were unofficially evacuated children. 78 were inoculated against diphtheria. A March 1947 blizzard reduced numbers to 37, and September saw a national milk shortage and no free milk for a fortnight, but November brought a day's holiday for Princess Elizabeth's wedding. A report described the building as very good for a small school. The children now attended the Modern School

Committee and to numerous other important committees.

Mr W R Jones, the new Head, had electricity and mains sewerage installed, introduced nature studies and initiated a joint Sports Day with the County Modern School (now ages 11-15) and an Open Evening for parents. Installation of a heating system delayed the beginning of the 1957 Spring Term, but generally the building was showing its age - a whole top window fell out - and a herd of cows destroyed the main gate. 1957/8 saw hot water and a drinking fountain provided. In 1959/60 the

Infant classes transferred under Mrs M Whitehead to the former, now modified, Secondary Modern School, to become the Silverstone County Infants School. The former inmates had to travel to Towcester. The Green Lane Junior School roll was now 96, divided into three groups, including children bussed in from Abthorpe and Wappenham.

In 1964 Remedial Services and the School Nurse began regular visits and by 1968 a Crossing Patrol operated on the A43. A request for a high boundary fence to protect the housing development in Graham Hill was refused by the Authority to the inconvenience of all concerned ever since. Its lack inhibits ball games and P.E.

In the Summer of 1969 Mr Jones became ill and retired, leaving "one of the best of village schools" to his successor, Mr D White. Swimming lessons in the Sponne pool were added to the curriculum in 1972. The roll had now reached 100. Thanks to the parents a black-and-white TV was acquired. During 1973 stringed instrument instruction became available and the Choir sang at Evensong in each catchment village. In September 1973 Mr J J Amos became Head. 1978 saw 139 on roll in a school built for 120. Sadly Mr Amos died before the end of the school year, to be succeeded in 1979 by Mr C Bray, who revived the House system and inaugurated a Parent-Teacher Association, "Friends of Silverstone Junior School", which over the years organised many social and fund-raising events.

In the early 1980s government initiatives and paperwork increased, as did the use of reprographics and staff in-service training. The school was now used for evening classes and clubs. Looking further outwards a link was established with the Langenheim Grundschule in the German Westerwald, and a Nikolausfest play was performed by the children for the Twinning Committee in Northampton.

The School has seen many changes in its long and illustrious history. The present environment has been adapted to cope with the demands of the National Curriculum; there has been an increase in the range of resources - including computers - to meet the needs of the technological age. Many of the traditions which have long been associated with the School continue to be observed and links with the Church are willingly maintained. The approach of the next millennium will see further changes as the village expands and develops. A new School might well replace the existing ones as the children of the community face fresh challenges.

Abridged by Nigel Read from "75 Years in Green Lane 1912-1987" by Colin Bray, Headteacher 1979-94, with a postscript by the present Headmaster Peter Chivers.

SCHOOL MEMORIES

Mrs May Whitehead was born into one of Silverstone's timber families, the Wests, in a house on the Brackley Road. May was one of the first pupils to attend the Church School when it moved to Green Lane from the Church, as an infant in 1912. There was great rivalry between Church and Chapel schools, the girls enjoyed watching the fights between boys of the two schools. Mr. Rodda was the Headmaster from 1914 for thirty-seven years. He was very keen on discipline but fair and much liked. May's brother was the first pupil to get a scholarship to go on to Towcester Grammar School.

May stayed on to become a pupil teacher, in those days a two year training in the classroom. Mr. Rodda advised her to gain experience in another school, so she taught at West Haddon near Rugby for nine years. He then got in touch with her when a vacancy came up at Silverstone and asked if she would like to apply.

Mr Rodda was a great committee man, involved on national and international teaching bodies, for which he received an

OBE. It often fell to May to be deputy Head during his frequent absences. May remained at Green Lane until 1960 when the Infants became a separate school. She was appointed the Headmistress and moved to the present site with Mrs. Middleton. She retired from a long teaching career in Silverstone in 1968.

News & Views 1992

REMEMBERING SILVERSTONE COUNCIL SCHOOL

Many of us from Silverstone will remember Mr & Mrs J.P. Osborne, also old classmates from Whittlebury and Abthorpe at the time. For many years Mr & Mrs Osborne were headmaster and mistress.

The rules were:- the highest standards of cleanliness must be maintained; hair must always be neatly brushed and combed; shoes were inspected regularly - had we polished the heels as well as the toes? Heaven help us if we had not! Nothing escaped their watchful eye. The day started with assembly in the hall, a prayer and a hymn, finally a song which would be changed weekly. Among the songs were Old Father Thames and The Garden Where the Pirates Grow, this one being quite humorous.

Among his many skills, Mr Osborne was a keen gardener and artist, also woodwork master. The school garden was beautifully kept and according to the seasons, flowers were placed upon the War Memorial from the School garden every Friday. Mr & Mrs Osborne were country lovers. Each child kept a little notebook and every day had to write a detailed account of work on the land, for example ploughing, hedgecutting and ditching, haymaking and harvest, also notes on birds, trees and flowers and the weather.

On Mondays, if we were not very brisk after the weekend, we were told we could not have a "Cobblers Monday". This saying, they explained, meant that the "Cobblers" rested on Monday after their football match at the weekend.

Our headmaster and mistress were very hardworking and won our respect and admiration, that is for sure. After the Second World War they left and went to Eastbourne to spend their retirement. They will be long remembered.

Vera Petcher, News & Views, December 1994

SILVERSTONE INFANT SCHOOL 1960-1989

A summary by Nigel Read of the Silverstone Infants' School Log Book (January 1960 to April 1989) covering the headships of Mrs Whitehead (1960-68) and Mrs Purser (1969-89) and ending with a paragraph by the present head, Mrs Norgate.

The Log Book records little of the classroom activities of the children, but does mention the introduction in 1970 of vertical grouping, which gave each class a cross-section of ages, and in the 80s the arrival of the first computer. It concentrates rather on the non-routine: open days, parents' evenings, visits to farms, harvest festivals, parties and carol singing for the elderly, outings, for example, to the Royal Show, the Royal Tournament, the Cotswold Wildlife Park, London Airport, Derngate and the Theatre Royal and the recurring scourges of measles, mumps and chicken pox. Also looming large are the regular visits of Nurses Mowbray, Irwin and Jones, of the medical and dental officers, educational psychologists, speech therapists, opticians and audiometric nurses, who screened new pupils.

The star of the Log Book is undoubtedly the school building, a cantankerous, moody, old prima donna, that, aided and abetted by the weather, demanded constant attention from County architects and tradesmen to the despair of caretakers and frustration of Headteachers.

The School building, already old in 1960, had previously housed the Secondary Modern School. The long harsh winter of 1962 froze the pipes throughout January and February. In 1963 part of a classroom ceiling fell down, a recurring problem. The toilets froze up again in 1968 and 1969. The boiler room flooded in in the 1969 storms while the boiler's unreliability was made worse by County bureaucracy taking two weeks to get valves changed. After refurbishment in the Summer holidays, windows would not shut properly, so that temperatures of 44° Fahrenheit (7° centigrade) were recorded in classrooms in January 1970. A new lavatory door had already fallen off by December. A typically slow response from County saw convector heaters installed in March, making the Staff Room warm for the first time since October.

During the installation of oil central heating in 1970 the sewer was damaged and blocked. In January 1971 the School closed for two days as an unofficial strike delayed oil ordered in December. The parents provided convector heaters, which were sadly largely useless during the three-day week and power cuts of February 1972.

A relatively uneventful 1973 saw one lad get a crayon stuck up his nose, and in May 1974 the School Association, a Parent Action Committee, was inaugurated. During the 60s the number on roll had ranged from 36 to 62. By April 1975 the roll was up to 90 with classrooms adequate for 29 - no wonder the ceiling fell in again. During 1975/6 the boiler room and three classrooms were flooded, the waste pipes froze and the boilers broke down again. More pleasantly, in 1977 the School celebrated the Jubilee with the crowning of a Rose Queen on Stocks Hill and a procession to the Playing Fields of the children, all dressed in red, white and blue.

The School shut for five days in 1978 during the oil tanker drivers' strike, and again a year later during the "winter of discontent", when a belated oil delivery provided heating and a succession of burst pipes. School returned to "normal" on 29th January, but two weeks later the mains pipe in the roof had frozen and snow had to be removed from the loft.

Later in 1979 wiring for 2kw heaters was installed in each room for emergency use. Early in 1980 the boiler was playing up again: a leaking water main was replaced, during which the oil feed pipe got fractured, only to be discovered when a whole delivery of oil, thousands of litres, simply vanished. The botched repair work continued through 1980 with failing canteen boiler, leaking oil, leaking roof, overflowing tanks, blocked drains and half finished work. The parents acted positively, redecorating part of the School and organising their annual fete to raise funds. One might think that the School just staggered from crisis to crisis. One suspects however, that the majority of children noticed little, for in spite of working in what were far from ideal conditions, they were enjoying a good education, as the following excerpts from a letter in the Daily Express of 12th March 1981 bear out:

Shabby school - but it shines for the teaching

Nowhere would you find a more loving and caring infant school than the one here in Silverstone, but we have no new teaching equipment, no school hall, no sports facilities and the classrooms have not been decorated for at least 11 years, the Local Education Authority, for some reason, priding itself on being bottom of the education spending league.

This year the county have offered us a choice of new books or re-decoration. Of course the books will be requested; the re-

decoration will be the job of willing parents during the summer holidays.

But apart from the dilapidated surroundings, the children are extremely happy and well cared for, as well as receiving a high standard of education. This is due entirely to the three teaching staff. What better start could a child have in its school life?

Mrs M. Heath, Silverstone, Towcester, Northants.

The 80s were much like the 70s. In spite of a new boiler and radiators in 1982, the boiler continued to fail regularly and the ceiling continued to fall. 1983 saw two arrivals: a mobile classroom, which soon let in water, and a 480Z computer that went down six months later. September 1984 saw the roll at 89 and concerns centred on lack of space and heat loss. By 1985 another freeze-up prompted many visits from County personnel about improvements and a new building. Perhaps they were ceasing to rely on the fact that 20 pupils equal one kilowatt.

During the 80s the School Managers became School Governors and included elected parent representatives. 1987 saw the first Annual Parents' Meeting and the first of the five annual teacher training days (taken from the holidays), initially called "Baker Days" after the Minister or more disrespectfully "bidets". Teaching staff were increasingly absent on courses on the National Curriculum, multicultural education and such like, which meant the School had to rely more on supply teachers. A sad comment says it all: This is the second day in over a year that all staff, teaching and non-teaching, have been present. The reward for all this effort was a visit from an education officer about minor improvements to the buildings, as a proper remodelling with extensions had been deferred.

During the last twenty years education has seen radical change. The world of education has become a microcosm of new inventions, each one more complicated than before. Learning to cope and to use them has become an essential part of the education, not least in Silverstone. The world has become a smaller place, a world of travel, a world of computerised digital communications where E-mail contacts can be made with Africa, America and other far flung places. These changes have not passed Silverstone Infant School by. The 80s saw the establishment of the National Curriculum with its ten subject folders, each subject demanding as much time as any other. Then came the new condensed curriculum in one document! Learning objectives, whole school improvement planning and Key Stage assessment tests changed education forever, all accompanied by the computer, the essential new learning tool.

Office for Educational Standards (OFSTED) inspections revealed weaknesses and strengths in the education system. The School experienced its first inspection in 1996. The report was favourable but highlighted some areas for improvement. The second inspection in December 1998 indicated that the school came in the top 5% of similar schools in the country. This excellent outcome has secured the school's future. The original Silverstone School has seen many changes, but one thing remains constant - children. Despite the changes in modern life children remain essentially the same - bright, garrulous, infuriatingly active and wonderfully inventive! It is therefore our privilege, duty and aim to continue to maintain Silverstone Infant School as a bright beacon for the education of future generations of the village's children.

MR JOHN DENNEY

At the close of the 19th century a book entitled "Our County" was published to celebrate Northamptonshire. An article was included on the schoolmaster at Silverstone, John Denney. It began as follows: Aristocratic eyebrows may possibly rise at the inclusion in "Our County" of a plain village schoolmaster of the Wesleyan persuasion, but no estimate of the factors which combine in our public life should omit the quiet and permeating forces of Methodism - forces pointedly shown in the position of Mr. John Denney, of Silverstone. The district which he pervades is one somewhat out of the common. No resident squire has for ages guided the destinies of Silverstone, though Whittlebury is within sight, and has sometimes tried to make itself felt. The curate-in-charge is shed annually like the oak-leaves of the surrounding woods. Accordingly, deprived of the blessings which flow from clerical influence and Tory domination, Silverstone is a hotbed of Radicalism and schism, and finds its leader in the experienced and canny schoolmaster of the local Methodists.

SILVERSTONE AT WAR

The British Army Captures Silverstone

In 1913 the annual army manoeuvres took place in Buckinghamshire and Northamptonshire, in part, no doubt, because of the barracks and military installations at Weedon. The Naval Air Service was involved flying army officers on observation duties. The Naval Wing sent six aircraft, a Short S.78 flown by Parker, a Bleriot XI-2 (Briggs), a Short S.75 (Courtney), a Sopwith D.1 (Davies), a Caudron G.3 (Marix) and a Short S.67 (Littleton). They flew to Lilbourne, near Rugby and motor transport was hired from Hertford Motor Carriage Company of Mayfair. It consisted of a couple of Napier lorries and two Napier touring cars. They also had camping equipment hired from the Army and Navy Stores, including a tent-hanger 250 feet long. By Sunday, 21 September, they had all arrived, including Flight Sub-Lieutenant Reginald Marix who had brought his Caudron up as a reserve aircraft.

The armies that faced each other were the Brown force, based on Aylesbury and Leighton Buzzard and the White Force with headquarters at Daventry. The progress of the manoeuvres was reported, with particular attention given to that most modern arm of the forces, the air service, in the October 9 issue of The Aeroplane, a weekly magazine sold for one penny.

Operations began at 7am on Tuesday, and the Brown cavalry under General Edmund Allenby was covering the River Ouse, unobserved by White Force aircraft. Meanwhile White cyclists had advanced as far south as Whittlebury. The two cavalry forces met south of Whittlebury and the Browns were driven back through Lillingstone Dayrell where they held and counter-attacked, taking Silverstone by nightfall.

On Wednesday morning the Browns held a line Helmdon-Wappenham-Abthorpe-Towcester and the Whites were centered on Blakesley with their flanks at Fosters Booth and Byfield. The Brown infantry pushed along the Woodford Halse road on the west and struck for Maidford from the east, but the toughest fighting was just west of Blakesley. By the end of the day the Whites had been driven back to a line from Charwelton through Everdon to Weedon. The chief lesson of this exercise was thought to be the need to co-ordiante cavalry with aircraft for a war of movement; nothing like the war that was to follow.

Sources: The archives of the Fleet Air Arm Museum, Yeovilton; Northamptonshire Public Library, Towcester; The Aeroplane magazine; Cross & Cockade magazine, Vol. 24, No. 2, 1993.

Silverstone War Memorial

When first I asked someone about the names on the war memorial, who these men were, where and how they died, I was met with a sense of wonder that I should ask at all, and a declaration of ignorance about them. Not even a confession of ignorance, just a bald statement that seemed to me to set the loss of these men in the service of

Western Front Association. The regimental museums, where the man's regiment is listed, also helped. The other source was the list of burials and memorials maintained by the Commonwealth War Graves Commission which I was able, with Rio Fanning's help, to access on the web (www.cwgc.org). Finally, once the basic data had been obtained, people in Silverstone added their memories. Many

A First World War photo, taken at The Walnuts, and captioned in pencil: Will Liddington, 1st Horse (Joe Webb?).

their country at nothing. But these are, in many cases, the fathers, brothers, uncles, husbands, grandfathers and great uncles of people living in Silverstone today, and that "today" will still be relevant decades from now.

The research carried out has been assisted by many other people. The starting point for the First World War was the publication *Soldiers Died*, which was first issued in the 1920s and is now available on compact disc (see www.great-war-casualties.com). It attempts to give information about everyone who was killed in the services in that war and is fairly accurate. The next-of-kin entries, where they exist, help pin-point our people as opposed to others of the same name. I was helped in this by the local branch of the

men served in the Northamptonshire Regiment, and George Durrant at the Museum of the Northamptonshire Regiment dug through the records to provide considerable information. Where the regimental archivist of other units contributed, a note is made.

For the First World War the memorial offers a surprisingly thorough, though not entirely complete, story of the war. The entries that follow are therefore arranged in chronological order to make the narrative easier to follow. Unless specially noted all these men died on the Western Front in France or Belgium. The three men who died in the Second World War are listed as they appear on the monument. The style chosen is to give the hard facts of the official record first and to follow that with what additional information I have been able to compile.

Jack Harris

Identification uncertain, but possibly: Born Stoke Goldington, Bucks. Son of Charles and Kate Harris, The Square, Stoke Goldington; husband of Clara Harris, Spring Cottages, Stoke Goldington, Newport Pagnell. Enlisted Northampton. Private, 7072, 1st Northamptonshire. Killed in action 17/09/14, aged 31 years. Memorial: La Ferté-sous-Jouarre, Seine-et-Marne, France.

When the Germans launched their invasion of France with the Schlieffen Plan, the small, professional army of the British Expeditionary Force fell back from Mons to Le Cateau and eventually to the River Marne east of Paris before taking part in the final, near-failure of the battles of the Marne and the Aisne, the two rivers that formed natural lines of conflict. Here the French, with what support the British could offer, held and threw back the German advance. Here the 1st Northamptons lost, on 17 October 1914, one officer and 54 other ranks killed, and of their wounded that day another four died. While Jack Harris certainly served with the county regiment, it is hard to see why, from the information given here, he appears on the Silverstone War Memorial, assuming we have the right man.

George Varney

Born Silverstone. Enlisted Northampton. Private, 3/9592, 1st Northamptonshire. Died of wounds 06/11/14. Buried in Poperinghe Old Military Cemetery, Belgium.

A casualty of the First Battle of Ypres, see under Albert Dudley below.

Albert Dudley

Born Silverstone. Son of William and Emma Dudley (stepmother), West End. Enlisted Northampton. Private, 9604, 1st Northamptonshire. Killed in action 14/11/14, aged 19 years. Memorial: Menin Gate, Ypres. Panel 43 & 45.

After the failure of the Schlieffen Plan, Germany's attempt to enfold Paris in a matter of days, a great void existed in north-west France and southern Belgium. Each army attempted to outflank the other, starting from a point near Paris and ending with the "race to the sea". On 21 October the Belgians flooded the land between Nieuport and Dixmude (Diksmuide), concentrating the conflict on the town of Ypres. A dramatic and close-run battle ensued which was just, and only just, won by the French and British under Douglas Haig. By the end of the fight, in mid-November, grooms, cooks and anyone who could hold a gun were in the front line. On 14 November the 1st Northamptons lost eight men, of whom Albert Dudley was one. His grave is not known.

Forester Roberts

Born Silverstone. Enlisted Towcester. He was a reservist, recalled, and rejoined 4 November 1914. Private, 3/9440, 2nd Northamptonshire. Killed in action 16/11/14. Memorial: Le Touret, near Neuve Chapelle, Panel 28/30.

War was declared and the first elements of the British force sent to France in August 1914. The 2nd Battalion, as part of 24th Brigade British Expeditionary Force, moved into the trenches for the first time on 14 November, just ten days after Roberts rejoined. They were in the area of Estaires, some 20km (12 miles) west of Lille, at Pont-Logy. On 15 November three men were killed and 12 wounded and on the following day more were wounded and just one, Forester Roberts, was killed. He had served for 12 days.

Thomas Lovell

Born Silverstone. Son of James and Sarah Lovell, Old Post Office, Silverstone. Younger brother of James Lovell. Enlisted Northampton, 4 July 1912, aged 19 years 6 months. Guardsman 15943, 1st Grenadier Guards. Killed in action 10-14/03/15, aged 21 years. Burial place or memorial not known.

Thomas Lovell joined the Regular Army as a Grenadier Guardsman on 4 July 1912 in

Northampton. He had been employed as a timber carter and the medical details on his attestation (entry form) say that he was five foot eight and a half inches tall, weighed 147 pounds and had a chest measurement of thirty-seven and a half inches, with a two-inch expansion on breathing in. His complexion was fresh, his eyes hazel and his hair light brown. He gave his religion as Church of England. He was passed fit for the Army and undertook short service of three years with the Colours and nine in the Reserve. His education evidently continued as his record shows, under Army School, the entry "3rd Class, 4.12.12." The 1st Battalion, Grenadier Guards went to France on 19 October 1914 and by March 1915 were serving with the 8th Division on the Neuve Chapelle sector of the front that now ran from the North Sea to the Swiss border. The German positions in the village were attacked on 10 March with the intention of breaking through to the Aubers Ridge beyond. At about 8 a.m., after a brief, 35-minute, bombardment, the Garwhal Brigade, the assault group of the Indian Corps, attacked from the west and the 7th and 8th Divisions came in from the north-west. Surprise was achieved and by noon the village had been taken. The artillery barrage now falling beyond the village was too thin to keep the Germans away and reserves were brought up, including the 6th Bavarian Reserve Division. The Grenadier Guards, in reserve on the first day, moved into the front line on 11 March. A major German counter-attack took place on the 12th, but made no progress. However, the British advance was stalled and the line remained where it was, an improvement of some 1,200 yards in depth on a front of about 4,000 yards. The British suffered 11,652 men killed, wounded and missing. While the date of Lovell's death is officially 10 March, his regimental record says 10-14 March. He was probably killed sometime between the Grenadiers coming into the line on the 11th and the end of the battle on the

14th. The failure of the artillery was held to be the result of too few shells being manufactured in Britain, and Lloyd George was appointed Minister of Munitions to improve production. One of his first acts was to introduce laws limiting the hours pubs were allowed to open, so the next time the pub closes, remember Thomas Lovell. (With thanks to the Guards Museum, Birdcage Walk, London.)

Tom Lovell

When the names on the memorial were first being investigated for this book, it was tempting to think that Thomas Lovell and Tom Lovell were the same person, repeated in error. However, it is clear that this is not so. It is said that Tom Lovell went to enlist at the same time as his cousin Thomas, but was rejected as being too young. He refused to accept being turned away, and resolved to go elsewhere and join up; possibly under an assumed name and giving a false age. No more than that is known at the time of writing. Where and when he died and with what regiment he served remain to be discovered.

William Spencer

Born Silverstone. Son of Mrs Mary Ann Spencer, Little London. Enlisted Northampton, 10/03/15. Private, 16573, 2nd Northamptonshire. Killed in action 09/05/15, aged 19 years. Memorial: Ploegsteert Memorial, Belgium (just north of Armentières, near Lille) Panel 7.

As the British steadied after the first gas attack at Ypres in April, General Haig felt able to support French eagerness to attack the Germans by launching an assault on the Aubers Ridge, a mild uplift in the landscape south-east of the River Layes and north-east of Neuve-Chapelle on the flat, boggy land between Béthune and Lille. The winding road north out of Aubers turns east before it gets to the river. From this point the 2nd Northamptons attacked, hopelessly, against the dominating positions of the Germans on

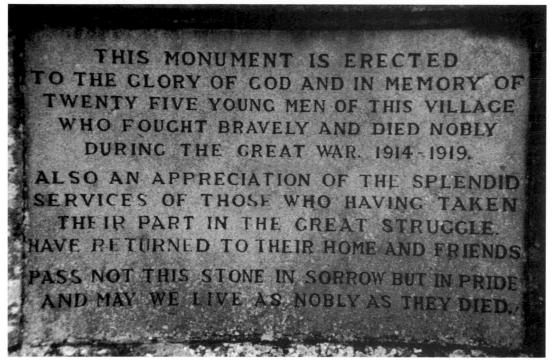

The dedication panel on Silverstone War Memorial.

the ridge to the south-east. Eight officers and 184 other ranks were killed that day and another 11 men died of wounds later. The attack was abandoned the next day after the British had suffered 458 officers and 11,161 men killed, wounded or missing. No advance was achieved. From Silverstone three men were killed here, William Spencer, who had served just two months, Frank Chapman and Charles Osborne.

Frank Chapman

Born Silverstone. Son of Joshua Chapman, Cattle End. Enlisted Northampton. Private, 9504, 2nd Northamptonshire. Killed in action 09/05/15, aged 24 years. Memorial: Ploegsteert Memorial, Belgium. Panel 7.

Frank Chapman died in the same action, the Battle of Aubers Ridge, as William Spencer and, like him, has no known grave.

Charles Osborne

Born Silverstone. Son of Mrs Charlotte Linnell, Mill View Cottage, Little London. Enlisted Towcester. Private, 9451, 2nd Northamptonshire. Killed in action 09/05/15, aged 21 years. Memorial: Ploegsteert Memorial, Belgium. Panel 7.

Charles Osborne was mobilized with the 2nd Northamptons, in which he was already serving, on 4 November 1914. His record shows that he was admitted to hospital on 12 February 1915 with myalgia (muscle pain) and returned to duty on 14 March. He, together with William Spencer and Frank Chapman, died in the attack on Aubers Ridge.

James Whitlock

Born Silverstone. Son of William Whitlock, Gravel Walk. Enlisted Towcester. Private, 16934, 1st Northamptonshire. Died of wounds 26/09/15. Buried in Lapugnoy Military Cemetery, Pas-de-Calais, France. Grave I.C.37.

In May 1915 the Russians were subjected to heavy losses in fighting in the Polish-Hungarian sector of the eastern front. The transfer of German troops to make up their losses and exploit their advantage gave the Allies' Senior Commander, Joffre, the advantage on the Western Front, or so he thought. As part of the series of attacks the British undertook the Battle of Loos in the flat, coal-mining country north of Vimy Ridge. The British attempt to use poison gas resulted in the fumes being blown back over their own men and the artillery barrage failed to destroy the German lines entirely, so the reserve troops were wasted in attempting to overcome the surviving positions. General French was held to be responsible for holding back the major part of the British reserves, thus ensuring failure, and was relieved of his post as Commander of the British Expeditionary Force. General Haig took over. The 1st Northamptons lost 33 men in action at Loos and three more, including James Whitlock, died the next day, 26 October.

Fred Wootton

Born Silverstone [Frederick George]. Enlisted Bletchley. Private, 19402, 1st Oxfordshire and Buckinghamshire Light Infantry. Died of wounds, Persian Gulf 31/03/16. Memorial: Basra, panel 26 and 63.

In November 1914 the 6th Indian Division fought its way up the Shatt al-Arab waterway from the Persian Gulf to take Basra, the key to securing the oil supplies from Persia (now Iran) along the pipeline from Ahwaz to the north-east. In May 1915 a reconnaissance in force was undertaken up the Tigris with the eventual successful defence by the Turks at Ctesiphon, just outside Baghdad. The British were forced to withdraw to Kut, about 160km (100 miles) back down the river and here they were besieged. Repeated efforts were made to relieve them, but when casualties amongst the rescuers had reached nearly twice the number of the besieged garrison, the attempts were abandoned and, on 29 April 1916, the British surrendered to the Turks. It seems likely that Fred Wootton was

wounded in the operations of the second week of March, the second of the three major efforts to raise the siege.

Joseph Hinton

Son of William Leonard and Amelia Hinton, 23 Brackley Road, Silverstone. Sapper, 2394, 1st West Riding Field Company, Royal Engineers. Killed in action 08/07/16, aged 26 years. Buried in Puchevillers Military Cemetery, north north-east of Amiens, grave ID37.

The Battle of the Somme began on 1 July 1916, when the French were bending, but not breaking, under the onslaught of the Germans at Verdun. It was the first major engagement of Britain's volunteer army, "Kitchener's Army", and uncertainty about the steadiness of these unprofessional soldiers led to a change of tactics. The advance was to follow days of artillery bombardment which, it was thought, would destroy the German defences, allowing the soldiers to advance securely at a walk. The artillery failed to wipe out the Germans in their deep dug-outs or to cut the barbed wire. The British were cut down in their thousands by German machine-gun fire and counter-barrages. Those killed or died of wounds amounted to 19,240. The wounded numbered 35,493; the missing 2,152 and those taken prisoner 585. Never before, or since, has the British Army suffered such casualties in a single day. The battle continued until November by which time the German casualties came to about 500,000 and the Allies to some 625,000. Joseph Hinton died on the eighth day of this terrible fight.

John Whitlock

Born and resident Silverstone. Next of kin: Mrs Clara Whitlock, West End. Enlisted Oxford. Private, 12737, 5th Oxfordshire & Buckinghamshire Light Infantry. Died of wounds 24/08/16. Memorial: Thiepval, pier and face 10A and 10D.

On Thursday, 24 August 1916 the 5th Ox

& Bucks were involved in an attack to clear Delville Wood of the Germans, part of the continuing battle of Guillemont (itself part of the Battle of the Somme) which started on the 18th. Their left flank was on the road from Longueval to Flers. The wood was finally cleared on Sunday, 27 August, by the 10th Durham Light Infantry, but by then John Whitlock had died. As he died of wounds one would have expected him to be buried nearby, but he is only commemorated on the Thiepval Memorial, as if he had never been found.

John Henry Timms

Born Bodicote, Oxon. Son of W. T. and Ann Timms, 4 Paradise Row. Enlisted Towcester, Private, 22204, the Northamptonshire Regiment, later:- Private, G/10391, 10th Queen's (Royal West Surrey). Killed in action 07/10/16, aged 18 years. Buried A. I. F. Burial Ground, Flers, Somme, grave II.B.8.

After the encouraging advance made with the assistance of tanks towards Flers on 15 September 1916, the Battle of the Somme continued with attacks on Thiepval, which was first assaulted on 1 July, and on the various strongpoints on the Transloy Ridge, across which the road from Albert to Bapaume runs. On 7 October the 23rd Division attacked and took the village of Le Sars on that road. The 10th Queen's sustained heavy casualties, of whom John Timms was one. (See also John Adams, below.)

Arthur Warman

Born Silverstone. Son of Silas and Emily Warman (entered as Warren in CWGC records). Enlisted Towcester. Private, 5120, (formerly 4036) 4th Suffolk. Died of wounds 19/02/17, aged 26 years. Buried St Sever Cemetery Extension, Rouen.

In the early months of 1917 the British maintained their pressure on the Germans on the Somme front. On the night of 17/18 February the Fifth Army attacked at Miraumont, astride the River Ancre, and gained both ground and over 700 prisoners of war. The Germans counter-attacked on the 18th and attacked further south the next day. The pressure forced the German High Command to accelerate the withdrawal to the Siegfried Stellung, known to the British as the Hindenburg Line, a complex fortification to the east which shortened the line they had to defend and was state-of-the-art as First World War trench, dugout and barbed wire systems went.

Fred Rush

Born Silverstone. Enlisted Northampton. Private, 16697, 2nd Northamptonshire. Killed in action 04/03/17. Memorial: Thiepval Memorial, Somme, France, panels 11A/11D.

Fred Rush was posted to the 2nd Battalion on 25 November 1915 and arrived on the 30th. His records show that he was admitted to hospital four times; first on 4 April 1916 with scabies (a contagious skin disease caused by a mite) and other ills - he returned to duty on 29 July, on 9 November with trench feet (chilblains and severe swelling from standing in water) and he was back on duty nine days later, on 4 December with a cut head for two days and on 26 January 1917 with impetigo (a skin disease), returning to duty on 11 February. On 4 March 1917 the British 8th Division captured Bouchavesnes, suffering 1,137 casualties. The 2nd Northamptons lost four officers killed and five wounded, and of other ranks 88 killed and died of wounds and 145 wounded. The position was held against six German counter-attacks. The modern village is called Bouchavesnes-Bergen because of a Norwegian's gift of a statue of the French Marshal Foch to commemorate the French capture of the same place on 12 September 1916 during the Battle of the Somme. On 1 September 1918 the British took the village yet again. The village is north of Péronne, just off the A1 Autoroute south of Bapaume. Fred Rush, because his grave is not known, is commemorated at Thiepval, near Albert.

Arthur Farey

Identification uncertain, but probably: Born Chelsea, Middlesex. Son of Samuel and Sarah Lavinia Farey, owners of the White Horse public house. Enlisted London, residence Towcester. Gunner, 42738, Royal Garrison Artillery. Died of wounds 05/05/17.

Fred Linnell

Born Silverstone. Son of Edward and Anne Linnell and husband of Mrs J. L. Linnell, Paradise Row. Enlisted Northampton. Private, G/20059, 23rd Duke of Cambridge's Own, Middlesex Regiment. Killed in action 07/06/17. Burial place or memorial, not known.

At the beginning of 1917 the German U-Boat campaign was starting to cause serious shortages in supplies reaching England. The French general, Robert Nivelle, had launched a disastrous attack on the Chemin-des-Dames in April as a result of which the French army mutinied. It was up to the British to keep up the pressure on the Germans. For more than a year before this, on a front facing the low ridge on which Messines stands, south of Ypres, the British had been tunnelling and now 21 huge explosive charges were at the ends of those tunnels, directly under the German lines. At 3.10 a.m. on 7 June the charges were ignited with a roar and shaking of the ground that was felt and heard in London. The troops poured forward, virtually unopposed by the dazed and shattered Germans. As the day dawned resistance increased, but the ridge was taken that same day. The 23rd Middlesex were on the northern end of the line near St Eloi, attacking Oasis and Oar trenches. They found them destroyed, but the line known as DammStrasse was strongly contested and here the 23rd suffered most of their casualties. By 4.30 a.m. they had taken their objectives and were consolidating their line, but by then Fred Linnell had probably died.

Septimus Roberts

Born Silverstone, 1st name George. Son of Mr & Mrs J. Roberts, Cattle End. Enlisted Northampton. Private, 16575, 1st Northamptonshire. Died of wounds 07/07/17, aged 21 years. Buried in Coxyde Military Cemetery, Belgium. Grave I.C.40.

No details of the cause or occasion of his wounds have been found at the time of writing. The 1st Northamptons were part of a force that took over the front line at Nieuport, where the Western Front met the sea, from the French and on 6 July 1917 the Germans shelled the area heavily. Roberts may have been wounded at that time. He joined up on the same day as Tom Roberts and William Spencer.

Stanley Heritage

Born Silverstone. Son of Walter and Susannah Heritage, Silverstone. Enlisted Towcester. Private 28136, 1st Northamptonshire. Killed in action 10/07/17, aged 21 years. Memorial: Nieuport Memorial, Belgium.

Three days after Septimus Roberts died at Nieuport [Nieuwpoort], the Battle of Dunes began. There was a massive artillery barrage by both sides, and the German Marines advanced on a 1,400 yard front at Lombaertzyde [now called Lombardsijde] north of Nieuport and east of the canal where the British forward positions were. Except for nine men who escaped by swimming the canal, all the 1st Northamptons in the line were either killed or captured. The dead numbered three officers and 95 men.

Edward Davis

Born Reading, Berks. 2nd name George. Son of William and Caroline Davis of Cattle End. Enlisted Northampton. Private, 17393, 7th Northamptonshire. Killed in action 31/07/17, aged 22 years. Memorial: Menin Gate, Ypres, Belgium. Panel 43 & 45.

In 1917 Field Marshal Haig was under tremendous pressure to agree to the British bearing the burden of the fighting. After the failed Spring Offensives planned by General Nivelle, part of the French Army had mutinied, fortunately without the knowledge of the Germans. In addition, Haig wanted to advance into Belgium to cut off the North Sea ports from which it was believed, U-Boats were operating against Allied shipping, threatening to deny Britain supplies. After the success of the Battle of Messines Ridge the British paused to build up supplies of men and munitions before launching the Third Battle of Ypres on 31 July 1917 - just as the rain began, the worst in 75 years. The 7th Northamptons were in 73 Brigade, 5th Army, and attacked with the 2nd Leinsters from Mount Sorrel through Shrewsbury Forest, south of the Menin Road and Sanctuary Wood. They were stopped by the pill-boxes at Lower Star Post and fell back somewhat to dig in. The 7th Northamptons lost four officers killed and eight wounded, and approximately 240 other ranks killed and wounded. The battle dragged on until four days after the taking of the village of Passchendaele by the Canadians on 4 November. The total casualties (killed, wounded and missing) by that time were approximately 244,900 British, 8,500 French and 230,000 German. The British abandoned the ground gained when the Germans attacked in Spring 1918.

Sydney Davis

Born Ditchley, Oxon. Son of William Davis, Silverstone. First name given as Sidney in CWGC records. Enlisted Wolverton, Bucks, residence Stony Stratford, Bucks. Private, 265204, 6th Oxfordshire and Buckinghamshire Light Infantry. Killed in action 20/09/17, aged 22 years. Memorial: Tyne Cot, near Ypres, panel 96 to 98.

The Third Battle of Ypres, known to many as Passchendaele, started on 31 July 1917, and continued in weather of unprecedented foulness. The rains of August exceed all records and the battlefield became a morass in which men were as likely to drown as to be killed by enemy fire. Lieutenant General Sir Hubert Gough was relieved of his command and the methodical Sir Herbert Plumer took over, planning a fresh attack in what became known as the Battle of the Menin Road. A break in the weather allowed him to reorganise his forces and, on 20 September, the attack went in. The 6th Oxfordshire and Buckinghamshire Light Infantry were in the north of the battlefield, advancing towards Langemark. The first obstacle they had to face, together with 12th Rifle Brigade, was Eagle Farm, which they took, but further progress that day was halted by the determined German defence against 11th Rifle Brigade on their left. Private Davis died in this fight, and, having no known gave, is remembered together with 34,984 other missing on the great memorial wall at Tyne Cot Cemetery, the largest Commonwealth War Graves Commission cemetery in the world. It has 11,908 graves.

Tom Roberts

Born Silverstone. Son of Mrs S. Roberts, Cattle End. Enlisted Northampton. Private, 16574, 1st Northamptonshire. Died of wounds 19/04/18. Buried Cambrin Military Cemetery, Pas de Calais, France. Grave N.46.

On 9 April 1918 General Erich Ludendorff launched Operation Georgette, his third great attack on the Allies that spring. In what they called The Battle of the Lys the British were pushed back from the gains of the Third Battle of Ypres (Passchendaele) of the previous autumn and there was a very real danger of the Germans breaking through to the Channel. They were held in a number of desperate fights, of which the Battle of Béthune took place on 18 April. Thirteen men of the 1st Northamptons were wounded that day, and Tom Roberts died the day after. The Cambrin cemetery is on the N41 between Béthune and La Bassée, only a couple of miles from the A26 Autoroute and about 40 minutes drive from Calais.

George Webb

Born Silverstone. Enlisted Towcester. Sapper, 213571, Corps of Royal Engineers 371st Forestry Company. Died 01/09/18. Memorial on father's gravestone in St Michael's churchyard, Silverstone.

The British Expeditionary Force needed materials for revetting (shoring up) trenches, building shelters, making roads and countless other purposes. Three quarters of the materials were timber products, supplied at first by civilian efforts from Britain, but later, starting in the winter of 1915-1916, by units of the Royal Engineers in France. Number 11 Forestry Company was formed in June 1917 and was renumbered 371st in October. It was posted to France in August 1917 and worked in the Forêt de Lyons and was quartered around Menesqueville. The strength was five officers and 120 men, though there were rarely that many of them. As well as felling trees, they operated sawmills and a light railway to transport their output. In Spring 1918 they prepared to join the front line as infantry opposing the massive German attacks, though they never actually had to take up arms. In August that year they were badly hit by the "Spanish" influenza epidemic, and it is likely that George Webb died of this illness, like thousands of his fellow serving soldiers. (With thanks to the Royal Engineers Museum, Chatham, Kent.)

Jack Rush

Born Silverstone. Enlisted Northampton. Private, 58883, 1st Northamptonshire. Killed in action 29/10/18. Buried in Cross Roads Cemetery, Fontaine-aux-Bois, near Landrecies, Nord, France.

In late September 1918 the British, Australian and American forces broke through the Hindenburg Line north of St Quentin and the general, slow collapse of the German defences began on this front and elsewhere. A month later the Germans were still holding on the line of the River Sambre (which joins the Meuse at Namur in Belgium) and the Canal running south from it passing east of St Quentin. On 29 October 16 men of the 1st Northamptons, including Jack Rush, were fatally wounded on the Sambre Canal. A major attack on 4 November took the position, but cost the life of the poet Wilfred Owen. The war ended on 11 November, 1918.

Men of Silverstone not shown on the memorial

Arthur Adkins Pittam

Born Silverstone. Son of Joseph Pittam, Stony Stratford and husband of Caroline Ellen Pittam, Silver Street, Stony Stratford. Enlisted Northampton. Private, 8051, 1st Northamptonshire. Died of wounds 14/05/15. Buried in Chocques Military Cemetery, Pas-de-Calais, France, grave I.A.119.

The 1st Northamptons were also in action at Aubers Ridge (see Spencer, Chapman and Osborne above) losing eight officers and 261 men on the day and a further 13 men who died of wounds, of whom Arthur Pittam was one.

George Pittam

Born Silverstone. Son of Mrs Pittam, 92 Church Street, Wolverton, Bucks and of the late Mr W. Pittam. Enlisted Wolverton, Bucks. Private, 12882, 6th Oxford and Buckinghamshire Light Infantry. Killed in action 03/09/16, aged 26 years.

John Adams

Born Silverstone, son of John Adams. Husband of Mrs E. A. Simpson (formerly Adams), 4 Brickyard, Scarborough Road, Norton Malton, Yorkshire. Enlisted Malton, Yorkshire. Private, G/18286, 11th Queen's Own (Royal West Kent). Killed in action 07/10/16, aged 26 years. Memorial: Thiepval Memorial, IIC.

The Battle of the Somme had begun on

1 July 1916 (see Joseph Hinton above). Advances were made chiefly in the southern part of the battlefield, north-east of Mametz and La Boisselle, while the German positions at Thiepval and Beaumont Hamel held for months. On 15 September a new factor entered the war, the tank. An attack led by 25 of these new weapons advanced an impressive distance - all of 2,000 yards - to enter Flers and come within 1,000 yards of Le Sars on the road to Bapaume. The Thiepval Ridge was, however, still in German hands and the successful battle to take it began on 26 September. October brought the rain and the soldiers struggled knee-deep in mud - on the roads. Off the road the mud was waist-deep in places. A man might drown in it, certainly would if shot. Then it also got cold, even down to freezing. It was in these conditions that the Battles of the Transloy Ridges were fought and, on 7 October, the Royal West Kents captured Le Sars. Their casualties were heavy, and included Private Adams. (See also John Henry Timms, above.)

Thomas David Richardson

Born Silverstone. Enlisted Bristol, residence Winterbourne. Private, 242333, 2/5th Gloucestershire (Territorial). Killed in action 31/09/18. Memorial: Villers-Brettonneux Military Cemetery.

On 31 September 1918 the British were celebrating the break-through on the Hindenburg Line north of St Quentin. It seems likely that Thomas Richardson died in that action.

Roll of Honour 1939-45 - The Second World War

Francis Edward Rodda

Born Whittlebury, 1915, son of William James Rodda (schoolmaster in Silverstone) and Gwendoline Mary Rodda, and husband of Ethel Marion Rodda, née Paterson, of Syresham (married 15 June 1941). Flying Officer, Royal Air Force Volunteer Reserve.

172 Squadron, Coastal Command. Died Tuesday, 24 August 1943, aged 28. Buried St Michael's, Silverstone, grave 401.

As a boy Francis Rodda lived in the stone cottage next to George Lovell's house at the bottom of Little London and went to the Church of England school. His best friends were Sonny James and Vic Linnell. He then went to Towcester Grammar School where he was called Sam, because his father was born in America. He joined the Metropolitan Police in 1934 and was posted to "R" Division in south-east London. When the war started he became involved in rescue work, once getting the shoes burned from his feet while getting people out of bombed flats.

He joined the RAFVR as soon as the police were permitted to volunteer and had completed basic training by March 1942, when he was in Manchester, waiting to go to Canada. After crossing the Atlantic on board the Queen Mary he arrived at CRAF (Canadian Royal Air Force) Moncton, Canada, in April. The following month he was sent to Grosse Ile, Michigan, USA for training. On 4 June 1942 he was transferred to Pensacola Naval Air Station, Florida. Here he trained on old seaplanes and on Catalinas. He was there until November, homesick and fretting to get back. On 9 October he got his wings; one of the few men to complete the course. He was commissioned on 19 November. More training followed - nine weeks on navigation, for example - in Charlottetown, Prince Edward Island, Canada. A letter from him in February 1943 reported that Frank Lovell's younger son was there as a Pilot Officer Observer. On 17 March 1943 he was back at Moncton for repatriation and sailed on the Queen Elizabeth.

On his return he was posted to RAF Abingdon where he came across Sheila Hinton who was serving in the WAAFs. He was then posted to Coastal Command, Devon. From RAF Chivenor, on the north bank of the River Taw, west of Barnstaple,

Francis Rodda in uniform and his gravestone in St Michael's churchyard.

he flew with Wing Commander Musson in Wellingtons on missions seeking German submarines, U-boats. On 29 July 1943 they sank U.614 in the Bay of Biscay. On 24 August they took off in foggy weather at 11.35 p.m. and crashed ten minutes later. Their slow rate of climb caused them to hit telephone wires some three miles inland of Clovelly, 13 miles (21km) south-west of Chivenor. They had two depth charges on board which exploded, killing the crew instantly and setting the aircraft on fire.

Francis's wife, Ethel, his son Derek and his grand-daughter Joanne, who was then in the Air Training Corps, attended a ceremony 50 years later at which the British Legion of Upper Clovelly dedicated a monument, a boulder with a plaque bearing the names of the crew. Joanne later qualified as a pilot. (From information provided by Mary Rodda, sister.)

Arthur Leslie Turnell

Husband of Bertha, née Osborne of Silverstone. Flight Sergeant, Royal Air Force Volunteer Reserve. 120 Squadron. Died Sunday, 1 October 1944. Buried Northampton (Billing Road) Cemetery, grave no.14547, but gravestone now moved.

"Tiny" Turnell was a Northampton man who worked for W. H. Smith in their newspaper distributing business. He met Bertha at the Weston Boat Club when she was working as a nursemaid for the Douglas family. They were married on Empire Day, 24 May, 1937. She was 23 and he was 22 years old. Before the outbreak of the war they had two sons, Dick and Roger. Tiny played rugby for Northampton and his sons were to do likewise in due time. In 1940, aware that he would be due for conscription in the next wave of call-up, Tiny volunteered, thus gaining the advantage of being able to select the arm in which he would serve, and chose the R.A.F. He was stationed in Ballykelly, Northern Ireland, and flew for some three months of the year from the American Air Force base at

Tiny Turnell and his wife, Bertha.

anything but easy. (Based on information given by his widow, Bertha Turnell of Murswell Close.)

Albert Edward Roberts

Son of Frederick and Gertrude Roberts of Cattle End and husband of Daphne Rose Roberts of Northampton (née Varney of Little London, Silverstone). Lance Corporal, Royal Army Service Corps. Died 07/02/45, aged 25 years. Buried Sai Wan War Cemetery, Hong Kong, grave VI.H.4.

Albert Roberts worked at Stowe School and then in a factory in Roade. He married Daphne at St Matthew's Church, Northampton after he had joined the army. They had no children. He was sent to Singapore, it is thought, and was captured. He was killed when a British bombing raid hit the camp or possibly the ship in which he was imprisoned. His younger brother James (Jim) also served in the army in the

Keflavik (west of Reykjavik) in Iceland. It was too cold for year-round operations because the aircraft iced up. On 30th September 1944, at 2 p.m., Tiny and the rest of the crew of nine men took off in their Liberator, an American aircraft, on patrol as part of their Coastal Command duties. It was a 12-hour flight and when, on the Sunday morning, 1 October, they landed Tiny was entirely exhausted. More than half asleep, he walked into a revolving propellor. Bertha was given the chance to have him brought home and of the crew two Australians, one New Zealander, one Canadian and some British came as well. He was buried with full military honours. Bertha was left with little boys of five and six years of age, a war widow's pension of 36 shillings (£1.80) a week plus 11 shillings (55p) a week for each of the boys. Life was

Albert and Daphne Roberts at their wedding.

Far East, but he survived and lived until 1988. The youngest of the three sons of the family was John (Jack) who worked for the Tustians for 43 years and was forced to retire when arthritis restricted his activity. He recollects his mother being summoned to the butcher's shop, Barratt's, near the Old Oak pub, to take a telephone call. She went from the house in Cattle End and received the news of Albert's death. So distraught was she that young Jack promised that he would never leave his parents, and he kept that promise, living with them until they went to old people's homes in Daventry; she, aged 91, to one, he, 86 years old, to another. They never saw each other again. They died three weeks apart. (Based on information given by his brother, Jack Roberts of Kingsley Road.)

Martin Marix Evans

SAILOR'S RETURN

Just before the Second World War, Silverstone teenagers walked up Gulliver's Hill by Hazelborough Wood, and their friends walked from Syresham to join them on Sundays. That was how Mrs Margaret Whitehead met her husband Maurice. He joined the Navy and Margaret saw him off on the train at Blisworth Station, then walked back to Silverstone. By a remarkable coincidence, on a visit to America with his ship, he met his cousin Frank Whitehead, also from Syresham, and in the Navy. Maurice's ship HMS Penelope was sunk later in the War but he was one of the survivors. During his special survivor's leave in 1944, he married Margaret.

Early in the War, Margaret joined the Army in the NAAFI, the canteen section of the Services. She was sent on a catering course to Stoke Bruerne and after 12 months was cook charge hand. There were times when she cycled to the Bank in Towcester with over £1000, a lot of money in those days. The King's Royal Rifles, the Royal Electrical & Mechanical Engineers and the Royal Engineers were stationed here.

Mrs Whitehead remembers that the archway opposite Croft's shop was part of Mr Jeffery's butchers shop. A group of children would lead and drag a bullock into the yard for slaughter, and after listening for the shot of the humane killer, watch the beast being bled and hung up. The drain can be seen to this day.
Colin Hughes

BOB GILES

Bob Giles was born on Boxing Day 1921 near Hungerford. He came to the Silverstone area with his family after serving in Burma as a muleteer in the Second World War to be near his parents and married sister in Adstock near Buckingham. In 1959 he applied for a job as a tractor driver on the Circuit, or so he thought, but ended up in charge of a grass drier for a concern called Green Crop Conservation: "You were drying the grass and that was coming out as dust and dried grass and then you were making pig pellets and chicken pellets which was all on the farm and all. And that was how I was operating the grass drier from April right through to October, nearly 7 days a week, 13 hours a day. It got a bit rank in the end.

At that time it was more of a farm than a Circuit. We called it the Ministry Yard. It was right in the middle of the Circuit, by the farm house and near the board fence. In there were all these sows and those gates were tied up with blinking wire, string and everything. A farmer named Graham farmed that. Then Jimmy Brown of the BRDC [British Racing Drivers Club] took over. When you say to people, in them days we had 2,000 pigs, we had a club circuit, we had a British Racing Drivers Club circuit, the Grand Prix Circuit and we also had the farm to run and everything, they wouldn't believe it. You know, we had a grass drier belting out smoke and steam, and all the steam's going across the track and the Formula 3's and all are coming around and took no notice. The marshals were more interested, during the dinner break in coming and watching me work the grass drier. Jim Clark, the racing driver, who had won the Indianapolis Grand Prix, he came up the next week testing, and that was when the testing was done by the hangar. All the cars lined up by the hangar and they came across out onto the track past the hangar. Jim Clark was a farmer and during the dinner break, I see him come in up the steps where I was, operating this machine. And he said "I hope you don't mind, but I'm very interested in

Bob Giles, in white shirt with push chair, in the primitive spectator enclosure in the circuit's early days.

this machine. Every time I come up I like to have a look round it." I set it in motion, on automatic pilot and I said "I'll take you round." I took him round: to the furnace, 120 degrees that were down at the other end. He was enthralled by it all. The grass going up and underneath, the bed and the fans working and drying it, then going back through the bottom one and going through the cyclone and then being drawn by air into the other building into these big silos and then from the silos it went into a big hammer mill and it was all ground up like that. "That was very interesting" he said. "I appreciated that." And then I said "Is there any possibility for me to have your autograph." He said "I'll do better than that." And he gave me an autographed photograph of when he won the Indianapolis the week before.

I've seen bad accidents. Terrible. When they used to come round at speeds of 100

m.p.h. and that was fast, so that when you had come through Club and you were coming up to Abbey, you had to put your foot down to get through Abbey, and then if you put your foot down too much the back end swung out and you ended up in the sleepers. This particular day this old boy put his foot down and the back end swung round and threw him and the car, and the steering wheel went right through his chest.

On motor cycle meetings they used to take the catch fencing down and protect instead with bales, so if a motor cycle hit the bales, it didnt hit the catch fencing, and they were all right. So after this particular meeting the motor cyclists had all got back to square one, testing, only testing. People were coming up and testing cars and this old boy at about 90 m.p.h., I reckon, on the Grand Prix Circuit, and somehow or the other his steering locked just before he'd gone under the bridge just before he got to Woodcote. He went straight into the concrete wall head on. It smashed the car up, and me and my mate we rushed round to see what had happened because we saw the dust and all that blown up. By the time we got there the sheets were all round. His girl friend was on Woodcote corner and saw it happen.

On another particular day, these people came up testing and they were these old-fashioned cars with a roll bar over the top, open but strapped in. We never understood how they went through the scrutineering bay with this particular car and never noticed it. Well, the fittings on the seat belts were nearly rusting away, and when he went into Maggotts going round the corner, everything went. The car tipped over, went from Maggotts to Becketts him with his head on the side. I don't want to put you off but they found his head, still in his helmet at the other side of the Circuit. Now Melvyn Payne was the first on the scene, he jumped over the barriers and only went and picked up this bloke's head in his helmet. He's the track manager up there. I admire the bloke, because he's only a young chap.

When I first started at the Circuit, the runways were all there. And even the main runway where the planes land today, that was all runways during the war. The hangars were all there. Down Hangar Straight was a big hangar which they demolished and took out to Holland. Of course, the main hangar which is up near the Circuit is still there and they have go-cart racing there now. And then one Grand Prix, they had these jets up demonstrating and that. Well this vertical take off jet - the Harrier Jump Jet - you couldn't hear yourself speak. It suddenly come in over the Circuit to land to get its bearings for the Grand Prix and as it landed, it took half the runway up - the jets burnt the runway, all the grass and all the hay and it did a hell of a lot of damage. Only just landing like that. I expect the Air Ministry put it right.

There was no end of things, because Jimmy Brown, he was in Spitfires during the war and that's how he was so interested in all these planes. In those days the Spitfires used to fly around here and Jimmy used to go and have a word with them and pilot them as well.

In the early days all the marshalls had was a green flag and a red flag, and a blue one for anybody passing and a yellow and black flag for oil on the surface. They had a hell of a responsibility every time. About five or six year ago, this car came off the track going into Becketts and there was an opening for the marshals fire tender to stand in but out of view of the track, so that if anything came off they'd be there to deal with it. Well, this particular day, this silly devil wasn't in the opening - he was way back out of the opening and this Formula One came off and hit the fire tender. He wasn't in it. I don't know what he was doing, but it hit the fire tender and caused a pile up there. He got the sack straightaway. He should have been in the fire tender not taking note of what was happening. It made a hell of a mess of my grass. I'd only cut it the day before.

I've met some famous people - Jim Clark and Jack Sears with his son David: he runs a racing team now, the touring cars. I know them well. Jack Sears he was one of the big directors. He used to come down once a month and do you know the first thing he done? He didn't bother going into the house for a drink with the family - Browns and that. He used to get out of his car - he came in a different car every time: he had a Rolls and he had all these different old fashioned cars. You never knew what he was going to pull up in. He'd get out of his car and he'd walk the whole way round that circuit. It was 3 mile you know, round that circuit, more now. And every so often he'd look to find out where I was. If I was out there mowing, he'd come straight across to me and compliment me on my work and that - everso friendly he was. And going back over the bridge one night on my bike, he caught me up and he stopped and he said Bob, I see you take as much pride in your bike as you do in your tractor and your equipment. That was another feather in my cap. He was very complimentary.

I never actually met Graham Hill. But I'll tell you what happened to him one day. He came up there testing and he came from Stowe down into Club, and he lost control or something went wrong with the car, and a whole lot of dust went up. He'd hit the bank. Course nobody expected to see him alive when they got down. You know what he was doing? Sitting on the side of the bank reading a book. There were sleepers in front of the bank. And he'd hit the sleeper round about 100 m.p.h. and gone up onto the bank.

But there was a very bad do that we had: Nicky Fauston - she's top dog at Brands Hatch and she's after this place - this particular day, her father had this big old-fashioned souped up Bentley. It would do about 200 m.p.h. on the straight. And they noticed as he came round Copses, there was sparks coming from underneath out of the engine. They didn't take any notice, but he come into Stowe and he came down into Club and the throttle, the carburettor got stuck. A little bit of metal, when they found out the reason, got stuck in the butterfly which opens and shuts. That was full open and he went headlong into the sleepers, straight over the catch fence which was then about 10 foot high and landed in the car park. He was killed outright. Car burnt out. But the thing about that was, they couldn't get any marshals. So they used to have farm hands doing the marshalling. That was a hell of a responsibility. You never had no training. All they did to you was to say "Right you're down at Stowe, you're at Club. Use your radio, keep in touch." and that's it. Now they've got 50 or 60 marshalls round the track and they're paid top rates.

Abridged from a 1999 interview with Elaine Lovell

CHAPEL GREEN

Motor-racing enthusiasts all over the world will be familiar with Chapel Curve which is part of the Silverstone Motor Racing Circuit. Few of them know that there was once a Methodist Chapel and a group of cottages huddled together beside a copse in a tiny settlement called Chapel Green. A double fronted house, Maggots Moor Lodge, used as a game-keeper's cottage, stood a little way off at the entrance to a riding into the Whittlebury Forest. Legend has it that a chapel dedicated to St Thomas-a-Becket, no longer visible, was built in earlier times, hence the name Chapel Copse. The Methodist Chapel and the cottages on the Green were all demolished in 1939, somewhat urgently, to make way for the building of a wartime airfield. After the war the Royal Automobile Club acquired the land with its runways to found the famous Silverstone Motor Racing Circuit, now home of the British Grand Prix.

Lily remembers how, on Summer Sunday evenings, she and her school friends, in those far off unsophisticated days of the 1920s, used to walk more than a mile by field and footpath to attend service in the tiny Chapel. They were Florrie, May, Ellen, Violet, and sometimes Dora if she managed to get ready in time. As far as Lily remembers there were no boys in the party. I imagined high jinks on the way home but apparently not. The twelve-year-old girls were quite content to be on their own.

The Chapel was a very small room in part of a cottage occupied by Mr Jim Philips. There were proper pews, a reading desk and a small harmonium. Services had to be held in day light as there was no lighting. Mr and Mrs George Payne lived next door to the chapel. George's brother Harry had one of the cottages at nearby Luffield Abbey Farm, with his wife, Liz, and three sons Frank, Arthur, and Lewis. Harry played the harmonium and led the singing. He was very strict with the children and woe betide anyone who behaved irreverently. Sometimes Mrs Payne deputised for her husband by playing with one finger. The Payne boys grew up in the tradition of going to chapel and they all had good voices, especially Arthur who was greatly in demand for village concerts. Their father offered to teach them to play music, but Lewis regretted that none of them took up the challenge.

The chapel was part of the Towcester Methodist Circuit and was a favourite place for preachers to go on a Sunday, especially as Mrs George Payne put on such a splendid tea in her cottage next to the chapel. The highlight of the tea was Albert Markham's dough cake from the village bakery in Silverstone. Markham's delivered to the outlying farms and cottages three times a week by horse and cart. John and Linda clearly remember driving the horse and cart through rough farm roads with many gates to open. They sat on a high seat above the carefully protected bread which was tidily stacked in the well of the vehicle, and carried to the houses in market baskets. After Luffield Abbey Farm and its cottages the next stop would be Chapel Green, then through other farms to Lillingstone Dayrell.

Emily Hinton remembers her father taking her to chapel when she was a little girl. She enjoyed the walk across the fields and will always remember seeing the preacher arriving on horseback.

So now, when you listen to Murray Walker commentating on the progress of Nigel Mansell or Ayrton Senna negotiating Copse Corner, Maggotts Curve, Becketts or Chapel Curve, spare a thought for the people who lost their homes and their little Chapel to make way for the war effort and, later, the Silverstone motor racing circuit.

As told by Lily Hitchcock to her friend Gwen Cox, with additional help from Lewis Payne, John and Linda Markham and Emily Hinton.

THE AIRFIELD

Silverstone airfield was constructed in 1942 by John Mowlem & Co. Ltd.and in April 1943 was taken over by No.17 Operational Training Unit, which had been formed in 1940 at RAF Upwood, where they had trained aircrew on Blenheim bombers. At Silverstone and later also at Turweston, a satellite airfield, No. 17 O.T.U. developed rapidly with eventually over 50 Wellington bombers and some 2,300 RAF and WAAF (Women's Auxiliary Air Force) personnel under the command of Group Captain K P Lewis.

Pilot Officer Priest writes: "An Operational Training unit existed to receive aircrew personnel who had successfully completed individual basic training as pilots, navigators, bomb aimers, wireless operators and air gunners and who were now gathered to "crew up" and receive further training to include night flying, air gunnery, bomb aiming exercises etc. before joining an operational squadron. The procedure for crewing up seemed and perhaps was an haphazard arrangement with the men left to themselves to form a

crew. It was a hit or miss affair, but on the whole was acceptable and worked successfully in most cases".

On each 12-week training course, and there were over 60 of them in the three years at Silverstone, were twelve crews. Training included "Erics" (dummy attacks on Westminster Bridge) and "Bullseyes" with various legs e.g. Goole, Ely, Pershore, ending with the bombing of Kew Bridge. The success or otherwise of these exercises was determined by use of a camera to shoot the bombing. Also important were fighter affiliation (fighter evasion practice), synthetic night flying trials, "Nickel" (leaflet dropping sweeps over France and the Low Countries), and "Window" dropping sorties. Window was strips of aluminium foil dropped to give a false image on enemy radar screens to confuse the defence. "From time to time", P/O Priest reports, "there would be an Air/Sea Rescue Search, usually off the Norfolk coast seeking possible survivors or evidence of aircraft wreckage from a previous night's bombing operation, a tense, sad event, a tedious and frustrating seeking and searching that was almost always unrewarding."

Aircraftsman Plonk writes: "Our job as ground staff was to service the aircraft and keep them flying. This entailed getting to the Flight Huts at 8 a.m. If there had been night flying the previous night, the aircraft would have been refuelled and faults reported on landing. A flight consisted of a Flight Sergeant, a Corporal Fitter and a Corporal Rigger. Depending how many planes we had, it varied between 8 and 10, there would be a compliment of engine fitters, riggers, electricians, radio bods and all other ancillary trades. Normally a fitter and rigger would have their own aircraft to service. Each aircraft would have a daily inspection (D.I.), which meant the fitter checking the engines and the rigger checking the airframe. If you were satisfied the aircraft was serviceable, you signed the F700, which was a record of the plane's

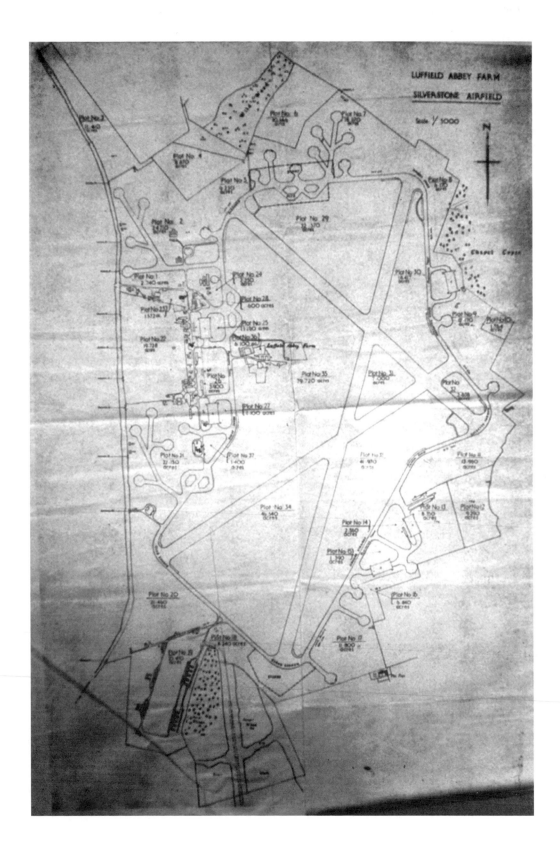

Map of the airfield and Luffield Abbey Farm. (NRO/SPR 76).

flying hours and faults.

"As to the social life on camp, there was a centre which catered for dances, cinema and ENSA concerts. I remember Joe Loss and his band coming. Also there were dances in the local villages around Silverstone and, of course, in the pubs.

"The Summers were pretty good, but in the really cold, hard Winters we more or less lived in our gum boots and leather jerkins. I think night flying was worst,

living quarters were dispersed in Hazelborough Wood, where the concrete bases of the huts and occasional descendants of the garden flowers planted by the wartime inmates can still be seen.

P/O Priest reports: "The walk to the showers and latrines was far from fun in the frost and snow or rain and mud. The working day started at 8 a.m. and finished at 6 p.m. Evening classes and correspondence courses were popular, especially towards

Wellington bombers at Silverstone.

seeing aircraft to dispersal; if one went off the perimeter onto the soft ground up to its axles, it was a tractor and a lot of pushing and shoving to get it out. Refuelling was another hazard, walking along the wings to the fuel tanks, especially if it was frosty, was usually very dodgy. But all pulled together to get the job done. We did not see much action, but it was a job that had to be done and I don't think we did it badly."

Life was considered reasonably pleasant at Silverstone in the Summer, but in the Winter it was found very cold: there was no heating in the hangars for instance and once the ink froze in the inkwells. Metal became so cold that it would stick to bare flesh and tear the skin away. For a time coke from the Northampton Gas Works was in short supply and had eventually to be got in from Birmingham by rail to Towcester. Married airmen lived mainly off base in the villages, but for the single men and women

the end of the war when servicemen were thinking of future careers."

To deal with personal and social problems a Personnel Panel was set up, on which there was no WAAF representative, although there were 200 WAAFs on site. Generally WAAF discipline was less harsh than the RAF's. WAAFs who went absent without leave were just given a good telling off. When two WAAF corporals were discovered in bed with two RAF officers dressed only in their socks, the two WAAFs were reduced to the ranks, while the two officers were dismissed the service, perhaps for not wearing full uniform.

In preparation for the June 1944 Normandy landings, the carpet bombing of German cities was interrupted and training concentrated on precision bombing of targets marked by pathfinder aircraft. Navigational training was also becoming more technical with the development of airborne radar navigational and target location aids such as GEE. Hurricanes were now also based at Silverstone for fighter affiliation training.

On the afternoon of 23rd September 1989, a memorial to the men and women of No 17 OTU was dedicated at the old entrance of Silverstone Circuit by Father Kenneth Ward. The dedication was attended by about 45 people, many of them former personnel of the unit, including the Commanding Officer Group Captain K. P. Lewis. The memorial stone was erected in memory of all who had served and trained with this Bomber Command Operational Training Unit at RAF Silverstone and RAF Turweston.

Based on an account of 17th OTU by Roger Saunders, individual memories and News & Views articles by Colin Hughes and Tony Townsend

THE CIRCUIT

October 2nd 1948, the day which so dramatically changed the future of Silverstone, will go down as one of the most significant days in its history. Previously famed locally for its numerous woodyards, it was on that date transposed to national and international acclaim as the Home of British Motor Racing. The story starts much earlier, when during the early part of World War II the Air Ministry, wishing to build an airfield locally, sought and acquired the land of Mr. Kinningstone's Luffield Abbey Farm along with some adjacent farmland for their Wellington Bomber Training Station. Using land to the south of the village and east of the Dadford Road, John Mowlems constructed a three runway airfield. Residential facilities were erected in the nearby Hazelborough Forest to the west of the Dadford Road completing the complex. The airfield was operational from April 1943 to November 1946 and at its peak it had a population of some two thousand personnel. Here, trained airmen were

received and welded into an harmonious crew through a residential course of 12 weeks.

With the war over and a wish to get back to normal activities, the hunger to kick start the British motor sport calendar was paramount to the RAC [Royal Automobile Club]. They started to look around for a suitable venue to host a Grand Prix. The circuits of the pre-war years were no longer available. Donnington Park had been requisitioned by the government and was in disrepair, Brooklands, having been sold to Vickers Armstrong in January 1946 was now being used for industrial purposes. The RAC found two possibilities, the airfields at Silverstone and Snitterfield, near Stratford-upon-Avon. Thankfully they chose Silverstone. At the end of the war, with the

Marshalls refresh themselves in preparation for a Grand Prix of the 1950s. From left to right: Bill Startin, Bill Gascoyne and Pierre Cantin.

departure of the RAF, the former airfield at Silverstone was being used by the Rootes Group for storage and the international packing of their Hillman Minx, Sunbeam Talbots and Humber Snipes. With only six weeks notice Silverstone Aerodrome was confirmed as the venue to host Britain's first post war Grand Prix. A busy time lay ahead and under the control of its first manager, a former RAF pilot Jimmy Brown. The task was formidable. As a result of his planning, drive and determination Silverstone was transformed from a redundant aerodrome

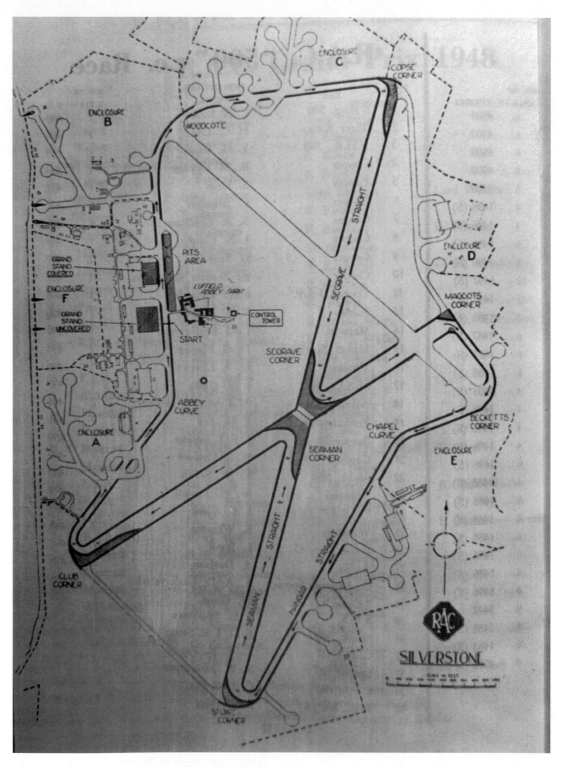

The circuit for the first Grand Prix at Silverstone, 1948.

being used for growing crops and vegetables through a War-Ag. initiative into an arena that would one day become a major sporting venue. These six crucial weeks saw the coming together of the infant Silverstone Circuit and the community that proudly shares its name.

Stories abound of local and contracted workers grafting all hours to prepare our circuit for that crucial day, October 2nd. On reflection it was important to everyone that the RAC appoint the right man. Fifty years later both Silverstones, the circuit and the village, have good reason to thank the RAC for their skill in making that crucial choice. Spectators were eager to see the best in motor sport after the barren war years. On that day they swarmed from all points of the compass to descend upon rural Silverstone. The main contenders, in the principal race, were the teams of the Italian Maseratis and French Lago Talbots. Battling against these two giants of their day were the privately entered home-grown ERAs. The British drivers and their mechanics were working under great pressure as they were having to use pre-war cars as opposed to the modern technology available to the factory teams of their immediate competitors. The day was outstanding. It attracted an enormous crowd, far greater than Jimmy and his gallant team could have envisaged. Thanks to his great leadership and the efforts of his team their apparently impossible goal was achieved. After the race it took some people until midnight to clear the car parks, such had been the magnitude of this sporting event.

The first post-war RAC Grand Prix resulted with a 1-2 for the works Maseratis driven by Luigi Villeresi and Alberto Ascari, both outclassing the valiant Bob Gerard piloting his privately owned pre-war ERA to a creditable third spot. Another significant event was in the warm up race. The 500cc race saw a certain 19-year-old, Stirling Moss, in his Cooper JAP. He was to record the fastest practice lap and lead the race until transmission trouble put him out of contention.

After such a busy period Jimmy Brown and his gallant crew could not rest on their laurels. The next Grand Prix was only 7 months away. May 14th 1949 was to see Silverstone host its second Grand Prix and move along the path to establish it as Britain's premier circuit - a position it still proudly holds 50 years later.

The 1949 Grand Prix brought back the crowds and another Maserati victory. Baron de Graffenried of Switzerland showed off his supreme driving skills in another Maserati 4CLT. Bob Gerard put in another fine performance giving him second place despite his outdated pre-war ERA. With two Grand Prix run, 1950 was just around the corner bringing with it the supreme day in the early life of Silverstone.

Motor racing history was made on Saturday, May 13th that year with a series of impressive firsts. The Grand Prix was honoured by a visit of King George VI, Queen Elizabeth and Princess Margaret. This was the first time a reigning monarch had attended a motor race and Royal Silverstone was born. The Federation Internationale de l'Automobile honoured Silverstone with the status of Grand Prix d'Europe, a first for a British circuit. If this was not enough, 1950 was also the first year of the World Drivers' Championship with Silverstone heading the Grand Prix to count in that year's championship. In addition it was the first of many times the great talent of Juan Manuel Fangio was to be seen in England.

Silverstone by now was establishing itself on the sporting calendar and year by year changes were gradually made to transform the ex-airfield into a prestigious theatre for motor racing excellence. This was helped by the BRDC buying the lease of the farm from the incumbent Mr. Graham in the late fifties. The farm and infield were being used for pigs, cattle and chickens as well as milling of the cattle food along with

Silverstone's fine
SUCCESSFULLY DELIVERED BY DR. FRANK NEWTON

JAMES HUNT OPENS SPORTS PAVILION — FUNCTIONS HALL

Exchanging gifts — Dr. Newton (left), James Hunt and Lord Hesketh.

EX-WORLD motor racing champion, James Hunt considers Silverstone his spiritual home as a driver and if ever he needed a positive demonstration of his popularity in the village it came on Saturday.

It seemed that the entire community turned out to see him unveil a plaque and officially open the proud new Silverstone Recreational Association pavilion and function room.

The villagers had spent years scrimping and scraping funds together to make the building of the facility possible.

What a compliment that their first guest should be a celebrity such as Hunt who arrived, characteristically dressed in jeans and running shoes, accompanied by the lovely Jane Birbeck and his great friend Lord Hesketh.

SHORT NOTICE

Remarkably, the whole occasion was envisaged and arranged with only five-days notice and, fittingly, the initiative was taken by Dr. Frank Newton, chairman of Silverstone Recreational Association, and the man whose energy, ingenuity and persuasiveness had guided the pavilion project to success.

Dr. Newton's commitment to the project was aptly described by Dr. Geoff Lidgard, the first chairman of the Silverstone Recreational Association, who said: "Frank has almost lived on the site and it got to the stage where a person had to lay 50 bricks to get a consultation at his practice."

Mr. John Tustain, chairman of Silverstone Parish Council, echoed the sentiment when he remarked that "were it

not for Dr. Newton's enthusiasm and leadership this building would not be here today."

Introducing James Hunt, Dr. Newton commented on the parallels of progress between the racing driver and Silverstone Recreational Association.

"It was in June 1973," he said, "that 100 Silverstone villagers first decided to buy a sports field. About the same time James Hunt let the throttle out of his racing career by finishing third in the 'Race of Champions' at Brands Hatch.

PROGRESS

In March 1974, a village meeting was told that a field had been purchased, while at the same time Hunt gained his first Formula One racing success with victory in the Daily Express International at Silverstone.

Things progressed from there — Hunt going on to win the world motor racing championship, and Silverstone Recreational Association eventually amassing sufficient monies to build something to go with their field.

Said Dr. Newton: "It soon became obvious we would not get an early village hall grant allocation from South Northants District Council.

"So, with the aid of a Sports Council grant, we modified our plans and decided to build a pavilion first and, hopefully, the sports/village hall later."

PACKED HALL

Opening the pavilion, James Hunt congratulated everyone on their splendid efforts and, looking at the hundreds who had crammed themselves in to see him, hoped they would not all come to use the place at once.

Hunt went on to describe the "great warmth and friendship" he always experienced in coming to the area and said that through the Silverstone people and Alexander, Lord Hesketh, he would always consider the area to be his base in motor racing.

STIRRING DEEDS

"Besides", he quipped, "Silverstone is the one circuit in the world where I could drive down the outside of the traffic jam if I was late for a meeting and not be arrested."

Parish council chairman John Tustain, in thanking Hunt, described the debt owed to him by saying: "Through his connections with Lord Hesketh and his stirring deeds on the race-track, he has done a great deal to make this area known and respected throughout the world."

PRESENTATIONS

There were various presentations.

Dr. Newton received a large bottle of whisky and a mounted trowel in

baby
AND VILLAGERS

thanks for his efforts; there was a traditional bottle of champagne for Hunt as he stood on the visitor's rostrum borrowed from Silverstone circuit, and the Hesketh team presented a framed picture of Hunt with their championship winning formula One.

AUTOGRAPHS

And, as Hunt obliged the many autograph hunters by signing copies of his book, 'Against All Odds', a bouquet was given to Dr. Newton's wife by Katherine Townsend, and a posy to Jane Birbeck by Lucy Bignell.

Afterwards, at a sherry reception, Dr. Newton described the building of the pavilion as "rather like a pregnancy with nine months hard labour and a fairly quick delivery."

NEXT STOP

"Now we must look after the baby," he said, emphasising that he will continue to remain actively involved in seeing the building function successfully and seeing that the whole village hall project is completed.

Now complete with a kitchen and bar, the pavilion will be base for 26 clubs of which the Sports and Social Club, which will be open four nights a week, is just one — but certainly the most significant financially.

FUNCTIONS

It will open on Wednesdays, Fridays, Saturdays and Sundays, although anyone wishing to have a function on one of those nights would take priority.

Management will be through the Recreational Association committee, of which Dr. Newton is chairman, and which comprises one member of each organisation using the facility.

Dr. Newton talked glowingly about the efforts made by local people in raising funds and providing help with construction.

In particular, he praised Silverstone Circuits for helping to promote the raffle of two cars to raise funds and allowing other events on the circuit including last year's athletics spectacular when 2,500 joggers turned up for their own footslogging Grand Prix.

ALL HELPED

By now there will hardly be a Silverstone resident who has not contributed directly towards building of the pavilion.

But even the comparatively modest 2,200 square feet of space

provided would have cost far too much had it been built by paid contractors.

VOLUNTEERS

Instead the villagers and friends helped themselves, doing all the work for little more than the cost of materials.

People like Frank Plummer who did the wiring; Halam Carr who was spare time plumber; Vic Lovell, Albert Taylesure and Rodney Hinton (bricking); Alex Bennett, Gerald Lovell, Bob Smith, Ted Harper, Mr. Clark, Mr. Churchill, Fleming Bros., and Ash Interiors/Richard Roberts Associates.

YEARS TO COME

The result of their effort was considerable, and justly rewarded by the opening ceremony by James Hunt, and the lasting pride in creating a community facility which the whole village can enjoy for years and years to come.

SILVERSTONE Recreational Association have come a long way since they agreed to pay £10,000 to Northamptonshire County Council for seven acres of land which was to serve as the village playing field.

The 50-year mortgage they had to take out for that expensive piece of ground has hardly been scratched in six years of

paying through the rates.

But, still the community has found cash to maintain the field and still they have banked by one means or another, the £22,000-odd needed to build their pavilion, opened on Saturday.

What they have today is a building of Banbury construction; 2,200 square feet shaped 72 feet by 32 feet.

An important feature — the bar.

Inside is a hall, 34 feet by 32 feet, suitable for disco's, wedding celebrations, meetings and other reasonably large functions.

KITCHEN

There is a good-sized kitchen adequate for serving cold buffets and a reasonable selection of hot snacks; men's and women's changing rooms big enough for two teams each, and served by four shower units altogether.

As well as the normal male and female toilet facilities there is a toddlers' toilet and wash basin, further touches

being the stone-built front porch and suspended ceilings.

Heat is provided via three separate plumbing systems with showering sportsmen paying for their hot water through a meter, kitchen users drawing from a separate immersion heater and a third system warming the main building.

The bar is 'disguised', when not in use, by a large notice board which stradles the front. Otherwise it will serve Tartan and Harp on tap and Litchbrough Ale from two old pumps which have china handles and brass fittings and which

once served in the now closed 'Compasses' pub in Silverstone.

Theoretically, the pavilion represents stage one of a two-phase project to provide community facilities for Silverstone.

After two or three years the intention is to get a village hall grant from the local authorities (if such grants still exist) build a sports hall big enough for badminton and other indoor sports, suitable for stage productions and with a committee room and perhaps some storage space.

That will cost at least another £20,000!

grass drying. In 1969 the purchase of the freehold of the land from the Ministry of Defence allowed more freedom to expand and develop their asset. This was done while the threat of being the site for London's third airport hung over its head. Under the ownership of the BRDC and the management of Jimmy Brown, dramatic changes took place. Jimmy in his wisdom used local labour to facilitate the early changes which I am sure not only saved him money but proved to be a bonding process between both the new and old Silverstones. The local people took both Jimmy and the Circuit to their hearts. Initially he and his wife Kay lived in the village before moving to Luffield Abbey Farm. Silverstone people were heavily involved in many aspects of Circuit life both as full time employees and as part-time workers on the big days. First full-time employees were Carroll Hinton and Ivy Cakebread from Dadford. Both served the Circuit loyally and became stalwarts of Silverstone Circuit. After the racing came the clean up with an army of paper pickers. May Adams, Mrs. Coleman then Kath Walker recruited a posse of ladies to perform the many tasks. In the early days the ladies armed with wide brooms even swept the circuit and pits. Toilets in the early days were not connected to the main sewer, which resulted in Silverstone ladies having to empty the basins. To show their appreciation the spectators put coppers into a waiting empty Oxo tin. The contents of the Oxo tin was eagerly awaited back at home. Children were more willing to go down the shop and do general errands when the Oxo tin was full. Bed and breakfast, now such a thriving trade at the major meetings, had an interesting start. The need to put up scaffolders from Mills of Coventry before the Grand Prix and cockneys employed by the Daily Express and Daily Mail as newspaper sellers meant any back bedroom brought in a welcomed revenue. At the other end of the scale racing drivers did stay locally too. The most noteworthy being Graham and Bette Hill who once stayed at Ira and Bette Davis's house in Brackley Road. The date of their stay is vague, they say that it could have been around nine months before the birth of Damon! If so, it would give a new slant to his 1994 Silverstone British Grand Prix victory on his home circuit in front of his home crowd! In the early days the drivers used to frequent the village pubs. The White Horse was often the venue for off-circuit refreshments and along with the Royal Oak had close links with the Circuit. Tales of meeting the likes of Graham Hill, Mike Hawthorn, Roy Salvadori, Jack Brabham and Ron Flockart were common. [See Plate 24.] The ace drivers of their day would come off the circuit for Flora Webb's renowned Ploughman's which would replenish the stomach and Sid Webb's best bitter which quenched their thirst. Silverstone Circuit was becoming an important part of the social history of the village.

It was not until the Grand Prix were moved from Saturdays to Sundays and the race enthusiast following was boosted by the Lord Hesketh/James Hunt factor that media coverage increased. Joe Public then started to make a week-end of the British Grand Prix taking advantage of the local hospitality. This has brought an ever increasing amount of revenue to the village. The local farmers welcomed the need for extra car parking and camping, the pubs and shops the increase of trade and local organisations and individuals an opportunity to earn an extra shilling. A good example is Silverstone Recreational Association which has in its 25 years transformed a 7.1 acre field to a facility which now hosts a village hall and playing field of which it is very proud. This is with thanks primarily to funds raised at the Circuit through the annual Grand Prix Raffle, camping and philatelic projects.

Over the years the circuit has been used for a wide range of activities other than motor racing. These have added to the richness of village life for those who have wished to avail themselves of them. In the sixties the film The Green Helmet was filmed partly at Silverstone with local people as extras. James Bond in Thunderball used Hanger Straight as the M1 to fire a rocket from a motor cycle to destroy a car. Sneaking into a hanger with Nicholas Whitehead, a schoolboy friend, to sit in James Bond's Aston Martin is still one of my cherished memories. Famous advertisements too have been filmed at the circuit. Joan Collins and Leonard Rossiter came to Silverstone to film one of their series of Martini advertisements.

As we now reflect and look ahead to the new millennium, the fifty-year marriage of the two Silverstones is as strong as ever. Since the early days (when Jimmy Brown stated: *We relied on faith, hope, charity, rope and posts!*) the circuit has been transformed beyond recognition, to a sophisticated, highly professional, forward-thinking business. It continues to project the name of Silverstone to every country in the world, while keeping faith with the village that shares its name.

Gerald Lovell

APRIL 1982: WHAT IS A VILLAGE?

We all think we know the answer. But there are two reasons why change is on the way. The first is that the current County Structure Plan comes to an end in nine years (1991), so the next County Structure plan will be in preparation in only five or six years time. The second reason is the proposed new bypass road, which will take a lot of traffic off the stretch of the A43 that passes through Silverstone.

The County Structure Plan decided how much building and development could take place in each village. In this village small scale developments, up to 6 houses, have been allowed on little patches of land dotted around here and there. Before the sewers were expanded the amount of new building was very restricted, but the sewerage capacity is now great enough for Silverstone to grow much bigger.

When the bypass is built, a lot of land will no longer be affected by the dense stream of traffic, and the village could then grow rapidly into a small town, perhaps even as big as Towcester. When will the bypass be built? Official sources have stated that it will be very soon, or maybe by the end of the century.

There are various possibilities for the future of Silverstone. No growth at all seems most unlikely. We could have a steady trickle of growth, or a rapid and massive expansion. We can sit back and see what fate (and the speculators) decide, or we can do some deciding and choosing for ourselves. The first stage of action is in your hands right now, your free copy of your village paper, with this important question to think about: What do WE want for Silverstone?

The next stage will be a questionnaire, to be distributed and collected, so that we can find out the opinions of Silverstone people. The answers will provide facts about how we all feel, and that will be much more useful than vague impressions. Armed with these facts we will be ready for a village meeting, where we might decide on a further stage of action that many other villages have found useful - a Village Appraisal.

A Village Appraisal is a report based on the facts of the village and the opinions of the villagers. For instance, there has recently been some disquiet about the amount of new building in the village. Can young Silverstone couples afford these houses? If there are to be so many new homes, (perhaps hundreds more when the bypass is built) will the school children have to be bussed to another village? The Infant

School is already nearly full. What about newcomers to the village who bought their houses for the sake of country views and greenery and who see these views vanishing? If there are to be more people, should we perhaps encourage planning permission to be given to provide more jobs in the village?

BILL COOK

Reading the last News Letter regarding driving sheep on the notorious A43, brought back memories of Bill Cook. Many old Silson folk will remember Bill, who regularly drove cows to be milked from the small holding on the A43, now farmed by the Coles family, to the top of Little

The Winterhills/Brackley Road junction, the houses of Murswell Lane beyond.

There will be plenty of other questions that will occur to you, this is something for us all to share and work at.

If we can produce a sensible report about the village, then we can present it to the County Planners, and hope to have some say in our future. If we ignore the whole business and say, "It will all be the same in 100 years", we may discover that in far less than 100 years, it is not at all the same. Instead of a village, we might have an isolated suburb or a small town. Is this what we want? We cannot bring back the "good old days", or even the "bad old days", but we can do something about the quality of life in Silverstone in years to come.

London (1930-1940s).

Bill was blind and did this job unaided apart from his white stick. Bill was also a skilled cane worker, and there are still shopping baskets he made in use in the village today.

The A43 is getting worse all the time, accidents almost daily. Come on by-pass, or do we have to wait another 20 years?

A Silverstone Pensioner.

THE SILVERSTONE BY-PASSES

In January 2000 the completion of the dualling of the A43 between the M40 and the M1 finally got the official go-ahead. The need had been evident from the 1970s.

Already in the early 1980s the A43 was being described by the police as one of the busiest non-motorways in Europe. By the mid 1990s it looked, after public exhibitions on the choice of route and the felling of a swathe of trees in Hazelborough Wood adjacent to the road, as if construction would start. However, the Labour General Election win in 1997 brought a review of all road schemes in a climate that was increasingly anti-road and anti-car. It was at this point that the

The new by-pass will, of course, not be Silverstone's first. Colin Hughes wrote in News & Views in 1992:

It must have been an upheaval for the village and a topic of conversation in 1930 when the by-pass was built. Even though the amount of traffic was only a fraction of what we have today, the old road, the main Oxford to Northampton road, was totally inadequate for the lorries negotiating the narrow road past the Post Office and along

The view north towards Catch Yard Farm (left) and Windmill Farm (centre, on horizon) on the route of the planned by-pass.

Silverstone By-Pass Action Group, which had already been campaigning for a number of years, called a Village Meeting. The major outcome was a stream of letters to Ministers. Civil servants were reportedly impressed, and perhaps the depth of feeling recorded by so many, plus, of course, the many very good and telling objective reasons for dualling, saved the A43 scheme, while others were abandoned.

Little London. There does not appear to have been so much controversy about the route, though it must have been hard for those losing almost all their gardens in the days when home-grown vegetables were so important to the weekly budget. One house had to be demolished and the house now at the corner of Winterhills was built instead. Some people had to cross the by-pass to a well, instead of just across their garden for water. The new road was of concrete and rather bumpy for a 16 year old girl and her father, cycling off to work in service at Grafton Regis, perhaps the first to ride along it before the road was quite finished and officially opened.

The first by-pass brought its problems. The second one, while improving life for residents in the Brackley and Towcester Roads, removing the barrier that separates Kingsley from the main village and providing easier vehicular access into and out of Silverstone, will, no doubt, have its downside. An Advanced Technology Park linked to motor racing will get the go-ahead on the completion of the dualling, providing employment and possibly attracting further housing, commercial and industrial development. The old Silverstone of wood yards has already largely gone, mourned by many. In spite of the changes the fact remains that many find Silverstone a very pleasant and fulfilling place to live.

Nigel Read

SPRING INTO BUSINESS

Until the mains water finally reached this village, fifty years ago (-ish), there were scores of wells, springs and pumps supplying the water to village homes.

Running through limestone, the water here was supposed to be very good, high in beneficial minerals such as manganese. "That's why there are so many long-lived folk among Silson people," I was informed. So if you are tired of paying inflated prices for spring water, how about restoring the pump in my barn, and going into business to market Silverstone Water.

The pump needs reassembling. It is under cover (or could be replaced with an electrical pump) and there you go.

P. Baker, News & Views, June 1986.

PART 6 💻 The Village in 2000

AGRICULTURE, COMMERCE AND INDUSTRY

Scriptwriter and novelist Rio Fanning in his workroom at Hall End Cottage.

In the first half of the 20th century the farms that circle Silverstone provided the local employment that, along with the wood yards, made Silverstone reasonably prosperous and kept the village and its shops going. At the end of the 20th century farming became a less labour intensive industry. Oppressed by competition from more gentle climes, the BSE crisis and an unfavourable economic climate, prices for livestock fell very low, so that many farmers, not helped by European Union and government bureaucracy, had to look for alternative sources of income. The wood yards reduced to one, Linnells, processing more imported wood than in the past. Although a significant number of inhabitants ran small businesses, some from home - from high quality joinery and machine parts production to publishing and TV script writing - Silverstone became a largely dormitory village with most of the employed driving to work in the neighbouring big and expanding towns.

Barry Linnell at the entrance to the new retail facility at Linnell Bros Ltd.

For some years, of course, the biggest enterprise had been Silverstone Circuits, and if not all employed there lived locally, the many events brought a lot of custom to local shops and boosted the income of those farmers providing camping and parking facilities, and of those householders offering accommodation. With the growth of Jordan Racing and the planned High Technology Park at the Circuit employment opportunities look set to expand in the future.

Apart from the farms, constants over the years have been Linnells Woodyard and local builders.

Linnell Bros Ltd

The history of Linnell Bros Ltd, Timber Merchants has been given in Part 4. As the new century opened, the area in front of the older buildings, in the past used for timber storage, was cleared to make way for a great wooden building, a massive log cabin, to provide retailing space for the expanding business in material and equipment associated with the use of timber.

P.V.Hinton (Builders) Ltd

After the severe winter of 1962/3, Peter Hinton, having had twelve weeks on the dole, was offered work by various people. Work continued to progress and in 1966 his brother, Rodney, joined him and the firm of P.V. Hinton (Builders) Ltd was formed.

In those days grants were available to farmers for the concreting of yards and roads and the re-roofing of existing buildings. This formed a substantial part of their work. Also, at this time, Local Authority grants were made for the installation in substandard houses of bathrooms, flush toilets, hot and cold water and the re-slating of roofs. Modern steel-framed farm buildings were also grant-aided, and work was available for concrete floors and walls to these buildings.

Maintenance work was important too, notably the twenty-four years they carried out all building work, including extensions, at the Green Man Inn, Syresham.

The first dwelling the firm built was in 1968. The firm progressed to employing six people, some of whom came straight from school to learn a trade. New houses continued to be built, for private customers, in Wappenham, Syresham, Whittlebury, Silverstone and Wicken. A total of twelve houses were built by the firm. Alterations and modernisations were also carried out.

Peter Hinton recalls building one house in Whittlebury with bedrooms on the ground floor and living accommodation on the first floor, which was called the upside down house by an old village resident, who visited daily while work was in progress.

After thirty-five years came the retirement of both partners and the company ceased to trade.

From a 1965 invoice:

One bag of cement cost: 8s.3d (41p)

Half a gallon (2.25 litres) of white paint cost: £1.10s.6d (£1.52)

Lorry load of building sand cost: £8. 19s. (£8.95)

Ten gallons (45 litres) of petrol cost: £5.7s.6d. (£5.35)

Price of our first dwelling built: £3,100 (complete)

Hinton Bros, Building Contractors

Hinton Bros was started by Mr. Dan Hinton and two brothers in the 1930s. After a while Mr. Dan Hinton ran the business by himself. The business, based in what is now the Post Office Stores, was very successful, with work carried out in Silverstone and many surrounding villages and at the Circuit, from when it first opened in 1947. The company also acted as funeral directors for some considerable time.

When Dan, in 1973, decided to retire at the ripe old age of 80, Mr. William John Coleman bought the business. He is the fourth generation of stonemasons and

Chris, left, and John Coleman creating a subtle, curved roof at 1 Murswell Lane in 1998.

bricklayers of Silverstone who date back to 1857. The firm is still very successful today, although it is now based in Towcester. Shortly John Coleman's son Christopher, the fifth generation of the Coleman family and partner in the company, will take over the reins and continue the good name of the family as stonemasons and bricklayers.

Paul Smith, Builder

Paul Smith relates that he started his working life at Hartridges in Buckingham, with whom he gained an HNC in Mechanical Engineering at Wolverton College. Determined to work for himself and in pursuit of an ambition nurtured from childhood, he set up on his own in 1987, doing firstly subcontracting work, mainly roofing for contacts he had cultivated in the building trade. He discovered the pitfalls of subcontracting when re-roofing the Saracen's Head at Towcester, when the lead contractor went bankrupt. Fortunately they did not owe him too much. Renovation of a couple of houses kept him in business until he was able to develop his father's wood yard at West End, near Blackmire's Lane

with two houses for sale and one to the rear for his and his family's use. He has ambitious plans for the future and is engaged at present in preserving one of the last old cottages at the top of West End, for which Silverstone must be thankful.

Graham Churchill Plant Ltd

Graham Churchill, another example of local boy made good, started at Silverstone C of E School in 1956. His parents had arrived in Silverstone in 1947 and his father was given the task by the Ministry of Agriculture & Fisheries, for whom he worked, to return Silverstone Aerodrome to agricultural use. They lived in Luffield Farmhouse for about 3 years and then moved in 1951 down to Winter Hills where they live today.

He moved on to Towcester Secondary Modern School, and could not wait to leave! 1966 saw the end of his school years but he had no intention of working for anybody else - he had decided long ago that he had to be self-employed. So he started buying and selling agricultural tractors and machinery for about twelve months, and then started working a second-hand digger that he bought for £185, lent to him by his father. He started working on the new housing development in Silverstone at Hillside for a company called Alfred James from Northampton. Houses were selling there for £5,500 in 1968.

In 1969 he bought his first new digger for £3,600 and in 1970 he was joined by Mick Tew from Kingsley Road. Mick is a first class machine operator and by working all the hours they could, they made the company grow slowly with other local drivers joining over the years. By the early 1980s the company employed about seventeen people and became Graham Churchill Plant Limited in 1986, slowly moving into tipper lorries as well as excavators. In 1998 the firm moved into new workshop and office premises at Winter Hills owing to the Silverstone by-pass being squeezed between the old yard and Winter Hills Farm, the old Grade 2 hunting lodge where he lives.

Graham Churchill Plant Ltd currently operates fifteen excavators and twelve tipper lorries and employs around thirty people.

SHOPS

In the early part of the 20th century Silverstone was largely self-supporting for everyday goods, although the carters still had plenty of trade fetching and carrying people and goods to and from Towcester and Northampton. At that time there were general stores in both Cattle End and West End, there being a good many more cottages there then than now, housing in many cases largish families. Many cottages were condemned and demolished and with the reduction in clients and the advent of wider car ownership these very local shops disappeared.

Before the second world war there were more shops in the centre of the village. At the top of Stocks Hill stood a haberdashers shop, and where Croft's is now was a bakery, while across the road to the right of the archway was a butcher's and further down Church Street at No.7 a cobbler's, at one time also a cake shop, opening onto Paradise Row, itself a line of nine cottages, the first of which was inhabited until 1969. Now the terrace has been converted to a barn and stores for the nearby farm.

There was the Post Office at various locations in the lower High Street, and at the higher end of the High Street was the Top Shop, a general store, which served not only its immediate neighbours, but also those cottages on Chapel Green situated on what is now the Circuit. On the Brackley Road stood and still stands a butcher's shop. On the Kingsley Road estate where the first houses were built just before the war, there

was also a shop until 1991.

Now with the steady centralisation of the retail trade, most of these shops have closed and Silverstone is left with just three: C. B. King Butchers, the Post Office Stores and Matthew Croft Stores.

The Butcher's Shop, Brackley Road

According to the late Lewis Blencowe, butcher on these premises from Autumn 1948 to Summer 1971, there was a butcher's shop here from at least the early 1900s, when a William Culley ran the business, followed by the Lovells in the early 1920s. Johnny Barratt took over in 1923 and stayed until 1948, when Lewis Blencowe moved from his Syresham butcher's shop and 100 acre farm. In 1948 rationing, which had been introduced in the war to ensure a healthy diet for all amid acute shortages of many foodstuffs, was still in force during the post-war period of austerity. The weekly meat ration per person was 8d (about 3p in modern money), lower in fact than during the war itself. This obviously restricted trade and many country butchers disappeared. Under rationing the distribution of meat was closely controlled by an army of inspectors. Cattle were graded, each butcher receiving a share of the best and inferior animals and of foreign meat. At this time the animals were still brought to the shop to be slaughtered, and to ensure the business would survive Lewis Blencowe, unlike many others, had his slaughter house brought up to standard.

By 1952 when meat rationing ceased, Lewis Blencowe's shop was the only true country butcher's for many miles around. He would typically slaughter each week two bullocks, ten lambs and six pigs, all local animals from Silverstone, Whittlebury, Chackmore, Whitfield and Foscote, and make three hundredweight of pork sausages. A bullock could be bought for £80 and a pound of rump steak would set you back all of 12 shillings (60p). Animals were delivered three times a week. At peak periods he would serve up to 200 customers a day, delivering twice a week to a further

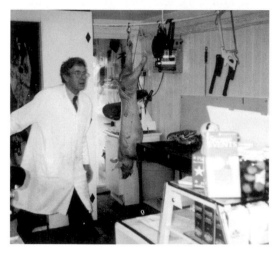

Colin King hurries to serve a customer.

100 as far afield as Buckingham. Lewis Blencowe, along with his wife, employed an assistant, but it was above all a family business with his daughters, Jill helping to cut the meat and Heather doing the accounts. There was another butcher's in Silverstone, De Groot's at 5 Stocks Hill.

In 1967 the Blencowe slaughterhouse had to be shut, owing to ever tighter regulations, and with it went much of the pride, knowledge and skill that made the trade so absorbing. Meat was now slaughtered in Northampton.

In February 1971 decimalisation required a new set of scales, which Lewis had bought the previous October for £450. By the February they had gone up to £500! With the coming of more central control Lewis Blencowe retired in July 1971, the business being taken over by Tapp and Beagin until 1985, when the present butcher Colin King arrived from a Hertfordshire family of butchers. Colin King maintains the finest traditions of the trade, dealing only in the best meat.

Lewis Blencowe had strong views about the changes that have taken place over the last 50 years: he deplored factory farming which is not kind and robs meat of its flavour. He was against artificial breeding and beef mountains in cold store where the meat gently deteriorates. BSE was the result of years of malpractice and unnatural feeding. Eating habits had changed too, with the emphasis on fast foods. In the old days people used to take their joints to the baker's to be roasted and in the war everyone kept a bacon pig, which was fed on all the scraps and vegetable waste from gardens and allotments.

The Post Office Stores

Joy and Tony Townsend moved to Silverstone from Birmingham in 1966 and bought the shop in the High Street. They acquired a little later the Post Office which had previously been at 1, High Street. The original shop was small, selling all manner of goods, with a chewing gum machine on

Anne Riley inside the protective screen within the Post Office.

the front wall. (See plates 34 and 35.)

About 1980 they bought Dan Hinton's workshop and converted it into the present shop. Before being a builder's workshop this building was a bakery, with the stoves still present at the date of purchase.

Through the years the Townsends added onto the back of the shop and the house and transformed the garden. The barn, now converted into a house, used to be the school years ago, but in the Townsend's time, it was Tony's bee loft. The shop offered home delivery, free range eggs from their own hens, local honey made by Tony Townsend and a full range of food products, gas heaters and basic camping equipment, as well as full Post Office services, not to mention the advice available from Joy Townsend, who as District Councillor had her finger on the pulse of village affairs and seemed to know everyone.

In what had been the original shop, they had a coffee shop for a number of years, which, an alternative to the White Horse, provided a central meeting point for the locals, to catch up on gossip and news.

The Townsends retired in October 1994 to live in the newly converted house adjacent to the shop. Sadly neither Joy nor Tony enjoyed a long retirement together.

The shop was taken over by Nigel and Anne Riley, who have maintained the quality of service. It has not been easy for them, the garden, much storage space, some customer parking and the bee-loft having passed into the hands of developers.

Matthew Croft Stores

Matthew Croft Snr opened for business in the present shop on Stocks Hill in 1976, after operating for ten years from the former butcher's shop, now converted to a house, across the road to the right of the archway.

In 1982 the shop front was altered, with the entrance door moved from the corner to the right hand side for safety reasons: traffic from the West End direction had increased, making it a particularly dangerous corner. In 1996 the shop front was altered again, this time to retain the character of a village store. In November 1998, when Matthew Croft Snr went into semi-retirement, the business was acquired by his eldest

Sally Cann and Matthew Croft hold a book signing for military history author Martin Marix Evans while Theo de Clermont looks on.

daughter, Sally Cann and Matthew Croft Jnr.

In the late 80s on the retirement of the Dodwells, who had run a newsagent's at 15 Little London, Croft's expanded to become a newsagents as well as a general store, selling anything from ping-pong balls (one delivered to the door personally by Sally one Christmas Eve to the delight of one cat) to underpants (to the relief of one wedding guest). (See plates 32 and 33.)

The Top Shop

Mary Varney, a resident at Clare House, refers to this shop as "Heritage's". She is going back to the period before and after the first World War, when Mr Heritage first managed, then owned a general store and grain merchant's. He advertised in an issue of the Towcester Wesleyan Magazine in 1905 that he sold groceries, ironmongery, bicycles, cooking and heating stoves, as well as grain and meal. Orders of 1/- (1 shilling or 5p in modern currency) and over would be sent anywhere in the Towcester district free of charge. This was done by horse and cart. The old stable was demolished in 1987, along with the "Meal Store". The "Corn Warehouse" had been converted into a granny flat with storage space beneath in 1976.

The shop was bought by Mr and Mrs Potter in the 1930s. To their daughter Alice, brought up in a town, Silverstone seemed primitive and she was dismayed at the move. Wartime was stressful, with their son Les away, serving in the Navy, and the difficulties of rationing. Mr Potter died in 1944. Mr D'Olyly, father of Daphne Tustian, helped Mrs Potter and her daughter to keep the shop going until Les was home. He and his wife Violet continued for a few years before selling to Archer Bros. Mr Bert Archer ran the "Top Shop" while Jack Whitehead managed the "Bottom Shop" (Crofts). The Archers' big innovation was to install two petrol pumps in the late 1950s.

Colin and Sara Hughes bought the premises at the end of 1970. During the eighteen years they were in the shop, shopping habits changed. During the 1970s, large orders went out at the end of each week, but as supermarkets opened locally, the orders diminished and it became more of a "top up" shop. Petrol sales varied with market conditions. Sometimes they could compete on price, other times they were selling lots of single gallons to enable people to travel to cheaper outlets. However, it was always a useful adjunct to the shop which did good business at Grand Prix time and on midweek practice days when the Track pumps were not open. The pumps were almost antique by the 1980s and were sometimes photographed by tourists. (See plate 22.)

The Hughes retired and sold to Janet Drage in 1988.

Petrol retailing became uneconomic for small outlets and the pumps closed early in 1991. The shop was not viable on its own and that closed in the November of the same year to stand empty until February 1998, when the shop area was rented out to Mrs Claire Payne, who with the support of her mother opened a bridal shop under the name of "Absolutely". On display were at least ten dresses, examples of those that Mrs Payne's mother makes to order. The shop also offered a wide range of accessories - shoes, hats and bridesmaids dresses - as well as waistcoats for the men. Only-used-once dresses were on sale too on commission.

Although a bridal shop seems an unusual enterprise for a place of the size of Silverstone, business was reasonably brisk at first, attracted through wedding exhibitions, the press and the yellow pages. Sadly the early promise was not fulfilled and, in 2000, Claire was obliged to close, defeated as much by the crushing burden of business rates as any other factor. Another example of enterprise frustrated by an environment hostile to small business.

RECREATION IN SILVERSTONE

Before the 1970s organised sport in Silverstone appears to have been confined to football. Other sports must have been played, for there was, for example, a cricket pitch. The 1970s, however, saw a flowering of sporting activity: not only the re-founding of the Football Club, but the setting up of the Swimming Club, the inauguration of the Silverstone Recreational Association, which has been the catalyst for so much more, the founding of the new Cricket and Joggers Athletic Clubs, followed in the 80s by the Aikido and Tennis Clubs and in the 90s by the Short Mat Bowls Club.

The football team, 1982.
Back Row: Barry Williams, Rodney Hinton, Pat Prestige, Vic Holt, Melvyn Bignell, Bernard Neil, Tom Hampton, Bobby Fleming, Brian Whitlock, Terrence Varney.
Front Row: Mickey Fleming, Richard Blackwell, Dave King, Dave Rush, Mickey Spencer, Richard Hayle.

Football

As early as 1903 the Silverstone Reading Room Football Club was affiliated to the Northamptonshire Football Association and played for a good many years on one of Linnells fields halfway down the Pyghtle, which doubled as the cricket field. Perce Adams remembers first playing for the village team in the 1922/23 season along the Towcester Road at the top of Shacks Barn, where they had to beat Shutlanger 20-0 to win the league, which they duly did!

Unfortunately further information about the 20s and 30s is scarce. Good old Silverstone names appear in the list of club secretaries: W. H. Hinton 1920/21. H. E. Adams 1921/22, J. P. Osborne 1922/23, G. E. Hockham 1923/24, H. E. Coleman 1924/25, A. J. Linnell 1925/26.

After the War in 1948 the British Legion Football Club was started, playing in the Brackley & District League with the Reserves in the Weedon & District League. The 1st team won their League in 1948/49 and 1949/50. They also won the Northants Lower Junior Cup with 650 people watching. Alec Hayle, who had played for the Boys' Brigade 1937-39 at the age of 15, was Club Secretary for 12 years.

After a gap of four years the present club was formed in 1971, when thirty people attended a meeting in the White Horse pub. A. Osborne became Secretary, B. Whitlock Treasurer and R. Humphries Chairman. The Club was accepted into the North Bucks League, but for three seasons played in the Central Combination League, returning to the North Bucks League for the 79/80 season, where it has played ever since. The team moved to the village playing field in Church Street for the 1974/75 season. At last the Club had a home.

In 1985/86 the Club started a Sunday League team. Over the twenty-seven years of its history the present club has been fairly successful, the various teams winning no fewer than 28 sets of medals. The best season was 1989/90 when the 1st team (Manager: D. Rush) won 4 cups and came Runners-up in the North Bucks Premier League. One of the greatest games was in 84/85 in the Northants Junior Cup away to Northampton Spencer who at the time were the United Counties League Division 1 leaders, which Silverstone won 3-2 in a great game!

The Club has enjoyed a lot of support from the people of the village over the last 27 years and devoted service from its secretaries: A.Osborne 1971-74, D.Rush 1974-75, R.Humphries 1975-77 and B.Whitlock 1977- .

The official history does not mention one incident, which has come to the editors' notice and which encapsulates the famous independent bloody-mindedness of Silsonites: when one Silverstone team objected to a penalty awarded unfairly to their opponents, they disdained any attempt, as is now fashionable with professional footballers, to browbeat the referee. They simply walked off with the goal posts.

Brian Whitlock (Football Club Secretary 1977 - to date)

Swimming

The Silverstone Swimming Club was originally started in 1973 by Patricia Baker, Iona Humphries and Jeny Newton as a means of organising transport and creating a social occasion. Twenty families went to Sponne School pool every Sunday evening for a good number of years until the pool closed and the Club transferred to Brackley.

Today the Club is still going strong with twenty families of all ages participating. Brackley Pool has the added bonus of the sauna, where the parents can disappear for a little while!

In twenty-six years little has changed, except that the reminder notes are now done on the computer instead of being hand-written.

John Fowler

SILVERSTONE RECREATIONAL ASSOCIATION

The Silverstone Recreational Association (S.R.A.) was formed in 1974 to administer the village Playing Fields. The work involved in planning this new village facility was initiated by Dr. Frank Newton, the village G.P. and undertaken by a team of local willing volunteers under his leadership. Much time and effort was involved and grants were obtained to assist with costs boosted by major fund raising activities. A Management Committee was formed from representatives of village organisations and co-opted members and this Committee continues to function today, helping to maintain and improve the village sporting and social activities.

In 1980, following the building of the Pavilion (Phase 1), the Silverstone Sports and Social Club was formed and officially opened by James Hunt (Formula 1 Champion 1976) together with Lord Hesketh and Oscar the dog in January, 1981. The Club helps to fund the S.R.A., providing a social side for its members and for those who join the numerous sporting activities. The annual membership fee is very small and the Club welcomes more local members. The Club has a pleasant and roomy bar area and there are many in-house activities, including skittles, darts and pool plus regular entertainment evenings throughout the year. Originally the Bar was run by volunteers but in recent years a full-time Steward has been employed. The Club is open every evening apart from Monday and at weekend lunch times.

Over the years, the sporting activities have developed well with both the Cricket and Football Clubs entering teams in local Leagues with a good degree of success. Phase 2, the Sports Hall, was completed in 1983 and opened by the Hon. Gerald Lascelles, President of the British Racing Drivers Club. Further major fund-raising in the late 80s enabled the construction of the tennis courts and the formation of an active Tennis Club. The Short Mat Bowls Club was started in 1993 and is an excellent recreational pursuit for all age groups within the community. Sadly, the Badminton Club, which had functioned for many years closed down in 1997 due to lack of support. Various initiatives led to the formation of Junior Badminton and Table Tennis Clubs over the years, but as with the Youth Club and Junior Football these have ceased to function. The Silson Joggers continue to meet at the S.R.A. for training runs.

During the years since its inception, the S.R.A. Committee has continued to work steadily towards the improvement of the facilities by promoting many fund-raising activities, including our annual Grand Prix Draw, our Special Event and First Day Autographed Covers so ably produced by Gerald Lovell, our annual Fete, Tabletop Sales, quizzes and social events. Latterly our funds have been boosted by the money raised from Grand Prix camping and breakfasts with the kind co-operation of the King family of New Rookery Farm.. The money raised, together with local grants, has enabled us to maintain and improve the Sports Field and its equipment, to provide new drainage, to build a new Hall toilet block and store extensions, to refurbish the Hall kitchen, to install new Hall heating and boundary fencing, and most recently to resurface the car park. Until 1996 the children's Play Area was funded and cared for by the S.R.A. but then the Parish Council took over the responsibility.

The S.R.A. depends entirely on villagers' support to maintain and improve its facilities. The Committee were encouraged by the formation of the Silverstone Amateur Dramatic Society, which has put on excellent productions in the Pavilion in 1998/9.

Ann Pullen

Cricket

Silverstone Cricket Club was formed in 1974 under the Presidency of D. W. Dodwell and Chairmanship of J. C. Johnson. Edna Dodwell followed in her late husband's footsteps as President, retiring in 1997 in favour of the current President John Johnson.

The Club initially concentrated on friendly games and in their first season played nineteen games with the first game against Syresham which Syresham won easily. However, two games later Marsh Gibbon provided Silverstone with their first victory.

In 1981 after six seasons of friendly games the Club joined the South Northants League. Since that year the Club has seen both promotion and demotion. A steady improvement in ability of players over the years has seen the Club advance to their current position in the First Division following two seasons in the Premier Division.

The Club has now expanded from its early beginnings and fields a second team in the Fourth Division of the South Northants League. The Club has always been keen to take on young players and the Under 13 team was formed in 1998.

The Club's home ground is on the village playing fields and as well as having a grass square with room for eight wickets it has recently installed an artificial wicket which is primarily used for Under 13 and friendly games.

The Club welcomes players of all ages and abilities with Silverstone residency no longer a Club requirement. Under 13 players

The cricket team, 1977.
Back Row: Norman Blackwell, Victor Lovell, Paddy Johnson, Kevin Brown, John Tolson, Jim Flannigan.
Front Row: Paul Smith, Steven Rush, Richard Hayle, Aled Roberts, Tim Cowley.

have practice sessions during the week during the summer with league matches on Sundays. First and second team games in the league are played every Saturday from the first Saturday of May to the end of August. Occasional friendly games are played on Sundays and midweek.

The Club is financed through membership fees, match fees and the generosity of local sponsors which allows the Club to provide equipment and tools for pitch preparation.

Clive Trundle

Jogging

The Silson Joggers Athletic Club was the brainchild of Dr Frank Newton, who prior to the Joggers formation, could be seen jogging around the village with Gerald Lovell and John Denney in his wake.

During the winter of 1976-77 it was Dr Newton's view that some of Silverstone s middle-aged residents lacked fitness: a leaflet was delivered to all male residents of the village aged 25-45. In February 1977 a meeting in the Church Rooms was followed by the Club's first training run in April at Bucknell Woods, a venue still used today during the summer months. Winter training then, as now, was based at Silverstone Motor Racing Circuit.

The Club has each year prided itself on staging a high quality race with Silverstone Circuit providing an excellent venue. In the early years the race was in the format of age-graded relay races; for the past twelve years, two laps of the Grand Prix Circuit have been used to give the Club one of the largest and most respected 10 Kilometer road races in the Midlands.

Several Cross-Country races have also been staged by the club with varying successes, with courses at three different venues on the edge of the village.

Following the Club's formation the first race entered was the County Cross-Country Championships in Badby Woods. The joggers surprised some of the larger athletic clubs by coming home with silver medals and the second team prize. Since that day the men have brought back silver on one occasion and three bronze medals. The ladies have had three bronze successes. The club has also had eight different athletes go forward to represent the County following these championships.

The Club's greatest hour remains at being promoted to Division 1 of the Chiltern Cross-Country League in February 1996, a league that the club has been a member of since 1988.

Many green vests can be seen participating in local road races of varying distances up to and including the marathon with London having its full quota of Silson athletes. Members are also prepared to travel further afield to participate, with groups taking in the New York Marathon, Paris - Versailles and the Bruges Half Marathon.

Recently the club has been hiring Sixfields Stadium Athletics track for coaching sessions suitable for children and adults alike during the months of April, May and June. In general racing on the track has interested the younger runners rather than the senior members.

The Club will be celebrating its 25th anniversary in April 2002 and is planning a get-together of athletes past and present.

Graham Linnell

Aikido

Silverstone Aikido Club, was founded in April 1983, with the members training under the tuition of Arthur Bignell at the Sports Pavilion.

In 1984 the Club was offered the facility of a permanent, matted Dojo (place of practice) in the old function room above the White Horse pub. The members practised here twice a week until 1989, when a new landlord decided to convert the room into a restaurant. The Club moved back to the Pavilion for a short period and then to the Church Rooms in 1990. Finally, in 1991, we were able to secure a permanent home at the Whittlebury Reading Rooms, with storage facilities available for the practice mats.

The Club, which is a senior club for those over the age of 16, practises the traditional style of Aikido and is part of the Kai-Shin-Kai group of the British Aikido Board. Aikido is a defensive martial art originating in Japan and can be performed by both men and women. Current members travel from as far as Bicester and Oxford to train regularly of a Friday evening.

Mike Wilkins

Tennis

Silverstone Tennis Club was founded in 1989 with the provision of two En-Tout-Cas All Weather Courts. These were provided for the village, through an active fund-raising period of some eight years, by the SRA. Its first Chairman Martyn Dearsley devoted much hard work to the Club.

Today, ten years on and with a current membership of 153, the Club continues to serve the inhabitants of the village (family annual membership for village residents is £25) and also allows restricted membership to inhabitants of the neighbouring villages of Whittlebury, Abthorpe and Wappenham.

The Club aims to encourage members

of all ages and skill levels to participate and enjoy the game of tennis. It achieves this by organising tournaments, club evenings, Ladies mornings and children's coaching sessions. The club is tremendously fortunate in having Stephen Mills as a member: Stephen has been the driving force behind the highly popular children's coaching sessions.

There are also social events such as barbecues and fun sports evenings that are held at the courts, on the playing field or at members' homes in the village.

The Club and the courts are extremely valuable assets for the village, and they need continued support to maintain this excellent facility.

With the possible expansion of Silverstone, the Club is in a position to change direction to fit the needs of the village in the future. At present the Club strives very hard indeed to run a relaxed, loosely structured club with the emphasis on family participation. However, if in the future there is a need or a demand for a more structured club, then with the right leadership, this could be accomplished with the organisation of inter-club leagues, tournaments and matches. But, with this type of club, there would be a real risk of elitism, by placing too much emphasis on serious competition. It is important that however high the standard of play reaches, it must always be remembered that it is a village club, for village members and there must always be a time and place for those less skilled to participate.

The committee is in place to serve its members and respect their wishes. The Club will evolve in line with the needs of its members and the village.

Richard Odell

Judo

Judo first arrived in Silverstone during 1989, when classes commenced at the Church Rooms under the tutoring of Jan Saul, subsequently to become Jan Gascoigne-Rice, at that time a 3rd Dan who had represented her country and had been a former British Judo Council National Ladies Champion.

Classes catered for a wide age range from 5 years old upwards including adults and were relatively successful with many children achieving a green belt, nearly the highest award that can be achieved under the age of 16, while the highest achievement in the adult category was a 1st Dan belt.

Under the name Zanshin Judo Club, Silverstone was represented at many competitions throughout the country, winning numerous medals. One achievement being a bronze medal in the British Judo National Championships.

Sadly in 1996 the club closed due to falling numbers and the remaining members transferred to the Towcester club.

However, in 1998 local parents asked if it would be possible to start an after-school judo club for the children. This first took place at the Infant School, but after problems with the floor, its future was again placed in jeopardy. Fortunately, the Junior School allowed the club to move to their premises in 1999.

The class has gone from strength to strength with numbers increasing and entering once again into the competition scene. Recently it took part in a friendly match with Blakesley School for a trophy, narrowly failing to win, in what we hope will become an annual local event.

Jan Gascoigne-Rice

Short Mat Bowls

An idea conceived by Silverstone Infant School in 1992 led to the S.R.A. organising an introductory evening on Short Mat Bowls at the Pavilion where a representative of the local Leisure Services (Pauline Tong) came to demonstrate and talk about the fun we could have in playing this game which was new to all of us. A goodly number of interested local folk came along and weekly sessions were organised, and eventually a Club and Committee were formed. Mats and bowls were initially on loan from the County but by grants and fund-raising the Committee was able to purchase these and new mats and further desirable equipment. Some items were made by members and storage facilities were built into the Pool Room at the Pavilion.

Since its inception the Club has grown in confidence and stature if not in membership and we now enter the county leagues and many individual competitions. Indeed some of our members now play for the Northants County team. Results in recent years have been very encouraging: 4th in the Southwest League in 1995/96 and 1st in 1996/97, 2nd (only needed 1 point to be champions) in the South League in 1997/98.

Members of the club have entered many tournaments where they have competed against many County and England players. Tournaments consist of Round Robins where you play for points and the mat winners proceed to the knockout stages. Club members rarely have problems getting to the knockout stages and have returned with many runner-up trophies from the final stages, but have never yet picked up the main one.

Meeting on a Thursday evening the members are a small select band who would dearly love to grow and have all the equipment and facilities to support a larger and more active membership. They pride themselves on their friendliness and sense of fun and particularly on the fact that there are members from 12 to over 80 who all play happily together.

The junior sessions are held on a Tuesday evening and provide the basic conception of match play. The summer season of 1998 saw the juniors successfully challenge local clubs in both home and away friendly matches.

Ann Pullen

CULTURAL AND SOCIAL ACTIVITIES

The oldest associations still running are the Boys' Brigade, founded in 1929, and the Women s Institute, founded in 1932. There were almost certainly others at that time which like the Horticultural Society and the Village Show were brought low by the Second World War.

As with the sporting clubs there was a burst of activity in the 70s, when a number of organisations, the Brownies and Guides, the Housewives' Register, the Playgroup, News & Views, Age Concern and the Summer Playscheme were all set up to answer the needs of all ages in the community, to be followed in the 90s by the Needlework Group and the Amateur Dramatic Society. Sadly the Guides and the Summer Playscheme have faded away, not so surprising when one considers the commitment needed and the responsibility assumed by those who are prepared to organise young people today.

The Women's Institute (W.I.)

The Silverstone branch was formed in 1932 with Miss McFerran as President and approximately thirty members. The meetings were held on the second Tuesday of each month, in the afternoon, at the Church Rooms. To this day, meetings are still held on the second Tuesday, in the same place, but in the evening. Then, as now, the meeting consisted of business, a talk or demonstration, sometimes a competition, ending with tea and general chat.

Talks have been very varied over the years: Poultry Dressing (1935), Care of the Feet (1935), Evelyn Home of *Woman* magazine (1972), Gardeners Question Time with Radio Northampton (1995) and a Refugee from Nazi Germany (1997). Competitions are still occasionally held, but in the early days the themes were very different: supper for 2 not to cost over 1 shilling (1935), darn the size of a penny on wool (1936) and gentleman's collar to be washed, starched and ironed (1938).

The W.I. in Silverstone still thrives, with a membership that peaked at eighty some years ago, and is now approximately forty. Besides the Jam and Jerusalem image, members take part in many pursuits, and have entered County Tournaments in Scrabble, skittles, rounders, darts and short mat bowls, having several successes at County level.

Over the years there have been a choir and active drama groups, taking part in village concerts and with one appearance, in 1989, at the Royal Theatre, Northampton, in an old time music hall. One of the plays, some years ago was *Venison and Vengeance*, adapted by one of the members from a story in Old Oak.

To celebrate the 40th anniversary members created the garden around the War Memorial and have maintained it ever since, recently planting new shrubs. A seat was added in 1975 and shortly afterwards, a litter bin. For many years groups have regularly walked local footpaths, ensuring that they are kept open and reporting any difficult points of access. Members enjoy outings to theatres and places of interest, give support to village events and award annual bursaries to help members attend residential courses at W.I.'s own college, Denman.

Branches are invited to send a delegate to meetings of the Federations at County and National levels, to discuss and vote on resolutions on topical issues, which if passed, are followed up and brought to the attention of a higher authority.

Playing its part in helping the less fortunate at local, national and international level has always been important to

Silverstone W.I. Examples of this side of the W.I. include entertaining boys from a community school in Brackley to an afternoon in Bucknell Wood, followed by a tea, and packing parcels of clothing, food and medical requisites for deprived and war-stricken areas of the world.

The W.I. offers different opportunities for every member to pursue skills and interests; it gives friendship and the chance to participate in village, county and national issues - something beyond the home and family.

Margaret Bignell, Rosemary Osborne and Margaret Floyd

Brownies

In 1972 Carole Flynn, Marion Austin, Joan Lidgard and Margaret Floyd, all having daughters who wanted to be Brownies, decided to start a pack in the village, and so the 1st Silverstone Brownie pack, was formed. Over the years many girls passed through the pack, working for Interest Badges, doing craft work, singing, country dancing and generally learning useful skills and having lots of fun. The pack helped at many village events, raised money for charities and regularly picked up litter around the village, long before the Council organised Operation Springclean. Such activities enabled the girls to fulfil their Brownie Promise and Law: A Brownie Guide thinks of others before herself and does a good turn every day.

Some leaders changed, as some moved on, while some stayed a decade. For many years the highlight was Pack Holiday - a week away from parents, learning to live together as a large family. Those weeks were great fun for all, but hard work for the leaders. The girls had to help with all the daily household chores of cooking and cleaning as well as enjoying games, outings and creative activities.

So many girls wanted to join that

eventually the 2nd Silverstone Pack was formed. Sadly the 1st Pack had to close in 1996 owing to a lack of adult leaders. Fortunately the story of the 1st Pack is well documented in five large scrap books and more importantly in the memories of the girls who were part of it.

Margaret Floyd

Guides

Silverstone Guides started in 1976, shortly after which Rita Betts (née King) and Carolle Wilson became the guiders until 1982, to be followed by Jill Brown and Dee Miller, and then Liz Tattersall. After a brief closure in 1989, Rita Betts and Barbara Malcomson re-started them in 1990 only to close again in 1998 because of other commitments, with nobody coming forward to keep the Guides going.

Right from the start the Guides have always had the opportunity to camp, be it on a Stowe School rugby pitch, or at Foxlease, a Guide House in Hampshire, or at Youlbury Scout site in Oxfordshire, or locally in Silverstone or the county. Guides attended International Camps in Northamptonshire in 1991 and 1997, where they were amongst over 1,000 girls from all over the county as well as other countries.

Two girls, Liz Bucklow and Fiona Reid, gained their Baden Powell Award, the highest award in the Guide section.

Most years the girls have entered the County Youth Service Sun Trek in Bucknell Wood, and have come very well up in the scoring, one team winning in 1990. Most years there has been a joint trip with the Brownies to the Derngate pantomime. The Guides have taken part in District events such as an International Party to celebrate Thinking Day or a Night Hike. They have raised money for charities, including a sponsored walk around Silverstone Circuit. They have enjoyed activities such as abseiling, archery, water sports and go-

karting, as well as roller and ice skating and bowling. They have challenged Whittlebury Scouts to outdoor cooking competitions. Many brave souls, both Guides and families, have enjoyed a dawn hike. The Guides have tried belly dancing, fashion and beauty evenings, aerobics, as well as taking various badges. For several years the Guide Pantomimes were famous.

Barbara Malcolmson

Housewives' Register

The National Housewives' Register was started in 1976 by Val Currie and Chris Craven. The group was open to housewives living in Silverstone or the surrounding villages and the rule was no talk about babies or nappies. The group continued until 1981 when it was decided to break away and form the Silverstone Housewives' Register. The group has continued to meet on alternate Thursday evenings during the school terms.

We have invited guest speakers to give talks on: self defence, first aid, graphology, coping with stress, planting hanging baskets, bee keeping, home security, bats, reflexology, knowing your rights, psychometric testing.

Following demonstrations we have had the opportunity to practise making saltdough models, festive floral creations, sugarcraft designs, flowery greeting cards and decorative Easter eggs.

We have been bowling, had a tour of the Royal Mail Sorting Office, visited the Body Shop for a talk on aromatherapy and much much more.

In 1997 the group started to meet during the day on alternate Tuesdays because a lot of housewives were unable to attend in the evenings. This has included trips to Oxford and Stratford-on-Avon, country walks, a tour of the Royal theatre, making Christmas decorations and a talk on the history of Silverstone.

In 1998 the group decided to meet in the school summer holidays with the children. We arranged walks, cycle rides, swimming, kite flying, roller skating, and a trip to Daventry Country Park.

Yvonne Reed

Age Concern

Silverstone Age Concern was formed in October 1977 . There had been two previous organisations which faded out due to lack of support. With the backing of Age Concern and a grant of £50, a Committee was set up under the Chairmanship of Mrs Elsie Torr.

At first, the Monday meetings were held in Silson Surgery, by kind permission of Dr Frank Newton. This was a logical arrangement as many people were waiting for chiropody; also the pharmacist, Ron Garner was present, which facilitated repeat prescriptions. Bingo was the name of the game, other board games were tried but had no appeal. In time Age Concern grew out of the restriction of the Surgery, so crossed the road to the Church Hall, where the Monday Bingo meetings are still held to this day.

In twenty-one years there have been lots of successful coach outings and one seaside holiday. It is difficult to think of a place Age Concern has not been to: Hunstanton, Spalding bulb fields, Weymouth, Weston-super-Mare, Bournmouth, Newmarket, King's Lynn, Malvern, Ely, Stratford-upon-Avon, Woburn, the Cotswolds and the Burford Wild Life Park. Basfords, then Jeffs coaches, have served Age Concern well, but unfortunately coach travel is becoming more costly, and careful thought is needed before taking to the road.

Special events as a change from Bingo have always been a feature of the activities. There was a time when a lunch with a speaker could be arranged, but at present there is no day when the room is available.

Several helpers have opened their gardens for an afternoon tea party, a notable one being at the home of Mr and Mrs Warren, Forest House.

Silverstone Circuit have hosted a Christmas Party for twenty years. It is a regular date, the first Wednesday in December. All the over-60s are invited, so even though a lot cannot come it is a big occasion. In 1998 Whittlebury and Dadford were invited, so it was even bigger.

Age Concern is not a Club. There is no subscription.

Gwen Cox

Playgroup & Pre-School

Silverstone play group was established in 1970 to provide the children of the local area with a secure environment in which to learn and play with their peer group. Over the years it has grown enormously and now caters on average for 35 children. Sessions are nearly every weekday depending on demand, either in the Chapel Rooms or in the Infants' School. The emphasis is still on play, but the early learning voucher scheme (see below) has focused the group on the pre-school educational criteria to which it must adhere. The Pre-school, as it was renamed in 1997, had also, as a charity, to provide a much more educationally competitive environment in order to attract children eligible for vouchers, without whom it would not have been possible to offer very low cost and often subsidised pre-school education to local children. Apart from the paid staff, the Pre-school is supported by a volunteer committee and parents as voluntary helpers.

The Pre-school has seen many changes over the years, not least the refurbishment of the rooms themselves, which took much fund raising by committees and parents and hard work by the Methodist Chapel. Anyone walking into the rooms after the refurbishment would have found it hard to believe that it was in a very poor state only 12 months previously. With a very dedicated staff, a committed supervisor and a hard working committee, the Playgroup/ Pre-school has coped with all challenges.

Vouchers: The equivalent of Vouchers are now passed direct to the Pre-school by the Local Education Authority for all children over 4 for up to five sessions a week. The original scheme, introduced in the mid-90s, distributed vouchers direct to parents.

Gail Toms

News & Views

Silverstone News & Views was first published on 1st June, 1979, although it did not then have a name. This was provided by Mrs Petcher from numerous other suggestions including 'Ard 'Ood & Faggots (Hard Wood & Faggots for non-natives) which was a village slogan familiar to older residents. It was started in response to many complaints about meetings clashing, people missing functions or hearing about them only after they had happened.

Quoting from the very first front page:-
If you have any happy or sad family events, items to sell or services to offer, a note or a phone call can get you into print. You can ask people to join clubs or weed your garden, to play in orchestras or cricket matches, you can tell us about events you are organising, or make comments and complaints about aspects of village life - it's your paper.

The objectives have not changed to this day - but the problem is as before - the editors need the information if they are to print it.

The October 1997 Issue Number 111 (but wrongly numbered 110) was a special free issue funded by increased advertising and the Parish Council who delivered them to every house in the village. It was designed to introduce the paper to new residents and to those older residents who had never heard of the paper. Some increase in circulation was achieved but survival without a price increase was not possible.

Every attempt is made for the paper to appear on the first day of the even numbered months and anything to be included should be delivered to the Post Office or one of the editors by the 20th of the odd numbered months. Blasphemous, party political or anonymous material is not printed. If the writer wishes to remain anonymous in print, that can be arranged, but the editors need to know from whom copy originates.

News & Views is usually on sale at the Post Office, Crofts and the Surgery. The editors are grateful to them for this facility.

June and Eddie Tuck

Summer Playscheme

The Summer Playscheme was started in the late 70s by a group of parents for activities for school-age children. It consisted of organised trips and activities and was funded by a sponsored bike-ride around the Circuit, until expenditure did not match sponsorship. From 1979 to 1996 a cup named after a Silverstone schoolboy, Nigel Tann, was awarded for the number of laps completed, the amount of sponsorship and the condition of the cycle.

Over the last ten years participation has dropped from over 150 turning up for the bike ride to only about 20 in 1998. The Scheme was suspended in 1998, owing to the final two organisers having alternative responsibilities. The balance of funds was handed over to the Parish Council.

Martyn Dearsley

Gardening Club

Compared   to   some   of   the   other

organisations in the village Silverstone Gardening Club is still in its infancy. It was formed in January 1996, with an encouraging number of people at the inaugural meeting and has gone from strength to strength. The aims of the Club are:

1) to promote the enjoyment of gardening,

2) to encourage the sharing of expertise and interest in a variety of plants and good garden practice,

3) to arrange talks and demonstrations on various aspects of gardening,

4) to organise plant sales, visits to gardens and other places of interest to Club members.

Regular monthly meetings are held, with speakers on many aspects of gardening, often in response to suggestions from members. There is always a chance to ask questions, and sometimes there are assembled a panel of experts to answer members' queries. Each year several outings are organised, sometimes on a Summer evening to local gardens of interest or demonstrations, and some being full day trips to more distant venues. Being members of the Royal Horticultural Society, visits to their gardens at Wisley are always popular. When these events include arrangements for refreshments so much the better! Refreshments always play an important part in our social events, at which members enjoy meeting up on an informal basis.

The emphasis is definitely on enjoyment, (and hopefully, education) but at the same time the Club makes a useful contribution to the village. The annual Daffodil Show in April is a very cheerful event, and the Horticultural Show in September is an important date in the village calendar. Many of our events are accompanied by a plant stall, to which members bring any surplus plants and cuttings - a very valuable service! Club members can also buy seeds, plants and bulbs at discounted prices and receive discounts at various local garden centres. The Club has purchased reference books and videos, to form the basis of a library for members' use.

In Spring the appearance of Silverstone has been much enhanced by the planting of 16,000 daffodils and narcissi, donated by Silverstone Circuits and planted by SGC members.

Members include people who have recently come to live in Silverstone, as well as many established residents, young and older, and members from outside the village are also welcome. Recent events have been attended by visitors from Germany and Japan!

Joan Lidgard

The Village Show

A newspaper report of August 1897 records the second annual exhibition of flowers, fruit and vegetables being held in conjunction with Silverstone Horticultural Society. The Village Show in its present form dates from 1984 when Edna Dodwell gathered a group of friends (Margaret Bignell, Ivor Floyd, Tony Townsend and Clive Trundle) together to reinstate a village tradition that had lapsed forty-five years previously. Today the show also includes sections for wine making and the full range of culinary skills. It is technically a closed show, i.e. restricted to village residents, with a fine array of cups and trophies, donated by local organisations and individuals. From time to time, funds have accumulated sufficiently for donations to be made to the village, e.g. the churchyard seat. Three of the original group are still organising the show, but Edna is no longer involved owing to ill health and Tony Townsend is no longer with us. Members of the Gardening Club formed in 1996 now assist in the running of the event which takes place annually in the Church Room at the beginning of September.

Ivor Floyd

Needlework Group

The idea of a needlework group was conceived through chatting to like-minded people who felt they wanted to learn new skills, but in an informal atmosphere. Sue had just finished her City and Guilds in Embroidery and felt that this would be the way forward for her. On a wet April morning in 1996 five eager ladies came expectantly into her kitchen. It was nerve-racking for her, but hopefully a learning experience for them.

The Group tackles any technique from making boxes to dyeing fabrics, appliqué to stumpwork, all achieved in an atmosphere of fun and laughter. Numbers have grown and coffee mornings are held to show the village what the Group has achieved, which is also exhibited at the Church Fete. The Group caters for all abilities: people work at their own level and pace, whilst enjoying each other's company.

Sue Fowler

Amateur Dramatics

The S.A.D. Theatre Company was founded on May 7th 1998 by Gail Toms and Elaine Lovell. The main aim was to provide a village-based opportunity for people with an active interest in amateur dramatics to have a go. The first few months were just spent working on loosening up inhibitions and on improvisations, but it soon became clear that with the cast available there was the makings of a very creditable team for a show.

The majority of the Company were under 16, so the first show had to be adaptable to incorporate the differing ages of the group. It was therefore incredibly good fortune when Peter Fordon's spoof *Murdered to Death* was discovered in Northampton Library. It was exactly right for the Company and promised everyone a good laugh. So in September, 1997 serious rehearsals started. It was not all plain sailing; there was the difficult task of finding a suitable and affordable local venue. Sponne School was initially booked, when the Company was relieved and delighted to discover a much unused stage nearer home, at the S.R.A pavilion. After many setbacks, including the sad departure of Elaine, owing to increasing commitments to other projects, the show went on in May 1998. It was a complete sell-out; there was standing room only. Due to its popularity, it was decided to put on an impromptu performance the following evening, when a further 60 people attended.

Rehearsals then started for the second show, a comedy by Frank Vickery called *Family Planning*, which was premièred in March 1999. A youth version of the same play was also produced giving the adult performers a real run for their money.

The Company hopes to keep the village rolling in the aisles or sobbing into their hankies for years to come.

Gail Toms

SILVERSTONE 1982-1998: A COMPARISON

In 1982 and again in 1998 a questionnaire was issued to every household in Silverstone in an attempt to discover what people thought of their village and what provision should be made for housing and employment opportunities, and what measures should be taken to improve leisure facilities and the quality of life, and in the case of the 1998 survey to provide a statistical base for grant applications.

The percentage of households returning a completed form was more or less the same on both occasions, with a 50% return in 1982 and a 49% return in 1998.

The questions asked in 1998 were different from those put in 1982, so that statistics are not always strictly comparable.

Population: The 1981 figures are based on the 1981 census, while the 1998 figures are the actual survey returns doubled:

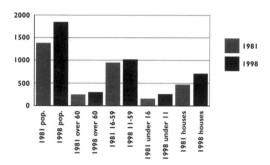

The figures above show that Silverstone has half as many houses again   in 1998 as it had in 1981, while the population has not grown so fast, which bears out the national trend of more 1 and 2-person households. The 1982 report reckoned that of the 250 (18% of the population) over-60s the majority would have been born and bred in Silverstone. The 1998 survey showed 22% (175 people) of all ages being born in Silverstone, while 32% were born within 10 miles of the village. Only 8 respondents (2%) had lived in Silverstone for more than 50 years.

Age of Houses: In 1981 nearly half of respondents lived in a post-1962 house and 10% lived in one over 200 years old. There was much the same picture in 1998, when again nearly half lived in a post-1971 house and 8% in 200 year old houses.

Cars: In 1982, 25% of households had no car, 50% had one car, 25% two or more cars. By 1998, 95% of households owned at least one car, with an average of 1.9 per household, the vast majority being kept in a garage or off the road.

Shopping: In 1982 30% of respondents did their main shopping in the village, thanks, it was thought, to the good range of shops and mobile shops serving the village. By 1998 about three quarters of respondents did their main shopping in Towcester, Northampton or Milton Keynes, leaving barely a quarter to shop in Silverstone - a result of wider car ownership and the demise of the "Top" Shop and the Kingsley Road shop. Between two thirds and three quarters of respondents visit the Post Office and Crofts' Stores regularly, with King's the butchers having a smaller but regular clientele and the mobile shops having steady, if unspectacular support.

Employment: In 1982 25% of respondents named Silverstone as their place of work, but by 1998 this was down to 20% with 18% working in Milton Keynes, and 30% working to the south and east of the A43. This shift is supported by a 1998 survey conducted for South Northants Council which showed that the majority of recent immigrants to Silverstone worked elsewhere, using their cars to get to work. In 1982 19% were self-employed which it was reported proudly *"fits in with Silverstone's legendary reputation for independence".* This has dropped to 11% by 1998, with 16% retired, but thankfully just 1% unemployed.

Housing: Attitudes to new housing changed markedly between the two surveys. In 1982 very few welcomed large estates, favouring individual houses and conversions (59%) and to a lesser extent small developments (24%) , with only 19% wanting no development at all. By 1998 the village had grown by over 200 houses and the County Council Structure Plan 1996-2016 was threatening Silverstone with a 1000-house development plus 20 hectares (50 acres) for industrial/commercial purposes. Consequently 59% of respondents wanted no growth at all, 17% welcomed 50 extra dwellings, 12% between 100 and 200, while just 2% welcomed 500 plus. At the same time, somewhat contradicting the above, 35% of respondents thought the village needed homes for young people, 25% for local people, 17% for the elderly and 13% for low income families. Interpreted that means that the village would welcome restricted development for special sections of the community.

Local Employment: Here again attitudes have hardened in the intervening years, owing to the changes proposed by the planners: in 1982 80% of respondents wanted to see more local employment, especially in the form of craft workshops and small factories, shops and services. In 1998 66% were against the proposed 20 hectare industrial/commerical site, with 22% in favour.

Bus Services: In 1982 14% of respondents used the bus service once a week. By 1998 3% used it more than once weekly and 13% used it less than 5 times a month. Both surveys recorded a need for a cheaper and more frequent bus service and for a service to Milton Keynes. Weekly buses to Milton Keynes and to Banbury were in fact introduced in late 1998 thanks to a Government subsidy to improve rural public transport.

Road Safety: In both 1982 and 1998 cars parked in the road were thought to constitute a danger in some parts of the village and requests were made for pavements where there were and still are none. By 1998 traffic calming was seen as a solution to the above problems. Concern was also expressed about the dangers of children crossing the A43 to get to school, as the crossing patrol has been discontinued because of the speed of the traffic.

Street Lighting: There were complaints in both surveys about street lighting: in 1982 about lighting in West End and Little London; in 1998 about lighting in Green Lane, Church Street, especially near the

Pavilion, West End and Hillside Avenue.

Dog Fouling: In both 1982 and 1998 dog fouling, or rather dog owners who permitted their dogs to foul pavements and footpaths without clearing up after them, were condemned roundly.

Opinions of Silverstone

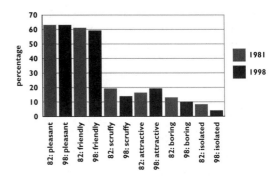

Nigel Read

1998 SILVERSTONE VILLAGE APPRAISAL; SUMMARY

Population: 350 households returned a completed questionnaire out of 715 on the 1998 Electoral Register: a 49% return.

926 were living in those households, of whom 797 (i.e. those over 11) were eligible to answer in Part 2, while there are 1493 (18+) voters on the electoral register.

Of those answering 51% were male, 49% female.

201 (26%) respondents were in the 22-39 age group, 312 (40%) in the 40-59 age band, with 147 (19%) over 60 and 116 (15%) in the 11-21 age band. Not included in the survey were 129 under 11s.

22 respondents were registered disabled.

72% of households have lived in Silverstone for less than 16 years, 38% for less than 6, while 8 (2%) have lived here for over 50 years.

32% or respondents were born within 10 miles of the village, 22% in Silverstone.

Housing: The majority of households live in owner-occupied (85%),detached (68%) or semi-detached (20%) houses (85%) or bungalows (13%) with either 3 (36%) or 4 (37%) or 5 (10%) bedrooms.

48% of respondents live in post-1971 homes, 8% in pre-1800 and 8% in 19th century houses.

Only a quarter belong to a Neighbourhood Watch scheme.

A fifth of houses have been extended.

Energy saving features are common: over 90% have a lagged water tank, loft insulation and double or secondary glazing; 46% have cavity wall insulation.

Severe flooding problems have affected 11 properties.

10 households recorded members leaving Silverstone because of a lack of suitable, affordable housing, 4 because of lack of local jobs/opportunities and 3 because of transport problems.

96% of respondents considered their accommodation suitable for their needs: of the 27 looking to move, 22 wanted to buy a 2/3 bedroom house in Silverstone or within a 10 mile radius. Nobody recorded the need for sheltered housing or residential care.

Education: Only a very small number of pre-school children will not go on to local state primary schools.

29 children are recorded as attending nursery/play school.

18 households recorded difficulties with after-school activities, mainly because of lack of public transport, but also because of road safety hazards and distance from school.

64 households had members following higher or further education courses.

Transport: 335 households possessed 640 vehicles, of which 190 are kept in a garage, 220 off the road and 37 in the road.

Of the 727 who responded to the public transport question, 602 (83%) never used the bus service, 96 (13%) used it less than 5 times a month, 18 (2%) used it between 5 and 10 times a month with only 6 (1%) using it more than 20 times a month.

465 (71%) went to work by car, 49 (7%) by bus, 5 (1%) by train, 30 (4%) walk.

Village Development: 428 respondents (59%) did not want the housing stock to increase, 124 (17%) thought 50 extra dwellings reasonable, 66 (9%) considered 100 extra and 23 (3%) 250 extra acceptable, while 17 welcomed 500+.

243 respondents (35%) thought the village needed housing for young people, 170 (25%) for local people, 116 (17%) for the elderly and 92 (13%) for low income familes. Only 266 (38%) thought no housing was needed, which seems at odds with the answers to the previous question.

Employment: 440 (59%) of respondents are employed or self employed, 119 (16%) retired, 96 (13%) in full-time education and 57 (8%) unwaged housewives/husbands. 11 (1%) are unemployed.

Of 163 who are looking or may be looking for work 59(36%) wish to work at home or in Silverstone, 53 (33%) within 10 miles and 44 (27%) within 30 miles.

64% thought a local job vacancy board very useful or quite useful.

460 (66%) were against a 50 acre industrial/commercial site in Silverstone, 153 (22%) were in favour.

Work Places: 93 (20%) of respondents in work work in Silverstone, 81 (17.5%) work in Milton Keynes, 138 (30%) work to the south and east of the A43.

189 (41%) of those in work probably use the A43 corridor at some stage, i.e. those working in Towcester, Brackley, elsewhere in Northants, Oxfordshire, elsewhere in the U.K. 59% therefore do not commute via the A43.

Footpaths: 460 (62%) use the public footpaths daily or weekly, a further 147 (20%) monthly. 585 (83%) could follow them without difficulty.

A vast majority would welcome a village map of public footpaths.

Opinions of Services	Good		Reasonable		Poor		None	
	Total	%	Total	%	Total	%	Total	%
Road maintenance	39	5	252	35	388	54	34	5
Road cleaning	59	8	402	56	209	29	43	6
Verge maintenance	59	8	341	48	245	34	66	9
Refuse collection	553	78	128	18	14	2	18	3
Street lighting	157	22	347	49	197	28	12	2
The provision of litter bins	95	13	263	37	294	41	60	8
Telephone kiosks' reliability	48	7	129	18	46	7	482	68
Community Police Officer	99	14	238	34	161	23	205	29
Winter gritting	57	8	248	35	313	44	88	12
Public transport	1	0	74	10	438	61	200	28

Use of Retail Services	Daily		Weekly		Monthly		Less Often		Never	
	Total	%	Total	%	Total	%	Total	%	Total	%
Silverstone Post Office & Stores	107	15	357	49	103	14	123	17	46	6
Matthew Croft Stores	190	26	363	50	73	10	58	8	49	7
C.B King Butchers	0	0	43	6	41	6	125	17	517	71
Fruit & Veg Mobile Shop	1	0	32	4	1	0	23	3	669	92
Fish Mobile Shop	0	0	22	3	5	1	48	7	650	90
Butcher's Mobile Shop	2	0	19	3	0	0	9	1	695	96
Mobile Library	1	0	13	2	25	3	22	3	664	92
Fish & Chip Van	1	0	35	5	46	6	134	18	510	70
White Horse Public House	6	1	82	11	103	14	268	37	271	37
Royal Oak Public House	3	0	32	4	36	5	137	19	517	71

Opinions of Silverstone

	Total	%
Attractive	134	19
Scruffy	98	14
An isolated backwater	25	4
Friendly	406	59
Posh	5	1
Pleasant	434	63
Ugly	15	2
Boring	72	10
Exciting and go-ahead	15	2
Stuffy	31	4

Number of people who answered the question: 693

There were some unclear signposts, unsafe bridges, stiles and barbed wire; some paths were too narrow for push chairs; kissing gates restricted push chair access.

Recycling Centre: 534 (74%) used or intended to use the new village Recycling Centre.

Shopping: Towcester, Northampton and Milton Keynes attracted as main shopping centres about a quarter of the 724 respondents each.

Social Activities: The Gardening Club (91) was the most popular, with the WI (35) and Age Concern (29) also with significant numbers.

Sporting Activities: The Tennis Club (60) attracted the largest number, with the Sports and Social Club (48), the Swimming Club (34), Cricket Club (26) and SRA (24) also having significant support.

Social Activities for the Young: Of the 50 respondents for this question 10/11 youngsters supported each of the Guides, Boys' Brigade and Y.O.B.S.

Recreational Activities outside Silverstone: The replies covered a huge range of activities that took place at all points of the compass, so that an analysis is impossible.

The Towcester Leisure Centre alone attracted signficant numbers: 76 for swimming and 47 for gym/keep fit activities. The response explains why it is so difficult to cater for individual needs in a relatively small place like Silverstone.

News & Views: 398 (55%) read every issue, 250 (35%) read it sometimes, only 73 (10%) never read it.

Local Government: Of 702 respondents 284 (40%) were prepared to pay a slightly higher parish council tax to meet some of the needs of the village, 266 (38%) were not, 152 (22%) were of no opinion. Some respondents said it depended on what the money was for. (N.B. Silverstone Parish Precept for a D-Band property is at present £17.86. For comparison: Towcester's is £51.31, Potterspury's £43.58, Whittlebury's £19.75, Greens Norton's £17.12)

Facilities lacking in Silverstone generally: A reliable, affordable, early-to-late bus service calling in the village was top of the list. Pavements for safety reasons were needed in Little London, West End, down Church Street to the Pavilion and along Dadford Road to the Circuit. There were many other suggestions, too numerous to include in a summary like this. Many of them were interesting and worth considering.

Hurdles are still, in 2000, to be seen in the hedgerows. These are in Cattle End.

Facilities for the school-age population: The greatest need was seen to be a base with a good range of facilities where youngsters could go in the evening, at the weekend and during the holidays.

Facilities for the disabled: Access to shops, post office, pub, church rooms needed to be improved, and kerbs dropped at strategic points.

Sports Pavilion Improvements: Decoration, heating, kitchen, bar and acoustics needed improving. Badminton Club should be resurrected. A greater variety of facilities were needed, but which was not clear.

Sports Field Improvements: The car park should be resurfaced, more litter bins and benches provided. Drainage should be improved. Help with pitch preparation is required.

Church Rooms Improvements: Total refurbishment was needed, together with lighter furniture for ease of arrangement. Chapel Rooms: There was only praise for these recently refurbished rooms.

Improving the quality of life and the environment: The overriding need for the by-pass has been recognised by the Government.

There was widespread condemnation of dog owners who permit their dogs to foul pavements and footpaths, particularly near the schools, without clearing up after them. They saw the solution as the provision of more poop-scoop bins and the reporting and prosecution of offenders.

Many requested some traffic calming measures especially on Crofts' corner, along Church Street, High Street, West End and the A43 (This may be just as necessary when the present A43 is detrunked). What sort of traffic-calming was not mentioned and this could be a very contentious issue.

There were many complaints too about the village's road surface.

Some thought there should be more social events to involve new people, and open discussions on village issues.

Views on the Circuit: Generally there was strong support for the Circuit, as a provider of employment and for bringing business and money to the village. The Circuit did not escape criticism, many thinking that it should do more for the village, for example, by taking steps to reduce noise pollution in the village, by providing public toilets at GP time and cleaning up afterwards, and by offering discounts.

Nigel Read

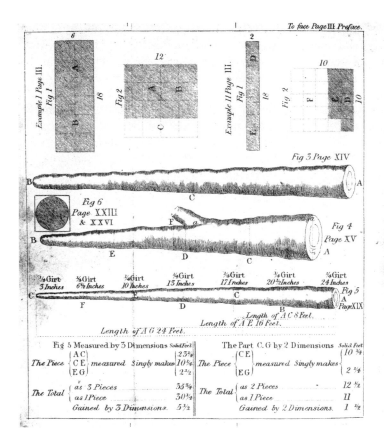

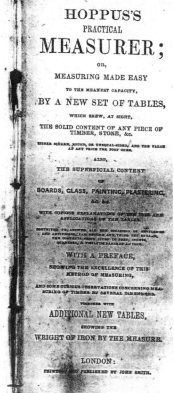

SILVERSTONE THANKS EDWARD HOPPUS

No self-respecting Silverstone person should contemplate going down the High Street, let alone into Bucknell Woods, without a Hoppus. So what is a Hoppus?

Edward Hoppus wrote a book of tables used to obtain the volume of a solid shape from certain laid-down measurements, as the title page of the copy lent by Vic Lovell makes clear. He was given his copy by Mary Varney of West End. Before that the book had been the property of her brother George, who was himself given it at Christmas 1938 by "A.J.H." A Silverstone woodsman needs three things: a good eye, a quarter girth tape and the faithful Hoppus. The good eye is to measure the height of the tree from base to crown. Instruments are available to do the job, but the experienced eye is as trustworthy and easier to use in the confines of a wood. A quarter girth tape is a measuring tape marked on one side with conventional feet and inches, but on the other with a scale which reduces the reading by a factor of four, so that eight feet comes back to two feet, that is, twenty-four inches. Thus a tree that measures eight feet in circumference at chest height gives a reading of 24 inches on the quarter girth measure. Note: the delightful diagrams facing the Hoppus title page are for other purposes than the one now being described.

So, let's suppose our woodman judges the height of his tree to be 40 feet. He then measures the quarter girth and gets a reading of 24 inches. As this is the reading at chest height he has to estimate what it would be if measured halfway up the tree and the rule is that he must deduct one measure of quarter girth for every twenty feet of height. So the reading on a 40 foot tree must be reduced by 2 to give 22 inches.

A section of quarter girth tape.

CONTENTS IN HOPPUS FEET

Quarter Girth 22"	Girth 22¼"	Feet Long	Quarter 22½"	Girth 22¾"
3·36	3·44	1	3·52	3·59
6·72	6·88	2	7·03	7·19
10·08	10·31	3	10·55	10·78
13·44	13·75	4	14·06	14·38
16·81	17·19	5	17·58	17·97
20·17	20·63	6	21·09	21·57
23·53	24·07	7	24·61	25·16
26·89	27·50	8	28·13	28·75
30·25	30·94	9	31·64	32·35
33·61	34·38	10	35·16	35·94
36·97	37·82	11	38·67	39·54
40·33	41·26	12	42·19	43·13
43·69	44·69	13	45·70	46·72
47·06	48·13	14	49·22	50·32
50·42	51·57	15	52·73	53·91
53·78	55·01	16	56·25	57·51
57·14	58·44	17	59·77	61·10
60·50	61·88	18	63·28	64·70
63·86	65·32	19	66·80	68·29
67·22	68·76	20	70·31	71·88
70·58	72·20	21	73·83	75·48
73·94	75·63	22	77·34	79·07
77·31	79·07	23	80·86	82·67
80·67	82·51	24	84·38	86·26
84·03	85·95	25	87·89	89·85
87·39	89·39	26	91·41	93·45
90·75	92·82	27	94·92	97·04
94·11	96·26	28	98·44	100·64
97·47	99·70	29	101·95	104·23
100·83	103·14	30	105·47	107·83
104·19	106·58	31	108·98	111·42
107·56	110·01	32	112·50	115·01
110·92	113·45	33	116·02	118·61
114·28	116·89	34	119·53	122·20
117·64	120·33	35	123·05	125·80
121·00	123·77	36	126·56	129·39
124·36	127·20	37	130·08	132·98
127·72	130·64	38	133·59	136·58
131·08	134·08	39	137·11	140·17
134·44	137·52	40	140·63	143·77
137·81	140·96	41	144·14	147·36
141·17	144·39	42	147·66	150·96
144·53	147·83	43	151·17	154·55
147·89	151·27	44	154·69	158·14
151·25	154·71	45	158·20	161·74
154·61	158·14	46	161·72	165·33
157·97	161·58	47	165·23	168·93
161·33	165·02	48	168·75	172·52
164·69	168·46	49	172·27	176·12
168·06	171·90	50	175·78	179·71
Girth 7' 4"	Girth 7' 5"		Girth 7' 6"	Girth 7' 7"

Now he turns to his Hoppus and looks down the column headed 22" (i.e. 22 inches) until he gets to the line opposite 40 in the Feet Long column, where the final result can be read off as 134.44 Hoppus Feet. As the value of the tree relates to the volume of commercially useful timber the Hoopus Feet content provides the basis for the final calculation as our woodman knows the price per Hoppus Foot.

Gerald Lovell and Martin Marix Evans

WEIGHTS, MEASURES AND CURRENCY

Long Measure

12 Inches = 1 Foot
3 Feet = 1 Yard
5.5 Yards = 1 Rod, Pole or Perch
4 Poles = 1 Cahain (of land, i.e. 22 yards)
10 Chains = 1 Furlong (ie 220 yards)
8 Furlongs = 1 Mile (ie 1760 yards)
3 Miles = 1 League

Land or Square Measure

144 Square inches = 1 Square Foot
(eg 12*12 ins)
9 Square Feet = 1 Square Yard (eg 3*3 feet)
30.25 Sq.Yards = 1 Rod, Pole or Perch
40 Rods,Poles,Perches = 1 Rood
4 Roods = 1 Acre (ie 4,840 sq yds)
640 Acres = 1 Square Mile

Timber Measure

100 Superficial Feet of Planking = 1 Square
120 Deals = 1 Hundred
108 Cubic Feet = 1 Stack
120 Cubic Feet = 1 Cord
50 Cubic Feet (Squared Timber) or
40 Cubic Feet (Unhewn Timber) = 1 Load or
Ton or 600 Feet of 1"(1 inch) Planking

Capacity

4 Gills = 1 Pint
2 Pints = 1 Quart
4 Quarts = 1 Gallon

(Dry Measure)

2 Gallons = 1 Peck
4 Pecks = 1 Bushel
8 Bushels = 1 Quarter

(Ale and Beer)

9 Gallons = 1 Firkin
2 Firkins = 1 Kilderkin
2 Kilderkins = 1 Barrel

Imperial to Metric

Linear Measure

1 Inch = 25.400 Millimetres
1 Foot = 0.30480 Metre
1 Yard = 0.914399 Metre
1 Fathom = 1.8288 Metres
1 Pole = 5.0292 Metres
1 Chain = 20.1168 Metres
1 Furlong = 201.168 Metres
1 Mile = 1.6093 Kilometres

Square Measure

1 Sq.Inch = 6.4516 Sq.Cms.
1 Sq.Foot = 9.2903 Sq.Decimetres
1 Sq.Yard = 0.836126 Sq.Metres
1 Perch = 25.293 Sq.Metres
1 Rood = 10.117 Ares
1 Acre = 0.40468 Hectare
1 Sq.Mile = 259.00 Hectares

Avoirdupois Weights

1 Ounce (oz.) = 28.350 Grammes
1 Pound (lb. - 16 ounces) = 0.45359243
                          Kilogram
1 Stone (14 lbs.) = 6.350 Kilograms
1 Quarter = 12.70 Kilograms
1 Hundredweight (Cwt.) = 50.80 Kilograms
                        or 0.5080 Quintal
1 Ton = 1.0160 Tonnes or 1016 Kilograms

Capacity

1 Pint = 0.568 Litre
1 Quart = 1.136 Litres
1 Gallon = 4.5459631 Litres

Monetary Conversion

In February 1971 the UK converted to the new decimal currency. Some of the interviewees in this book refer to payments or prices in what soon came to be known as "Old Money". In the old system one Pound consisted of 240 pennies. A Penny was usually written as a "d.", (deriving from the ancient Roman denarius). Twelve pence made 1 shilling (1s.), 2 shillings were a florin, 5 shillings were a Crown, so 2 1/2 shillings were "half a crown", and 10 florins, or 8 half crowns, made a pound.

A convention arose over the years for prices of goods in shops and markets to be shown using oblique strokes to separate these various units. One shilling and sixpence was 1/6 and one pound and ten shillings and sixpence was £1/10/6.

When Decimalisation came along all these conventions were thrown out of the window. The pound remained unchanged, but was now divided into 100 new units called New Pence (NP) to distinguish them from the old Penny.

So a New Penny (100th of a pound) was = 1 NP (2.4d). A new Twopence coin was worth = 2 NP (4.8d). A new Fivepence coin was worth = 5 NP (1 Old Shilling), and a Florin (24 old Pence) became = 10 NP (2 Old Shillings)

Not long afterwards, the "NP" name became shortened to a "p.", as it still is today.

So when you read that someone received a "bob" (1/-) it means 5p, "five bob" (5/-) means 25p, "ten bob" (10/-) means 50p, and "seventeen and six" (17/6) means 87.5p.

Quite easy if, as some of us were, you were brought up on it!

Joe da Casa

GENERAL GLOSSARY

3 Hen.3 = in the third year of the reign of Henry III.

abbat = abbot.

advowson = patronage of a church office.

alienation = transfer of land ownership.

amerciaments = fines.

amphora = two-handled, narrow-necked jar for oil or wine.

Angevin kings = Henry II, Richard I, John, Henry III, Edwards I, II and III, Richard II.

appendant = attached.

assize = trial or inquest.

assize of bread and beer ordinance = regulating weights and measures.

before the Conquest = before 1066, in Anglo-Saxon times.

blodewite = penalty for bloodshed.

bordar = villein of the lowest rank.

cartulary = collection of records and documents.

carucate = measure of land; originally what could be ploughed by an eight-oxen team in a year.

chancery rolls = legal records.

chapel of ease = chapel built for the convenience of parishioners who live far from the parish church.

common of pasture = right to pasture.

contumely = insulting language or behaviour.

conventual = belonging to a convent.

copyhold = tenure less than freehold, evidenced by copy of the manorial court-roll.

demesne = land belonging to a lord or the king.

demise = transfer of land by will or lease.

depredator = pillager.

Domesday survey = carried out by William I s commissioners in 1086.

dower = portion of a deceased husband's estate that the widow has for life.

easement = right to use another person s land.

escheated = reverted to the feudal lord in absence of legal heirs or on outlawry of tenant.

escheator = agent who seized property for the feudal lord.

exility = poverty.

extraparochial = outside the parish.

farm = fixed charge imposed on town or county.

fealty = obligation of fidelity on a feudal tenant or vassal to his lord.

fee = land granted by a lord to his vassal.

feme covert = married woman.

fief = see: fee.

fine = sum paid to a lord, especially for a privilege.

forest = not necessarily woodland, but land reserved for the King s hunting; usually under Forest Law controlled by the Forester instead of the Sheriff. Forests are never mentioned by name in Domesday except for the New Forest.

frank-almoin = free alms or land given to a religious body.

frank-pledge, = view of court held periodically for the production of tithes.

free-bench = estate in copyhold lands that a widow has for her dower.

furlong = measure of length: quarter of a virgate, 220 yards, similar to the modern furlong used in horse racing.

garth = enclosed yard or garden; cloister garth: an open courtyard enclosed by a cloister.

haybote = right to take wood for the repair of fences.

heriot = death duty paid to the lord by relatives.

hide = measure of land: 120 acres, although this could vary; originally the land required to support a family and its dependants. Domesday hide values were not real measurements of land, but figures on which tax (geld) was based.

hidage = tax payable on a hide.

hold of = have title of land from a lord.

housebote = right to take wood for the repair of houses.

hue and cry = pursuit of criminals with loud cries to sound the alarm.

hundred = subdivision of a county with its own assembly or court of notables and village representatives.

in capite = to hold directly from the crown.

inquisition = judicial inquiry, investigation.

knight s fee = amount of land for which the services of an armed knight were due to the sovereign.

Knights Templar = military religious order.

jointure = provision made on marriage by husband for wife s use after his death.

laund = open space in woods, clearing.

liberties = district within a county exempt from the jurisdiction of a sheriff.

leat = trench or ditch that conveys water to a mill wheel.

ley = grassland.

manor = unit of territorial organisation, consisting of the lord s lands and lands from whose holders the lord has the right to exact fees and fines and where he has privileges. It has its own court and probably its own hall, but not necessarily a manor house as such. The manor was the basic unit of Domesday.

mediety = half.

mesne estates = land held by a mesne lord who holds an estate of a superior lord.

messuage = dwelling and its adjacent buildings and land.

meoiety = half.

muniments = title deeds.

natives = relatives.

overplus = surplus.

perambulation = inspection.

pillory = wooden frame on a post with holes for offender s head and arms.

pollard = cut branches back to encourage a more bushy growth.

prescription = claim to ownership based on uninterrupted possession.

quo warranto = by what warrant: writ calling upon a person to show by what authority he makes a claim.

scutage = payment to lord in lieu of military service.

seised, seized of = in possession of, holder of (in feudal terms).

sere = dry, withered.

sergeanty, serjeanty = form of land tenure where the tenant rendered service only to the king.

service of suit = attendance at a lord s court.

tallage = tax levied on Crown Lands by monarch or toll levied by lord on tenants or vassals.

temporalities = revenues and material possessions of a church, convent or abbey.

tithes, tythes = tenth part of annual produce or income set apart as an offering to God for the support of religious establishments.

toft = homestead.

tumbril = cucking or ducking stool.

vassal = man who paid homage and fealty (loyalty) to a lord in return for protection and often a fief.

verderer = official responsible for law and order in the royal forests.

view = by view of: formal inspection of.

vill = territorial unit consisting of a number of houses and their lands.

villein, villane = peasant bound to his lord to whom he paid dues and services.

virgate = quarter of a hide.

waiff, weyf = ownerless property which, if unclaimed, falls forfeit to the lord.

GLOSSARY OF VILLAGE PLACE NAMES

August Grounds = Field on the west side of the Abthorpe Road, just past the stream.

Barrack Row = Cottages that used to stand at the far end of Cattle End.

Blackmires = Isolated farm standing between Bucknell and Hazelborough Woods, reached via the lane at the side of The Chequers in West End.

Blackwel = Well or spring on Bufton.

Bleak Hall = Farm on the Dadford Road near the A43.

Bluebottle Row = Cottages east of the A43, now listed as part of Murswell Lane.

Brickle or Brick Yard, =

expired clay pits on the corner of West End and Church Street, now a pocket park surrounding the ponds.

Bufton = Land behind Mayo's timber yard in West End.

Bunny Lodge = House east of the A43 opposite the junction of the High Street and the 'main road'.

Cats or Catch Yard = Small farm and land in the hollow on the eastern side of the A43 and to the rear of Bluebottle Row.

Chequers, The = Former public house on the corner of Blackmires Lane.

Cockshoot End = Southern part of the High Street from the A43 to just below the entrance to Graham Hill.

Compasses, The = Former public house, now a private home, whose name is thought to derive from "The Lord Encompasseth Thee'; situated on the west side of the High Street close to the beginning of the Pyghtle path to the south of the Post Office.

Cooke's Close = Land on the western side of Cattle End; a house taking this name has since been built here.

Coronation Terrace = Houses built by the council in 1937 on the west side of West End.

Crarves, The = Footpath running south from the Infant School through to West End.

Cricket Field = Field next to

the Pyghtle footpath bounded to the west by the stream.

Cut Throat Lane = Green lane running from Abthorpe Road beyond Challock Farm to Pits Farm on the Towcester Road.

Fish Ponds = Mediaeval ponds, the remains to be seen to the north of the churchyard.

Fishwaters = Field lying in the valley at the bottom of the bridle path north of New Rookery Farm, bounded to the north by a high bank, formerly mediaeval fishponds.

Frank's Lane = First and eastern part of Blackmires Lane.

Frog Hall = Group of modern houses off Whittlebury Road, that takes its name from the old cottage retained in the development.

Grafton Leys = Land at the very end of Cattle End,which contains two stone dwellings, the home of Dr. Frank Newton.

Gravel Walk = Footpath from Church Street to the Infant School.

Green Lane = At one time main thoroughfare for those on foot or horseback; heavier traffic would have used the Old Riding that runs down to West End.

Greens Norton = In 1369 Silverstone Burnham was in the manor of Silverstone and Luffield, owned by Sir Henry Green.

Kruger's Den = Land in the

hollow between the A43 and Cat's Yard. A reference to the leader of the South African Republics in the Boer War, perhaps?

Little White Horse = Former beer house at 28 Little London in Tinkers Lane.

Meeting Hill = Part of High St. now called Chapel Hill.

Missionary Row = Group of cottages on the east side of West End, north of the exit to the Crarves footpath; now demolished and redeveloped, but once known for the old apple orchards behind them, recalled by modern house names e.g. Applegarth, Orchard View.

Munges = Fields on the south side of Church Street, between "Brickle" and Linnell's Farm.

Murswell Lane = At one time, during the enclosures, private road "of ancient breadth".

Old House = House by Varney's Barns, or perhaps the barns themselves.

Old Lane = Footpath from Pump Corner crossing the Crarves and possibly going on to West End.

Old Riding = Southern part of West End from "Varney's Barn" to the A43.

Olney = Brackley Road from the Royal Oak to the Dadford Road junction, at one time all cottages and small allotments. The name means "lonely clearing or lonely wood".

Paradise Row = Terrace of cottages running off

Church Street near Linnell's farm, now used for storage.

Pits Farm = Site of the old gravel pits, formed by the glaciers in the last ice age. The gravel was used to make the Turnpike road.

Pound, The = Walled enclosure hard against the barn wall of Rookery Farm in Puddledock. Originally used for keeping stray animals, it was also at one time a rubbish dump. Now it is a grassy corner by the barn conversion. Another pound was in the yard of No 5 Little London.

Puddledock = Church Street from the farm to West End, so called because in the years before it was metalled, the area from the Rookery to the S.R.A. would flood, looking like a large puddle.

Pump Corner = Junction of Green Lane with High Street.

Pyghtle, The = Footpath leading from the Infant School to West End.

Ridges, The = Fields on the south side of Whittlebury Road opposite Windmill Farm.

Sawyers Close = Land behind the police house in Church Street, running from the churchyard to Rookery Farm, so called because it was where sawyers sawed up wood into planks; often confused with 'Sayers Close' in Cattle End.

Shacks Barn = Former field barns to the north of Kingsley Road, demolished to make way for a straightened A43.

Stone Pits = Land and houses on the corner of Whittlebury Road [Cat's Yard side] and the A43, now known as Clare House.

Terrace, The = or Terrace Villas, now discovered to be two separate groups of buildings: the Terrace was a row of houses at the top of the High Street opposite what was the 'Top Shop'; Terrace Villas were four houses beyond 58 - 64 High Street.

Tinkers Lane = Narrow lane running from opposite the Council flats in Little London through to Orchard Cottage.

Turnpike = Road created through the village in the 1770s to accommodate the growing timber and haulage trades.

Varney's Barns = In Varney's wood yard, where Hazelwood is now.

Watergate = Cottage on the Abthorpe Road, West End, by the stream which marks the Abthorpe-Silverstone boundary.

Water Lane = Footpath running along the stream just off Little London.

Winter Hills = Land and cottage on the east side of the A43 opposite High Street, running from Bunny Lodge through to a Circuit entrance at its end. It may have got its name from the mediaeval annual collection of cattle for winter feeding; in the 20th century it became the winter quarters of Cody's Circus.

LIST OF SUBSCRIBERS

Chris & Steph Abraham
Mrs M. Adams
Miss Winifred Adams
Mrs A.L. Allen
The Austins Family
P. Baker-Cassidy
Mr & Mrs G. Ballinger
Mrs P. Barrett
Mr B. Baud
Keith Baughan
Mrs L.P. Bayliss
Sylvia Bebbington
Paul & Miki Bennett
Judy Berry
Gill & Paul Bevan
Mr K. Bignell
Mrs M.P. Bignell
Andy Billingham
Geoff Billingham
Pam Billingham
Joe Birch
A. Blackwell
Mr Graham Blackwell
Mr G.W. Blackwell
N.J. & D.. Borshell
Neil & Wendy Bosher
A. J. Bradshaw
Mr Russell Bridgeman
Nick & Laura Broomhall
P.G. & V.W. Broomhall
C. & J. Brotherton
Eb & Dorothy Brown
Ian Brown
Jem Russell Brown
Mrs K. Brown
Miss R. Bryan & Mr J. West
Margaret Budd
Dave & Elaine Burford
Mr & Mrs R. Burns
Mr & Mrs H. Carr
Jane Castle

Joanna Castle
Sarah-Louise Castle
Simon Castle
Violet Causebrook
Charles & June Challinger
Dr M.J. Chappell
Mr N. Charles
Mr G. Churchill
P.A. Coles
Paul & Pat Collins
Mr P.J. Collins
Mrs Wendy Collins
Mrs G.J. Cox
Brenda Crowther
Mrs Val Currie
Mr J.D. da Casa & Ms P. Higgins
Mrs A.W. Davies
M. Dearsley
Anastasia de Clermont
Gillian de Clermont
Theodore de Clermont
Kerris & Colin Denley
J.L. Denney
Miss M. Denney
Edna Dodwell
B.H. Douglas
Miss T. Dowle
Norman William Durran
Elaine Dyer
Mr R. Eames
Mark Evans
Mrs Carol Eves
Mr G. R. Fleming
Ivor & Margaret Floyd
Sue Fowler
Mr & Mrs R.T. Gascoigne-Rice
Mrs P. Gaysher
Mr Robert Henry Giles
Mr & Mrs J.V. Godfrey
Mike Goff & Ghislaine Davies-Goff
Trevor F. Goode
Alexandra Goodfellow
Amy Goodfellow

Mrs J. Hamer
A.J. Hamp
Mrs A. Hardy
Darren Harris
Jim Harris
John Harris (Junior)
John Harris (Senior)
Mrs D. Hayle
Edna Hayward
Mrs M. Heath
Tony Henderson
Mr W. Hickman
Mrs Elsie Higgins
Irene Hill
Mr S. Hill
Mr & Mrs Harvey Hine
Mr B. R. Hinton
Mary Hinton
Mr & Mrs Peter Hinton
Mrs Judith Hodges
Margaret Holland
David & Pam Holton
John Hughes
Sara Hughes
Bunny Hutchings
Mrs G.M Ibbotson
John & Heather Illingworth
John & Jane Jacobs
Chris & Pat Japp
Mr Andrew George Jeacock
Peter Jeacock
Sue Jennings
John Johnson
Ken Jones & Tere Cugno
S.H. Jones
Win Kelf
Mr & Mrs J.L. Kimber
Mr & Mrs Kirkbride
Roy & Carol Knight
Audrey & Jim Lambert
Miss Angela Linnell
Mr Barry A. Linnell
Don Linnell
Mrs J. Linnell

K.H.Linnell
David Lofty
Carolyn & Gerald Lovell
Chris & Elaine Lovell
Mr David Lovell
Joe Lovell
Jonathan Lovell & Diana White
Neil Lovell
Nicholas Lovell
Sidney Lovell
Vic Lovell
Mr & Mrs J. Lyons
Mervyn & Sophia Maddison
J. Maleham
G.M. & M.F. Marix Evans
David Markham
Linda Markham
Mr M. Maxwell
David McCabe
Mrs Valerie McDonald
Paul Meaden
Anita Measey
Vicky & David Meek
Dr Frank & Mrs Jeny Newton
Bill Nicholson
Richard & Kim Nike
Mrs P. North
Beryl & John Oates
Jonathan Odell
Libbi Odell
Richard & Helen Odell
William Odell
Mrs R.D. Osborne
R.L. Palmer
Mrs S.A. Parish
Margaret Parker
Mrs Jean Partridge
Andrew Payne
Stephen Payne
Susan Payne
Mrs Vera Petcher
Mary & Alan Pickles
Mr & Mrs M.V. Piggott
Mrs Sheila Porter

Adrian Potter
Nicholas Potter
Richard & Mea Potter
Bim Prentice
Anne Pullen
Ian Ratcliffe
Pat & Nigel Read
Ruth Reddall
Barbara & Tony Redhead
Yvonne & Dave Reed
A.S. Reeve
Jane Rimell
John F. Roberts
Mr & Mrs R.G. Roberts
R.J. Roberts
Alan Robertson
Mrs Rachael Robinson
Mr R.F. Rogers
Steven Rush
Mr M. Sales
Silverstone C.E. Junior School
Mr Dennis Sleep
Mrs Georgina Smart
David Smith
Graeme & Anne Smith
Pam & Bernard Smith
Margaret & Bob Southgate
Mr D. Sparrow
David Gordon Spencer
Mr Donald Spencer
J. Spittles
Desmond & Jean Statham
Mrs M. Sturges
Mr Harold Summers
Mr N.H. Sutton
Mrs Pat Tattersall
Ken & Chris Taylor
Mr & Mrs M. Taylor
Mr Matthew Taylor & Miss Sharon Childs
Mrs Gail Toms
Mr A.R. Travill
Dr & Mrs E.A.M. Tuck
Mike & Gill Tucker

Mrs B. Turnell
Mr & Mrs Peter Turton
D. Tustian
John Tustian
Eileen Tyrrell
Erik Van Kampen
Mr T. Varney
Mr N. Wallace
Mr & Mrs D.J. Wallen
J. Warren
Raymond Webb
D.F. Wesley
Mr Kevan West
Leslie & Edith West
John Whitehead
Margaret L. Whitehead
B.W. Whitlock
Mrs Sue Whitlock
Peter & Audrey Wiles
Mr & Mrs D. Willers
Mr P. Williams
R.A.F. Williams
Shirley & Martin Williams
Mrs A.E. Willis
Mike & Pat Willis
Christine Wilson
Jeff Wilson
Keith & Joy Wilson
Leonie Yeates

INDEX